Pentecostals in the 21st Century

Pentecostals in the 21st Century

— Identity, Beliefs, Praxis

EDITED BY
CORNELIU CONSTANTINEANU
CHRISTOPHER J. SCOBIE

CASCADE *Books* · Eugene, Oregon

PENTECOSTALS IN THE 21ST CENTURY
Identity, Beliefs, Praxis

Copyright © 2018 Corneliu Constantineanu and Christopher J. Scobie. All rights reserved. Except for brief quotations in critical publications or reviews, no part of this book may be reproduced in any manner without prior written permission from the publisher. Write: Permissions, Wipf and Stock Publishers, 199 W. 8th Ave., Suite 3, Eugene, OR 97401.

Cascade Books
An Imprint of Wipf and Stock Publishers
199 W. 8th Ave., Suite 3
Eugene, OR 97401

www.wipfandstock.com

PAPERBACK ISBN: 978-1-5326-1671-6
HARDCOVER ISBN: 978-1-4982-4066-6
EBOOK ISBN: 978-1-4982-4065-9

Cataloguing-in-Publication data:

Names: Constantineanu, Corneliu. | Scobie, Christopher J.

Title: Pentecostals in the 21st century : identity, beliefs, praxis / Corneliu Constantineanu and Christopher J. Scobie.

Description: Eugene, OR: Cascade Books, 2018 | Includes bibliographical references.

Identifiers: ISBN 978-1-5326-1671-6 (paperback) | ISBN 978-1-4982-4066-6 (hardcover) | ISBN 978-1-4982-4065-9 (ebook)

Subjects: LCSH: Pentecostalism | Pentecostal churches—Doctrines | Christianity—21st century

Classification: BX8762.Z5 C66 2018 (print) | BX8762.Z5 (ebook)

Manufactured in the U.S.A.   01/02/18

In loving memory of Dr. Miheal Kužmič (1943–2005), who with his wife Helena and family pioneered the Pentecostal church in Ljubljana, 1966.

Contents

Contributors | ix

1 Introduction: Pentecostal Identity, Spirituality, and Theology | 1
   CORNELIU CONSTANTINEANU AND CHRISTOPHER J. SCOBIE

2 Pentecostal Identity | 14
   VELI-MATTI KÄRKKÄINEN

3 Some Aspects of Hermeneutics in the Pentecostal Tradition | 32
   ROGER STRONSTAD

4 Sacrament or Ordinance? A Pentecostal Approach to a Contentious Issue | 59
   JEAN-DANIEL PLÜSS

5 Towards a Pentecostal Perspective on Salvation | 76
   EDMUND J. RYBARCZYK

6 How, Why, and When Should Someone be Baptized? What Is Its Relationship to Salvation? | 94
   GLENN BALFOUR

7 The Baptism in the Holy Spirit | 111
   FRANK D. MACCHIA

8 The Gifts of the Spirit | 122
   KEITH WARRINGTON

9 The Church | 141
   CECIL M. ROBECK JR.

10 A Pentecostal Proposal for Discipleship | 158
    CHRISTOPHER J. SCOBIE

11 Fulfillment of God's Promise
    in the Soon-to-Return King | 181
    VAN JOHNSON

12 Pentecostalism and Ecumenism:
    Past, Present, and Future | 202
    AMOS YONG

13 The Theological Motivations for Pentecostal Mission | 237
    WONSUK MA

14 Mission, Education, and Public Engagement:
    A Case Study in Romanian Pentecostalism | 255
    CORNELIU CONSTANTINEANU

Contributors

Glenn Balfour (PhD Nottingham University) is an ordained minister with the AoG UK, and is Principal of Mattersey Hall, UK.

Corneliu Constantineanu (PhD OCMS, Oxford & Leeds University, UK) is Professor of Theology at "Aurel Vlaicu" University, Faculty of Humanities and Social Sciences, Arad, Romania.

Van Johnson (ThD Wycliffe College, University of Toronto) is Dean of Masters at the Pentecostal Seminary, Toronto, ON, Canada.

Veli-Matti Kärkkäinen (Dr Theol., Habil. University of Helsinki) is Professor of Systematic Theology at Fuller Theological Seminary, Pasadena, CA, USA, and Docent of Ecumenics at University of Helsinki, Finland.

Wonsuk Ma (PhD Fuller Theological Seminary), former Executive Director of the Oxford Centre for Mission Studies, UK, is Distinguished Professor of Global Christianity at Oral Roberts University, Tulsa, OK, USA.

Frank D. Macchia (ThD University of Basel) is Professor of Christian Theology at Vanguard University, Costa Mesa, CA, USA.

Jean-Daniel Plüss (PhD Catholic University of Louvain) is Chair of the European Pentecostal/Charismatic Research Association in Zürich, Switzerland.

Cecil Melvin Robeck, Jr. (PhD Fuller Theological Seminary) is an ordained minister with the AOG, USA. He serves as Professor of Church History and Ecumenics and Director of the David du Plessis Center for Christian Spirituality at Fuller Theological Seminary, Pasadena, CA, USA.

Contributors

Edmund J. Rybarczyk (PhD Fuller Theological Seminary) is an ordained minister with the AOG, USA. Professor of Historical and Systematic Theology, Vanguard University, Costa Mesa, CA, USA.

Christopher J. Scobie (PhD University of Ljubljana, Theological Faculty) is ordained minister and serves in the local church in Ljubljana, Slovenia.

Roger Stronstad (DD Christian Bible College) is Director and Associate Professor in Bible and Theology at Summit Pacific College, Abbotsford, BC, Canada.

Keith Warrington (PhD Kings College, University of London) is Vice-Principal and Director of Doctoral Studies at Regents Theological College, Malvern, UK.

Amos Yong (PhD Boston University) is Professor of Theology and Mission and Director of the Center for Missiological Research at Fuller Theological Seminary, Pasadena, CA, USA.

1

Introduction

Pentecostal Identity, Spirituality, and Theology

Corneliu Constantineanu
and
Christopher J. Scobie

The Pentecostal movement worldwide, even though only a century old, represents one of the most remarkable phenomena of global contemporary Christianity, with an amazing dynamic of growth and a formidable potential for mission and Christian witness in today's world. This book is a delightful collection of expert contributions produced by some of the world's preeminent Pentecostal theologians and offers a wonderful window into some of the unique features of the phenomenon of twenty-first-century Pentecostalism. The contributors were invited to reflect on various, important issues regarding Pentecostal identity, beliefs, and praxis. This is not a book of systematic theology. It is rather a collection of essays addressing important theological themes that pastors, theologians, and lay leaders are grappling with in this early part of the twenty-first century. As the world-renowned, Slovene-born, Croatian theologian Peter Kuzmič, agreeing with Karl Bath, would often remind his students, "The expositor today must preach holding the Bible in one hand and the newspaper in the other!" Inherent in his remark is the continuing need for the contextualization of the sacred texts. A newspaper informs us of contemporary issues and challenges, the drift and direction of society; the Bible, when contextualized with the Spirit's illumination, speaks authoritatively, informatively, and wisely and offers comfort, support, hope, and direction to the people of God so that the community of faith may be truly God's instrument for the redemption of the world, thus sharing God's heart and His ultimate desire to redeem the whole of creation.

It is often claimed that Pentecostalism has its roots in the book of Acts, although it is commonly considered to have been birthed as the Spirit fell in Topeka, Kansas (1901), and Azusa Street, Los Angeles (1906). The Holy Spirit fell upon believers and breathed a new wind of renewal and commitment. Followers were empowered for witness and evangelization as a new wave of evangelism and church planting was birthed. This young movement, now only a little over one hundred years old, has now touched every country on the globe. Most believers are found in small churches (eighty to one hundred people), yet large churches like *Hillsong* and *Vineyard* for example, have emerged, and have influenced much of the church's music. According to Marc Cortec of Wheaton College, in 2014 there were 631 million Pentecostals in the world comprising one quarter of all Christians, which is forecast to grow to 800 million by 2025.[1] Pentecostalism started in the new world, yet recently its most significant growth has occurred in the Global South, as South America and Africa have experienced substantial growth in Pentecostal Christianity. China and much of Asia have also not been left out, with large growth, and in some situations it has been growth in the midst of great persecution. Now, as we move through the second decade of the twenty-first century, Europe and North Asia will surely not be passed over.

We are greatly indebted to each of the contributors, who have most graciously committed their time and labors towards this outstanding contribution. We are absolutely convinced that this book will encourage and exhort the Pentecostal leaders of local churches and inform and engage those interested in matters of faith and social engagement. The latter, social engagement, continues to be an avenue where much growth will occur in the coming years. Pentecostalism has much to offer the world, and we believe that by sharpening and strengthening the identity, faith, and praxis of our churches we may indeed bring a significant contribution to the Christian witness in our troubled and desperate world. Towards that end we seek the particular guidance and empowerment of the Spirit and so continue to sing that old song of the early Pentecostals, "Come, Come Holy Spirit, Come!" Each chapter in the book focuses on a particular aspect of Pentecostal identity, belief, and/or praxis. Readers may choose to move backwards and forwards as each chapter is largely self-contained. In what follows, we offer a brief summary of the contributions in the book, highlighting the major emphasis of each chapter.

1. See Cortez, "The Growth of Global Pentecostalism."

Identity

We begin with the issue of identity. Veli-Matti Kärkkäinen, the world-renowned Finnish scholar, seeks to define the basis of the distinctive Pentecostal spirituality and discusses the question of what makes Pentecostals Pentecostal. The importance of religious identity cannot be overstated here, as it is a crucial issue that shapes the ways we interact with the world, highlights our particular theological and spiritual contribution, and gives us our specific place in the world. The relative newness of Pentecostalism as a movement, the lack of uniform Pentecostal doctrine across adherents, various theological extremes (examples of both fundamentalism and liberalism can be observed), and the fact that church ecologies (in relation to governance and authority) are diverse, all conspire to create a significant challenge to any attempt to speak about identity.[2] In addition, the task is made even more difficult and elusive by the fact that early Pentecostal theology was developed in oral and other non-discursive forms, such as experience.

Kärkkäinen shows us that the critiques of Pentecostalism as an over enthusiastic spiritual movement do not accurately reflect Pentecostals. Pentecostalism is decidedly more shaped by its Christology, which holds to the fivefold role of Christ as: Justifier, Sanctifier, Baptizer with the Spirit, Healer, and Soon-to-return King. Pentecostal spirituality is a spirituality that reflects a "full gospel"—it is Christocentric in nature and charismatic in expression. The worship service is a setting where adherents encounter the risen Christ, which emphases the possibility of experiencing God mystically. Kärkkäinen concludes that a better understanding of our own spirituality helps Pentecostals to (re)define who they are in ever-changing contexts for survival and flourishing. Furthermore, establishing strong identity acts as a preventative measure, supporting congregations by assisting them in avoiding any drift into "strange waters." Perhaps of key importance is also an improved self-understanding, this clarification is necessary in order to relate to other Christians and work towards the unity for which Christ himself prayed.

Hermeneutics

In theology, hermeneutics is the interpretation of the ancient biblical texts, which were written in times far removed from our contemporary society. It first seeks to establish what the original author intended to communicate to his audience and then to make application for contemporary society.

---

2. See Scobie, "The Body of Christ in 1 Corinthians," 28.

Early claims that Pentecostals were fundamentalists who distort the hermeneutical process failed to recognize the contribution of Pentecostalism to theology. Among these claims was the charge of a failure of interpreters to separate early writers and their limitations from the source of inspiration, the limited capacities of the original writers, and the failure to recognize the literary forms and patterns of thinking over long periods of time.[3] However, with the emergence of generations of highly trained and skilled theologians in the Pentecostal tradition, this claim no longer holds water.

Pentecostals hold to the conviction that authority comes from God alone, and the Holy Scriptures are God's self-revelation to humanity; Scripture alone is authoritative.[4] Amos Yong, a leading Pentecostal thinker, speaks of a theological and philosophical approach to hermeneutics in which there is a relationship between the Spirit, the Word, and the Community (when the history of interpretation is heard), where no hierarchy is established.[5] This triadic negotiation of Spirit, Word, and Community to produce a single unified interpretation is now repeated enough to be considered the Pentecostal hermeneutical approach.[6]

Early Pentecostal theologies were heavily influenced by the reading of Acts, which records the historical account of the first thirty years of the church. Roger Stronstad, an authority in hermeneutics, lays to rest the argument that Luke-Acts is limited to historical narrative. Luke is shown to "rival Paul as the greatest theologian and teacher in early Christianity." Stronstad's skillful contribution is aimed at helping contemporary readers become better interpreters of Luke-Acts, which forms a significant part of the basis for Pentecostal doctrine.

When readers are able to establish Luke as more than a historian, but also a theologian and teacher, rich theological contributions are produced. Stronstad argues that in Luke's theology there is an "antecedent spiritual state" as a prerequisite to "Spirit baptism." There remain scholars who are adamant that Luke's use of Spirit is limited to the description of regeneration. However, Stronstad shows that those who experience the activity of the Spirit for vocational use had subsequent spiritual regeneration. Stonstad concludes that Luke makes a compelling case that "Spirit baptism" *must* be read as a vocational commissioning empowerment.

---

3. See Pontifical Biblical Commission, "Interpretation."
4. Duffield and Van Cleave, *Foundations of Pentecostal Theology*, 16–18.
5. Yong, *Spirit-Word-Community*, 17–18.
6. Scobie, "The Body of Christ in 1 Corinthians," 55–58.

Sacraments vs. Ordinance

This has been a delicate and controversial subject, which is skillfully addressed by our colleague Jean-Daniel Plüss. The term "sacrament" has tended to be avoided by Pentecostal communities as it communicates something more than they intend to give church rites. The word sacrament does not appear in the English Bible but first made its way into the Latin Vulgate to translate the Greek word *mystērion* into *sacramentum*. Sacrament is commonly understood as something sacred, an efficacious sign of grace through which the divine life is mediated. The sixteenth-century Reformation rejected the notion of signs mediating God's grace for salvation, preferring to hold to the belief that grace is mediated from God by faith in Jesus Christ through the Holy Spirit. Thus, Pentecostals have largely followed a Zwinglian memorial meal, which reflects an ordinance theology. The term "sacrament" tends to reflect a ritual, which contains a sanctifying effect, while "ordinance" reflects a practice ordained by God.[7]

Jean-Daniel Plüss encourages Pentecostals to discover the deeper dimensions of liturgical practice rather than simply celebrating a rite. In some quarters, the individualization of faith of Protestantism has detracted from the value of community fellowship in and with Christ. "If general worship among Pentecostals is geared towards encounter," says Plüss, "how much more would this be the case during the celebration of Communion?" As Christ is present at the meal, there is an exhortation to rediscover the *charismata* available through the encounter with the risen Christ.

Soteriology

The field of theology that examines the doctrine of salvation through Christ is called soteriology. Dealing with salvation, we are indebted to the work of Edward Rybarczyk, who first deals with the need for salvation from the evil that has affected the entire human race. Atonement is made by Christ's substitutionary death on the cross, which is at the heart of Christianity.

For Pentecostals, salvation is not limited to simply the forgiveness of sin and entry into a new relationship with God through Christ. Atonement is the basis of healings, a new life in the Spirit, and eschatological realities of hope, joy, trust, and love in the present. Traditional Christianity has at times limited the effects and benefits of salvation to the forgiveness of sin and a life hereafter, however, the craving of the human heart is for a deeper reality. The pneumatological emphasis of Pentecostals represents an existential

---

7. Kärkkäinen, "The Pentecostals View," 120.

reality open to believers to experience this authenticity as a result of the soteriological encounter. It is the Holy Spirit who plays the mediating role in the process of salvation. Edward Rybarczyk emphasizes the free nature of the choice to participate with God in salvation, a process of which God is the first mover.

Baptism

Glenn Balfour produces a very helpful contribution enumerating key canonical texts which describe the Pentecostal position on water baptism. Water baptism is a prominent ritual among all Christian traditions, yet through the passage of time, the practice and understanding of it have significantly varied from what Jesus spoke of, and about which Luke and Paul wrote. This wonderful contribution answers questions like: How should we baptize in water? What is the proclamation over the baptismal candidate? Why? When? What is the re-generational effect of baptism? Moreover, Glenn Balfour touches on the controversial issue of *paedobaptism*, which is a predominant practice among the historical Christian traditions. Those who differ from this understanding of baptism in contemporary communities will have to ask themselves questions regarding the role and authority of Scripture. When Jesus instructs his followers to go and baptize, did he mean it and did the early believers follow this example? Glenn Balfour answers with a resounding "Yes!" and gives sound exegetical reasons for this.

Baptism in the Spirit

Perhaps no other aspect of faith identifies Pentecostals as "People of the Spirit" more than the belief and practice of Spirit baptism. Evangelicals have commonly held Spirit baptism and the initial reception of the Spirit, upon initial faith, to be one and the same. Some sacramental theologies include Spirit baptism as part of water baptism (or perhaps confirmation). Still, some other charismatics have sought a middle ground by defining Spirit baptism as incorporation "in Christ" through baptism, yet released later. This is perhaps similar to some "third wave" evangelicals who believe the Spirit is received in salvation but released subsequently.

Frank Macchia prefers to use the language of "the Spirit continually coming upon us . . . ," which while rooted in the born-again experience is a subsequent experience of power, "at the moment of one's charismatic gifting and call to witness." This experience subsequent to salvation cannot be neglected when one carefully examines the Spirit's role in empowering the church for a witness, which is reflected in Luke-Acts. Frank Macchia cites the scholarly support of Stronstad and Menzies in their work showing that Luke's pneumatology reflects the charismatic and missional nature as opposed to the soteriological nature, which we see in Paul. Frank Macchia provides a corrective to classical Pentecostals who have insisted that "speaking in tongues" is the "initial sign" of Spirit baptism. Rather, he follows the influential Jack Hayford, who claims Spirit baptism opens the individual to the possibility of "speaking in tongues," but such speech is not necessarily characteristic of Spirit baptism. Moreover, "Spirit baptism" does not exalt the individual, but, as a "calling forth of love," is love in action, empowering in effect, missional in activity, and accountable in community.

Gifts of the Spirit

The Spirit's roles in enabling people to function charismatically is as old as time itself. Pentecostals have always rejected cessationism, the idea that the supernatural phenomena ended with the passing of the apostles, as though the Spirit's activity was only for the birth of the church. Keith Warrington demonstrates why Pentecostals can confidently assert the present-day activity of the Spirit in *charsmata* (spiritual gifts) and *pneumatikoi* (spiritual utterances of discernment). Warrington continues to provide some parameters for the use of the diverse spiritual gifts present to believers, which are to be used for the benefit of the church and wider community, and shows that "Pentecostals prefer to accept that the *charismata* are on loan from the Spirit; they are manifestations of the Spirit through believers that are expected to be used in ways that are appropriate to his character and will." Warrington lays aside the claim that prophecy is intrinsically superior to the other speaking gifts. He notes simply that prophecy is more valuable since it is understandable and therefore more beneficial to the community.

Pentecostals acknowledge that the Spirit empowers believers to function beyond their natural powers. The Spirit may enable them to utilize gifts that they have already been granted as part of their person. Keith Warrington finds that Paul explicitly mentions "nearly thirty different gifts." Many of the gifts are self-explanatory, yet a sustained discussion on *glossolalia* is helpful and informative. The Holy Spirit has unlimited resources for believers. Pentecostals are expected to make themselves available for use and with these gifts to benefit the church and wider community.

Ecclesiology

While the birth of the church is commonly recognized as taking place on the Day of Pentecost (Acts 2), various models of decision making can be inferred from Scripture (Episcopalian, Presbyterian, Congregational, or Spiritual in guidance). Scripture does not prescribe a formula for the church governance or order of service.

Cecil Robeck finds that the church is the people of God, who are indwelt by the Spirit. The church was guided by the *apostolic teaching*, the teachings of those who had been with Jesus for three years, learned from him, and seen him in action. The church in its early days focused on the oral narrative of the testimony of the apostles, people responded with faith to this testimony, and relationships among believers formed a *koinōnía* (fellowship, participation in and with one another). It was a sharing of life together where they sustained one another with prayer and open sincerity. What is perhaps notable is that while God has one people and one body, there was a remarkable *continuity* with Israel, which soon moved to a *discontinuity* with Israel as the Christians continued within larger boundaries than the Jewish communities permitted. Contributions from John and Peter together with some early fathers accentuate the focus on relationship with one another and thus the spirit and character of church leaders.

Robeck shows that since this initial Pentecost, the church continues to "finds its strength, its power, its purpose, its proclamation, its fellowship, its table, its prayer today in 'Pentecost.'" From these metaphors and images, we are forced to ask what is important in meeting and what is to take priority in community life.

Discipleship

Ultimately, one could argue that to make disciples is a key purpose of the church. At Jesus' ascension, he left this final command to his followers. Jesus did not say "Make churches, Bible schools, hold evangelistic meetings, concerts, youth group meetings, etc." While these may be useful strategies, Jesus said: "Make *disciples* . . . teaching them to obey" (Matt 28:20). False disciples were a challenge to the early church, as were threats of heresy, cultural values creeping into the church, and socioeconomic challenges. These are all similar challenges that we face today, to which we might also add denominational distinctives, all conspiring to derail the process of disciple making.

Christopher Scobie has reviewed some developments among some early Pentecostals in discipleship. Finding a significant growth and development in Pentecostalism, possibilities for theological contributions are reaching for new horizons. This chapter shows that the stool of discipleship in contemporary Pentecostal communities rests on four legs: faith, the Spirit, Scripture, and community. Faith is the starting point for this journey with Christ as humans respond to God: yet this faith must be mentored, encouraged, and given room to grow. The role of the Spirit is unquestionably necessary as leaders allow the work of the Spirit in the lives of disciples. But what is the Spirit doing in disciples? When Paul said to his beloved brethren in Colossae "Let the word of Christ richly dwell within you . . ." (Col 3:16), there is the sense that what is sought is a life of obedience, a life that conforms to Christ's. Pentecostals can agree that discipleship is the process of sanctification. In order to give structure and form to this idea of sanctification this discussion examines Paul's first epistle to the Corinthians, which was written with the intent of bringing sanctification to a community embroiled in conflict, disunity, and spiritual misuse. Using a deliberative methodological analysis, the author shows that Paul's argument was intended to bring the community in Corinth to maturity (sanctification) "in Christ" through a process of eight key steps. The final aspect of discipleship is community. One could here agree with the French novelist Marie-Henri Beyle, who famously wrote: "One can acquire everything in solitude except character." Community is essential to create disciples.

Pentecostalism today has a significant advantage in discipleship because its hermeneutic avoids the rigid dogmatism of the early evangelicals of the modern scientific era, and provides freedom of the Spirit to lead in congregations while allowing the community to participate in the process. However, while the growth is certainly massive, we must not become complacent, but discover a new urgency to see Christ formed in the lives of followers through personal faith, the work of the Spirit, Scriptural formation, and a life lived well in community. This is the mission of leaders within Pentecostalism.

Eschatology

As we think of New Testament eschatology, we are considering what God has already done and what he is yet to do. The study of eschatology has been plagued by difficulties and misinterpretations. Think, for instance, of the dispensationalism of the mid-1800s, which gained a hearing throughout Western Christianity and is typified in the "Left Behind" series of novels. The examination of apocalyptic literature has always produced a mixed variety of results, in part because such texts remain cloudy until readers appreciate their context and form. Apocalyptic literature has a specific apocalyptic genre, it has a specific purpose, and it was written with symbols and images used to convey what the writer had seen. To read literally that which is meant symbolically is to invite confusion and mistake.

Van Johnson's thoughtful contribution reminds us that Pentecostalism has always identified closely with eschatology. Pentecostals claim what happened on the Day of Pentecost also happened to them. Early Pentecostals were greatly encouraged in evangelism and witness because of the new outpouring of the Spirit. Events such as Azusa Street were seen as the "latter rain" which would precipitate the soon-to-return Christ. While Pentecostals tend to read the millennial reign of Christ on earth literally, when the dispensationalism that produces Pentecostal beliefs about the rapture and seven years' tribulation, etc., is removed, so also is some of the scheme for the raptures. While the conviction that Jesus will soon return predates dispensationalism, Van Johnson laments that its capitulation will erode the urgency for evangelism that Pentecostals experienced in the past. Eschatology has played a significant role within Pentecostalism and has perhaps been a significant catalyst for the enormous and dynamic growth this last century, as the King's return is eagerly anticipated. The imminent return of Jesus to rule remains the great hope for all believers; however, if the "imminent" is removed so too may the passion and excitement for witness. Apocalyptic literature was written some 2,000 years ago to encourage believers in very trying and discouraging situations. Pentecostals need to rediscover this same encouragement and exhortation so that the present-day sufferings are not felt to be in vain.

Pentecostalism and Ecumenism

The modern ecumenical movement is said to have started in 1910, emerging from the World Missionary Conference in Edinburgh.[8] The Pentecostal-Catholic ecumenical dialog, which started in 1972, is the oldest inter-denominational dialog in existence. It should be pointed out that not all people were happy with this. David du Plessis (1905–87) had his ministerial credentials from AOG withdrawn as a result of his involvement. (They were later restored to him.) Currently, the dialog is in its sixth phase, which is led from the Pentecostal side by Cecil Robeck.

Some Pentecostals have questioned the validity of ecumenical work and have raised objections to engagement with other churches. Pentecostals believe the Christ is recognized spiritually not visually and accuse some

8. Vondey, *Pentecostalism and Christian Unity*, xiii.

churches of betraying essential elements of the gospel. Moreover, the Pentecostal experience is deemed to have breathed life into the church as the church is known only by the Spirit, those without the Spirit may be devoid of life (apostates).

The well-known and highly acclaimed theologian Amos Yong claims that a biblical case for ecumenism can be established on the basis of metaphors used by Paul, which speak of the unity of the church. Moreover, the prayer of Jesus in John 17, the unity demonstrated between the Father and the Son, and the love that characterizes the Trinitarian relationship all point to unity intended in the church.

The ecumenical movement is able to affirm differences rather than force uniform liturgies, traditions, and expressions. One does not need to be naïve to suggest that embracing different spirits includes the potential for problems; however, Yong concludes that Pentecostals need the larger church as the larger church needs Pentecostalism and its contribution. Yong encourages ecumenical reach on all levels: academic, church leadership, institutional-denominational, and personal. He also finds that Pentecostals have a responsibility to educate themselves, to reach out towards other Christians and support leaders to build inter-denominational relationships. This, of course, is done without compromising one's own beliefs and convictions.

Pentecostals and Missions

Traditionally, Pentecostals have been concerned with the spread of the gospel cross-culturally. The growth of the Pentecostal movement over the past hundred years has significantly contributed to the growth of Christianity. Evangelism and church planting have been an integral part of Pentecostalism as it is intimately connected with the outpouring of the Spirit in Acts 2. As Pentecostalism has developed, missions has moved from evangelism and church planting to social engagement in various ways, all with the end goal to make converts. For Wonsuk Ma, this call to missions emphasizes the purpose of the outpouring of the Spirit in Acts 2. Accordingly, this Spirit baptism was closely linked with witnessing as contemporary Pentecostals were able to identify intimately with the first church (closing the time gap between then and now). Moreover, the early hermeneutic, which included a literal reading of Scripture, explained individuals personal experience as a work of the Holy Spirit. What occurred in Acts, was now occurring again in their presence, thus emphasizing the call to "witness"-missions. Thus, this experience with God gave greater motivation and encouraged participation in missions.

In his thoughtful contribution, Wonsuk Ma identifies the theological resources that have sustained Pentecostal missions. These include Spirit baptism and the prophethood of all believers, as the community is incorporated in the work of the Spirit. Furthermore, early eschatological presuppositions ignited an urgency towards the task of missions as the "hour was late." Finally, the influence of the social gospel did not evade Pentecostalism, and thus many social programs combine to advance Pentecostal missions. Helpfully, Wonsuk Ma does not brush over challenges that Pentecostals need to face as some eschatological expectations, the ugly "prosperity gospel," consumerism, and some cultural manipulations demonstrate the need for greater theological reflection and coherence. Spirit baptism, the Bible and its authority, locally grounded and relevant theologies, the role of community, and experience will continue to play vital roles. Theologies will grow as theologians mature, soul-winning will remain a priority in Pentecostal missions, whether evangelism, church planting, or social engagement.

Mission, Education, and Public Engagement

In a contextual reflection from Romania, Corneliu Constantineanu presents some unique features of the Pentecostal church in Romania, one of the largest and most vibrant among the Pentecostal churches in Europe. He shows that after a rather difficult period of persecution and marginalization in the decades of the communist regime, the Romanian Pentecostal church has developed to become, currently, the fourth largest Christian denomination in Romania and is the only church in the context of Central and Eastern Europe to have had significant growth in various respects in the last ten years. Beyond numerical expansion, the church has also made significant progress with regard to several other areas, such as foreign missions, education, economic, social, and political engagement, as well as Roma Christianity. This is significant as the case study on the Romania Pentecostalism could be a model for the Pentecostal contributions to the economic development of local communities, advances in education, and unique mission impetus in the region.

Having taken a little time to sketch the shape of what is to come, it is time to jump in to the chapters themselves. Enjoy!

Bibliography

Cortez, Marc. "The Growth of Global Pentecostalism." *Wheaton Theology Conference* 4 (2014). http://marccortez.com/2014/04/16/growth-global-pentecostalism-wheaton-theology-conference-4.

Duffield, Guy P., and N. M. Van Cleave. *Foundations of Pentecostal Theology*. Los Angeles: L.I.F.E. Bible College, 1983.

Gee, Donald. *Now That You've Been Baptized in the Holy Spirit*. Springfield, MO: Gospel Publishing House, 1972.

Hayford, Jack. *The Beauty of Spirit Language*. Nashville, TN: Thomas Nelson, 1996.

Hollenweger, Walter J. *Pentecostalism: Origins and Developments Worldwide*. Peabody, MA: Hendrickson, 1997.

Kärkkäinen, Veli-Matti. "Free Churches, Ecumenism and Pentecostalism." In *Toward a Pneumatological Theology: Pentecostal and Ecumenical Perspectives on Ecclesiology, Soteriology, and Theology of Mission*, edited by Amos Yong, 53–64. Lanham, MD: University Press of America, 2002.

———. "The Pentecostal View." In *The Lord's Supper: Five Views, Roman Catholic, Lutheran, Reformed, Baptist, Pentecostal*, edited by Gordon T. Smith, 117–35. Downers Grove, IL: IVP Academic, 2008.

Macchia, Frank D. *Baptized in the Spirit: A Global Pentecostal Theology*. Grand Rapids: Zondervan, 2006.

Menzies, Robert. *Empowered for Witness: The Spirit in Luke-Acts*. JPTS Series 6. Sheffield, UK: Sheffield Academic Press, 1994.

Pontifical Biblical Commission. "The Interpretation of the Bible in the Church, Methods and Approaches for Interpretation" (1993). http://catholic-resources.org/ChurchDocs/PBC_Interp1.htm.

Robeck, Cecil M. J., and Amos Yong, eds. *The Cambridge Companion to Pentecostalism*. Cambridge: Cambridge University Press, 2014.

Scobie, Christopher James. "The Body of Christ in 1 Corinthians: A Fresh Reading, Implications for Faith Communities, and an Ecumenical Dialog between Catholics and Pentecostals." PhD diss., Faculty of Theology, University of Ljubljana, 2015.

Stronstad, Roger. *The Charismatic Theology of St. Luke*. Peabody, MA: Hendrickson, 1988.

Warrington, Keith. *Pentecostal Theology: A Theology of Encounter*. London: T. & T. Clark, 2008.

Yong, Amos. *The Spirit Poured Out on All Flesh: Pentecostalism and the Possibility of Global Theology*. Grand Rapids: Baker Academic, 2006.

———. *Spirit-Word-Community: Theological Hermeneutics in Trinitarian Perspective*. Reprint. Eugene, OR: Wipf & Stock, 2002.

———. *Who is the Holy Spirit? A Walk with the Apostles*. Brewster, MA: Paraclete, 2011.

Volf, Miroslav. *After our Likeness: The Church as the Image of the Trinity*. Grand Rapids: Eerdmans, 1997.

Vondey, Wolfgang, ed. *Pentecostalism and Christian Unity: Ecumenism Documents and Critical Assessments*. Eugene, OR: Pickwick, 2010.

———. "Pentecostal Identity and Christian Discipleship" (2013). http://www.pctii.org/cyberj/cyberj6/vondey.pdf.

2

Pentecostal Identity

VELI-MATTI KÄRKKÄINEN

Introduction

IN RESPONSE TO HIS own question about what the meaning of "time" is, St. Augustine famously responded that if no one asks, he knows what "time" means, but should someone ask him to define it, he doesn't know how to do so (book 11 in his *Confessions*). I wonder if something similar applies to the issue of defining Pentecostal identity. Other Christians certainly have a fairly accurate intuition of what Pentecostalism is—notwithstanding many misconceptions! However, when asked to give a definition, they might be at their wit's end. Not only that, but it seems to me that perhaps most Pentecostals themselves feel the same kind of dilemma. Every Pentecostal (I guess!) possesses a fairly accurate idea of what makes one a Pentecostal. Yet when asked what Pentecostalism is—apart from the standard "Spirit baptism" and "charisms"—they may not be well prepared to respond, particularly in our current times when there are crowds of other Christians who similarly speak of Spirit baptism and in whose lives charismatic gifts seem to be at work.[1]

The question of Pentecostal identity, hence, is not a simple one. It is complex and includes various facets and viewpoints. At the same time, it is a crucial topic as it has implications for both Pentecostals' spiritual life and other Christians' perceptions of the distinctive features of this youngest Christian family.

---

1. Just think of the vast and wide Roman Catholic charismatic movement, whose membership with over 100 million adherents surpasses that of any single Protestant denomination!

In this essay,[2] I will first seek to define Pentecostalism on the basis of its distinctive spirituality. Thereafter, to specify in some detail what kind of distinctive spirituality that is, I delve into the topic of "full gospel," the shorthand for Christ-centrism in faith and spirituality. Following that is a look at the importance of the worship service for understanding Pentecostal identity: namely, that it is in liturgy, prayers, and praise, in which Christ is encountered through the Holy Spirit, that the distinctively Pentecostal spirituality is manifested. Finally, before a short conclusion, the Pentecostal conception of the Holy Spirit and Spirit baptism with a view to identity receive a focused discussion.

Charismatic Spirituality as the Key to Defining Pentecostal Identity

While nothing like a uniform definition of Pentecostalism exists, a helpful orientation to the complex topic is provided by the terminology adopted by *The New International Dictionary of Pentecostal and Charismatic Movements*,[3] the standard and most authoritative source of knowledge about Pentecostalism. Its typology divides it into three interrelated categories. The first category is "(Classical) Pentecostal" denominations, such as the Assemblies of God or Foursquare Gospel, owing their existence to the famous Azusa Street Revival in Los Angeles, California, in 1906 (and in Topeka, Kansas, a few years earlier). Most of the European Pentecostal movements—many of which, particularly in the former Eastern Europe, are known under the nomenclature "Apostolic Church"—belong to the first category even when a direct link to the said American revivals is lacking. (My homeland, Finland, serves as an illustration: its roots and birth are independent of American Pentecostal bodies in the sense that the movement, similarly to other Nordic countries, was established by local leaders rather than international ones; yet the inspiration and prompting came from contacts with Azusa Street Pentecostals.) The second category is "charismatic movements," Pentecostal-type spiritual movements within established churches (the largest of which is the Roman Catholic charismatic renewal). The third category is "Neo-charismatic" movements, some of the most no-

---

2. This essay depends heavily on and borrows largely from my previous publications, See Kärkkäinen, "Free Churches, Ecumenism and Pentecostalism"; Kärkkäinen, "Identity and Plurality"; Kärkkäinen, "Pentecostalism and Pentecostal Theology in the Third Millennium."

3. Burgess and van der Maas, eds., *The New International Dictionary of Pentecostal and Charismatic Movements*.

table of which are the Vineyard Fellowship in the United States, African Initiated Churches, and the China House Church movement, as well as an innumerable number of other independent churches and groups all over the world. Number-wise, the charismatic movements (about 200 million) and Neo-charismatics (200–300 million) well outnumber Classical Pentecostals (75–125 million).

Even after this clarification of various categories under the nomenclature "Pentecostal-charismatics," there is much diversity within each category, including the first one. The diversity within worldwide "Pentecostalism" has to do with two dimensions: the cultural and the theologico-ecumenical. Pentecostalism, unlike any other contemporary religious movements, spread across most cultures, linguistic barriers, and social locations.[4] Related to this is the theological and ecumenical diversity, which simply means that there are several more-or-less distinct Pentecostalisms. Thus, speaking of Pentecostalisms (in the plural) would be valid; but for the sake of convenience, the singular form is usually preferred. How different in ethos, manifestation, and to some extent in theology are, for example, Yoido Full Gospel Church in Seoul, Korea (the world's largest church with more than one million adherents) from the African American (Black) Pentecostal churches of the US South, and how different are both from the small Pentecostal congregations in any European country, and so on. Even concerning Pentecostalism in Europe, there are vast differences between, say, the Pentecostal Church of Finland (my homeland) which displays heavy influences from Lutheran and Eastern Orthodox traditions, British Pentecostal movements (Assemblies of God and Elim), which are deeply indebted to American influences, and say, Pentecostal movements in Romania (with the largest number of adherents in all European countries), which finds itself in an Orthodox and Reformed environment. And so forth.

In other words, the question of what makes Pentecostalism—what constitutes its identity—is a notoriously difficult one.[5] There are a number of reasons for the difficulty in addition to those mentioned above. Unlike, say, Lutheranism or Roman Catholicism, Pentecostal identity is not based on creeds or shared history. This is not to say that Pentecostals have no written statements of faith. Yes, they have. However, even the oldest ones are very young in comparison to traditional churches, and they are far less detailed in their stipulations. Nor can Pentecostal identity be based on ecclesiastical structures since you can find the whole repertoire of them

---

4. The diversity is well documented. For an up-to-date account, see e.g., the annual statistic lists in the January issue of *International Bulletin of Missionary Research* compiled by David B. Barrett and Todd M. Johnson.

5. Kärkkäinen, "Free Churches, Ecumenism, and Pentecostalism."

from the most local-church autonomous models (Scandinavia) to congregationalist (Continental Europe and England) to presbyterian (White Pentecostals in the USA) to episcopal (Black Pentecostals in the USA and elsewhere) to other types.

Consequently, most theological observers of Pentecostalism nowadays prefer a criterion for identity that is centered on spirituality rather than history, creedal statements, or church structures.[6] To be more precise: the most distinctive feature of Pentecostalism is Christ-centered charismatic spirituality going back to the classical "full gospel"[7] template in which Jesus is perceived as Savior, Sanctifier, Healer, Baptizer with the Spirit, and the Soon-returning King.[8] Spirituality, thus, is the key to "defining" Pentecostal identity.

Walter J. Hollenweger, the most well-known analyst of Pentecostalism, has for decades insisted on its spirituality as the most distinctive feature of Pentecostalism. Unlike many others, he argues that the early years of the movement, which were characterized by intense spiritual experiences and charismatic gifts, are not necessarily to be taken as the "childhood" of the movement out of which it should grow, but rather the defining period of identity formation. The first decade of the movement, says Hollenweger, forms the heart, not the infancy, of Pentecostal spirituality. Features such as orality of liturgy; narrativity of theology and witness; maximum participation at the level of reflection, prayer, and decision making in a community characterized by inclusion and reconciliation; inclusion of dreams and visions into personal and public forms of worship; and a holistic understanding of the body-mind relationship reflected in the ministry of healing by

---

6. Albrecht speaks of an "underlying or core spirituality" among various types of Pentecostalisms. See Albrecht, *Rites in the Spirit*, 28. Harvey Cox, the informed observer of Pentecostalism from Harvard University, is on to something significant in claiming that Pentecostals have a distinctive way of constructing reality and that it has influenced their understanding of mission and social concern. Cox posits that at the heart of the Pentecostal movement is a restoration of what might be termed "primal spirituality." See Cox, *Fire from Heaven*, 81. Cox also speaks about "primal piety." Ibid, 99 and "primal hope" in relation to distinctive Pentecostal spirituality. Ibid., 111–22.

7. The term "full gospel" derives from American Pentecostalism in which, in the 1940s or so, an influential movement under that nomenclature emerged, particularly among Christian businessmen, but not limited to them. That nomenclature, however, has much wider attestation in Pentecostal history. Its roots go back all the way to the very beginnings of Pentecostalism when movements such as the Foursquare Gospel arose. That classical movement (which nowadays is known globally as the International Church of the Foursquare Gospel) began to speak of the core of Pentecostal preaching and belief in terms of the "full gospel" as outlined above.

8. A definitive study of the main motifs of "full gospel," See Dayton, *Theological Roots of Pentecostalism*.

prayer—these were all formative in the beginning of the movement.⁹ For Hollenweger, thus, Pentecostalism represents a religious movement *sui generis*, "a new confession," which cannot be reduced to fundamentalism, evangelicalism, or even to Protestantism as such.¹⁰ It was brought into existence, not by rational theological analysis, but a sudden outpouring of the Spirit. Experience was first, then came doctrine. This was well captured in the statement called "Essence of Pentecostalism," which sought to define the basic identity of Pentecostalism:

> It is the personal and direct awareness and experiencing of the indwelling of the Holy Spirit by which the risen and glorified Christ is revealed and the believer is empowered to witness and worship with the abundance of life as described in Acts and the Epistles. The Pentecostal experience is not a goal to be reached, not a place to stand, but a door through which to go into a greater fullness of life in the Spirit. It is an event which becomes a way of life in which often charismatic manifestations have a place. Characteristic of this way of life is a love of the Word of God, fervency in prayer and witness in the world and to the world, and a concern to live by the power of the Holy Spirit.¹¹

Another way of formulating the importance of spirituality to Pentecostal identity is with reference to distinctive Pentecostal hermeneutics. This is done by the American Pentecostal theologian Kenneth J. Archer, who speaks of the "Pentecostal Story as a Hermeneutical Narrative Tradition":

> The Pentecostal community is a distinct, coherent narrative tradition within Christianity. Pentecostal communities are bound together by their charismatic experiences and common story. The Pentecostal narrative tradition is one embodiment of the Christian metanarrative. Yet, because the Pentecostal community understands itself to be a restorational movement, it has argued that it is the best representation or embodiment of Christianity in the world today. This may sound triumphalist; yet, Pentecostals, like all restorational narrative traditions of Christianity, desire to be both an authentic continuation of New Testament Christianity and a faithful representation of New Testament Christianity in the present societies in which they exist. Of course, the understanding of what was and should be

---

9. Hollenweger, *The Pentecostals*, 551; Hollenweger, *After Twenty Years' Research on Pentecostalism*, 6; Land, *Pentecostal Spirituality*, 14, 47.

10. Hollenweger, *The Pentecostals*, 265.

11. Kärkkäinen, *Spiritus ubi vult spirat*, 50–51.

New Testament Christianity is based upon a Pentecostal understanding. Moral reasoning, which includes biblical-theological interpretation, is contextualized in the narrative tradition of the Pentecostal community. Pentecostals will engage Scripture, do theology, and reflect upon reality from their own contextualized communities and narrative tradition.[12]

"Full Gospel": A Christ-Centered Spirituality

Against common assumptions, then, the center of Pentecostal spirituality and theology is not the Holy Spirit but rather Jesus Christ. Yes, Pentecostals love to speak of the Holy Spirit and to highlight the work of the Spirit in personal and church life. The Holy Spirit, however, is not the center of their message or preaching any more than it was that of the New Testament Christians: early followers of Christ did not go out to preach the Holy Spirit as Savior and Lord but rather Jesus Christ. Pentecostalism is, therefore, first and foremost *a Christ-centered movement.*[13] If you attend a Pentecostal church meeting, you will hear the name of Jesus over and over again in prayers, praise, and sermons; "Holy Spirit" is mentioned far less often.

This is exactly what Donald Dayton, in his seminal work *Theological Roots of Pentecostalism* has argued.[14] According to him, Pentecostals ought to understand themselves through a paradigm involving several theological factors. The four he identifies were present in a slightly different form in the American Wesleyan/Holiness Movement of the nineteenth century, but they were reconfigured in Pentecostal thinking and used in a powerful way in the form that Aimee Semple McPherson, the founder of the Foursquare Gospel, one of the oldest and largest Pentecostal bodies, popularized them: Jesus was understood to be Savior, Baptizer in the Holy Spirit, Divine Healer, and Coming King. To these were added still one aspect, rooted in the Holiness Movements from which Pentecostalism came, and consequently Pentecostals were known as "Full Gospel" Christians. This full gospel consisted of five theological motifs:

1. Justification by faith in Christ,

12. Archer, *Pentecostal Story*, 40–42.

13. For a fine account of key themes and orientations in Pentecostal spirituality see Spittler, "Spirituality, Pentecostal and Charismatic." In the past, a typical way of dismissing Pentecostals in terms of deprivation theory was the norm among sociologists of religion, often with little or no firsthand knowledge of the movement itself. For a balanced critical discussion see Miller, "Pentecostalism as a Social Movement."

14. Dayton, *Theological Roots of Pentecostalism*.

2. Sanctification by faith as a second definite work of grace,
3. Healing of the body as provided for all in the atonement,
4. The premillennial return of Christ,
5. The baptism in the Holy Spirit evidenced by speaking in tongues.

A look at any Pentecostal doctrinal manual shows that four or five of these motifs are at the core of theological developments (that in turn are supposed to authentically reflect the underlying spirituality). Yet, as any movement, Pentecostalism employs the categories of the fivefold gospel in a creative and not always constant way. Typically, the distinctive features—especially Spirit baptism and charisms, healing, and eschatology—receive separate treatments.[15] Justification by faith is either assumed or mentioned in passing, except for those Pentecostal movements—such as the one in my homeland, Finland, a predominantly Lutheran land—where it belongs to one of the key doctrines embraced.[16] Holiness is another topic, widely debated among early Pentecostals (depending on their relation to the preceding Wesleyan Holiness Movements),[17] which either is taken for granted (closely related to the typical Protestant two-stage soteriology, as a next step from justification)[18] or allocated a separate treatment. Take, for example, the book recently produced by British Pentecostals titled *Pentecostal Perspectives*.[19] There are chapters on Spirit baptism, eschatology, as well as healing and exorcism. The topics of justification and sanctification do not receive separate treatments even though they are assumed. Interestingly, a chapter on revelation and the Bible has its own locus, reflecting the strong emphasis on biblical authority among Pentecostals, linked with the close relationship with the fundamentalist movement in the early decades (which, ironically, otherwise resists the core charismatic spirituality of Pentecostalism).[20]

So, if Christology rather than pneumatology is at the center of Pentecostalism, we have to say that the common criticism of the movement

---

15. A good example is the widely used Pentecostal manual in the United States written by two leading Foursquare theologians. See Duffield and Van Cleave, *Foundations of Pentecostal Theology*.

16. Kuosmanen, *Raamatun opetuksia*, 88–96; Viksten, Mauri, *Terveen opin pääpiirteitä*, 70–74.

17. See Dayton, *Theological Roots of Pentecostalism*, chs. 2 and 3.

18. For basic orientation to Pentecostal soteriology see, Hollenweger, "Pentecostalism: Origins and Developments Worldwide," ch. 19.

19. See Warrington, *Pentecostal Perspectives*.

20. For an enlightening analysis of the uneasy relationship between Pentecostalism and fundamentalism, see Sheppard, *Pentecostalism and the Hermeneutics of Dispensationalism*, 5–34.

as an enthusiastic "Spirit movement" is not accurate. Rather, Pentecostal spirituality is embedded and anchored in an encounter with Christ as Christ is being depicted in his manifold role of Justifier, Sanctifier, Baptizer with the Spirit, Healer of the Body, and the Soon-coming King. Christ is being encountered in the power of the Holy Spirit.

I am of course aware that at times the term "full gospel" is used by Pentecostals in a way that borders on ideology, the implication being that other churches' gospel is not as "full" or as complete. While that kind of implicit critique no doubt was in mind by those who coined the term, in its best theological sense, it is rather an attempt to identify the basic elements of a biblical gospel. As such it needs to be heard both as a legitimate self-identification and a call to other churches to pay attention to what Pentecostals perceive to be forgotten or lost parts of the gospel.

So far, my analysis of the core themes of Pentecostal spirituality has strongly reflected Euro-American roots. There is no denying that the Azusa Street[21] and thus American influence has been determinative in the birthing of Pentecostalism, even when its Black (African American) contributions are properly acknowledged. Nevertheless, it is also a fact that various Pentecostalisms of the world—as established above, there is a need to speak in the plural because of the sheer diversity of Pentecostalism[22]—represent significantly different, yet not totally unrelated, spiritual movements from their Western counterparts. While indigenous and local Pentecostalisms are flourishing all over the world, much work is yet to be done in terms of recording their relation, on the one hand, to the roots of the movement and, on the other hand, the ways they are critiquing and expanding Pentecostalism.[23]

---

21. For an authoritative account see Robeck's *Azusa Street*. This book is the first fruit of a massive, meticulous study project on the origins of Pentecostalism in Southern California and beyond.

22. For a recent discussion of emerging global Pentecostalisms see, Anderson and Hollenweger, *Pentecostals after a Century*. Note the statement by C. M. Robeck: "Pentecostals are multi-cultural . . . if for no other reason than that they are found around the world," he argues, and therefore he, among others, suggest that we need to speak of Pentecostalisms rather than Pentecostalism (as a single phenomenon). Robeck, *Taking Stock of Pentecostalism*, 45.

23. For a helpful beginning, see Anderson, *An Introduction to Pentecostalism*. The main challenge faced by theological analysts of Pentecostalism is that despite the rapid growth of academic theology and theologians in the past two or three decades, still so much of Pentecostal spirituality exists in oral or other nondiscursive forms, especially from the early formative years and in traditions outside the West. The comment by J. Hollenweger, however, is a healthy reminder to us: Taken seriously this offers a real possibility of discovering a methodology of theology in an *oral* culture where the medium of communication is—just as in biblical times—not the definition, but the description;

"Meeting with the Lord": A Profile of Pentecostal Worship Service[24]

We have established so far that, at its core, Pentecostalism can be defined in terms of spirituality that is Christ-centered and that a major way Pentecostals seek to encounter Christ is the worship service. Let us deepen our analysis of Pentecostal spirituality by looking at the importance of liturgy and worship. In the words of the researcher of Pentecostal spirituality and ritual Daniel Albrecht,

> In a very real sense the Sunday services of . . . [Pentecostal] churches are designed to provide a context for a mystical *encounter*, an experience with the divine. This encounter is mediated by the sense of the immediate divine presence. The primary rites of worship and altar/response are particularly structured to sensitize the congregants to the presence of the divine and to stimulate conscious experience of God. . . . The gestures, ritual actions, and symbols all function within this context to speak of the manifest presence.[25]

The centrality of the worship service as the place of meeting with the Lord for Pentecostals is not diminished by the obvious fact that its forms vary greatly because of cultural and historical reasons. Whereas at the beginning of the movement, even in the United States and Europe and currently in numerous churches in the Global South, very charismatic, nonstructured, and enthusiastic worship patterns are common, most liturgies in the Global North (Europe and the United States, particularly the former) nowadays differ only slightly from other Protestant and evangelical styles. A visitor to a typical Pentecostal worship service on Sunday morning in my homeland does not necessarily see much difference from services in other Free churches, say, Baptists or Methodists. It has to be added, however, that at its very core Pentecostal spirituality and worship employs "bodily" and "kinesthetic" features in which raising the hands, bodily movement, touching (for example on the forehead of the sick person in the prayer for healing),

---

not the statement, but the story; not the doctrine, but the testimony. Whoever denies that one can do proper theology in these categories will have to prove that the Bible is not a theological book. Our way of doing theology is a culturally biased form (yet necessarily so, in our culture!). There are other equally relevant forms of doing theology. Pentecostalism offers raw materials and elements for such an alternative methodology." Hollenweger, "Charisma and *Oikumene*," 332–33.

24. This section is taken primarily from my "Encountering Christ in the Full Gospel Way."

25. Albrecht, *Pentecostal Spirituality*, 121.

and similar aspects communicate what the Catholic tradition would call "sacramental principle" (that the divine appears in the bodily or physical) and what in the wider theological sense could be called "an incarnational principle." The whole body, not only the mind, is part of the encounter with the Lord. To put it another way, for Pentecostals "worship" is another way of saying "presence of God."[26]

Related to the centrality of the longing for meeting with the Lord is the centrality of spiritual experience.[27] While *experience* is a loaded term in contemporary theology, it is impossible to understand Pentecostal spirituality and the full gospel apart from this category. Elsewhere, I have recently argued that the worship service with its expectation of this encounter is the structuring principle of Pentecostal spirituality:

> The stress on experience can of course at times lead to overemphasis on emotionalism. However, it still is the case that even to begin to understand this spiritual tradition, speaking of experience is essential. . . . Spontaneity and openness to the leading of the Spirit characterize church life. Even where worship services are being planned, the focus is on being open to the leading of the Spirit. Therefore, those who come to the worship prepare themselves by praying to God for his manifestation. . . . Encounter with God is the central feature of the Pentecostal-Charismatic spirituality. The goal of the sermon is not only to share spiritual teaching; the ultimate goal of a Pentecostal sermon, similarly to prayer and praise, is an authentic and fresh meeting with the Lord. This is of course not unrelated to the emphasis on experience. A typical Pentecostal worship meeting culminates in the altar call where people are being invited by the preacher to come forward to be prayed for in order to meet with the Lord, be it about becoming a believer, healing a sickness, or getting help with finances.[28]

The expectation of and prayer for divine healing is a powerful way of encountering the Lord, the Healer in the power of the Spirit.[29] As the

---

26. Albrecht, *Pentecostal Spirituality*, 109.

27. For the centrality of experience in the spiritual life, see the important works by the Jesuit Donald L. Gelpi, no stranger to charismatic spirituality (while not part of the movement itself). See Gelpi, *Experiencing God* and Gelpi, *The Turn to Experience in Contemporary Theology*. From a Lutheran perspective with a view to Lutheran charismatics, see Antola, *The Experience of Christ's Real Presence in Faith*, ch. 2.

28. Kärkkäinen, *Vapaakristillisyys, helluntailaisuus ja baptismi*, in Teoksessa *Kirkkotiedon kirja*, 312, translation mine.

29. For a fascinating, delightfully critical theological look at the topic of healing, including abuses of healing practices among some Pentecostal healing preachers, see

British Pentecostal New Testament scholar Keith Warrington notes, "The prime motivational force has . . . been the fact that Jesus healed, and the record of the Gospels that he healed all who came to him. Jesus is seen to be the paradigm for the contemporary Christian."[30] This holistic Pentecostal worldview, by "its belief in and experience of the paranormal," can legitimately be called an "alternate *Weltanschauung* for our instrumental rational modern society."[31] While Pentecostals do not usually resort to the language of sacramentality, the sacramental principle of embodiment—Word becoming flesh in the incarnation—is clearly operating here.[32] The healing and restoring the power of the Spirit as experienced in the encounter with Christ the Healer is the hallmark of this holistic spirituality. With all its anti-sacramental mindset, there are times when, especially at the Eucharistic table, there is an expectation of being touched by the healing power of Christ.[33]

Other ways of meeting with the Lord are being appreciated and sought for among Pentecostals, such as empowerment with spiritual gifts in order to be equipped for service and witnessing as well as in one's prayer life. For the purposes of this essay, however, enough has been said of the underlying core motif in Pentecostal spirituality that reflects the full gospel. While it can easily degenerate into an exercise in individual piety, from the beginnings Pentecostalism has been a thoroughly communal spirituality. The paradigm of the early church as recorded especially in the book of Acts—the favorite book of Pentecostals—is communal in orientation.[34] What the Reformed theologian Michael Welker of Heidelberg says about the importance of communion in a biblical theology of the Spirit can easily be applied to the Pentecostal emphasis on community:

Hollenweger, *Pentecostalism: Origins and Developments Worldwide*, ch. 18.

30. Warrington, *Pentecostal Perspectives*, 147. For the influence of the divine healing movements of the nineteenth century on Pentecostalism, see Dayton, *Theological Roots of Pentecostalism*, ch. 5.

31. Cargal, *Beyond the Fundamentalist-Modernist Controversy*, 163.

32. There have been attempts by some Pentecostal theologians to find commonalities between Pentecostal spirituality, especially its emphasis on *glossolalia*, speaking in tongues, as a way of "securing" the divine presence and sacraments as "signs" of the divine presence. While there are some connecting points, I also think the differences are so dramatic that at the most one can only point to some common underlying motifs behind *glossolalia* and, say, the Eucharist, see Macchia, "Tongues as a Sign," 61–76.

33. This motif was discussed in the Catholic-Pentecostal dialogue. Kärkkäinen, *Spiritus ubi vult spirat*, 397–406.

34. This was widely discussed in the Catholic-Pentecostal dialogue. The third round of talks concentrated on the topic of *koinonia*. It was also part of the fourth quinquennium when missionary implications of *koinonia* were discussed. Kärkkäinen, *Ad ultimum terrae, Evangelization, Proselytism and Common Witness in the Roman Catholic-Pentecostal Dialogue*, 109–13.

The Spirit produces a new unanimity in the people of God, frees the people from the consequences of the powerlessness brought about by their own "sin," and raises up the life that has been beaten down by oppression.... In all the early attestations to the experience of God's Spirit, what is initially and immediately at issue is the restoration of an internal order, at least of new commitment, solidarity, and loyalty. The direct result of the descent of God's Spirit is the gathering, the joining together of people who find themselves in distress. The support of their fellow persons is acquired; a new community, a new commitment is produced after the descent of the Spirit.[35]

So far, this essay has emphasized the centrality of Christology and charismatic spirituality as the key to defining Pentecostal identity. That pneumatology may not be the focus of Pentecostalism, however, is not to undermine its importance. It just has to be placed in perspective. Let us reflect briefly on the nature and role of the Holy Spirit and pneumatology for Pentecostalism. That discussion will also give occasion to say something more of Spirit baptism, the most well-known—and often widely debated—claim of Pentecostalism. Since another essay in this collection delves into many details of the topic, let it suffice to be brief here and highlight the importance to understanding Pentecostal identity.

Holy Spirit and Spirit-Baptism[36]

As is well known, Pentecostals love the book of Acts. The reason is simply that it tells the story of the first Christian churches having been born as a result of the Pentecostal pouring out of the Spirit. The promise in Acts 1:8 was taken literally by Pentecostals and believed to be happening "here and now": "But you shall receive power when the Holy Spirit has come upon you; and you shall be my witnesses in Jerusalem and in all Judea and Samaria and to the end of the earth" (RSV). What is significant about this Pentecostal experience and expectation of the Spirit was succinctly captured in the beginning of the Roman Catholic-Pentecostal dialogue in a Pentecostal position paper: "It may hardly be gainsaid, that the Pentecostal revivals of the present century have taken the *koinonia* of/with the Holy Spirit out of the cloistered

---

35. Welker, *God the Spirit*, 52, 57.

36. This section is based on my two essays, Kärkkäinen, "The Spirit Poured Out on All Flesh"; Kärkkäinen, "Pneumatologies in Systematic Theology."

mystical tradition of the Church, and made it the common experience of the whole people of God."[37]

Speaking of the power of the Holy Spirit in the life of the church and individual Christians was of course nothing novel in the history of Christianity. What was dramatically novel was Pentecostals' claim not only that all Christians, men and women, poor and rich, educated and uneducated, white and black, should expect the empowerment by the Holy Spirit, but that it is the *normal* mode of typical Christian life! Hence, we can speak of this Pentecostal expectation as a form of democratization and reconciliation: not only is there access to God and "holy things" for all men and women, but also access to ministry and leadership. It is not about education, status, or wealth, but about the empowerment of the Holy Spirit.

This is what Pentecostals call "empowerment" and was named "primal spirituality" by the noted observer of global Pentecostalism, Harvard theologian Harvey Cox. With this term, Cox refers to the largely unprocessed central core of humanity where an unending struggle for a sense of destiny and significance rages. For Cox, Pentecostalism represents a spiritual restoration of significance and purpose to lift people from despair and hopelessness.[38] Cox considers this emphasis on "primal spirituality" evident in the contemporary (postmodern) world—as well as among Pentecostals in the Global South—as the key to Pentecostalism's dramatic expansion.

Whereas for most other Christians the presence of the Spirit is just that, *presence*, for Pentecostals the presence of the Spirit in their midst implies *empowerment*.[39] While this empowerment often manifests itself in spiritual gifts, such as speaking in tongues, prophecy, or healings, it is still felt and sought for by Pentecostals even when those manifestations are absent. The main function of the Pentecostal worship service is to provide a setting for an encounter with Jesus, the embodiment of the full gospel (as outlined above) to receive the (em)power(ment) of the Spirit. As important as sermons, hymns, and liturgy are, they all take second place to the "meeting with the Lord," as they put it.

Pentecostalism has thus offered a grassroots challenge to established churches and theologies, especially those endorsing the so-called cessationist principle, which holds that miracles or extraordinary charismata ceased at or near the end of the apostolic age. Often ridiculed for emotionalism, Pentecostals introduced a dynamic, enthusiastic type of spirituality and

---

37. Ervin, "Koinonia, Church and Sacraments," 8–9.

38. Cox, *Fire from Heaven*, 81. See also Kärkkäinen, "The Re-Turn of Religion in the New Millennium," 469–96.

39. In this distinction, I am indebted to the Benedictine Catholic expert on Pentecostal-charismatic movements, Fr. Kilian McDonnell, OSB.

worship life to the contemporary church, emphasizing the possibility of experiencing God mystically.

While the experience rather than doctrine came first,[40] a novel and disputed doctrinal understanding of Spirit baptism emerged in the early years of the movement. While never uniformly formulated nor followed by the worldwide movement, it is only fair to say that for the large majority of Pentecostals, this view came to be known as the "initial physical evidence." This simply means that Pentecostals expect an external sign or marker of the reception of Spirit baptism, namely, speaking in tongues (*glossalalia*). Pentecostals claim this doctrine comes from the book of Acts and from contemporary experience. Theologically, the initial-evidence doctrine functions "sacramentally": it is an external confirmation of the inner grace received from God's Spirit. Pentecostals do not, of course, call it "sacramental," nor do they necessarily affirm the connection.[41]

Other gifts of the Spirit such as prophesying, prayer for healing, and works of miracles are enthusiastically embraced and sought for by Pentecostals. Belief in the capacity of the Spirit to bring about healing, whether physical or emotional/mental, is one of the hallmarks of Pentecostalism. In this, Pentecostals echo the postmodern insistence on a holistic understanding of the body-mind relationship. A related belief is the capacity to engage in "spiritual warfare" and exorcise demonic spirits, if necessary. This is a significant part of Pentecostal spirituality, especially in the Global South.[42]

All that said, however, it is interesting—and ecumenically important—to note that typically Pentecostal *doctrines* of the Holy Spirit (writings on pneumatology) fairly closely follow typical Protestant lines. Moreover, they are compelled to bring in their own distinctive contribution, namely, the dynamic and charismatic nature of the Spirit's ministry. Amos Yong summarizes it well:

> In Pentecostalism, as in most conservative, traditionalist, and evangelical Christian traditions, the orthodox doctrine of the Holy Spirit as divine person continues to prevail. Yet Pentecostals go beyond many of their orthodox Christian kindred to say that the Holy Spirit continues to act in the world and interact personally with human beings and communities. In this tradition, then, there is the ongoing expectation of the Holy Spirit's answer to intercessory prayer, of the Spirit's continual and

---

40. Plüss, "Azusa and Other Myths," 191.
41. Macchia, "Tongues as a Sign," 61–76.
42. See Onyinah, "Deliverance as a Way of Confronting Witchcraft in Contemporary Africa."

> personal intervention in the affairs of the world and in the lives of believers even when not specifically prayed for, and of the Spirit's manifestation in the charismatic or spiritual gifts (as enumerated by St. Paul in 1 Corinthians 12:4–7). Of course, amidst all that occurs in Pentecostal circles are some rather fantastic accounts . . . and discerning between the valid and the spurious is not always easy. Pentecostals face the tension of (on the one hand) accepting a rather traditional supernaturalistic worldview along with at least some of the more embarrassing claims that come with it resulting in their being excluded from scholarly or academic conversation, or (on the other hand) attempting to reinterpret Pentecostal testimonies within a more naturalistic framework so as to be able to proceed acceptably with rigorous scientific inquiry into Pentecostal spirituality and experience.[43]

In other words, on the one hand, Pentecostal theological works follow the traditional doctrine of the Holy Spirit and Trinity and usually employ categories and terms borrowed from others. On the other hand, Pentecostals go beyond the established contours of traditional theologies and push the boundaries of pneumatology based on their distinctive spirituality as described above.

Concluding Remarks

After the first century of its existence, Pentecostalism faces some significant theological tasks, including putting a coherent doctrine of its own in writing. Part of that work is also the continuing clarification of Pentecostal identity. That is important for two main reasons: first of all, for Pentecostalism itself. Only a spiritual movement that begins to understand itself is able to (re)define in ever-changing contexts what the key issues for survival and flourishing may be. A movement without the sense of self-identity may easily drift into "strange waters" and find itself stuck with debates that are foreign to it. Second, the clarification of identity is needed in order to communicate clearly to other Christians—and non-Christians—who they are. Particularly concerning spiritually enthusiastic movements such as Pentecostalism, there are some misconceptions and misunderstandings. It is not good for the movement's future to let others define who they are.

We have to be patient and give time to a young movement, such as Pentecostalism, to work on its identity, theology, and spirituality. Even those older traditions, such as Lutheranism or the Reformed churches still

---

43. Yong, "The Spirit Hovers over the World."

continue this task, after several hundreds of years of reflection. In that continuing work, the role of non-Western Pentecostalism (from Asia, Africa, and Latin America) will be defining for the third millennium as the epicenter of Christianity has already moved there. Most Pentecostals of the world are found elsewhere than in Europe and the United States and therefore we must look to "Majority-World Pentecostals" to help us understand what Pentecostalism is and who we are.

Bibliography

Albrecht, Daniel E. "Pentecostal Spirituality: Looking through the Lens of Ritual." *PNEUMA: The Journal of the Society for Pentecostal Studies* 14.2 (1996) 107–25.
———. *Rites in the Spirit: A Ritual Approach to Pentecostal/Charismatic Spirituality*. Sheffield, UK: Sheffield Academic Press, 1999.
Anderson, Allan H. *An Introduction to Pentecostalism: Global Charismatic Christianity*. Cambridge: Cambridge University Press, 2004.
Anderson, Allan H., and W. J. Hollenweger, eds. *Pentecostals after a Century: Global Perspectives on a Movement in Transition*. Sheffield, UK: Sheffield Academic Press, 1999.
Antola, Markku. *The Experience of Christ's Real Presence in Faith: An Analysis on the Christ-Presence-Motif in the Lutheran Charismatic Renewal*. Schriften der Luther-Agricola Gesellschaft 43. Helsinki: Luther-Agricola Gesellschaft, 1998.
Archer, Kenneth J. "Pentecostal Story: The Hermeneutical Filter for the Making of Meaning." *PNEUMA: The Journal of the Society for Pentecostal Studies* 26.1 (2004) 36–59.
Burgess, Stanley M., and Eduard M. van der Maas, eds. *The New International Dictionary of Pentecostal and Charismatic Movements*. Revised and Expanded Edition. Grand Rapids: Zondervan, 2002.
Cargal, Timothy B. "Beyond the Fundamentalist-Modernist Controversy: Pentecostals and Hermeneutics in a Postmodern Age." *PNEUMA: The Journal of the Society for Pentecostal Studies* 15.2. (1993) 163–87.
Cox, Harvey. *Fire from Heaven: The Rise of Pentecostal Spirituality and the Reshaping of Religion in the Twenty-first Century*. Reading, MA: Addison-Wesley, 1995.
Dayton, Donald W. *Theological Roots of Pentecostalism*. Grand Rapids: Zondervan, 1987.
Duffield, Guy P., and N. M. Van Cleave. *Foundations of Pentecostal Theology*. Los Angeles: L.I.F.E. Bible College, 1983.
Ervin, Howard M. "Koinonia, Church and Sacraments: A Pentecostal Response." Unpublished Pentecostal position paper read at the International Roman Catholic-Pentecostal Dialogue in Venice, August 1–8, 1987.
Gelpi, Donald L. *Experiencing God: A Theology of Human Emergence*. New York: University Press of America, 1987.
———. *The Turn to Experience in Contemporary Theology*. New York: Paulist, 1994.
Hollenweger, Walter J. "After Twenty Years' Research on Pentecostalism." *International Review of Missions* 75 (1986) 3–12.

———. "Charisma and *Oikumene*: The Pentecostal Contribution to the Church Universal." *One in Christ* 7 (1971) 332–33.
———. *Pentecostalism: Origins and Developments Worldwide*. Peabody, MA: Hendrickson, 1997.
———. *The Pentecostals*. Peabody, MA: Hendrickson, 1988.
Kärkkäinen, Veli-Matti. *Ad ultimum terrae, Evangelization, Proselytism and Common Witness in the Roman Catholic-Pentecostal Dialogue 1990–1997*. Studies in the Intercultural History of Christianity 117. Frankfurt: Lang, 1999.
———. "'Encountering Christ in the Full Gospel Way': An Incarnational Pentecostal Spirituality." *Journal of the European Pentecostal Theological Association* 37.1 (2007) 9–23.
———. "Free Churches, Ecumenism and Pentecostalism." In *Toward a Pneumatological Theology: Pentecostal and Ecumenical Perspectives on Ecclesiology, Soteriology, and Theology of Mission*, edited by Amos Yong, 53–64. Lanham, MD: University Press of America, 2002.
———. "Identity and Plurality: A Pentecostal-Charismatic Perspective." *International Review of Mission* 91.363 (2002) 500–504.
———. "Pentecostalism and Pentecostal Theology in the Third Millennium: Taking Stock of Contemporary Global Situation." In *The Spirit in the World: Emerging Pentecostal Theologies in Global Contexts*, edited by Veli-Matti Kärkkäinen, xiii–xiv. Grand Rapids: Eerdmans, 2009.
———. "Pneumatologies in Systematic Theology." In *Studying Global Pentecostalism: Theories and Methods*, edited by Allan Anderson, Michael Bergunder, André Droogers, and Cornelis van der Laan, 223–44. Los Angeles: University of California Press, 2010.
———. *Spiritus ubi vult spirat: Pneumatology in Roman Catholic-Pentecostal Dialogue (1972–1989)*. Schriften der Luther-Agricola-Gesellschaft 42. Helsinki: Luther-Agricola Society, 1998.
———. "'The Re-Turn of Religion in the New Millennium': Pentecostalisms and Postmodernities." *Swedish Missiological Themes* 95.4 (2007) 469–96.
———. "'The Spirit Poured Out on All Flesh': Pentecostal Testimonies and Experiences of the Holy Spirit." In Lord and Life Giver: Spirit Today. A special edition of *Concilium* 4 (2011) 78–86.
———. "Vapaakristillisyys, helluntailaisuus ja baptismi." In *Teoksessa Kirkkotiedon kirja: Ekumeeninen johdatus kirkkojen oppiin ja elämään*, edited by Pekka Metso and Esko Ryökäs, 283–324. Helsinki: Kirjapaja, 2005.
Kuosmanen, Juhani. *Raamatun opetuksia*. Vantaa: RV-Kirjat, 1993.
Land, Steven J. *Pentecostal Spirituality: A Passion for the Kingdom*. Sheffield, UK: Sheffield Academic Press, 1993.
Macchia, Frank. "Tongues as a Sign: Towards a Sacramental Understanding of Pentecostal Experience." *PNEUMA: The Journal of the Society for Pentecostal Studies* 5 (1993) 61–76.
Miller, Albert. "Pentecostalism as a Social Movement." *Journal of Pentecostal Theology* 9 (1996) 97–144.
Onyinah, Opoku. "Deliverance as a Way of Confronting Witchcraft in Contemporary Africa: Ghana as a Case Study." In *The Spirit in the World: Emerging Pentecostal Theologies in Global Contexts*, edited by Kärkkäinen Veli-Matti, 181–202. Grand Rapids: Eerdmans, 2009.

Plüss, Jean-Daniel. "Azusa and Other Myths: The Long and Winding Road from Experience to Stated Beliefs and Back." *PNEUMA: The Journal of the Society for Pentecostal Studies* 15.2 (1993) 189–201.

Robeck, Cecil M. *Azusa Street: Mission and Revival.* Nashville: Thomas Nelson, 2006.

———. "Taking Stock of Pentecostalism." *PNEUMA: The Journal of the Society for Pentecostal Studies* 15 (1993) 35–60.

Sheppard, Gerald T. "Pentecostalism and the Hermeneutics of Dispensationalism: The Anatomy of an Uneasy Relationship." *PNEUMA: The Journal of the Society for Pentecostal Studies* 6.2 (1984) 5–34.

Spittler, Russell P. "Spirituality, Pentecostal and Charismatic." In *The New International Dictionary of Pentecostal and Charismatic Movements. Revised and Expanded Edition*, edited by Burgess, Stanley M. and Eduard M. van der Maas, 1096–1102. Grand Rapids: Zondervan, 2002.

Viksten, Mauri. *Terveen opin pääpiirteitä.* Vantaa: RV-Kirjat, 1980.

Warrington, Keith, ed. *Pentecostal Perspectives.* Carlisle, UK: Paternoster, 1998.

Welker, Michael. *God the Spirit.* Translated by John F. Hoffmeyer. Minneapolis: Fortress, 1993.

Yong, Amos. "The Spirit Hovers over the World: Toward a Typology of 'Spirit' in the Religion and Science Dialogue." *The Digest: Transdisciplinary Approaches to Foundational Questions* 4.12 (2004). http://www.metanexus.net/digest/2004_10_27.htm.

3

Some Aspects of Hermeneutics in the Pentecostal Tradition

ROGER STRONSTAD

Introduction

IN A VARIETY OF ways every Bible reader is an interpreter. The task of interpretation began with the writers of the Bible, in whole (the canon) and in part (individual documents). No writer simply penned the "raw" data of events or episodes. Every writer processed the raw data according to a variety of cultural, historical, and theological presuppositions. In addition, the Hebrew and Greek Bibles were, sooner and later translated into the babel of the world's languages. In this context, every translation is an act of interpretation. And, of course, everyone who reads the Scriptures—in whole or in part; in the original languages or in translation—is an interpreter. However, not all interpreters are equally informed or skilled. The following discussion aims to help the twenty-first-century reader of the Scriptures to become a better interpreter of (specifically) Luke's two-volume book, Luke-Acts, which is the foundation of Pentecostal doctrine. The structure of the presentation is simple and straightforward: (1) Three Preliminary Considerations, (2) Luke Is a Historian, (3) Luke Is a Theologian, (4) Luke Is a Teacher of Salvation History ,(4.1) Luke's Use of the Old Testament/Septuagint, (4.2) Luke's Narrative Strategies.

1. Three Preliminary Considerations

The subject of the hermeneutics of Luke-Acts can be approached in a variety of ways. One of them is to briefly consider the human, divine, and ethical dimensions of the hermeneutics of interpreting the Bible.

1.1 The Human Dimension of Interpretation

The interpretation of Scripture, in whole and in part, is the process of translating the words/language of a speaker or writer into the words of the hearer or reader. This activity includes a minimum of five interdependent activities. First, it involves the *translation* of the Hebrew and/or Greek text into the native language of the interpreter. Second, interpretation involves the task, which is identified by another Greek loan-word, namely, *exegesis*, which begins with a detailed analysis of the text (either in the biblical language or in translation). Third, the process of interpretation sets the text under consideration into its *contexts* (immediate, book, and canonical). Fourth, the interpretation of select texts will, by a process of crystallization advance from analysis to synthesis—that is, from exegesis to *biblical theology*. Fifth, this process—from interpretation to theology–demands the relevant *application* of Scripture to the interpreter's life setting, for Christianity is a living, existential faith and not merely a set of doctrines.

1.2 The Divine Dimension in Interpretation

The task or process of interpretation which I have summarized in the preceding paragraph primarily involves the human side of interpretation. However, the interpretation of Scripture can never be limited to being human activity. This is because the text to be interpreted is not merely a human text but it is also a divine word. As a divine word, it needs a divine assistance when interpreted. The Scriptures, themselves, speak of this repeatedly. For example, on one occasion when Jesus was teaching some disciples he, "opened their minds to understand the Scriptures" (Luke 24:45). On an earlier occasion, Jesus had promised the disciples, "the Holy Spirit . . . will teach you all things, and bring to your remembrance all that I said to you" (John 14:26). Similarly, Paul insists, "the natural man does not accept the things of the Spirit of God . . . and he cannot understand them, because they are spiritually appraised" (1 Cor 2:14). These quotations illustrate that the interpreter must be a spiritual person, one who allows the risen Jesus to open his/her heart to understand the Scriptures, one who submits to the teaching of the Spirit just as a servant submits to his/her master, one who has been born again and lives and walks by the Spirit.

1.3 The Ethical or Moral Dimension of Interpretation

The Protestant Reformation transferred the interpretation of Scripture from the domain of the church to the domains of churches, movements, special interest groups and/or individuals. This effected some gains—the doctrine of *sola Scriptura*, but it also effected some losses. One loss is that it loosed upon Christendom a Pandora's Box of potential and actual Scripture twisting. This unintended consequence of the Reformation continues to the present. Yet, since Scripture is God's Word, and the interpreter is the servant of the Word, this interpretational anarchy is morally problematic. The interpreter has no moral right to "master" the Word—however well-intentioned (s)he may be. The interpreter is under the moral or ethical obligation to be a trustee of the Word. As a trustee of God's Word, the interpreter is morally bound to work toward a consensual understanding of Scripture, in whole and in part. When it comes to interpretation, there is no moral virtue in the pursuit of individual, idiosyncratic, and/or novel meanings. The goal is to teach "sound" words, that is, spiritually healthy words (1 Tim 6:3). The interpreter is to "guard through the Holy Spirit . . . the treasure [Scripture] which has been entrusted to him" (2 Tim 1:14). This is the ethical imperative that the interpreter, "handle accurately the Word of truth" (2 Tim 2:14).

When it comes to identifying the genre of Luke-Acts, interpreters have struggled to find appropriate terms. This is primarily because as a two-volume narrative, focusing first of Jesus and then of his followers, Luke-Acts is a very complex document. For example, earlier interpreters might simply identify Luke as "historian." However, by the 1970s, Luke had come to be identified as "historian and theologian." Now, in the twenty-first century, Luke has been identified as "storyteller, interpreter, and evangelist."[1] There is validity in all of these identifications, but for the purpose of this discussion about aspects of hermeneutics in the Pentecostal tradition I am identifying Luke as, "historian, theologian, and as teacher."

2. Luke Is a Historian

The Bible is a collection of books that were written over many centuries and in a variety of styles or genres. These include such genres as historical narrative, poetry, proverbs, prophetic sayings or oracles, letters, written sermons, and an apocalypse. In the New Testament, the most common literary style is the letter or epistle. Paul, James, Peter, John, and Jude all wrote

---

1. To illustrate this trend to increasing complexity, see Robertson, *Luke the Historian in the Light of Research*; Marshall, *Luke*; Parsons, *Luke*.

letters to individual churches, groups of churches, or to individuals. Further, though it is often classified as a letter, the book of Hebrews identifies itself as a "word of exhortation" or written sermon (Heb 13:22). In addition, the last book of the New Testament identifies itself as a revelation or an apocalypse (Rev 1:1). In contrast, the first five books of the New Testament are written as historical narrative. The church classifies the books of John, Matthew, Mark, and Luke as "good news" or gospels, and Luke's second book as the Acts of the Apostles. Luke, however, identifies both of his books, the Gospel and the Acts, as historical narrative. Luke, therefore, is a historian.

That Luke is a historian is self-evident from his narrative style. Luke was neither one of the Twelve nor one of the larger circle of Jesus' disciples. Therefore, as a later convert to Christianity, he was dependent upon earlier eye-witness reports for his information about all that Jesus said and did (Luke 1:1–4). Luke takes his sources, which most likely include Mark's Gospel, and sets the key events of the gospel in the context of the ongoing history of the Roman Empire. For example, he sets the birth announcement of John the Baptist in the days of King Herod (1:5). He also reports that the birth of Jesus happened when, "a decree went out from Caesar Augustus, that a census be taken of all the inhabited earth" (2:1). In addition, Luke reports that John began his prophetic ministry, "in the fifteenth year of the reign of Tiberius Caesar, when Pontius Pilate was governor of Judea . . ." (3:1). Much later, Paul takes the good news about Jesus throughout the Roman Empire, in the decades when Sergius Paulus is proconsul of Cyprus (Acts 13:7), the Emperor Claudius has recently expelled the Jews from Italy (Acts 18:1), Gallio is proconsul of Asia (18:12) and, in turn, Felix and Festus are resident governors at Caesarea (Acts 23–25). Self-evidently, Luke takes pains to show that the events of both the origin and the spread of the gospel are woven into the warp and the woof of the advancing history of the Roman Empire and its leaders.

It is not only self-evident from his style that Luke is a historian but the two prologues to Luke-Acts show that he is a deliberate, self-conscious historian. Luke opens his so-called gospel (i.e., The Gospel according to Luke) with a brief but formal prologue (Luke 1:1–4). This serves as the introduction to both volumes of his two-volume book. Luke begins volume 2, the so-called Acts of the Apostles, with a somewhat lengthier prologue (Acts 1:1–11). This prologue recapitulates the closing episodes of the first volume (e.g., the commissioning and the ascension) and also introduces the theme of Acts, namely, all that Jesus had begun to do and teach he will continue to do and teach by/through the Holy Spirit, his surrogate presence in and among his disciples and, later, their converts.

At the beginning of his first book, Luke identifies what he has written to Theophilus by the Greek word *diēgēsis* (Luke 1:1). This word means "account" or "narrative," and identifies not only the Gospel of Luke but also identifies its sequel, the Acts. The word *diēgēsis* is an *hapax legomena*, that is, it appears but once in the New Testament. Therefore, we must examine other Greek literature for help in determining its meaning.

The Liddell and Scott lexicon shows that the word *diēgēsis* is used from Plato onwards, including the first-century Jewish writers Philo and Josephus.[2] However, in the light of Luke's demonstrable dependence on the Septuagint (abbrev., LXX), the pre-Christian translation of the Hebrew Bible into the Greek language, we do not have to go further afield than this translation to understand how Luke uses the term. In the LXX *diēgēsis* has a variety of meanings: tale (Deut 28:37), byword (2 Chr 7:20), riddle (Ezek 17:2), and discourse (Sir 8:8, 9). More relevant to Luke's usage, the anonymous writer of 2 Maccabees describes the five books of Jason of Cyrene, which he proposes to epitomize into a single book as "narratives of history" (*tēs historias diēgēmasin*, 2 Macc 2:27). Moreover, *diēgēsis*, "is use *ter* (three times) in the letter of Aristeas to Polycrates (1, 8, 322) to describe the 'narrative' he has to unfold." It is this latter usage in Aristeas which most closely approximates its meaning in Luke's prologue, namely, to imply a full narrative.

In his second prologue, at the beginning of Acts (1:1–11), Luke identifies what he has written earlier as his "first account" (*proton logon*, 1:1). In his commentary on the Greek text of Acts, F. F. Bruce informs his readers: "*Logos* is used for a division of a work which covered more than one papyrus roll. . . . Lk. and Ac. covered one papyrus roll each."[3] As used in his prologue to Acts, however, *logos* means more than simply, "first papyrus roll." It also points to the genre of Luke-Acts. In similar contexts, such as in the earlier historian, Herodotus, for example, *logos* means either a complete historical work (*Hist.* 2.123; 6.19; 7.152), or else it means one section of such a work (*Hist.* 1.75; 2.38, *et al.*). In language which is similar to Luke's, Herodotus writes about, "the first book of my history (*en to(i) proto(i) ton logon*, 5.36), or the beginning of my history (*en toisoi protoisi ton logon*, 7.93). Clearly, in these contexts not only does *logos* mean papyrus roll, but it also means narrative history, whether it is viewed in whole or in its parts.

In the LXX, moreover, *logos* often translates the Hebrew word *dabar*, which can mean either "word" or "thing," to mean both "act" and "chronicle." For example, concerning David the Chronicler reports:

---

2. Liddell and Scott, *A Greek-English Lexicon*.
3. Bruce, *The Acts of the Apostles*, 65.

> Now the acts (*logos*) of King David . . . are written in the chronicles (*en logois*) of Samuel the Seer, in the chronicles (*logon*) of Nathan the prophet, and in the chronicles (*logon*) of Gad the seer (LXX 1 Chr 29:29).

Similarly, the acts (*logos*) of Rehoboam and other kings are written in the Chronicles of the prophets (LXX 2 Chr 12:15 *et al.*). Indeed, as designating the "acts of X" *logos* is synonymous with *praxeis*, and, as designating the "record about X," *logos* is synonymous with *biblio(i)* (2 Chr 13:22).

Obviously, Luke's use of the words *diēgēsis* and *proton logon* (Luke 1:1; Acts 1:1) means that Luke-Acts has affinities with the Greek histories of Herodotus *et al.* and, in the LXX with the Hellenistic Jewish history written by Jason of Cyrene and epitomized in 2 Maccabees, as well as with the sacred history, 1 and 2 Chronicles. Clearly, this evidence shows that Luke is a self-conscious historian, and his multi-volume book (Luke-Acts) is history. This means that we can no longer continue to classify Luke's first account *simply* as a gospel and Luke as an evangelist. Luke himself does not give us these options. Mark claims to have written a gospel (Mark 1:1), whereas Luke claims to have written a history. Thus, Mark is an evangelist, but Luke is not. Furthermore, Luke is a historian, but Mark is not.

These observations about Luke and Mark and the genre of their writings are supported by the early church historian, Eusebius of Caesarea (c. 265–339). Eusebius identifies Luke's two books by two terms. The first is the Greek word *historesen* (*Hist. eccl.* 1.195). This word means "written account," "narrative," or "history." Eusebius also identifies Luke's two books by the Greek word *praxeis* (*Hist. eccl.* 1.253). This word is usually translated into English as "acts." *Praxeis*, or Acts, is the traditional title of Luke's second book. Clearly, the evidence of these four terms, the two from Luke's prologues and the two from Eusebius, is unanimous and unambiguous. It is unfortunate that in the English Bible Luke's two books have different names, namely, the Gospel according to Luke and the Acts of the Apostles. Despite this, both separately and together Luke-Acts is to be classified as historical narrative or chronicle, history, or acts. This makes Luke, their author, the first but not the last historian of the church.

3. Luke Is a Theologian

As we have already observed, Luke identified his two-volume book to be historical narrative (Luke 1:1; Acts 1:1). This identification puts him in the context of earlier historiography, both secular and sacred. Except for the occasional eccentric modern interpreter, seemingly determined to be new and novel no matter how solidly grounded the current consensus about the genre of Luke-Acts is, no one disputes that Luke is a historian. However, when we turn from the subject of Luke the historian to the subject of Luke the theologian, it is an altogether different matter. There is as yet no scholarly consensus about Luke the theologian. Storm winds sweep across the interpretive landscape.

These winds relate to the issue of genre or literary style. We have observed that Luke writes as a historian and Luke-Acts is historical narrative. Typically, many New Testament scholars have repudiated the efforts of those who use historical narrative for theological purposes. However, something approaching scholarly consensus is beginning to emerge from the storm clouds of controversy. The following quotations illustrate the emerging consensus.

Luke-Acts provided historical definition and identity as well as theological legitimation for the author's conception of narrative Christianity.[4]

> History writing in antiquity had a didactic (instructional) quality and aim.[5]
>
> ... we reject Fee and Stuart's highlighted maxim that, "unless Scripture explicitly tells us . . . ." Though they do not intend it as such, this restriction implicitly contradicts 2 Timothy 3:16 and fails to grasp the key purpose of historical narrative.[6]
>
> There is nothing wrong in principle with deriving normative beliefs and practices from narratives.[7]

The quotations illustrate the perspectives of scholars from a variety of Christian traditions. Because they are observations about historical narrative rather than, for example, being attempts to espouse some particular view about deriving normative beliefs and practices from Luke's narratives, they represent a fresh wind in the study of Luke's historiography. Therefore, while in and of themselves these quotations do not prove that Luke is a "theologian" of salvation history, they do mean that the Pentecostal interpreter, proceeding with all due caution and diligence, may explore Luke-Acts as Scripture, which is much more valuable than mere historical narrative.

The interpreter who treats Luke-Acts as a document which has theological value for the modern Christian must answer a number of questions, both general and specific. For example, did Luke have a theology? Yes. Every

---

4. Aune, *The New Testament in Its Literary Environment*, 137.
5. Bruce, "First Church Historian," 13.
6. Klein, Blomberg, and Hubbard, *Introduction to Biblical Interpretation*, 349–50.
7. Michaels, "Evidences of the Spirit," 203.

biblical writer, indeed, every Christian has a theology or theologies. This is true whether or not it is a conscious or more unconscious theology; whether it is articulated or implied.

Acknowledging that Luke had a theology we may then ask: did he write Luke-Acts with a theological as well as a historical intent? Yes. His narratives report what Jesus, the prophet who was mighty in word and deed, had accomplished in bringing salvation to mankind, to both the Jew and the gentile.

Since Luke wrote as a theologian as well as a historian we must also ask, Is it possible for those who read Luke-Acts to discern his theology in his narrative, his history about all that Jesus began—and after his resurrection-ascension continued—to do and teach? Again, yes. Readers of Luke-Acts, both the lay person and the professional interpreter, will discern Luke's theology about Jesus as Savior, Lord, and Christ (Luke 2:11); his theology about God as Father and his complementary theology about the Holy Spirit, who is present to baptize, to empower, to fill, and to lead his disciples.[8]

These somewhat more general questions and answers lead to several more specific questions. For example, having asked the question, did Luke have a theology? and answered, yes, we must now ask, Is Luke a theologian in his own right? This is another way of asking the question, Is Luke's theology independent of Paul's theology? In other words, does Luke contribute fundamental theological perspectives, which though *complementary* to Paul's perspectives, are not *conformable* to Paul's perspectives? Typically, Pentecostals have answered these questions with a resounding yes. For example, they interpret Paul's Spirit baptism language in 1 Corinthians 12:13 to be about a person's conversion-initiation, but, in contrast, they interpret Luke's Spirit baptism language (Luke 3:16; Acts 1:5; 11:16) to be about commissioning-empowerment. In contrast to this, many non-Pentecostals insist that both the Pauline and the Lukan Spirit baptism must have the same meaning—conversion-initiation. Thus, many non-Pentecostals believe that the term always has a soteriological meaning whereas, depending upon Paul's and Luke's context, Pentecostals, believe the term may be *either* soteriological (1 Cor 12:13) *or* vocational (Luke 3:16; Acts 1:5; 11:16). This example illustrates that Pentecostals champion Luke to be a theologian in his own right, to be a writer with his own unique and independent contribution to the theology of the New Testament. Pentecostals insist that Luke is not to be pressed into Paul's mold.

---

8. Recent discussions about Luke as theologian include: Conzelmann, *The Theology of St. Luke*; O'Neill, *The Theology of Acts in Its Historical Setting*; Green, *The Theology of the Gospel of Luke*; Jervell, *The Theology of the Acts of the Apostles*; Bock, *A Theology of Luke and Acts*.

Understanding that Luke is a theologian is complicated by several facts, namely, that Luke wrote a two-volume book to which the translators and editors have given different names (unlike how they have handled Old Testament books such as 1 and 2 Samuel, 1 and 2 Kings and 1 and 2 Chronicles), whose names wrongly imply that Luke wrote each book in a different genre or literary style (The *Gospel* according to Luke and the *Acts* of the Apostles), and further said books have been split apart in the canonical shape of the New Testament by the ill-advised insertion of the Gospel according to John between Luke's first account (Luke) and his second account (Acts).[9] Many interpreters have adopted the stance that one can do theology (i.e., Christology) from the Gospel of Luke, even though it is a historical narrative, but that one cannot do theology (i.e., pneumatology) from the Acts of the Apostles, because it is historical narrative. If Luke, however, wrote his gospel as both a historian and a theologian then, by his own account, he was still a theologian as well as a historian when he wrote the Acts of the Apostles. In other words, if Luke's Gospel is a source for understanding Luke's theology-Christology, then the Acts is just as surely a source for understanding and applying Luke's theology-pneumatology.

To conclude, it is probable that the emerging consensus about Luke-Acts: 1) will put an end to the all-too-common artificial, arbitrary, and altogether false dichotomy which is made between history and theology in Luke-Acts; 2) will jettison the "cannon within a cannon" approach to theology whereby Paul determines what is normative and also determines what Luke means, and 3) will accord to Luke-Acts the unity of genre and the complementary unity of authorial theological intent from Luke's first to his second accounts about the origin and spread of Christianity.

4. Luke Is a Teacher of Salvation History

Luke is a historian, but he is more than a historian. At one and the same time, he is also an intentional theologian. But Luke is more than a historian who writes narrative theology. Luke is also, self-consciously, a teacher. In his first prologue Luke explains to Theophilus (and to everyone else who reads Luke-Acts) about his catechetical or instructional intentions: ". . . it seemed fitting for me . . . to write . . . so that you might know the exact truth about the things you have been taught" (*catechēsis* Luke 1:4). So, although Theophilus has been taught/instructed about all that Jesus had done and

---

9. *The Full Life Bible Commentary to the New Testament* follows the order, John, Matthew, Mark, Luke-Acts. See Preface (vii) for the explanation of this order. See Arrington and Stronstad, *The Full Life Bible Commentary to the New Testament*, vii.

taught, Luke, nevertheless, wrote his narrative about the origin and spread of Christianity to instruct him in a more orderly manner (Luke 1:3,4). In this regard, Theophilus seems to be like the earlier example of Apollos, whom Luke reported to have been instructed, catechized in the way of the Lord, but who, nevertheless, was given a more accurate teaching by Priscilla and Aquila (Acts 18:25–26). Luke does not tell his readers by what catechetical methodologies Apollos was instructed by Priscilla and Aquila, but his readers can observe by what genre and by what narrative strategies he, himself, instructed Theophilus.

As we have observed, Luke-Acts is a historical narrative that Luke has self-consciously, deliberately infused with a theological purpose. In order to instruct his readers, Theophilus, and every other reader, he uses a variety of narrative and instructional strategies. Several of these are directly rooted in Luke's own Bible, namely, the Septuagint translation of the Hebrew Bible. These include but are not limited to: 1) the use of OT/LXX terminology, 2) echoes of Old Testament typology and 3) reports of charismatic (i.e., Spirit-inspired) exegesis. Other strategies supplement Luke's indebtedness, both to the Hebrew Bible and its Old Testament translation. These include, though are not limited to: 1) programmatic episodes, 2) bracketing/*inclusio*, 3) prophecy-fulfillment, 4) parallelism, and 5) antecedent spiritual prerequisite themes. Without danger of contradiction, it may be said that Luke is a highly skilled, interesting, and effective instructor.

4.1 Luke's Use of the Old Testament/Septuagint.

Advancing from the prologue to Luke's Gospel, the reader, whether he be Theophilus in the first century or someone in the twenty-first century, plunges from one culture to another—from a culture at home in formal, classical Greek to a culture of Jewish piety. Luke begins his narrative in the world of Jewish piety, and whether the language is that of his sources or his own, it is laced with so-called septuagintalisms. These are the product of translating the Hebrew language into the Greek language. In chapter 1 of the Gospel, with its unexpected reports about the activity of the Holy Spirit, Luke shows a definite indebtedness to the LXX when he reports about the restoration of prophecy that is associated with the birth announcements of John and Jesus.

Old Testament/LXX Terms

The late fourth-century conquest of the ancient Near East by Alexander the Great (ca., B.C. 336–23), and the subsequent control of Judea by the competing Greek kingdoms of the Ptolemies in Egypt and the Seleucids in Syria brought about the Hellenization of many Jews, both in Judea and throughout the Diaspora. Thus, it was that to meet the synagogue needs of Greek-speaking Jews in Ptolemaic Egypt that the Hebrew Bible was first translated into the Greek language. This translation is called the Septuagint after the legendary number of translators—seventy. One hundred and fifty years later Greek-speaking Christians, both the Jew and the gentile, appropriated the LXX as their own Scriptures. Thus, the LXX was Luke's Bible, and it provided much of the theological terminology (Greek words; Hebrew meanings) that he used to report the origin and spread of the gospel, of Christianity. This is as true for his reports about the activity of the Spirit of God, beginning with the opening infancy narrative (Luke 1:5—2:52), as it is for his reports about the birth of Joshua (LXX, Jesus), the Messiah (LXX, Christ), i.e., Jesus Christ.

With one exception, namely John the Baptist's signature prophecy about being "baptized in the Holy Spirit" (Luke 3:16), every term which Luke uses to describe the presence, activity, and effects of the Holy Spirit is first found in the LXX. For example, with the birth announcements about the messianic messenger, and the coming of the Messiah, there is an unexpected, unprecedented outburst of the activity of God's Spirit. To describe this, Luke uses the term, "X was filled with the Holy Spirit" (1:15, 41, 67). Here Luke is borrowing the term from his Greek Bible, where it was used five times—all in some form of charismatic context (Exod 28:3; 31:3, etc.). Further, the Spirit will "come upon" Mary, Simeon, and others (Luke 1:35; 2:27), as it had earlier "come upon" the prophet Ezekiel (Ezek 2:2; 3:24). Jesus begins his public ministry only after he has been "anointed" by the Holy Spirit (Luke 3:22/4:18), the experience of the Spirit which Isaiah wrote about (Isa. 61:1). Immediately before Jesus launches his ministry, he is "led" by the Spirit (Luke 4:1), an experience of the Spirit about which Ezekiel wrote (Ezek 8:3; 11:1, etc.). Between the resurrection and the ascension, Jesus announces to his disciples that they will be "clothed" with power in the immediate future. In the Greek Bible, this had been the earlier experience of Gideon and others (Judg 6:34; 1 Chr 12:18; 2 Chr 24:20). The evidence for Luke's use of LXX terms permeates his narrative. In a brief survey such as this is, these examples must suffice.[10]

---

10. For more information about this Septuagintal terminology. Stronstad, *The Charismatic Theology of St. Luke*, 20–23.

Old Testament Typology

Luke's use of LXX terminology is a matter of record. Many interpreters, however, shy away from typology because it has all-too-often been practiced in ways that stretch their credibility. Nevertheless, biblical typology is legitimate and, like Luke's use of LXX terminology, is also a matter of record.

In a typological relationship there is a historical correspondence or pattern between two or more historically independent episodes. For example, in the Hebrew Bible, the parting of the Red Sea by Moses (Exod 14) and the parting of the Jordan River by Joshua (Josh 3–4) is an example of this, and it is made explicit by the author of the book of Joshua (4:14, 23). Further, there is a typological relationship in the transfer of the Spirit from one leader to another. Two examples illustrate this: the transfer of the Spirit from Saul to David (1 Sam 13:13–14), and from Elijah to Elisha (2 Kgs 2:9ff). The vantage point of typology is retrospective. In other words, it looks back to a historically analogous and relevant episode from earlier times. Of course, it is God, the Lord of history, who gives the typological correspondence between these historically independent episodes. The historian, however, occasionally may be consciously aware of the typological relationship between the present and the past and shape his narrative accordingly.

Examples of typology in Luke-Acts focus on, but are not limited to, the Moses-Wilderness events and Elijah-Elisha events. For example, the Spirit-led testing of Jesus in the wilderness for forty days echoes the God-led testing in the Wilderness for forty years (Luke 4:1–12; Exod 15:25; 16:4; Deut 8:2, 16). The transfiguration or metamorphosis of Jesus on the mountain, whereby "the appearance of his face became different," echoes the earlier transfiguration or metamorphosis of Moses on Mt. Sinai, whereby his face shone with the glory of God (Luke 9:24–36; Exod 34:29–35). Jesus is also the "prophet like Moses," who must be listened to, i.e., obeyed (Luke 9:35; Deut 18.15).

In addition to the Moses-Jesus typology, there is in Luke's narrative an Elijah, Elisha-Jesus typology. The first example is in the narrative where Luke reports Jesus' inaugural sermon in Nazareth (Luke 4:16–37). Jesus is about to be rejected as a prophet by his own townspeople with the result that he will minister to strangers just as earlier Elijah had gone to the land of Sidon and ministered to a woman and Elisha ministered to no one in Israel, but only to Naaman the Syrian (4:25–27). This Elijah, Elisha-Jesus typology pervades much of Jesus' Spirit-full, Spirit-led, and Spirit-empowered ministry. Jesus controls nature, particularly water, just as earlier Elijah and Elisha had performed miracles relating to water (8:22ff; 1 Kgs 2:8; 2 Kgs 2:19ff); Jesus multiplies food, just as earlier Elijah and Elisha were the agents by whom food was miraculously multiplied (9:12ff; 1 Kgs 7:16; 2 Kgs 4:3ff, 42ff). More dramatically, Jesus raised the dead, just as earlier Elijah and Elisha had raised the dead (7:14–16; 1 Kgs 17.17ff; 2 Kgs 4.34ff). Significantly, when Jesus raised the widow's son from the dead, the people exclaimed, "a great prophet has arisen among us" (Luke 7:16), and thenceforth Jesus had the reputation that he might be (the eschatological) Elijah (9:19; compare Mal 4:5).

This Moses-Wilderness and the Elijah/Elisha-Jesus typology, which Luke knits into the fabric of his narrative, come together dramatically in the Pentecost narrative. On that first post-Easter day of Pentecost, Jesus pours out the Holy Spirit upon his disciples who have gathered at the temple to pray. Two signs of theophany announce to the mixed crowd of the inhabitants of Jerusalem and devout Pentecost pilgrims to Jerusalem: a sound such as that produced by a gale force wind and flames like tongues of fire (Acts 2.2,3). These signs of theophany echo the signs of theophany, first in the time of Moses and then Elijah on Sinai, Horeb, that other mountain of God (Exod 19:16–18; 1 Kgs 19:11–12). In addition, the actual pouring forth of the Holy Spirit upon the disciples (Acts 2:4, 17–21) echoes the earlier transfers of the Spirit from Moses to the seventy elders, on one hand, and from Elijah to Elisha, on the other (Num 11:25–29; 2 Kgs 2:7–18). Many of the Jesus-Moses and Jesus-Elijah/Elisha typological correspondences embedded in the Pentecost narrative are implicit. Though they are implicit they are made certain by a large number of explicit typological correspondences and, further, they clarify and enrich the readers understanding of the Pentecost narrative.

Charismatic Exegesis

Luke not only describes the presence and activity of the Holy Spirit by terms that he found in his Greek Bible (LXX), and not only weaves typological correspondences between Jesus and Moses and between Jesus and Elijah and Elisha into the warp and woof of his narrative, but also uses what has been classified as charismatic exegesis. As defined by David E. Aune, "'charismatic exegesis' is an umbrella term for a variety of methods of biblical interpretation that share several core features: (1) it is *commentary*; (2) it is *inspired*; (3) it has an *eschatological orientation*, and (4) it was a type of prophecy prevalent during the late Second Temple period."[11] Luke reports several examples of charismatic exegesis in his history of the origin and spread of the gospel.

11. Aune, *The Westminster Dictionary of New Testament and Early Christian Literature*, 92.

Luke reports two examples of charismatic exegesis that are more important than the others for understanding his charismatic theology. These are 1) Jesus' inaugural sermon in Nazareth (Luke 4:16–30) and 2) Peter's inaugural sermon in Jerusalem (Acts 2:14–36). These sermons are at strategic locations in the parallel structure of Luke and Acts. In each case, the sermon follows a series of introductory episodes which lead up to the inauguration of the public ministry of Jesus and of his disciples, respectively. As the following chart illustrates, each sermon contains the features of Aune's definition of "charismatic exegesis," even when the defining feature may be implied rather than specific.

Charismatic Exegesis: Two Sermons

Defining Feature	Jesus' Inaugural Sermon Luke 4:16–30	Peter's Inaugural Sermon Acts 2:14–36
1. it is **commentary**	Quotes Isaiah 61. Announces, "Today this Scripture has been fulfilled in your hearing" (Luke 4:21)	Announces, "this is what was spoken of through the prophet Joel" (Acts 2:17). Quotes Joel 2:28–31.
2. it is **inspired**	Prior to the sermon Luke reports that Jesus was, "full of the Holy Spirit" (Luke 4:1). I.e., his sermon is a *pneuma* discourse	Prior to the sermon, Luke reports that Peter was, "filled with the Holy Spirit" (Acts 2.4), i.e., his sermon is a *pneuma* discourse.
3. it has an **eschatological orientation**	The outpouring of the Spirit associated with the birth of John and Jesus heralds the dawning of the new age (Luke 1). Jesus observes that John is the pivot point of sacred history (Luke 16:16)	The outpouring of the Holy Spirit on the day of Pentecost is an event in the *eschaton*, the last days (Acts 2.17)
4. it is a type of **prophecy**	Being a man of the Spirit, Jesus is a prophet (Luke 7:16; 24:19, etc.). His sermon is a *pneuma* discourse (Spirit-inspired speech)	Being a man of the Spirit, Peter is a prophet (Acts 2:17/18). His sermon is a *pneuma* discourse.

As examples of charismatic exegesis in Luke-Acts, these programmatic sermons illustrate Luke's awareness of the extent to which the coming of Jesus (Luke 4) and the pouring forth of the Holy Spirit upon the disciples on the day of Pentecost (Acts 2) fulfill Old Testament expectations.

4.2 Luke's Narrative Strategies

Whether it was at the conscious level or at the unconscious level, or some combination of the two, Luke's intimate and pervasive familiarity with the Greek Bible (LXX) and, in particular, with its sacred histories, shaped his own approach to writing this two-volume sacred history (Luke-Acts). Thus, as we have observed above (Luke's Use of the Old Testament/Septuagint), he used the Greek vocabulary which he found in his Bible to describe the presence and activity of the Holy Spirit in the new, messianic age; he shaped several of his narratives on the principle of typology, and reports several key sermons that are Spirit-inspired applications of Old Testament texts. In addition to this specific Old Testament influence, Luke also uses other narrative strategies that, when they are observed, not only sharpen the reader's exposition of the text but that also enrich the reader's appreciation of both Luke's narrative skills and the message of his charismatic theology. These narrative strategies include, but are not limited to his use of 1) programmatic episodes, 2) the prophecy-fulfillment theme, 3) bracketing, or *inclusio*, 4) parallelism, and 5) the "antecedent spiritual prerequisite" theme.

Programmatic Episodes

In his narrative strategy, Luke begins each of his two accounts about Jesus and his followers and their converts with a prologue (Luke 1:1–4; Acts 1:1–11). The actual narrative in each account begins with a series of transitional and introductory episodes (Luke 1:5—2:52; Acts 1:12–26). Following these introductory episodes, Luke reports about the inauguration of the public ministries, first of Jesus and then of his disciples (Luke 3:1—4:30; Acts 2:1–41). These are not simply important in themselves, but they are programmatic for the meaning and message of each account in its entirety. Appearing early in each account, these programmatic narratives introduce key persons and/or key themes.

Luke reports the inaugural sermon of Jesus in the synagogue in Nazareth and its aftermath. He begins his narrative at that point in the synagogue service when the synagogue official has invited Jesus to follow up the prescribed reading from the Law by reading the prescribed text from the Prophets. Taking the Isaiah scroll, Jesus reads the prescribed limit of two to three verses: "The Spirit of the Lord is upon me, because he anointed me to preach the gospel to the poor . . ." (Luke 4:18; Isa 61:1). Jesus then claims to fulfill what he has just read. He next provokes his townspeople to honor him as a prophet. He also challenges them to receive him in a manner differently than Israel had earlier received the prophets Elijah and Elisha. When, however, with murderous intention his townspeople reject him as a false prophet he leaves them to go and minister to strangers (Luke 4:16–30).

This narrative about Jesus' inaugural sermon is programmatic for Luke's reports about Jesus' entire ministry. As written about in Isaiah, Jesus is the Spirit-anointed Servant. He preaches good news to the poor (Luke 4:18; 6:20; 7:22). This good news includes the message that sins are forgiven (5:24; 7:48). This good news also includes a charismatic, Spirit-empowered ministry (4:14, 18), namely, *the* blind receive sight, *the* lame walk, *the* lepers are cleansed, and *the* deaf hear, *the* dead are raised up, *the* poor have the gospel preached to them (7:22). Luke's reports about the healing of the centurion's slave and the raising of the widow's son from the dead, respectively, echo the earlier ministry of Elijah and Elisha (7:2–27; compare 4:24–27). And so it goes throughout Luke's account about all that Jesus said and did. Jesus' ministry recapitulates themes that Luke has reported programmatically in the inauguration narratives. In other words, as Luke reports it, Jesus functions as the prophet like Isaiah, like Elijah and Elisha, and like the rejected prophets. He also functions as the prophet like Moses (9:28–36) and the prophet like David, that is, the royal prophet (19–23).

In his recent account of all that Jesus began to do and to teach, Luke reports the inaugural sermon of Peter at the temple in Jerusalem (Acts 2:1–41). On that day when devout Jews—those resident in Jerusalem and Judea and pilgrims from the Diaspora—have gathered at the temple, Jesus poured out his Holy Spirit upon the company of about 120 disciples. When Jesus poured forth the Spirit there were two signs of theophany (the noise like a violent wind and the flames like tongues of fire) and the attesting sign of being baptized in the Holy Spirit—the disciples worshiped God in languages which they had never learned (2:2–4). So unexpected and dramatic are these signs that, not surprisingly, the crowd which is gathered at the temple is bewildered, amazed, marveling, perplexed, and even mocking (2:5–13). Peter seizes the moment and, filled with the Holy Spirit, preaches to the crowd. Like Jesus' earlier inaugural sermon Peter's preaching is to be classified as charismatic exegesis (2:14–36). First, he appeals to the prophet Joel to explain what the crowd has just seen and heard (2:17–21). Next, he preaches about Jesus, about his divinely attested charismatic ministry, about his death by crucifixion, and about God raising him from the dead (2:22–36). The aftermath is that about three thousand accept Jesus as their Messiah, repent, are baptized, and added to the company of disciples (2:37–41).

Luke's report of Peter's inaugural sermon at the temple in Jerusalem on the day of Pentecost is programmatic for much of what he narrates in Acts. The pouring forth of the Holy Spirit upon the disciples (Acts

2:1–4) is programmatic for Luke's subsequent reports of further examples of the Holy Spirit being poured out upon disciples wherever the gospel spreads (8:15–17; 9:17; 10:44–48; 19:1–7). That the disciples on the Day of Pentecost were filled with the Holy Spirit and prophesied (2:4, 17–21) is programmatic for the many episodes throughout Luke's narrative when disciples, either in groups or singly, continued to be filled and prophesy—whether said prophesying was a *pneuma* discourse, bold witnessing, or prophetic judgment (4:8, 31; 9:17; 13:9, 52). Further, that Peter witnessed about Jesus as Lord and Christ to devout Jews from the nations of their Dispersion (2:9–11) is programmatic for the geographic spread of the gospel throughout the Roman Empire—from Jerusalem to Rome (2:28). In addition, Peter's witness about the resurrection of Jesus (2:24–36), is programmatic for the ongoing witness about Jesus (3:15; 4:33; 10:40; 13:30–37; 17:31; 23:6–10; 24:21; 26:8). There is, however, one major theme in Acts that is not found programmatically in Luke's report of Peter's inaugural sermon. This absentee theme is what may be called the "gentile mission." The table of nations in 2:9–11 is about the geographic spread of the gospel among the Jews of the Diaspora. Luke does not explicitly introduce the gentile mission until he reports about Paul's mission to bear the name of Jesus "before gentiles and kings and the sons of Israel" (9:15) and also when he reports about Peter's most reluctant visit to the household of Cornelius, the Roman centurion (10:1–11, 18).

Bracketing/*Inclusio*

In addition to using the narrative strategy of programmatic episodes, specifically, to reporting Jesus' inaugural sermon and, then, Peter's inaugural sermon (Luke 4:16–30; Acts 2:1–41), Luke also uses the narrative strategy of bracketing. This narrative strategy is commonly called *inclusion*.[12] This term is cognate to and may be recognized in such common English words as include and inclusive. With this narrative strategy, the narrator, in this case, Luke, brackets a narrative unit, which may vary from book-length to a single episode with a common theme, location, or word or phrase to signify the beginning and the end of the narrative unit.

Luke often uses the narrative strategy of *inclusio*. The following two examples—one from the Gospel of Luke and the other from Acts—illustrate but do no exhaust the number of times he uses *inclusio*. For example, in his first account about Jesus he brackets his report about Jesus' public

---

12. Aune, *The Westminster Dictionary of New Testament and Early Christian Literature*, 229.

ministry as the anointed prophet with explicit prophetic and programmatic references (see discussion above) in Jesus' inaugural sermon and the closing, retrospective reference at the end of his account about Jesus being, "a prophet mighty in word and deed in the sight of God and all the people" (Luke 4:24–30; 24:19). Thus, by the strategy of *inclusio* Luke shows that from first to last Jesus ministered as the Spirit-anointed prophet, i.e., as the prophetic Messiah or Christ.

Examples of *inclusio* are also to be observed in Luke's second account, namely Acts. For example, Luke introduces the ministry of Stephen by identifying him to be, "a man full of faith and of the Holy Spirit" (Acts 6:5). After reporting about Stephen's experiences twice more (6.8 [by implication] 6:10), Luke reports the ending of Stephen's ministry by martyrdom, observing that he was "full of the Holy Spirit" (7:55). Thus, in the same way that Luke showed that Jesus ministered by the Holy Spirit as the anointed prophet from first to last, so Luke showed that Stephen ministered being full of the Holy Spirit from first to last. In other words, this example of Luke's use of the narrative strategy of *inclusio* shows that all of Stephen's "great wonders and signs" and all of his words of "wisdom," not least of which was his defense before the Jewish Council, are full-of-the-Holy Spirit works and words.

Prophecy-Fulfillment

A third narrative strategy that Luke uses is prophecy-fulfillment. Of course, many of the events that are associated with the life, the message, and the ministry of Jesus and of his followers fulfill Old Testament prophecies. But Luke's prophecy-fulfillment narrative strategy is more than about that. It is that strategy whereby when Luke reports a prophecy of John the Baptist or of Jesus he also always reports its subsequent fulfillment in the lives of the disciples. This is a narrative strategy which is unique to Luke among the Gospel writers. It is a uniquely Lukan narrative strategy because he, and only he, completed his account about all that Jesus began to do and to teach with a complementary narrative about what his disciples, as heirs and successors to his ministry, continued to do and to teach.

One of the most far-reaching examples of Luke's prophecy-fulfillment strategy arises out of the ministry of John the Baptist. In common with Matthew, Mark, and John, Luke also reports a prophecy that John made about his successor. In contrast to himself, who baptized in water, the Messiah will baptize in the Holy Spirit and fire (Luke 3:16–17). Among these four writers, only Luke reports the fulfillments of John's prophecy.

But before he reports the fulfillments of John's prophecy he first reports that the Messiah, Jesus, renewed John's prophecy: "He commanded them not to leave Jerusalem, but to wait for what the Father had promised . . . for John baptized with water, but you shall be baptized with the Holy Spirit not many days from now" (Acts 1:4–5). And, indeed, a few days later Jesus poured forth the Holy Spirit upon the disciples, baptizing, empowering, and filling them with the Holy Spirit (1:4, 8; 2:4). John's prophecy is also fulfilled several years later. At that time, the Holy Spirit fell upon Cornelius and his household (10:44). When this happened, Peter, hearing Cornelius speaking in tongues and exalting God (10:46; compare 2:4, 11) remembered Jesus' words, "how he used to say, 'John baptized with water, but you shall be baptized with the Holy Spirit'" (11:16–17). In addition, though Luke does not use the explicit "baptized in water; baptized in the Holy Spirit" language of John's prophecy, he does, nevertheless, report one further example of John's prophecy and its fulfillment. This happened in the experience of some disciples at Ephesus. After Paul had baptized these disciples in water, the Holy Spirit came on them, and they *began* speaking in tongues (compare 2:4) and prophesying (Acts 2:17).

Luke's use of the prophecy-fulfillment strategy can also be illustrated from Jesus' teaching about the Holy Spirit. Luke reports that Jesus made six promises to his disciples about the Holy Spirit: three before the resurrection and three after the resurrection. Before the resurrection, he first promised his disciples that the Father would give the Holy Spirit, the superlative gift, to those who pray (Luke 11:13). In addition, he also promised that when the witness of the disciples about him would be opposed the Holy Spirit would teach them what to say in their defense, that is, Jesus (through the Holy Spirit) would give them words and wisdom (12:11–12; 21:14–15). Between his resurrection and the ascension, Jesus promised that his disciples would be clothed, witness; he renewed John the Baptist's prophecy about being baptized in the Holy Spirit and for a second time promised that they would receive God's empowering presence, namely, the empowering Holy Spirit (24:49; Acts 1:5, 8).

Having recorded these six examples—and they are but six out of many (note Peter's observation [Acts 11:15])—of Jesus' prophecies about the Holy Spirit, Luke, since he continued his first account with a second, *must* also report examples of their fulfillment. In fact, only by reporting fulfillment of these pre- and post-resurrection promises can he show that Jesus was a true prophet. Thus, the prophecy that the disciples will receive the Father's gift of the Holy Spirit was fulfilled in Jerusalem on the day of Pentecost (note 1:14) and later in Samaria (8:15). Further, the prophecies of the Holy Spirit's *inspiring* presence when the disciples were being opposed (Luke

12:11–12; 21:14–15) were fulfilled in the experiences of Peter and Stephen (Acts 4:8; 6:10). The two prophecies of the Spirit's *empowering* presence for witness (Luke 24:19; Acts 1:8) were repeatedly fulfilled (4:33 etc.). Finally, Jesus renewed John the Baptist's prophecy about being baptized in the Holy Spirit (Luke 3:16–17); a prophecy for which Luke reported two explicit fulfillments (Acts 1:4–5/2:4; 10:44–48/11:15–17) and two implicit examples (8:15–17; 19:1–7).

Clearly, Luke's prophecy-fulfillment strategy was neither incidental to his narrative nor insignificant for his message. Luke was intentional and his very intentionality points to the importance that he attached to the prophecy of John the Baptist and the promises of Jesus. It should be equally clear that Luke was a highly skilled narrator. Self-evidently, he crafted his narrative with much care. He introduced key themes in his two accounts by placing a programmatic narrative near the beginning of each account. He tied narrative units together by using the technique of bracketing or *inclusio*. He also repeatedly demonstrated that John the Baptist and Jesus of Nazareth were true prophets by the narrative strategy of prophecy-fulfillment. In addition to all of this, Luke also frequently used the narrative strategy which is identified by the term "parallelism." To a discussion of this, we will now proceed.

Parallelism: Doublets and Triplets

This is the most characteristic of Luke's narrative strategies. When Luke uses this strategy, he writes the second narrative in ways that directly, explicitly parallel the first. The parallelism may be as broad and complete as the fact that the thematic structure of Luke's "second account" (Acts) parallels the thematic structure of Luke's "first account" (Luke). It may include small narrative units within both Luke and Acts, such as the programmatic narrative about Jesus' inaugural sermon (Luke 4:16–31) and Peter's inaugural sermon (Acts 2:14–41). Or it may include parallels within either one of Luke's books, such as his descriptions in the infancy narrative about John and Jesus, and Luke's description of Peter's and Paul's experiences of being filled with the Holy Spirit. Luke's use of parallelism is so pervasive that it cannot be an occasional happenstance. Rather, it is the product of Luke's distinctive mindset or outlook about the origin and the spread of Christianity.

Several examples of Luke's parallelism figure prominently in his writings. These include 1) parallels between John's and Peter's preaching about salvation, 2) parallels between the lives and ministries of John and Jesus, 3) parallels between Luke's reports about Jesus' Spirit-anointing and the

Spirit baptisms of the disciples on the day of Pentecost and, years later, the household of Cornelius and 4) the parallels between the prophecy-sign motif in the Pentecost narrative and in the Cornelius narrative. In addition to the examples of Luke's narrative strategy of parallelism, which are discussed as part of the exposition about being baptized and filled with the Holy Spirit, there are many other significant examples of this narrative strategy. These will be identified, but, because of the limits of this chapter, will not be discussed.

1. Luke's thematic structure of his "second account" (Acts) parallels the thematic structure of his "first account" (Luke).

2. Luke's report about the pouring forth of the Holy Spirit on all people on the day of Pentecost (Acts 2:17–21) parallels his earlier report about the Spirit of Prophecy manifest through sons and daughters, young men and old men, and even upon male and female bond-slaves in his infancy narrative (Luke 1–2).

3. Luke's report about Stephen, his experience of the Spirit, his ministry, and his martyrdom (Acts 6:8—7:60) parallels important aspects of Jesus' earlier experience of the Spirit, his ministry, and his martyrdom (Luke 4–24).

4. Luke's report about the charismatic ministries of Peter and Paul, such as healing cripples and raising the dead, not only parallel each other but also parallel the earlier charismatic ministry of Jesus.

To aid the interpreter in understanding Luke's narrative strategy and the message(s) which it communicates, these examples of Luke's parallels are listed in Appendices 1–4. Luke's reports about Paul's three evangelistic tours (a.k.a. three missionary journeys), the three reports of his conversion, etc., continue to remind his readers that these parallel accounts are important signposts to what is important to Luke, himself.

Luke's strategic use of parallelism emphasizes that for him particular events, actions, and sayings not only have meaning in themselves but also have an enhanced meaning as part of the whole. Luke's parallelisms emphasize that sacred/salvation history is organic; it is more than individual episodes and independent facts. Further, since the Gospel and Acts are written as scrolls they are to be read linearly, i.e., from beginning to end, from Luke 1 to Luke 24, from Acts 1 to Acts 28, rather than by the more typical modern hunt-and-peck approach, the first episode provides a pre-understanding that the reader carries forward to the second, parallel narrative.

The "Antecedent Spiritual State" Prerequisite

The interpretation of Luke's data about being "baptized in the Holy Spirit" continues to create much conflict. One side of the debate is adamant that, for Luke, this term describes a soteriological experience, namely, "conversion-initiation."[13] Others are equally certain that it describes an aspect of the vocational activity of the Spirit, namely, commissioning-empowerment for witness.[14] More recently, others have proposed a theology that bridges the soteriological vs. vocational interpretations.[15] The best way to resolve the differences of interpretation is to put Luke's data about being baptized in the Holy Spirit into the complete context of Luke's pattern of the "antecedent spiritual state" prerequisite. The following chart outlines Luke's data.

Antecedent Spiritual State Prerequisites to Receiving the Holy Spirit

Character*	Antecedent Spiritual State	Subsequent Spiritual Experiences of the Holy Spirit
Elizabeth	Luke 1:6 righteous, walked blamelessly	1:41 filled with Holy Spirit and prophesied
Zacharias	Luke 1:6 righteous, walked blamelessly	1:67 filled with Holy Spirit and prophesied
Simeon	Luke 2:25 righteous and devout	2:25 led by the Holy Spirit and prophesied
120 brethren	Luke 6:13 disciples Acts 11:17 believers	1:5 **baptized in the Holy Spirit** 2:4,17 filled with the Holy Spirit; spoke in tongues = prophesied
5,000 disciples	Acts 4:4 believers	4:31 filled with the Holy Spirit and gave inspired bold witness
Samaritans	Acts 8:12 believers	8.15–17 received the Holy Spirit
Paul	Acts 9:15 chosen instrument to witness about Jesus	9:17 filled with the Holy Spirit (to witness)

---

13. See Dunn, "Baptism in the Holy Spirit."
14. See Menzies, "Empowered for Witness."
15. See Macchia, *Baptized in the Spirit*.

Character*	Antecedent Spiritual State	Subsequent Spiritual Experiences of the Holy Spirit
Cornelius' house church	Acts 10:2–4 God-fearers, righteous Acts 11:17 believers	11:16 **baptized in the Holy Spirit** 10:46 spoke in tongues = prophesied
Ephesian twelve	Acts 19:1 disciples Acts 19:2 believers	19:6 (implied) **baptized in Holy Spirit;** spoke in tongues and prophesied

* Because of their unique position in salvation history I have not included the examples of either John the Baptist or Jesus.

Apart from excluding John the Baptist and Jesus, the above is a comprehensive survey of the relevant data. For *everyone* who experiences the activity of the Spirit Luke *always* identifies their antecedent spiritual state. They are qualified to experience the Holy Spirit because they are *already* either "righteous" or "believers" (or both). In other words, no one experiences being "filled with the Spirit" or being "baptized in the Spirit" who is not already in right standing before God. This means that being "baptized in the Spirit" *must* be about commissioning-empowerment. As a corollary, the term "baptized in the Spirit" *cannot* be about conversion-initiation. Luke's data is compelling. The conversion-initiation interpretation of Luke's Spirit baptism episodes which many twenty-first-century Christians still espouse must be abandoned on the rubbish-heap of lost causes.

The discussion in this chapter about Luke as historian, theologian, and teacher shows that each narrative "account" in itself (i.e., Luke and Acts) and both "accounts" together (i.e., Luke-Acts) are, arguably, the most carefully crafted books in the New Testament. St. Luke, historian and theologian, is a skilled teacher *par excellence*. Indeed, an unprejudiced reading of Luke's two-volume account narrative shows that he rivals Paul as the greatest theologian and teacher in early Christianity.

APPENDIX

The following charts illustrate Luke's narrative strategy of parallelism.

1. The thematic structure of Acts parallels that of Luke.

Thematic Structure	The "First" Account	The "Second" Account
A "beginning" narrative	Birth, Spirit-anointing of Jesus	Spirit baptism, Spirit-filling of disciples
An inauguration narrative	Jesus preaches inaugural sermon in Nazareth	Peter preaches inaugural sermon in Jerusalem
Reports of confirmatory miracles	Jesus casts out demons and heals the sick (e.g., a cripple)	Peter and John heal the crippled beggar
The approval/disapproval response theme	Crowds are amazed by Jesus' ministry; Pharisees disapprove	Crowd is amazed by Peter's ministry; Jewish Council disapproves
Travel narrative	Jesus travels from Galilee to Jerusalem	Paul travels from Antioch to Rome
Trials narrative	Jesus is tried before the Jewish Council, Pilate, and Herod	Paul is tried before Jewish Council, Felix, Festus, and Agrippa

2. The pouring forth of the Spirit of prophecy on the day of Pentecost parallels the outburst of prophecy in the infancy narrative.

Representative Persons	Luke's Infancy Narrative	The Pentecost Narrative
sons	John is a son whose ministry is prophetic (1:15–17)	sons shall prophesy
daughters	Mary is a daughter whose song (1:46–52) must be identified as prophecy (compare 1:41; 1:67)	daughters shall prophesy
young men	John is a young man who is a prophet (Luke 1:76)	young men shall see visions

Representative Persons	Luke's Infancy Narrative	The Pentecost Narrative
old men	Zacharias (1:22; 1:67) & Simeon (2:25–32) are old men, who prophesy	old men dream dreams
male bondslave	Simeon is a male bondslave who prophesies (2:29)	male bondslaves shall prophesy
female bondslaves	Mary is a female bondslave who prophesies (1:38)	female bondslaves shall prophesy

3. Luke's report about Stephen parallels his report about Jesus

JESUS (Luke)	STEPHEN (Acts)
full of Holy Spirit 4:1	full of the Holy Spirit 6:3; 5:7; 7:55
he kept increasing in wisdom 2:52	full of wisdom 6:3, 10
Jesus returned to Galilee in the power of the Spirit 4:14	full of grace and power 6:10
miracles and wonders and signs which God performed through him Acts 2:22	performed great wonders and signs 6:10
accused of blasphemy 5:21	accused of blasphemy 6:11
rejected by elders, chief priests and scribes 9:22; 22:66	opposed by scribes and elders 6:12, false witnesses speak against him 6:13
speaks against Jerusalem and temple 19:41–46; 21:6	speaks against temple 6:13; 7:46–50
his face became different and his clothing white and gleaming 9:29	had the (white/radiant) face of an angel 6:15 (compare Luke 24:4)
rejection of the prophets motif 4:24–30	rejection of the prophets motif 7:51–53
trial: refers to the heavenly Son of Man 22:69	trial: refers to the heavenly Son of Man 7:56
crucified, cries out: Father, into thy hands I commit my Spirit 23:46a	dying, prays: Lord Jesus, receive my Spirit 7:59
crucified, prayed: Father, forgive them for they do not know what they are doing 23:34	dying, prays: Lord, do not hold this sin against them 7:60a
crucified: he breathed his last 23:46b	martyred: he fell asleep 7:60b

These parallels between Jesus, the charismatic Christ, and Stephen, the charismatic deacon, are like the earlier parallels between Elijah and Elisha, who both ministered to gentiles, multiplied food, raised the dead, and parted the Jordan, etc., but are more extended and are, if possible, of a higher order. The full significance of these parallels between Jesus and Stephen must forever remain locked in Luke's mind alone. The reader, however, can infer that their significance relates to their unique position in the unfolding of salvation history. It is through Jesus' ministry and death as the rejected prophet that the provision of salvation is made; it is through Stephen's ministry and death as a rejected prophet that Christianity begins its decisive break with Judaism and salvation begins to be taken to the Samaritans and ultimately to the gentiles.

4. Luke reports parallel ministry actions from Jesus to Peter to Paul.

Ministry Action	Jesus (Luke)	Peter (Acts)	Paul (Acts)
1. Heal cripples	5:17–26	3:1–10 9:32–35	14:8–10
2. Heal by objects	8:43–48 cloak	5:12–16 shadow	19:10–12 aprons
3. Agents imparting the Holy Spirit	Acts 2:33	8:15–17	19:1–7
4. Curse Opponents	11:45–52	8:18–25	13:9–12
5. Raise the dead	7:16	9:36–43	20:7–10
6. Take the gospel to the gentiles	(This is the disciple's task)	10:1—11:18	13:46–48
7. Criticized for doing #6		11:1–3	15:1–5

Bibliography

Arrington, French L., and Roger Stronstad. eds. *The Full Life Bible Commentary to the New Testament*. Grand Rapids: Zondervan, 1999.

Aune, David E. *The New Testament in Its Literary Environment*. Philadelphia: Westminster, 1987.

———. *The Westminster Dictionary of New Testament and Early Christian Literature and Rhetoric*. Louisville: Westminster John Knox, 2003.

Bock, Darrell L. *A Theology of Luke and Acts*. Grand Rapids: Zondervan, 2012.

Bruce, F. F. *The Acts of the Apostles: The Greek Text with Introduction and Commentary*. 2nd ed. Grand Rapids: Eerdmans, 1952.

———. "First Church Historian." In *Church, Word and Spirit*, edited by James E. Bradley and Richard A. Muller, 1–14. Grand Rapids: Eerdmans, 1987.

Conzelmann, Hans. *The Theology of St. Luke*. Translated by Geoffrey Buswell. New York: Harper and Row, 1961.

Dunn, James D. G. *Baptism in the Holy Spirit*. Studies in Biblical Theology, Second Series 15. London: SCM, 1970.

Green, Joel B. *The Theology of the Gospel of Luke*. Cambridge: Cambridge University Press, 1995.

Jervell, Jacob. *The Theology of the Acts of the Apostles*. Cambridge: Cambridge University Press, 1996.

Klein, W. W., C. L. Blomberg, P. and R. L. Hubbard. *Introduction to Biblical Interpretation*. Dallas, TX: Word, 1993.

Liddell, Henry George, and Robert Scott. *A Greek-English Lexicon*. 9th ed. London: Oxford University Press, 1968.

Macchia, Frank D. *Baptized in the Spirit: A Global Pentecostal Theology*. Grand Rapids: Zondervan, 2006.

Marshall, I. Howard. *Luke: Historian and the Theologian, Contemporary Evangelical Perspectives*. Grand Rapids: Zondervan, 1970.

Menzies, Robert P. *Empowered for Witness: The Holy Spirit in Luke-Acts*. JPTS 6. Sheffield UK: Sheffield Academic Press, 1994.

Michaels, J. Ramsey. "Evidences of the Spirit." In *Initial Evidence: Historical and Biblical Perspectives on the Pentecostal Doctrine of Spirit Baptism*, edited by Gary McGee, 202–18. Peabody, MA: Hendrickson, 1991.

O'Neill, J. C. *The Theology of Acts in Its Historical Setting*. London: SPCK, 1961.

Parsons, Mikeal C. *Luke: Storyteller, Interpreter, Evangelist*. Peabody, MA: Hendrickson, 2007.

Robertson, A. T. *Luke the Historian in the Light of Research*. Grand Rapids: Baker, 1977.

Stronstad, Roger. *The Charismatic Theology of St. Luke*. 2nd ed. Grand Rapids: Baker Academic, 2012.

4

Sacrament or Ordinance?
A Pentecostal Approach to a Contentious Issue

Jean-Daniel Plüss

Many Pentecostal and evangelical Christians feel uncomfortable in referring to baptism and the Lord's Supper as sacraments. They prefer to call them ordinances, as Jesus called his disciples to baptize and to come together in remembrance of him. They emphasize obedience to his commands and the memorial character of these actions. However, there have been Pentecostals who, from the beginning, maintained sacramental language when referring to rituals like baptism, foot washing, or the Breaking of Bread. What difference does it make if one chooses one term over against the other? What are theological implications? Before we can discuss the issue from a Pentecostal point of view, we need to clarify a few things.

Firstly, I would like to make clear that I will be using the terms Communion, the Lord's Supper, and the Eucharist interchangeably. They all have biblical roots and emphasize important aspects of that practice when Christians come together to remember that Jesus died on the cross in order to reconcile the world to God (2 Cor 5:18–20 and Col 1:20–22).

Secondly, we are well advised to look at how these ordinances or sacraments evolved. What are the biblical foundations and how have the views on baptism and the Lord's Supper developed from the beginnings of Christianity until today?

Thirdly, Christians from non-Reformed traditions sometimes wonder if Pentecostals have created a new sacrament when they speak about the baptism in the Holy Spirit. Is this experience of Pentecost to be compared with water baptism? If it is different, why is it called a baptism? We will have to address that question in due time.

Biblical Considerations

When the Lord Jesus Christ celebrated the last meal with his disciples, he was following a tradition that has its roots in Exodus 12:1–28, the Passover meal of the Israelites in Egypt. Many rites practiced by Christians have their roots in Jewish customs. We find, for instance, that baths for purification were built next to synagogues and "baptisms" were practiced in the Old Testament (Lev 13–15; 2 Kgs 5:1–14). Before the time of Jesus, Jewish groups like the Essenes practiced baptisms for the sake of purification and John the Baptist is recorded baptizing as a sign of repentance and for the remission of sins (Mark 1:4). Thus, when the disciples of Jesus baptized, the people were already familiar with this practice.

Similarly, elements of public worship, prayers, and invocations have biblical roots. Some psalms were written to be said on specific occasions in the temple worship in Jerusalem. Such texts are called liturgical because they are related to common worship. Thus, Zechariah is said to have returned home after this service (*leitourgias*) in the temple (Luke 1:23), and in Hebrews 8:6 we read that Jesus' ministry (*leitourgia*) was superior to that of the old times. Some contemporary Bible translations indent poetical and liturgical texts in order to show that they had a special function in the community of believers. In the letters of Paul, we find doxologies that were taken up by the early church (Rom 11:36; Gal 1:5; Eph 3:21). The clearly poetic character of Philippians 2:6–11 has convinced many interpreters of the Bible that we have here an early Christian hymn praising Christ's humility and exaltation. Moreover, we know from Colossians 3:16 that the believers encouraged each other with hymns and spiritual songs. Similarly, the words in Revelation 5:12 have been taken up by the early church as an expression of praise and submission to their Lord of lords and King of kings. We can say that early Christians worshiped in ways that expressed their common faith. Baptism and the Breaking of Bread were essential elements of worship from the very beginning (Acts 2:41f. and 1 Cor 10:1–22). Other rituals practiced were prayers for healing and the anointing of the sick with oil (Jas 5:16) and probably foot washing. Daniel Tomberlin, a Pentecostal minister, put it like this, "Whether or not we understand the mystery of how we encounter the grace of God through the sacraments, we cannot diminish their significance in the life of the early Christian community. To early Christians, participation in the holy sacraments was theology in action."[1]

---

1. Tomberlin, *Pentecostal Sacraments*, 77.

Historical Developments

As the church worshiped, liturgical elements and rituals developed as time went on. Justin Martyr was a second-century Christian apologist. In chapters 65 to 67 of his *First Apology*, Martyr explains the celebration of the Eucharist. It is considered to be one of the earliest Christian documents explaining the Lord's Supper, besides Paul's teaching in 1 Corinthians 11:17–32.[2] The person leading a worship service, he writes, is to give praise and thanks to God in a lengthy prayer as an expression that those who will partake of the Lord's Supper are considered worthy to do so (ch. 65). The food as a symbol of thanksgiving is explicitly called Εὐχαριστία, the Eucharist (ch. 66). The Greek verb *eucharistein* means "to give thanks" and is a direct reference to Jesus's prayer of giving thanks on the night that he was betrayed (1 Cor 11:24). The food that has been blessed is considered by Christians of that time to be the Lord's own flesh and blood, not just mere bread and wine. If we consider that many Christians between the first and third centuries were persecuted, we can understand a deep identification with their Lord who suffered for them and died on the cross. They took Jesus' words literally when he said "this is my body" and "this is my blood" in Mark 14:22–24 and Matthew 26:26–28.

In the *Apostolic Tradition* traditionally associated with Hippolytus of Rome,[3] written about sixty years later, the celebration of the Holy Communion is again referred to as the Eucharist. The giving thanks is explicitly stated three times at the beginning of the memorial supper (4:2, 3, 4). It is also a memorial meal (4:10–11) in accordance with 1 Corinthians 11:25. At the same time, Hippolytus stated that the partaking of the bread and chalice are holy mysteries and the Eucharistic prayer includes an invocation that the Holy Spirit may fill everyone that partakes of the meal so that the believer would be strengthened in faith.

The high respect given to the celebration of the Lord's Supper is further witnessed when Hippolytus says that new converts (catechumens) are not allowed to take part in the Lord's Supper (ch. 27). They first had to go through a three-year period of teaching before they could be baptized and only after that they were admitted to partake of Communion.[4] The Eucha-

---

2. The First Apology of Justin Martyr, dates probably from the middle of the second century. Justin Martyr, "The First Apology."

3. The *Apostolic Tradition* is an early Christian text dating from the very beginning of the third century AD.

4. Mentioned are elaborate details as to the catechumenate (ch. 17–20) and baptism (ch. 21). No unbeliever or any animal was allowed to eat from the bread as it is understood to be the body of Christ (ch. 37). Nor may anything be spilled from the cup as it

rist was considered a mystery and non-Christians had to be kept ignorant about its significance.

Although some of the aspects mentioned would be severely criticized by the Reformers in the sixteenth century, it is important to be aware of them as they include important thoughts that would lead Christians to call them sacraments.

The term "sacrament" is understood as pointing to a holy reality that is behind certain functions that Christians partake in. The beginnings can be found in the Old Testament as any ritual performed before the God of Israel had to be pure and worthy of God's holiness. Although there is no exact equivalent for the word "sacrament" in Hebrew, the rite of circumcision, ritual washings, and the Passover meal can be considered as holy actions that would correspond to a Christian understanding of sacrament. Augustine of Hippo (354–430) argued that the Old Testament had sacramental rituals, but that they were not very effective because they were performed in obedience to the law.[5] With regard to Christian rites, Augustine was convinced that they were visible signs, but that there was also an invisible reality behind them that had to be taken seriously.[6]

When Christianity became the official religion in the Roman Empire under Constantine and as the baptism of little children became the norm, baptism as such became the marker for salvation in Christ. Technically, one's faith was still a prerequisite, but practically faith was a given through the church. In the following centuries, the meaning of baptism and the Lord's Supper became ever more narrowly defined by the theologians of the Western Church. What was important was the "thing" itself. They believed that God's grace resides symbolically in every rite that was instituted by Jesus Christ. In the first centuries, the term "sacrament" could refer to the Bible, one's faith, or any cultic rite performed in a Christian manner. However, the number of sacraments was later limited to seven particular actions (baptism, confirmation, the Eucharist, confession, the anointing of the sick, holy orders, and matrimony). In Eastern Orthodox Christianity, a more open definition of sacrament was upheld. The seven rites just mentioned are considered by them as the major sacraments, but anything that is done by the church could be considered to be sacramental, that is, an expression of God's grace through the body of Christ.

---

is the blood of Christ (ch. 38). Hippolytus, *Apostolic Tradition of Hippolytus of Rome*.

5. Augustine, "Against Faustus the Manichaean," ch. 19. sec. 13.

6. Nicene and Post-Nicene Fathers, *On the Catechising of the Uninstructed*, ch. 26, sec. 50.

It does not surprise that the continuing restriction of what a sacrament was and did, led in the Middle Ages to the fact that such rites had received a quasi-magical property in the minds of the common people. Sacraments in themselves were now understood to be carriers of salvation because they were administered by the church.[7] God's grace in Jesus Christ and the faith of the believer were theologically still important, but speaking realistically, the people were only focusing on the value of external actions. An extreme development of that attitude was the introduction of plenary indulgences during the Renaissance period. They were letters granting eternal salvation based on large financial offerings. These were used by Catholic rulers to fund expensive building projects. It was high time for the church to experience a reform.

The Impact of the Reformation

It was Martin Luther's disgust with the use of indulgences as a means to secure one's salvation that caused him to write the ninety-five theses in protest. The Protestant Reformation brought about a new focus on the Bible as source of our religious understanding, the redemptive role of Jesus Christ, the importance of God's grace, the necessity of faith, and the fact that glory was not due to church leaders but to God alone.[8]

With regard to the sacraments, this re-orientation had the following consequences. Their number was reduced by most Reformers to two. It was argued that Jesus only instituted baptism and the celebration of the Lord's Supper.[9] Other practices like marriage, confession of sins, and confirmation were upheld, but not given the same status.

For Martin Luther, who originally had no intentions to break away from the Roman Catholic Church, but hoped to renew it from within, baptism and the Lord's Supper retained much of their traditional significance.

---

7. That the sacraments were carriers of grace was compounded by the teaching that the sacraments were efficacious regardless of the moral rectitude of the priest who administered them (ex *opere operato*).

8. These points of emphasis are nowadays referred to as the five *solae*; Latin phrases describing that "Scripture alone" was to be the source of God's teachings, that "by faith alone" one could receive salvation offered through Jesus Christ, that "by God's grace alone" one was justified in Christ and made a child of God, that "by Christ only" salvation was made possible, and that "only God deserves all the glory." These fundamental beliefs appear in the writings of the Reformers, although they were not listed as a set as we do today.

9. However, the washing of feet has also been commanded by Jesus in John 13:14. This is the reason why believers of the Anabaptist tradition and some Pentecostals do practice the washing of feet as a ceremony expressing humility as Christ did.

That means that the practice of infant baptism as an introduction to God's church continued. As the confession of faith could not be given by the baby, it was given by the godparents instead. Likewise, Christian teaching, that in antiquity preceded baptism, continued to be given once the baptized person was able to learn. Baptism was considered to be a visible sign of a covenantal relationship between the person and God. God would keep his promise.[10]

With regard to the Eucharist, Luther continued considering the Eucharistic host worthy of adoration. For him the consecrated bread and wine were in a real sense the body of Christ. Although one could still taste the bread and wine distinctly, the two elements together and by the power of God's Word, made Christ present in a sacramental union.[11] This view became known as consubstantiation as both realities were affirmed, the physicality of bread and wine as well as the real presence of Christ.

The Reformation at the beginning of the sixteenth century took place as natural sciences were rediscovered and Christian humanism gained powerful momentum. The Swiss Reformer Huldrich Zwingli was one such humanist and that to the bone. For him the problem of the old church was that it had gotten caught up in all manner of sacramentalism and external observances, like the wearing of ornate vestments and the adoration of pictures. For Zwingli, it was clear that Jesus' words, "This is my body" had to be understood metaphorically rather than literally. He therefore stressed that the value of celebrating the Lord's Supper was in its memorial character and denied that there was any real presence of Christ in the elements. Nevertheless, Zwingli maintained that Christ was present in a very real but spiritual way, namely in the worshipping community (Matt 18:20). John Calvin later introduced a new position maintaining that the elements were indeed carriers of grace, but not because they had been transformed. It can thus be maintained that Luther and Calvin spoke of baptism and the Lord's Supper as sacraments, whereas Zwingli considered them to be mere symbols.

The Anabaptists, who as radical Reformers were Luther's and Zwingli's adversaries, held the most revolutionary position. "Baptism shall be given to all those who have learned repentance and amendment of life, and who believe truly that their sins are taken away by Christ . . . ."[12] In other words, they put the understanding of baptism upside down. It had to be understood as a consequence of conversion and not as an introduction to faith. They argued one already had to be a believer before baptism would make sense, quoting

---

10. See Luther, *The Large Catechism*.

11. Luther, Martin. "Confession Concerning Christ's Supper," 13–258; Luther, *Luther's Works, American Edition*, 161–372.

12. Swiss Brethren Conference, "The Schleitheim Confession."

Bible verses such as Mark 16:16, Acts 2:38, 8:35–38. Hence, the Anabaptists claimed that only adults could take the decision to be baptized.

As the Reformation progressed, various groups developed the Zwinglian approach to the Lord's Supper. One of the reasons was due to the emphasis on the common priesthood of all believers, arguing that all baptized Christians are "priests" before the eyes of God (1 Pet 2:9). Some believed that it was no longer necessary that the Lord's Supper would be celebrated by an ordained priest. It could be done so by any believer in right standing before God. As a result, the Breaking of Bread was primarily celebrated as a communal memorial of Jesus. Later, Baptist groups and the Brethren preferred to speak about Communion rather than the Eucharist and they avoided the term "sacrament" by replacing it with ordinance. They simply argued that baptism and the Lord's Supper were ordained by Jesus Christ; not more—not less. They also claimed that a sacramental understanding of the Eucharist included an unnecessary repetition of a sacrifice that had once and for all been achieved in Jesus' death on the cross (Heb 10:10).

The Anglican Communion developed to be a church of the "Middle Way," that is, it incorporated ideas of the Reformation on the one hand and it maintained Catholic ideas on the other. Anglicans maintained that only baptism and the Lord's Supper were strictly speaking the sacraments that Christ instituted, but that other sacramental actions were known to the church, such as matrimony, confession, and ordination. Traditional Anglicans maintained that the sacraments were effective, based on the rites performed. Anglicans on the evangelical side maintained that sacraments had to be received with the right kind of attitude and faith in order to be received worthily. Reading the *Thirty-Nine Articles*,[13] which are foundational to Anglican teaching, one notices the balancing act performed between the old and a new tradition with regard to the nature and role of sacraments. On one side, it speaks about the Lord' Supper as partaking in the body and blood of Christ. On the other side, it claims that the body of Christ is given, taken, and eaten in a spiritual manner.

In the Methodist church, a revivalist movement that came out of Anglicanism, the celebration of Communion is seen as one of God's ways to make his presence and grace visible. God's presence is understood spiritually rather than physically. Without faith, the participation in the Breaking of Bread is an empty ritual. In faith, however, the Holy Spirit is understood to work signs of grace in the believer and the church.[14] In other words, salvation is by God's grace in Christ. It is grace that invites us to say "yes" to

---

13. Church of England, "The Thirty-Nine Articles of Religion."
14. Felton, *This Holy Mystery*, 5.

the offer of Christ. Therefore, participation in the Lord's Supper as such is not salvific, but it sustains and nourishes the believer in the walk of faith. In that sense, Methodists believe that in Communion we can receive and experience God's grace.[15]

A much more radical point of view was put forward by the Salvation Army, which was founded in 1865 by a former Methodist, William Booth. It was argued that the sacraments did not provide anything by way of spiritual substance that could not be found in their own worship services and private devotions.[16] Salvationists contend to this day that sacraments distract from the fact that God can meet anyone, anywhere, at any time. Hence they would not include elements in their worship services that hint at a mediated presence of the Lord. On the contrary, there were "signs and wonders" which were recorded in the 1880s taking place during meetings of the Salvation Army that are strongly reminiscent of Pentecostals gatherings.[17] According to them, these signs and wonders manifesting God's love happened because of the believers' readiness to be open to God's grace. They were not due to any sacramental rite.

It is from this array of doctrines and experiences of the churches that evolved of the Reformation that Pentecostals would eventually draw their own understanding of baptism and the Lord's Supper.

Pentecostals Caught between Ordinances and Sacraments

It is commonly affirmed that Pentecostals have a symbolic understanding of baptism and Communion. Many use the term "ordinance" deliberately in order to avoid any sacramental notions or misunderstanding that these religious rites automatically function as channels of grace.[18] Thomas F. Zimmerman, a former General Superintendent of the Assemblies of God in the United States of America, once stated, that their worship services are informal and non-liturgical and that the ordinances are symbolic rather than inherently efficacious. He stressed that baptism is essentially an act of obedience and profession of faith. For this reason, infants are dedicated rather than baptized. The Lord's Supper is considered a memorial of Christ's

---

15. Ibid., 7–8.
16. Salvationists, *The Sacraments. The Salvationist Viewpoint*, 35.
17. Bramwell Booth, *Echoes and Memories*, 67–72.
18. Bicknell, "The Ordinances: The Marginalized Aspects of Pentecostalism," 205.

death and a reminder of his second coming. Not membership to a church, but faith in Christ is the criterion for participation in this ordinance.[19]

Now, although such statements are generally accepted by Pentecostals around the world, it does not really do justice to the deeper reality experienced by Pentecostal believers when they are baptized or participate in Communion. Neither does it reflect the richness of traditions from which Pentecostals developed their theology. In recent times, many Pentecostal theologians have taken a fresh look at the ordinances and have discovered deeper dimensions in their liturgical practices than just the celebration of a memorial or the obedient response to an ordinance of Christ.[20] At the same time, some[21] have explained baptism in the Holy Spirit to be sacramental in nature because Spirit baptism is a gift from God that changes the believer and equips him or her with power from on high (Luke 24:49). The word baptism, derived from the Greek verb *baptizein* referring to dipping, is used metaphorically,[22] it does not refer to a function performed by the church like water baptism, but to an infilling by the Holy Spirit.

As a follow-up on the developments after the Reformation, let us look at some of the contexts in which Pentecostal theology developed. The establishment of Pentecostalism in Europe during the early years of the twentieth century shall be a point in case. The Norwegian Methodist minister Thomas B. Barratt, who had returned from an unsuccessful fundraising trip in the USA, approached his congregation in Oslo at Christmas 1906 and told them that he had received the "baptism in the Holy Spirit," an experience that many Methodists at that time were searching for without precisely knowing what to expect. Barratt had not come home with money, but with power from above, just as people at the Azusa Street meetings in Los Angeles had experienced. Thus, the message of Pentecost was introduced to Europe. Soon the news spread to countries like England, Germany, the Netherlands, the Baltic region, and other places. Barratt's personal contacts, and the activities of Scandinavian missionaries, were essential in the spread of the teaching about being baptized and empowered in the Spirit as the Book of Acts illustrates.

In northern England, an Anglican vicar named Alexander A. Boddy also experienced this charismatic infilling and began to have special

---

19. Zimmerman, "Assemblies of God Churches' Worship," 42.

20. For an introductory discussion on current reflections and good bibliographic material. See Warrington, *Pentecostal Theology*, 161–69; Tumberlin, *Pentecostal Sacraments*.

21. Tomberlin, *Pentecostal Sacraments*, 74; Macchia, *Baptized in the Spirit*, 247–56; Chan, *Pentecostal Theology and the Christian Spiritual Tradition*, 53, 92–96.

22. Macchia, "Baptized in the Spirit," 3–20.

meetings in his parish in Sunderland. A little later, the Lutheran pastor Jonathan Paul had the same experience. It is important to note that these three early Pentecostal pioneers came from church traditions that considered baptism and the Lord's Supper to be sacraments rather than just ordinances. They believed that these rites were more than just symbolic acts of obedience, confession, or memorial. Yes, it was true that human beings played a significant role, but their theological tradition emphasized that God was present as well and would act according to his good will and grace. The first to pick up the Pentecostal teaching in the Netherlands was Gerrit Polman. He had been raised in the Reformed church and joined the Salvation Army as a young man and became an officer in the same. Thus, when he became a Pentecostal he had come from a tradition that did not even practice baptism and Communion.[23] In Sweden, it was Lewi Pethrus, a Baptist pastor that took up the cause of the Pentecostal movement there. Like Polman, Pethrus grew up in a church that was officially non-sacramental. In Switzerland and France, some Pentecostal leaders were Reformed ministers and naturally predisposed to follow a Zwinglian view of the ordinances.[24]

As a consequence of these ecclesial origins, we find two different streams of thought in the early Pentecostal movement. One that respects traditional views, being open to an understanding of baptism and the celebration of the Eucharist wherein God is assumed to play an important role and the other stream that emphasizes the human agency in baptism and the Lord's Supper. This mix is an indication that Pentecostal theology is more than just an adoption of evangelical theology with a bit of pneumatology added. We therefore need to look at how Pentecostals worship; how they understand, celebrate, and experience water baptism and the Breaking of Bread and how they understand the Holy Spirit to be active in their lives.

A Pentecostal Phenomenology of Baptism and the Lord's Supper

What brought these diverse churchmen together was a commitment to Jesus Christ and a personal experience of the Holy Spirit. They had been influenced by nineteenth-century revivalism and the Holiness movement.

23. Although there are no baptismal rites nor the taking of Communion, the Salvation Army has its own set of ceremonies such as the dedication of children, the enrolment and uniform-wearing, funerals, etc. It should be added that members of the Salvation Army who seek baptism or wish to partake at the Lord's Supper are free to do so in other churches.

24. Robert Willenegger, Jean and Fritz de Rougemont in Switzerland were Reformed minsters and Louis Dallière was pastor of the Reformed church of France.

If only they could be part of a Pentecost like the first Christians. We can see from their personal biographies that these ministers of the gospel had a common vision and a prayerful desire to be used by the Holy Spirit. Theological nuances and liturgical distinctives played a secondary role. What mattered was to be close to God and to do his will. When they experienced the baptism in the Holy Spirit they felt a new confidence and an empowerment for service. They saw themselves like the first apostles in Jerusalem. Not only was this what the prophet Joel had foretold, this was that which the early Christians had experienced (Acts 2:16–18).

Accordingly, early Pentecostal worship consisted very much of praise and adoration in the presence of God, reading the Word and waiting. There was a great expectancy that the Holy Spirit would move. Testimonies were shared of what God had done in people's lives. Worship services did not follow a century-old protocol. Nobody could say for certain what would happen next. Somebody had a hymn or a reading. There was perhaps a prophecy addressed to the church or a vision shared. In other words, worship was not just about "doing the right thing." It was of the essence. Expectancy and encounter are still important attitudes that describe Pentecostal worship today.[25] This disposition leads Pentecostals to understand that when baptisms are celebrated, it is not just a ritual of obedience according to the precepts of the Bible, nor is it limited to a formal confession to the Christian faith as could be expected. Baptism is *more*. If there is a symbolic dying in Christ and raising in Christ, there is in a real sense a new beginning; a blessing that enables the believer to life a life in the power of the Risen One (Rom 6:1–14). Such an identification in Christ means that Christ is present in a real way. If the presence of the Lord were only symbolic, it would not have the same impact.

Adding to that, Pentecostals generally practice baptism by immersion, which implies the biblical idea of washing. Although it is clear that it is the blood of Christ that washes us from all sins (Rev 1:5; Rom 3:25), we find in the New Testament various passages that relate water baptism to a cleansing from sin (Acts 22:16; 1 Cor 6:9–11; Titus 3:5; Heb 10:22). It is common to hear Pentecostals say that when they were baptized they felt clean and ready for a new beginning. This perception is a sign that water baptism is understood to be more than just a symbol. Baptism is *both* a human decision *and* an act of God; a step in obedience and faith, but *also* a sign of grace; an ordinance as well as a sacrament.

If we turn to the celebration of the Lord's Supper, we find this conviction amplified. If general worship among Pentecostals is geared towards

---

25. Warrington, *Pentecostal Theology*, 219.

encounter,[26] how much more would this be the case during the celebration of Communion. The word "communion" expresses togetherness, the church as the body of Christ coming together in the name of their Lord to celebrate God's presence in the church through the Holy Spirit. Likewise, the designation "Lord's Supper" indicates that it is Jesus Christ who is the host that invites the faithful to participate at His table. Moreover, in fulfillment of time, the Lord of lords will invite the people of the kingdom, to attend the celestial banquet (Matt 26:29). If we consider the term "Eucharist," we see, as we mentioned before, that it is taken from 1 Corinthians 11:24 where the Lord is said to have "given thanks" before breaking the bread and blessing the cup, and sharing the Passover meal with his disciples. It is the meal that would symbolize the new covenant, not just a formal contract, but an intimate reality. It would be a pity if the celebration of Communion would lose this corporate character.[27] The fact that in certain churches the bread is no longer broken, but distributed in commercially produced little portions and the wine or grape juice is given in little plastic cups to be drunk at the person's personal convenience points to a tendency to individualize this important moment that should be an expression of community and fellowship with Christ.

Besides the communal aspect of partaking in the Lord's Supper, there is another important dimension. Because Pentecostals believe in the possibility of divine healing, there is a strong sacramental element in the celebration of the Lord's Supper. It focusses on the conviction that Jesus Christ did not only die on the cross in order to atone for our sins, but that we are also being healed by the wounds of the Suffering Servant (Isa 53:5). Hence, the celebration of the Eucharist is, on one hand, in thankful remembrance that in Jesus we have reconciliation with God, but it is also in anticipation that the restoration of communion with God can yield more. A healing of sickness—physical, mental, and social—is also anticipated. The Pentecostal belief that there is healing in the atonement is due to a literal reading of that text in Isaiah. The New Testament quotations of that passage do not primarily relate to Christ's atonement. In Matthew 8:14–17, the word of the prophet is mentioned in relation to the messianic ministry of Jesus, long before he died on the cross. Furthermore, in 1 Peter 2:24, we have the reference in the context of suffering and the forgiveness of sins and not with regard to physical healing.[28] Nevertheless, the idea that healing is part of God's restoration of his people is common in Jewish and Christian interpre-

---

26. Albrecht, *Rites in the Spirit*, 141.
27. Bicknell, "The Ordinances," 163.
28. Warrington, *Pentecostal Theology*, 270–74.

tation.[29] It is a fundamental element of eschatology, an anticipation and sign of the coming kingdom of God.

Perhaps the most convincing reason that an overwhelming majority of Pentecostals believe that there is healing in the atonement of Christ is based on personal application of Isaiah 53:5. Many can testify that they have been physically restored, or to give another example, that they experienced a healing from an unreconciled event in the past as they participated in the Lord's Supper and received a healing touch as a gift of God's grace. These people would claim that God's Spirit was truly present in their midst as they partook of the Eucharistic elements. The term "real presence" has a concrete meaning for Pentecostals even if they are not inclined to believe in transubstantiation.[30] Hence, to refer to the bread and wine as mere symbols does not satisfy the wider reality associated with the celebration of the Lord's Supper. However, it needs to be added that there should not be a magical misunderstanding either. The partaking in Communion does not automatically generate healing or restoration. The Swiss Pentecostal Jakob Zopfi argued that Christ's presence was intimately connected with the spiritual disposition of the ones partaking in Communion. He argues with Acts 2:42–43, that where believers fall short of devoting themselves "to the apostles' teaching, and to the fellowship, to the breaking of bred" there will also be a lack of "signs and wonders."[31] In other words, the Breaking of Bread is not just an element in the order of the service. It is an essential part of Pentecostal worship. Dale Coulter suggests in a similar vein that Pentecostals can relate the sacramental encounter with Christ in the Eucharist with the charismatic

---

29. The salvation and restoration of Israel was often referred to in terms of wholeness and healing, Isa 58:8f; Jer 8:22; 30: 17, Mal 4:2. We find also the idea of healing in the Christian tradition, so for instance in the Christmas hymn *Hark! The Herald-Angels Sing*, where the promise from Malachi 4:2 is resumed "Hail, the Son of Righteousness! Light and life to all he brings, risen with healing in his wings" or the hymn *Christ, the Great Physician*, where it reads, "Healed by the Great Physician, healed by the Great Physician, glory to God! He saves the soul, maketh the suff'ring body whole; thus at His feet my burdens roll, healed by the Great Physician."

30. The doctrine of transubstantiation refers to the belief that the substance of bread and wine used in the Eucharistic sacrament does change into the body and blood of Jesus Christ. Many Christians living in the twenty-first century find themselves in a situation where they would like to uphold Christ's real presence in the celebration of the Eucharist, but do not necessarily do so in a *physical* sense.

31. "Realpräsenz und Arbeitsgemeinschaft, – man kann die beiden Begriffe nicht trennen. Wo die Abendmahlsgemeinschaft unheilig ist, wird es eine Gnade Jesu sein, wenn er Seine Gegenwart zurückzieht . . . die Geistesoffenbarung zum Segen bleibt auch aus, dass Geistesleben der Gemeinde bleibt schwächlich. Organisation tritt an die Stelle des Wirkens des Geistes. Wo es am „Bleiben in der Lehre, in der Gemeinschaft, im Brotbrechen und Gebet" mangelt, mangelt es auch am Offenbarwerden vieler." Jakob Zopfi "Wunder und Zeichen," 15.

encounter with Christ during ministry time that follows the preaching of the Word.[32]

The classical discussion of whether one should call the Lord's Supper a sacrament or an ordinance could perhaps be overcome by remembering the biblical term *"mysterion,"* the Greek word for "mystery". We are to be ministers of the mysteries of God (1 Cor 4:1) and God's mystery is Christ in us (Col 1:25–28). It would be shortsighted to understand a mystery only in terms of knowing a truth that is hidden to others. As these verses seem to imply, there is more to it. There is an added dimension which is attributed to God. *Mysterion* was translated into Latin with the word *sacramentum*: ". . . when applied to the acts of baptism and eucharist this was intended to mean that in these events God's work in Jesus Christ is effected by the power of the Holy Spirit."[33] Pentecostals can appreciate this explanation that is deeply rooted in God's Trinity. The fact that they are not cessationists,[34] implies that God is free to act through the Spirit in the same way today as it happened during the ministry of Jesus and the early church. It is for this reason that Pentecostals pray for the sick, lay hands on them, and anoint them with oil. These sacramental actions are in line with the mystery inherent in the celebration of the Lord's Supper. Because God loves and cares for his creation, he enjoys being present in the midst of God's people and bless them; especially when they worship and glorify the Father, reach out to their neighbor in the name of Christ, and minister in the power of the Holy Spirit.

In Conclusion, the Role of the Holy Spirit

This brings us to some closing comments with regard to ordinances and sacraments. It can be argued that stressing baptism and the Lord's Supper to be mere ordinances undermines the role of the Holy Spirit in the teaching of the church. This claim cannot be made against the great Reformers. Calvin and Zwingli did emphasize that the Holy Spirit was at work in baptism and the memorial meal. However, in our time the attitude toward the ordinances can betray a certain doctrinal shallowness. A sense of mystery is lost. In some churches of the Reformation Communion is celebrated only four

---

32. Coulter, "A Liturgy, a Legacy, and an Anglican Band."

33. WCC, "One Baptism: Towards Mutual Recognition," 7.

34. Cessationism is a conviction that is found among strict Calvinists and certain Baptists. They basically argue that during the time of the first apostles divine gifts were signs validating the preaching of God's word and that divine miraculous activities have ceased as the biblical canon (the writings of the Old and New Testaments) has been fully received.

times a year or even less, and some attendants do not even participate when Communion is offered. Is it a rite they feel uncomfortable with? Could it be that it is so because they only follow the order of worship and mind what the other participants do, but are not really open to God being present? Another concern expressed is "that a trend has occurred within Western Pentecostalism that has resulted in the occasion being marginalized and swamped by singing, into which the partaking of the symbol is inserted rather than it being the central aspect of the event."[35]

In some churches, the Breaking of Bread seems void of an explicit liturgical context. As early as in the 1940s Donald Gee, a leading Pentecostal minister in Great Britain, issued a warning to those Pentecostal churches that wanted to celebrate the Eucharist in an unstructured way. He was convinced that such meetings boasting of freedom would only end up producing a stereotype that is more barren than the liturgical services they deprecate and consequently their meetings would also be aesthetically less appealing.[36] And we may add that such meetings would lack an awareness of God's loving grace here and now, the mystery of our faith.

Pentecostals can avoid commemorating the Lord's Supper in a superficial way. They can be consciously Trinitarian in their celebration. In their worship, they can give God the glory. In making recourse to the pertinent biblical passages, they can focus on the pivotal truth of Christ's atonement and resurrection. And by invoking the Holy Spirit's blessing, they can confess that without the Spirit's work Christ is not made present in our hearts.

Furthermore, as James Bowers has pointed out, there is a direct relation between living a Spirit-filled life and the life of the community. "The call to a Spirit-filled life is also fundamentally a call to covenant community of the Spirit."[37] And it is this covenant community that celebrates in the Lord's Supper its origin, its nurture, and its future in Jesus Christ and through the power of the Holy Spirit. It is this presence of God's Spirit that makes all the difference.

Bibliography

Allen, David. *Neglected Feast: Rescuing the Breaking of Bread*. Nottingham, UK: New Life, 2007.

Albrecht, Daniel E. *Rites in the Spirit: A Ritual Approach to Pentecostal/Charismatic Spirituality*. Sheffield, UK: Sheffield Academic Press, 1999.

---

35. Warrington quoting, Allen, *Neglected Feast*, 168.
36. Hollenweger, "Liturgies, Pentecostal," 241.
37. Bowers, "A Wesleyan-Pentecostal Approach to Christian Formation," 76.

Augustine, "Against Faustus the Manichaean." Christian Classics Ethereal. http://www.ccel.org/ccel/schaff/npnf104.iv.ix.xxi.html.

Bicknell, Richard. "The Ordinances: The Marginalized Aspects of Pentecostalism." In *Pentecostal Perspectives*, edited by Keith Warrington, 204–22. Carlisle, UK: Paternoster, 1998.

Booth, Bramwell. *Echoes and Memories, A famous classic reprinted for the 1978 International Congress of Salvationists.* London: Hodder and Stoughten, 1925.

Bowers, James P. "A Wesleyan-Pentecostal Approach to Christian Formation." *Journal of Pentecostal Theology* 6 (1995) 55–86.

Chan, Simon. *Pentecostal Theology and the Christian Spiritual Tradition.* Sheffield, UK: Sheffield Academic Press, 2000.

Church of England. *The Thirty-Nine Articles of Religion.* 1562. https://www.churchofengland.org/prayer-worship/worship/book-of-common-prayer/articles-of-religion.aspx.

Coulter, Dale M. "A Liturgy, a Legacy, and an Anglican Band." Blog on *First Things*. http://www.firstthings.com/blogs/firstthoughts/2013/12/19/a-liturgy-a-legacy-and-an-anglican-band.

Felton, Gayle Carlton. *This Holy Mystery: A United Methodist Understanding of Holy Communion.* Nashville, TN: The United Methodist Church, 2005.

Hippolytus. *Apostolic Tradition of Hippolytus of Rome.* Translated by Kevin P. Edgecomb. http://www.bombaxo.com/hippolytus.html.

Hollenweger, Walter. "Liturgies, Pentecostal." In *A Dictionary of Liturgy and Worship*, edited by J. G. Davies, 241. London: SCM, 1972.

Justin Martyr. *The First Apology.* http://www.earlychurchtexts.com/public/justin_eucharist.htm.

Luther, Martin. "Confession Concerning Christ's Supper." 1528. In *Martin Luther: Studienausgabe, Vol. 4*, edited by Hans-Ulrich Delius, 13–258. Berlin: Evangelische Verlagsanstalt, 1986.

———. "The Large Catechism." Translated by F. Bente and W. H. T. Dau. Penn State Classic Series Publication. http://www2.hn.psu.edu/faculty/jmanis/m~luther/mllc.pdf.

———. *Luther's Works, American Edition, Vol 37, Word and Sacrament, III.* Edited by R. H. Fischer. Philadelphia: Fortress, 1961.

Macchia, Frank D. *Baptized in the Spirit: A Global Pentecostal Theology.* Grand Rapids: Zondervan, 2006.

———. "Baptized in the Spirit: Towards a Global Theology of Spirit Baptism." In *The Spirit in the World. Emerging Pentecostal Theologies in Global Contexts*, edited by Veli-Matti Kärkkäinen, 3–20. Grand Rapids: Eerdmans, 2009.

Nicene and Post-Nicene Fathers. *On the Catechising of the Uninstructed.* Translated by S. D. F. Salmond. http://www.newadvent.org/fathers/1303.htm.

Salvationists. *The Sacraments: The Salvationist Viewpoint.* London: Salvationist Publishing, 1960.

Swiss Brethren Conference. *The Schleitheim Confession.* 1527. http://www.anabaptists.org/history/the-schleitheim-confession.html.

Tomberlin, Daniel. *Pentecostal Sacraments: Encountering God at the Altar.* Cleveland, TN: Center for Pentecostal Leadership and Care, Pentecostal Theological Seminary, 2010.

Warrington, Keith. *Pentecostal Theology. A Theology of Encounter*. London: T. & T. Clark, 2008.

World Council of Churches. "One Baptism: Towards Mutual Recognition. A Study Test, Faith and order Paper No. 210." 2013. https://www.oikoumene.org/en/folder/documents-pdf/One_Baptism_Corrected_for_reprint.pdf.

Zimmerman, Thomas F. "Assemblies of God Churches' Worship." In *A Dictionary of Liturgy and Worship*, edited by J. G. Davies, 42–43. London: SCM, 1972.

Zopfi, Jakob. "Wunder und Zeichen." *Die Verheissung des Vaters*, January, 1963.

5

Towards a Pentecostal Perspective on Salvation

Edmund J. Rybarczyk

Enough food is produced for everyone on earth but 21,000 people die daily from hunger; 7,665,000 million perish annually.[1] In North Korea alone—the planet's largest prison camp—thousands are imprisoned without trial, then tortured and murdered every year.[2] In short, we witness *macrocosmic* tragedy and unspeakable suffering. We all know something is wrong *out there*. But there is more. We watch daily as people whom we love do little things that lack integrity. Our neighbor lies for a job promotion. A sister shoplifts a small bottle of perfume. An uncle accepts a bribe in his government office. We see that there is something skewed in those who mean so much to us. Then, if we are honest, we realize that same brokenness abides *inside our own hearts*. We resent a cousin's recent business success or we covet the new television a friend of a friend just purchased. It becomes apparent, then, that there are also *microcosmic* problems in life. What is the source of all this?

Most everyone, religious or not, believes in evil. Bible-believing Christians believe that evil is more than either mere accident or the shadow side of life. The evil that ruins the planet is not just between people nor is it only inside our own hearts. This painful dynamic is so pervasive and so

---

1. See, Poverty.com, "Hunger and World Poverty." According to Statistic Brain, 65 percent of those who die from starvation come from just seven countries. See, Statistic Brain, "World Hunger Statistics." Too often the political dimensions of starvation are ignored: governmental tyranny and dictators brutalize the poor and suffering.

2. The North Korean government has been known to execute entire families for the crime of one member. See, Human Rights Watch, "World Report 2012: North Korea."

mysterious that it is best understood as something that involves and violates the most profound category known to humanity: God.

The Bible Teaches That Sin Confines the Entire Human Race[3]

Traditionally understood, sin is missing the mark (Exod 32:31; Lev 5:15; Prov 8:36; Isa 53:6; Luke 24:47; Rom 3:23; 1 John 3:4). Narrowly, sin is a violation of God's commands and will. However, because the Bible teaches that God is a God of love and because the church does not believe God is capricious, we believe that God has reasons for his commands—as creator he wants what is best for us, his creations. He built the universe and wisely knows how we should live inside that universe. So, when we violate God's will and ways we are really violating God's being and character. His commands issue from his character. Violating God's will and acting contrary to his character introduces sin into life; sin is like an infection that spoils reality and perverts relationships. When we sin we violate our God-given consciences, feel guilty, and morally twist our souls. What is the cure? Jesus' apostles believed that he came not merely to teach the gospel but *to be* the gospel (Matt 1:21; Acts 4:12; 10:43; Rom 5:10; 2 Cor 5:18–19; 1 Tim 2:5; Rev 1:5). Jesus is the source of life, the beautiful one who both brought and is salvation. The church, Christ's body, needs to think carefully and deeply about what it is that the Triune God has done for us in salvation. Roger Olson wrote, "Without the formal reflection on the meaning of the gospel of salvation that constitutes theology, that gospel would quickly devolve into mere folk religion and lose all conviction as truth and influence on the church or society."[4] For careful reflection's sake, we will explore various facets of the doctrine of salvation.

Salvation: Rooted in Christ

The New Testament reveals that Jesus is the solution to sin's shame, guilt, infection, and death. Why did the ancient Christians believe Jesus was Savior? The Hebrew name "Jesus" means salvation ("God saves"). In his own day there were many men named Jesus, but the apostles believed Jesus of Nazareth was unique: he spoke with amazing authority (Matt 7:28–29;

---

3. See Rom 11:32; Gal 3:22. Scriptures herein are provided as exemplary and not exhaustive.

4. Olson, *The Story of Christian Theology*, 14.

13:54; Mark 1:22; 6:2; 11:18; Luke 4:32; John 7:46), healed the paralyzed, blind, and dead (Matt 9:1–8; 20:29–34; Mark 5:21–43; 8:22–25; Luke 4:33–37; 5:18–26; 7:11–17; John 9, 11), had demons confess him as God's Son (Mark 1:21–28; 5:1–20; Luke 4:31–37), audaciously claimed both the power to forgive sins and judge the nations (Matt 9:1–8; 25:31–46; 26:62–6; Mark 2:1–12; Luke 7:36–50; 24:44–49; John 17:2; Acts 10:38–42), and then claimed to be starting a new covenant between God and humanity (Matt 26:26–28; Mark 14:24–25; Luke 22:20; John 3:16–18; 5:30–47; 6:32–69; 11:24–27; 14:6). Even more impressively, Jesus said he would die and rise again (Matt 20:17–19; Mark 8:31–33; 10:32–34; Luke 18:31–34; John 13; 16:7–33; 17:26), and then did just that (Matt 28:1–15; Mark 16:1–8; Luke 24:1–51; John 20–21; 1 Cor 15:4–6)! (Christian theology is inextricably bound to real events. No historical event = no theological truth.)[5] After his resurrection, he taught the disciples about the events concerning himself (Luke 24:27; Acts 1:1–3; 1 Cor 15:4–6), and then sent the Holy Spirit to empower them for the same kind of ministry Jesus himself had been doing (John 20:22; Acts 2; 3:1–10; 5:12–16; 8:12–40; 9:32–42; 10:17–48; 16:1–34; 1 Cor 14:20). Studying the Hebrew Scriptures while they were filled with God's Spirit, the apostolic community realized that Jesus was not only the Messiah prophesied by ancient Jews, but was God himself (Matt 26:26–28; Mark 4:33–41; Luke 5:17–26; 6:1–11; 22:14–20; John 1:1–18; 3:16–21; 8:58; 11:25; 14:6).

That same ancient Jesus-community furthermore believed that Jesus' death was no accident; instead it was the very God-promised means of salvation for anyone who will believe in their heart, confess with their mouth, and bow their knee to Jesus as Lord (Acts 2:38; 5:31; Rom 10:9–11; 1 Cor 15:3; Phil 2:10; 1 Pet 1:13; 1 John 1:7; 5:5; Rev 5:13). In the crucifixion, God made a level and humble place to meet us. The cross is a relational place between God and us that does not involve power or coercion. My Vanguard University colleague, Frank Macchia, wrote, "God does not commit violence on creation."[6] God made himself vulnerable and open at Golgotha and when we meet him there we likewise come to him in humility, vulnerability, and honesty.[7] That God would humble himself thus is stunning.

---

5. For example, see all of 1 Corinthians 15, but especially verse 14, "... and if Christ has not been raised, then our preaching is in vain, your faith also is in vain." Lesslie Newbigin notes that Jesus, who lived and died and was resurrected in history, came to redeem people like ourselves who indwell history. While history is not saving (only God saves), it does provide a field of continuity for relationship and theological development. Newbigin, *The Gospel in a Pluralist Society*, ch. 6, 9.

6. Macchia, *Justified in the Spirit*, 25.

7. Timothy Keller, a Reformed Pastor in New York City, rightly argues that there

God's humiliation in Christ expresses the wisdom of God. Indeed, St. Paul touched on this when he wrote, "we speak God's wisdom in a mystery, the hidden wisdom, which God predestined before the ages to our glory; the wisdom which none of the rulers of this age has understood; for if they had understood it, they would not have crucified the Lord of glory" (1 Cor 2:7–8). God is a beautiful God! He lowered himself to our level, he entered into our decrepit existence in order to make possible a loving relationship. Jesus is a beautiful Lord and he invites "whoever will believe" to join his love (John 3:15–16; 11:26; 1 Tim 2:4; 2 Pet 3:9). Because he died a shameful, illegal, and horrific death on a cross, no one will ever be able to say to him, "you don't understand what it's like." So great is his love that he embraced the worst of who we are and the most evil elements of our social constructs. He is indeed a beautiful savior.

It is easy to read the New Testament as literature and overlook the profound effect Jesus had upon his followers. They were constantly in awe of him. Frequently, they did not understand his actions or teachings. Nevertheless, Jesus' person and work combined to overturn their worldview and change their hearts as persons. Amazingly—as the culmination of all they had seen, heard, and *experienced*[8] about and through Jesus—this first Christian community worshipped the man Jesus as God, and we see this made evident across the New Testament corpus.[9] This chapter is not spe-

---

is no love, not even for God, without the risk of vulnerability. Love that is mandated, love that is required, is not true love. God makes himself vulnerable to us at the cross and reciprocally we must make ourselves vulnerable to him. No vulnerability equals no love. Keller, *The Reason for God*, 47–49, 76–85, 181–86. The Eastern Orthodox tradition has argued salvation similarly through the category of *kenosis*: the Son of God's self-limitation and humility (Phil 2:7). In Christ, God is a lowly God who invites—but does not force—us into relationship. Lossky, *Orthodox Theology*, 100. C. S. Lewis reminds us that Jesus is both a lamb and a lion. Jesus is now lowly and humble, but one day he will return as a lion to judge both every being who ever lived and every nation that ever existed.

8. The reader is reminded that theology is "faith seeking understanding," as Anselm put it. First, we experience something in life from, in, or about God and then, secondly, we seek to faithfully understand and explain that. For the Eastern Orthodox the very word "theology" is not an intellectual enterprise but an experience of the Triune God's being. Lossky, *The Mystical Theology of the Eastern Church*, 9, 38, 43, 65. Pentecostals would voice a hearty amen to Christianity first being an experience! Pentecostals also will do well to be able to understand, explain, and "give an account for the hope that is yours" (1 Pet 3:15).

9. That post-Babylonian-captivity, radically monotheistic Jews—Jews who were fully convinced that idolatry was an abomination—would do this staggers the imagination. It reveals to us again how preeminent Jesus was in the hearts and minds of the apostolic community. We note this against a 200-year-long spate of authors who believe Christians did not begin worshipping Jesus as God until after the Constantinianization

cifically about Christ Jesus, but if we fail to recognize the resolutely Christological foundations of New Testament teaching about salvation we will grotesquely misunderstand what Jesus' own followers witnessed, believed, and confessed. Lacking Jesus Christ there is no salvation. Philip Melanchthon (1497–1560) once aptly wrote, "to know Christ is to know his benefits." Agreed, Christ brought salvation and the many blessings that flow from that. Yet, we carefully add that Jesus *is himself* salvation and resurrection.

Salvation as Atonement

Something is askew both in society and inside persons. However, as the Bible teaches across it, there is more. By our sins, we have violated God's own character. We have damaged the arrangement God made between himself and us inside this universe. Here's an analogy. Over the last forty years, the United States government, for its own gain, has irresponsibly borrowed 17.3 trillion dollars. Today our national debt is almost as large as our annual Gross Domestic Product; the threat of economic collapse is looming.[10] It is possible, though unlikely, that another country might repay our enormous debt and if so everyone's problem would be solved. But it is impossible for our lenders to simply ignore our debt; if they did that they would go bankrupt. The answer? That debt simply *must* be repaid.

Sin incurs a cost both inside the universe and with God. Sin is the activation of ruination. The cost *must* be paid, the ruination stopped. Some wonder, why didn't God *simply speak* the words "you are forgiven"? After all, he is God, can't he do anything he wishes? Answer: no, he could not simply speak forgiveness because the cost of sin and sin's ruination would not be addressed with integrity. Similarly, America's debt-holders cannot simply *say*, "You don't have to repay your loans," because they themselves would go broke and the global economy might shut down; economic law demands repayment. God took action to deal with our sins: he became man, died in our place, was resurrected, and sent his Spirit. He thereby dealt with sin's debt and ruination. Put differently, God so respected the way he had built the universe that to solve the universe's plight he entered the universe to struggle with the problem. If he had simply spoken "I forgive you all," some might rightly accuse him by saying, "Hey, God, that's not fair. You have to play by the rules you established. Forgiveness has a cost. You can't

---

of Christianity in the early fourth century. The New Testament is nuanced and layered in its treatment of Jesus Christ; those layers show that there was an increasing awareness of Jesus' divinity.

10. Boccia, Fraser, and Goff, *Federal Spending by the Numbers*.

just *say* you're forgiven, someone has to *own* the debt." Jesus, the Son of God incarnate, owned our cost, took on our debt, and overcame the ruination; he atoned for our sins (Isa 53:5; Mark 10:45; John 3:16; 20:31; 2 Cor 5:18–19; Heb 9:12; Rev 5:9–10). God worked within the confines of the universe that he had built and with integrity forgave us.

However, there is still more beauty involved in God's atoning salvation. I compare what God did for us in Christ to a story from my own life. The son of divorced parents, I grew up with a marked sense of relational insecurity. When I asked some girl out for a date and she said no, I would never ask her again. Insecure, I could not stand being rejected. Later, while in college, I met Tawnya, the woman who is today my wife. I am embarrassed to report that before we were engaged to be married I broke up with Tawnya two times (she talked me out of a third time!). Wondrously, she lovingly reunited with me despite the fact that *if she* had said no to me, or broken up with me, out of insecurity I would not have accepted her back. Graciously, Tawnya forgave my impetuousness and we rejoined. God's salvation is like that. He did not wait for us to love him before he sought us for relationship. The apostle Paul wrote, "God demonstrates his own love toward us, in that while we were yet sinners, Christ died for us" (Rom 5:8). God is so secure in his love and God so yearns for restored relationship with us that he took the initiative to make atonement even before we knew about him (Eph 1:4–5; Col 1:13–14). Jesus touched on this dynamic when, speaking about God's kingdom, he told his disciples, "Go out into the highways and along the hedges, and compel them to come in, that my house may be filled" (Luke 14:23). Salvation involves not only atonement for our sins, it involves restored relationship.[11] God yearns to know and love us. Similarly, a jealous God, he yearns for us to know him, love him, and give our allegiance to him (Exod 20:5; Num 25:13; Deut 5:9; Matt 7:23–27; Mark 10:23; Rev 3:16).

Per the New Testament, Jesus' atoning work—his substitutionary death on the cross—is the very heart of Christianity. Indeed, Jesus is the Lamb of God who offers himself so that God's peace may embrace creation. The Baptist realized that Jesus would atone for the whole world's sin (John 1:29, also see Mark 10:45; Acts 8:32; Rom 8:32; Heb 9:14; 1 Pet 1:19; Rev 5:6, 8). In church history, atonement doctrine was famously forged by Roman Catholic theologians, Anselm of Canterbury (1033–1109) and Thomas Aquinas (1225–74).[12] Substitutionary atonement theory holds that our

---

11. Stated per that sentence, salvation involves both *imputed righteousness*, righteousness that is counted towards us in Christ (Rom 5:17; 2 Cor 5:21; Gal 2:16), and *union with God* (Matt 26:26–28; John 7:38; Eph 5:31–32); the New Testament teaches both.

12. Anselm focused on the Godward side of the question, while Aquinas focused

violation of God's law and honor must be remedied. Later, the sixteenth century Reformation Protestants put salvation—the atonement—at the heart of Christian theology. The centrality of Christ's offering for sin is offensive to some non-Christians today; it is viewed as religiously too exclusive. The apostles, however, recognized the excellency and preeminence of Christ Jesus. Peter, full of the Spirit, said, "there is no other name on earth by which men might be saved" (Acts 4:12). Our joy as Christ's followers is to faithfully proclaim God's saving act in Christ. Christ is not the property of Christians, nor is salvation. Our calling is to bear witness *in humility*, knowing it is not we that save ourselves, but instead we are saved by God's extreme mercy through Christ Jesus.

A few theologians today believe traditional doctrines of atonement through Jesus' crucifixion represents a kind of divine child-abuse: the angry Father punished his Son. Yet, to pose Christ's crucifixion that way fails to recognize that the Father was grieved for it all.[13] Moreover, it is to misunderstand both the problem—sin's insidious presence everywhere—and its solution—God offered himself for our restoration and justification. The problem was gigantic, corroding the entire universe. An enormous remedy was required and in Christ, the Chosen One anointed of the Holy Spirit, that remedy was effected. Martin Luther was thus correct: salvation is entirely the work of God. To experience true joy we human beings do not merely need our "self-esteem" raised, or reassurance that we "really are good people" as is so commonly stated in public discourse. We need to be forgiven by God. Jesus was no mere man whom God chastised, and the Father is not some sadistic being who delights in punishing sinners. In humble solidarity, God incarnate—the second person of the Trinity—bore our sins so that he could forgive us, and restore us to himself, to one another, and to ourselves. There is no abiding spiritual health outside of Christ. Let's explore that dimension further.

Salvation as Healing

In Western (Roman Catholic, Protestant, and Pentecostal) theology, the emphasis on Christ's salvific work has fallen upon the atonement as forgiveness. That is a good and faithful apostolic theological construction. Truly, forgiveness heals us! It sets us free from our guilt and restores wrecked relationships. However, there have been cultural-contextual

---

more on the anthropological dimensions of the question.

13. Moltmann, *Trinity and the Kingdom*.

reasons for that salvation-as-forgiveness emphasis: Latin culture,[14] even before Christianity was born, was very law-based, very legal-based. Latin culture is attuned to societal laws, fault, blame, responsibility, and the narratives that accompany those categories. We like understanding what the rules are and who is to blame, just as we like knowing who is not at fault. That Latin philosophical construction rather shaped the manner in which the Bible was read and interpreted.

A more recent theological emphasis views salvation as healing. In some regards, this is really not new. The Eastern Orthodox churches have, for some two millennia, understood Christ's salvific work in therapeutic categories. Even in the second century Irenaeus (130–202) taught that Jesus reversed the curse of sin; again sin is like an infection that ruins both us and God's creation. Building on Irenaeus' foundation, and profoundly rooting his own theology in the doctrine of the incarnation, Athanasius (293–373) wrote, "For he was made human so that we might be made divine. And he revealed himself through a body so that we might receive an understanding of the invisible Father. And he endured the mistreatment of humans, so that we might inherit immortality."[15] Athanasius did not mean we become little deities; he did believe that as we grow in Christ and as God's Holy Spirit grows us into Christ-likeness that we take on the character, quality, and likeness of God. Athanasius variously believed that God lowered himself in the incarnation (Gal 4:4; especially Phil 2:5–11) in order to raise us up in Christ's resurrection; that God's humility resulted in our glory; that God's varied condescension in the incarnation, Jesus' obedience, and crucifixion results in our being raised up as the immortal children of God. In all of this, Athanasius, unlike Anselm, did not portray Christ's death as a vicarious sacrifice, rather he portrayed it as the method for dealing with physical death. Jesus Christ heals us of death. And indeed, hope fills our hearts to know that death will not have the final victory! As the patristic fathers put it, "he conquered death by dying."

To more carefully understand that kind of incarnation-as-salvific theology we should note that the prevailing category for Greek philosophy has been "being." Greek philosophers, and those in their wake, have constantly asked what does it mean to *be*? What elements comprise *being*? And, from whence does death come? How should death, the great challenge to being, be understood? Eastern Orthodox theology, dialoguing with and thinking alongside Greek philosophy, understands God's incarnation as working

---

14. This traditionally involved all Romance-language (Latin, French, Italian, Spanish, Portuguese, and Romanian) societies and then the extension of those into the later non-Roman-language societies developed by Protestantism.

15. Athanasius, *De Incarnatione* 54 (p. 192).

healing for those in Christ. The incarnation is the union of the divine and the created, of eternity and time, and of God and man. Put simply, Christ's perfect divinity restores our fallen humanity. The Eastern Orthodox assert that when, by the Holy Spirit's agency (Matt 1:20; Luke 1:35), God's Son became Jesus of Nazareth, he sanctified matter and overcame physical death. The immortal one, God's holy Son, heals us of our mortality. This is why the Orthodox often say about someone who has died, "God bless her repose." They do not believe the dead are so dead as many evangelical Christians understand it. Instead, the dead in Christ are merely asleep: their bodies are dead or sleeping (euphemistically speaking) (Acts 7:60; 1 Cor 15:6, 18, 20, 51; 1 Thess 4:13–15; 2 Pet 3:4), though their souls/selves are alive in the presence of Christ (Luke 23:43; Phil 1:20–24; Rev 6:11; 14:13). Such incarnational theology roots salvation squarely *in the person*, first, of Christ. The *being* of Christ is emphasized *more than his work*, though his work—death and resurrection—are the means of Christ's victory on our behalf. Although the New Testament places the emphasis on our salvation within the historical event of Christ's crucifixion, death, and resurrection, this incarnation-as-healing theology reminds us that it is not our good deeds (even deeds inspired by the Holy Spirit)[16] or a body of secret knowledge, or even a compassionate attitude that saves us. Jesus of Nazareth, the great *theos-aner* (God-man), alone is Savior and his benefits always involve his person.

More recently, salvation as healing developed in the twentieth century among Pentecostals. Led by William J. Seymour (1870–1922), the Azusa Street Mission in downtown Los Angeles, the widely-recognized birth-place of Pentecostalism, drew large and international crowds for three straight years (1906–9) in large part due to the physical healings they witnessed in the services. Those early Pentecostals, though very exuberant in God's Spirit, nevertheless sought to ground their experience in the biblical witness. (Over subsequent decades, Pentecostals were steadily accused by the larger church of teaching and doing things contrary to Scripture. Of course, every movement has anomalies and those who err, but Pentecostals have consistently insisted on being biblical.) That they even prayed for, and laid hands on, the sick was because they read the apostles doing that in Acts. The Spirit of God in their hearts motivated those early Pentecostals to find biblical warrant for their actions and teachings.

Again, for Pentecostals physical healings are not accidental. Pentecostals know that it is the Holy Spirit who gives charismatic gifts—including healings and miracles—for the sake of gospel-mission, people's edification,

---

16. Macchia, *Justified in the Spirit*, 7.

and the glory of God. For this chapter's purposes, we note that most Pentecostal churches and denominations have argued that physical healings are grounded in Jesus' atoning work. Chiefly, they maintain that Isaiah 53:4–5 provides the context for understanding Jesus' healing work:

> Surely our sickness[17] he himself bore, and our pains[18] he carried; yet we ourselves esteemed him stricken, smitten of God, and afflicted. But he was pierced through for our transgressions, he was crushed for our iniquities; the chastening for our wellbeing fell upon him, and by his stripes we are healed. (Isa 53:4–5)

After Jesus healed a paralyzed man, healed Peter's mother-in-law, and freed many who were demonized, Matthew interpreted Jesus' work in 8:17 by quoting Isaiah, "He took our infirmities and carried away our diseases" (Isa 53:4). Thus, Pentecostals maintain that salvation is not only about being forgiven our sins, or given relationship with God, or knowing that because we are in Christ death will not have final claim on our bodies. More, salvation involves our bodies in this life. This is powerful! Salvation is not just a doctrine. Salvation is not just a future hope. Christ's salvation makes a difference in the here and now, even in our bodies. This salvation-as-physical-healing theological understanding is just one reason why Pentecostalism is exploding around the world. (Of course, leaders need to be ready to help explain why, and comfort hearts when, healings do not happen.) So prevalent is this salvation-as-healing Pentecostal theology that Frank Macchia wrote, "One is much more likely to hear a sermon preached to sinners from Pentecostal pulpits today about accepting healing by faith in Christ than about justification in the traditionally forensic sense of the word."[19] Pastors and missionaries in Africa, Latin America, China and elsewhere report powerful stories of physical healings and this news grips people's hearts and helps draw them to saving faith.

God's power to heal is real. I myself have experienced God's immediate healing touch. Months after a car accident I suffered when I was sixteen years old a visiting evangelist touched my arthritic, pain-filled, left ankle. (My left foot had been all but severed in that wreck.) Now, I did not want him to pray for me. Physically tired and sitting on the back row of church that evening, I just wanted to be left alone. However, at the behest of my compassionate dad, the evangelist knelt down and gently laid hands on my ankle and prayed. Immediately, I felt a warmth move into my ankle and the

---

17. Sometimes interpreted as "griefs."
18. Interpreted sometimes as "sorrows."
19. Macchia, *Justified in the Spirit*, 82.

pain was gone! Experientially I learned that God's healing power is real. In that event the Lord also taught me that he does not need my faith to move in my life, even though the Bible teaches that the Lord can do more in and through people where faith is present. Over the years, I've also learned to recognize that God, the giver of "every good gift" (Jas 1:17) also heals us indirectly. Regularly, I thank the Lord for doctors, medicine, technicians, anesthesiologists, and nurses. Too often Pentecostals overlook how God works indirectly in life through other people.

The benefits of Christ's work are manifold. The New Testament describes Jesus' work using many categories: election, adoption, redemption, justification, washing, purchase, liberation, union with Christ, baptism, and new creation. Just that small list shows how encompassing is Jesus' work regarding us. Christians, both to seek out God's life-encompassing work and to recognize the Spirit's already-occurring work, need a more fully orbed understanding of salvation as healing, perhaps like that held by believers in Africa. Independent Pentecostal Africans make healing central to their worship services and preaching. They also extend an understanding of healing to issues like "unemployment, family disputes, racism, marital discord" and tribal controversies.[20] God comes to heal relationships, needs, holes in our souls, abuses, addictions, and divergent wounding's. Salvation is not simply being forgiven; thank you, God, for forgiveness! We need to be healed, too. True, sometimes this salvation-as-healing-for-this-life position has resulted in the "prosperity gospel," the belief that God wants his children to be abundantly blessed in every earthly way—physically,[21] social status-wise, and monetarily. Again, all movements have their errors and over-statements. Yet, if we eliminate every issue that presents challenges we will have little remaining to avail ourselves. Too many daily vitamins are unhealthy, and anything can be turned into a falsehood.[22] The need for solid, mature, wise, and timely pastoral teaching is great.

---

20. Cox, *Fire From Heaven*, 254–62.

21. The history of monasticism also reveals this tendency. There have been monastic movements that have believed one can be so tightly united with Christ or so infused with God's Spirit that one will never physically die. This side of eternity, a now but not-yet perspective must be emphatically embraced. See more on this in the text below.

22. For decades, Pentecostal theologians and scholars have argued carefully against the prosperity gospel's over-reaching tendencies. See Fee, *The Disease of the Health and Wealth Gospels*. The prosperity gospel has both its American versions that are grotesque capitulations to ideological capitalism, and its African versions that seek to address the enormous poverty that besets so many nations on their continent. See Attanasi and Yong, eds. *Pentecostalism and Prosperity*.

Salvation as New Life in the Spirit

The traditional Western narrowing of salvation as forgiveness of sin and as justifying our legal status before God is not only biblically short-sighted, it is insufficient for what we human beings crave. Is forgiveness enough if, finally, we will die anyway? Is justification sufficient if this life is meaningless? The apostle Paul implies that the answers are "no" when he wrote that if Christ was not bodily resurrected then, our hope is in vain (1 Cor 15:14). Paul, though keenly aware of our need for forgiveness, did not stop his theological reflection at forgiveness. He understood an equally troubling challenge: this life, such as it is, is not enough. This life—created good though it is—is not enough. *We yearn not only for a life after this life, but we also yearn for more* in *this life.* For Paul, following Jesus Christ has the unprecedented, hardly expected, benefit of life in God's Spirit. The source of new life—the very life and power that resurrected Christ—is the Holy Spirit. God sends this Holy Spirit-ual power into our hearts, and we experience new life. Because many Christians overlook this element of new life, and so also miss the joy and hope it brings, we must go deeper hereon.

The beauty of Christianity is life, new life. Yes, forgiveness is marvelous and has healing effects; we celebrate that. However, Jesus also came to make possible our reception of God's Holy Spirit. Among Western Christians, St. Paul is famous for developing the doctrine of justification by faith. However, Paul wrote far more about life in the Holy Spirit than he did about forgiveness and justification.[23] Paul was a man vibrant in God's Spirit. Paul understood variously that God's Spirit is a new principle that works in our hearts and minds (Rom 8; Gal 3:1–14; 5:16–26; Phil 1:19), a down-payment on the Father's promise (Rom 8:23; 2 Cor 1:22; 5:5; Eph 1:13–14),[24] and the power of resurrection (Ezek 37:13–14; Rom 1:4; 8:11). Christ's messianic covenant is a channel of new life because Jesus sends the Spirit to indwell us. Just as he was baptized and received the Spirit, so too are we immersed in Christ who sends his Holy Spirit (Matt 3:13–17; Acts 2:1–21; 10:44–48; Rom 6:1–14; 8:1–17). *The indwelling Christ, the indwelling Spirit, is the very life of the new covenant, the law written on our hearts* (Jer 31:33; Rom 2:15; 1 Cor 2:11–16; Heb 10:16). In all of that we—as persons and as Christ's corporate body—were created to be living temples; that theological purpose and goal cannot be overstated amidst our reflections on salvation. God intends to make both

---

23. Fee, *God's Empowering Presence*.
24. Revelation 22, where that water causes all of creation to flourish.

people and creation his eternal dwelling place (1 Cor 3:16–17; 15:28; 2 Cor 6:16; Rev 21)![25]

Bishop Kallistos Ware tells an ancient story. "Tell us about the visions that you see," a monk once said to Abbot Pachomius (292–348). "A sinner like me does not expect to see visions from God," Pachomius replied, "but let me tell you about a great vision. If you see a holy and humble man, that is a great vision. For what greater vision can there be than this: to see the invisible God revealed in his temple, a visible human person?"[26] Sometimes today we church-folk can neglect how transformative the indwelling of God's Spirit truly is. Regularly hearing God's word preached, routinely studying the Bible, and commonly discussing the Christian life, we Christians can profane how spectacular it is when a person gives her allegiance to Christ as Lord. Familiarity breeds contempt; we can err and make the holy profane. I believe that in our churches we need to share regular reports, "testimonies" in older parlance, with one another about the Spirit's actions in our respective lives. We need to encourage one another that God is greater, that the Spirit is active amongst us, that God's *fons vitae* is really gushing in and through others. Scripture shows that the Spirit is always at work (Gen 1:2; John 3:8), but frequently we "quench" the Spirit by not sharing the good news of his activity with one another or by not seeking his presence and movement. The New Testament teaches us to "kindle afresh the gift of God which is in [us] . . . a spirit . . . of power and love and discipline" and to "stimulate one another to love and good deeds" (2 Tim 1:6–7; Heb 10:24; Jude 20). Sharing stories and praises with one another, forcibly pursuing God's kingdom and Spirit amongst us (Matt 11:12; Luke 11:9, 13), and praying with and in the Spirit (Rom 8:23, 26; 1 Cor 14:1–33; Jude 20) will stir our own hearts and spirits.

Salvation as new life in God's Spirit raises different appropriate pastoral questions. If indeed we have this new life, will believers still struggle with sin? Put differently, are Christians so suffused with God's Spirit that they are no longer tempted? Alternatively, if we are full of the Spirit will our bodies no longer suffer disease? To answer these kinds of questions, we recall the New Testament teaching on the eschatological dimensions of salvation in Christ.

Eschatology traditionally has to do with the study of "the end times" and "the last things" (death, resurrection, judgment, hell, the great completion of all history, and heaven-on-earth). However, among theologians, eschatological dimensions include both *how* and *that* the end has already broken into the present. It was God's Spirit who both conceived Jesus in Mary's womb and empowered Jesus' ministry. By using different parables

---

25. See Wright, *Surprised by Hope*.
26. Pachomius "First Greek Life of Pachomius 48," 62.

and by giving explanations of his signs, Jesus taught that with his coming the kingdom of God had begun to break into the present. The Spirit of God had come through Jesus' person and work, sometimes violently so (Luke 4:31–37; 8:26–39; John 2:13–17)! The Gospels themselves show us that Jesus frequently taught about an imminent-future day of judgment, commonly understood in the Hebrew Scriptures as the "day of the Lord." However, Jesus taught and acted in ways such that he believed that the end was *presently active* through his ministry and the people he touched. For decades, scholars have framed this dynamic as the "now-not yet" of God's kingdom. By the Spirit, Jesus had come into the present era; people could see the effects of the Spirit's presence when Jesus healed, cleansed, forgave, taught, and delivered people. In the Spirit, Jesus defeated demons, principalities, and powers, but he did not yet destroy them. By the Spirit, Jesus was raised from the dead, ascended to heaven, and accomplished our salvation. However, the finality, the *dénouement* of all history, awaits completion. The final battle looms; death, sin, Satan, and Anti-Christ have not yet been cast into the abyss. This now-not yet tension of Jesus' ministry thus has cosmic dimensions, but it has personal dimensions too.

As non-believers, when we are convicted of sin and truth, and when we are drawn towards Jesus as Lord, we experience something of God's kingdom, the Spirit's action, in our lives; something unique works inside us. Then, when we confess with our mouths and believe with our hearts that Jesus is Lord, we are born anew; we can feel amazingly different and/or be suddenly filled with hope, trust, joy, and love. Across the sweep of our lives in Christ we experience growth, we receive and exercise charismatic gifts, we live disciplined lives of holiness and learn to prefer others over ourselves (life in the Spirit is sometimes dynamic, but also sometimes mundane and even boring, yet it is all born of God's *ruach*);[27] there is growth in Christ-likeness. And yet, every Christian walking the planet will testify to an ongoing battle with temptation and sin. We know Christians who have failed (pastors and priests even) and ourselves experience failure to resist sin. How can this be? After all, God's Spirit lives inside us. There is a now-not yet dynamic quality to the work of God's Spirit. Indeed, Jesus is Lord, but not all beings, people, or nations bow their hearts or knees to him. Jesus came for the whole world, yet life's atmosphere is still infected with sin; we continue to live inside that befouled and infected atmosphere. John wrote, "Beloved, now we are children of God, and it has *not* appeared as *yet* what we shall be. We know that, when he [Christ] appears, we *shall be* like him, because we *shall* see him just as he is. Moreover, everyone who has this hope fixed on him purifies himself, just as he is pure" (1 John 3:2–3). By those verses, and

---

27. Levison develops how we can become people of God's Spirit through disciplined, not only charismatic, means. See Levison, *Filled with the Spirit*; Levison, *Fresh Air*.

later in the same passage, we see that John was aware that believers struggle with sin and impurity. Elsewhere, Paul touched on the now-not yet quality of the kingdom when he wrote, "For in hope we have been saved, but hope that is seen is not hope; for why does one also hope for what he sees?" (Rom 8:24). Paul's position on this was emphatic: the people whom God's Spirit indwells, "while we are in this tent, we groan, being burdened, because we do not want to be unclothed, but to be clothed, in order that what is mortal [infected by death] by be swallowed up by life" (2 Cor 5:4). The apostle himself struggle with temptation and sin, and yet his trust was in Christ's righteousness, not in Paul's own righteousness (Rom 7:7–25). Paul knew that there was a future final transformation that awaits those in Christ. We are *now* in Christ, but the completion of our salvation has *not yet* been fully realized. We *have been* saved by Christ at Golgotha. We *are being* saved by Christ in his Holy Spirit. We *will be* finally and fully saved by our Triune God and will indwell resurrected bodies in the New Jerusalem.

This salvation-as-new-life pneumatological emphasis is one ripe for plucking and juicing by Pentecostals. We have long emphasized the experience of God's Spirit as an existential reality; now we just need to apply that more carefully concerning the doctrine of salvation. For a century we have primarily, in our theologizing, focused on Holy Spirit-ual empowerment and gifts. That focus has benefitted the global church; we have reminded them all of the Spirit's ongoing dynamic activity in gospel proclamation and kingdom work. And yet when it comes to soteriology, the Spirit is still the "Cinderella of the Trinity." Fittingly, theologians have focused for two thousand years on the Father and the Son. The Father is Creator, and the Son is Redeemer. Further, the Scriptures more directly portray the Trinity's first two members than the Spirit. Moreover, we know from the Bible, that the Father and Son are persons: we read people conversing with them as persons. And although Jesus referred to the Spirit in personal terms the Spirit is more ambiguous, especially in the Old Testament. Reflecting the historic emphasis on the Father and Son, and reflecting some of the ambiguity about the Spirit in the Scripture, across some twenty years of theological instruction my theology students consistently refer to the Spirit as an "it." Depersonalizing the Spirit like that not only works against more vibrant Trinitarian constructions, it also causes pastors and disciples to more easily ignore the Spirit's role in salvation. The Spirit does not merely subjectively actualize the objective work of Jesus, as too many theologians have posited it. The Spirit is central to the work and life of salvation itself.[28]

Pentecostal theologian Frank Macchia argues that Jesus' Spirit comes to indwell believers and to bring them into right relationship within the

---

28. Steven Studebaker raises similar challenges. Studebaker, *From Pentecost to the Triune God*, 175–85.

effulgence of the Trinity. Not merely grace as a power, but God's very Spirit comes to indwell believers. Macchia quoted early Pentecostal pioneer John G. Lake (1870–1935):

> The medium by which God undertakes to bless the world is through the transmission of Himself. The Spirit of God is His own substance, the substance of His being, the very nature and quality of the presence and nature of God. Consequently, when we speak of the Spirit of God being transmitted to man . . . we are talking about the transmission of the living substance and being of God into your being and into mine. . . . That is the secret of the abundant life of which Jesus spoke. He said, "I have come that they might have life, and that they might have it more abundantly" (John 10:10). The reason we have more abundant life is that, receiving God into our being, all the springs of our being are quickened by his living presence.[29]

Macchia reasons that "the goal is to turn all of creation into a temple of the divine presence in the image of Christ and to the glory of the Father."[30] Again, this understanding of salvation exceeds that of an agreement between a judge and the accused, "but an intimate communion of love involving mutual indwelling," a making-right of all relationships, or what Macchia calls a "rightwising" of sinful flesh and existence.[31]

Salvation and the Human Role

God is the first mover in salvation. Secondarily we respond. God sent his Spirit and Son before we ever thought to receive salvation. God invites first. The Bible is clear that salvation is God's work. And yet our response is necessitated. Though of the Augustinian tradition, which frames salvation as a matter of God's eternal decree,[32] John Calvin nevertheless accurately summed up biblical teaching—salvation is God's work, but *he will not save us without us*. Salvation is entirely a gift of God. We did nothing to make or offer the gift. We are like street beggars whose only response is to say, "yes, thank you," to a free sandwich. Saying yes to the sandwich does not make

---

29. Lake, "The Ultimate Test of True Christianity," 65.

30. Macchia, *Justified in the Spirit*, 78.

31. Ibid., 8. "Rightwising" thus involves pardon, healing, sanctification, and the implementation of justice across all relationships. Macchia says, "The Spirit gave the Word a body so that those with bodies might receive the Spirit." Rogers, "After the Spirit," quoted in Macchia, *Justified in the Spirit*, 132.

32. In contrast to Augustine, Calvin believed God did indeed choose to damn some while saving others; this was an eternal decree (a *decretum horribile*, an awe-full decree), one made before time began. McGrath, *Reformation Thought*, 134.

the sandwich our cause. Our saying yes to God does not make us our own saviors or place any of salvation's honor, praise, or glory with us. Nevertheless, accepting the sandwich is necessary if we are to eat.

Put differently, as I teach my students, evangelicals like to say, "It's not a religion, it's a relationship." Relationships require mutuality, commitment, and vulnerability.[33] If God forced us into salvation it would neither be a relationship nor would it be loving; coerced salvation would be abusive. The essence of the Trinity is self-giving, so forcing us into salvation would violate God's own identity.

How much faith is necessary? Short, theologically correct answers would be, "as mustard seed's worth," or "enough." However, minimizing the issue with that question fails to understand what salvation in God truly means. Salvation is not about how little one has to do, but about how, out of gratitude, one can share God's love and giving.

When I was growing up in my boyhood Pentecostal church, our pastor would preach, "tonight, ladies and gentlemen, eternal salvation is at stake. God has one vote, and Satan has one vote. But you have a vote, too. How will you cast the deciding vote?" Construing salvation that way is evangelistically effective, but theologically grotesque. Satan is not God's equal. Salvation comes from God alone, and we have the joy of saying yes.

Finally, I simply must insist that salvation is for disciples. In the Great Commission, Jesus did not say "Go and make *converts* of the nations." He said, "Go and make *disciples* of the nations" (Matt 28:19–29). An important reason our societies are not well seasoned with the gospel or permeated with God's Holy Spirit, is that we have spent too long trying to meet some minimal legal-understanding of justification in order to "get people saved." Polls and studies constantly reveal that Christians divorce at the same rate as non-Christians, suffer addictions at rates close to those of non-Christians, and hold religious and philosophical views similar to non-Christians. How can this be? We have far too many nominal, half-committed, I-don't-want-to-go-to-hell Christians in the churches. My theology students frequently hear me say, "Converts get to go to heaven. Disciples get to change the world." Following the risen Jesus is not a *have to* but a *get to*. It is not our *duty* to proclaim the gospel—it is our *joy*! It is not so much a *burden* to be salt and light as it is an *adventure*. Help us, living God, to walk in faithfulness to you and your salvation!

---

33. See above Keller, *The Reason for God*, 47–49, 76–85, 181–18.

Bibliography

Athanasius. *De Incarnatione*. In *Patrologiae Cursus Completus, Series Graecae*, edited by J. P. Migne. 168 vols. Turnholti, Belgium: Typographi Brepols, 1978.

Attanasi, Katherine, and Amos Yong, eds. *Pentecostalism and Prosperity: The Socio-Economics of the Global Charismatic Movement*. Christianities of the World. New York: Palgrave Macmillan, 2012

Boccia, Romina, Alison Acosta Fraser, and Emily Goff. "Federal Spending by the Numbers, 2013: Government Spending Trends in Graphics, Tables, and Key Points." http://www.heritage.org/research/reports/2013/08/federal-spending-by-the-numbers-2013.

Cox, Harvey. *Fire from Heaven: The Rise of Pentecostal Spirituality and the Reshaping of Religion in the Twenty-first Century*. Reading, MA: Addison Wesley, 1995.

Fee, Gordon. *The Disease of the Health and Wealth Gospels*. Vancouver, Canada: Regent College, 1985.

———. *God's Empowering Presence: The Holy Spirit in the Letters of Paul*. Grand Rapids: Baker Academic, 2009.

Human Rights Watch. "World Report 2012: North Korea." http://www.hrw.org/world-report-2012/world-report-2012-north-korea.

Keller, Timothy. *The Reason for God: Belief in an Age of Skepticism*. London: Hodder & Stoughton, 2009.

Lake, John G. "The Ultimate Test of True Christianity." In *Spiritual Hunger, the God-Men. And Other Sermons by John G. Lake*, edited by Gordon Lindsey, 62–68. Dallas: Christ for the Nations, 1976.

Levison, John R. *Filled with the Spirit*. Grand Rapids: Eerdmans, 2009.

———. *Fresh Air: The Holy Spirit for an Inspired Life*. Brewster, MA: Paraclete, 2012.

Lossky, Vladimir. *The Mystical Theology of the Eastern Church*. Crestwood, NY: St. Vladimir's Seminary Press, 1976.

———. *Orthodox Theology: An Introduction*. St. Crestwood, NY: Vladimir's Seminary Press, 2001.

Macchia, Frank. *Justified in the Spirit: Creation, Redemption, and the Triune God*. Grand Rapids: Eerdmans, 2010.

McGrath, Alister E. *Reformation Thought: An Introduction*. 3rd ed. Oxford: Blackwell, 2002.

Moltmann, Jürgen. *Trinity and the Kingdom: The Doctrine of God*. Minneapolis: Augsburg Fortress, 1983.

Newbigin, Lesslie. *The Gospel in a Pluralist Society*. Grand Rapids: Eerdmans, 1989.

Olson, Roger. *The Story of Christian Theology: Twenty Centuries of Tradition and Reform*. Downers Grove, IL: IVP, 1999.

Pachomius. "First Greek Life of Pachomius 48." In "The Mystery of the Human Person," edited by Kallistos Ware. *Sobornost*, 3.1 (1981) 62–69.

Poverty.com. "Hunger and World Poverty." http://www.poverty.com.

Rogers, Eugene F. *After the Spirit: A Constructive Pneumatology from Resources Outside the West*. Grand Rapids: Eerdmans, 2005.

Statistic Brain. "World Hunger Statistics." http://www.statisticbrain.com/world-hunger-statistics.

Studebaker Steven. *From Pentecost to the Triune God: A Pentecostal Trinitarian Theology*. Grand Rapids: Eerdmans, 2012.

Wright, N. T. *Surprised by Hope: Rethinking Heaven, the Resurrection, and the Mission of the Church*. New York: HarperOne, 2008.

6

How, Why, and When Should Someone be Baptized? What Is Its Relationship to Salvation?

GLENN BALFOUR

Introduction

PENTECOSTAL CHURCHES CAN TRACE their modern historical beginnings back to Los Angeles in 1906. It was in this year that there was a dramatic experience of the Holy Spirit in the Apostolic Faith Mission, 312 Azusa Street, a church led by Pastor William J. Seymour. At the center of this experience was the phenomenon of "speaking in tongues." The experience was identified very quickly with the out-pouring of the Holy Spirit on the Day of Pentecost as described in Acts 2:1–4. And so the modern Pentecostal denominations began.[1] Since then, and during the last four decades in particular, Pentecostal churches have grown strongly.

The impact of its modern historical beginnings has had a noticeable effect on Pentecostal theology. In terms of Pneumatology—particularly in terms of an "empowerment reception" of the Holy Spirit that is distinct from a "soteriological reception" of the Holy Spirit—Pentecostal theology is unique.[2] It is also the case that this unique Pentecostal pneumatological

---

1. In fact, the origins of Pentecostal churches may be traced back to Parham, and the Topeka Outpouring of 1901. Nonetheless, it is with Azusa Street that the new Pentecostal churches truly began to spread globally.

2. This uniqueness has increasingly been "shared" with many churches that are not Pentecostal in name. These churches could broadly be described as "charismatic" in practice. One should not forget, however, how sharply different the Pentecostal position was from the cessationist position held by virtually every other major church grouping at the start of the last century.

nexus has had "knock-on" effects on various other aspects of Pentecostal faith and practice.[3] Beyond this pneumatological nexus, however, "Pentecostal theology" is, in fact, something of a misnomer. There are no other uniquely, or even distinctly, Pentecostal positions in any other area of Christian theology.

Undoubtedly, various socioeconomic or historical realities have led to various tendencies within Pentecostal circles. So, for example, the "disadvantaged" socioeconomic reality of many early Pentecostals contributed towards an imminently futurist eschatology. This undoubtedly was fed by the "ostracism" many early Pentecostals felt by the wider church, and by some of the awful historical realities of two world wars. However, these tendencies are fundamentally incidental. This is borne out by the fact that they can go as quickly as they came. So, for example, as Pentecostal generations have felt the socioeconomic benefits of the "Redemption Cycle," they have adopted with ease a more inaugurated or even realized eschatological position.

In reality, Pentecostals are mainstream when it comes to the three central pillars of systematic theology—Trinity, incarnation, and atonement. Indeed, despite its radical pneumatological distinctives and charismatic practices, Pentecostal theology is intrinsically conservative and biblically oriented. To this extent, it could be described as traditionally Protestant or evangelical. And this applies to its position on water baptism.

The Pentecostal Position on Baptism in Water

There is, then, no uniquely—or even distinctly—Pentecostal position on baptism in water. Rather, Pentecostals adhere to a fairly standard non-conformist evangelical position, which is epitomized by the Baptist tradition within Christian circles. So, for example, the relevant AoG GB Statement of Faith reads, "We believe that all who have truly repented and believed in Christ as Lord and Savior are commanded to be baptized by immersion in water." Other Pentecostal church groupings use different phraseology, but the central facet is the same: *full immersion in water is a required act of obedience for everyone who has made a conscious decision to follow Christ.*

Some fairly standard New Testament proof texts are used to support this position. Three, in particular, are Matthew 28:19, Acts 2:38, and Acts 10:47–48. In the first of these, Matthew 28:19, the final command of the

---

3. For example, Christology within Pentecostal circles tends to be more "kenotic" in emphasis (rather than "hypostatic union"-ist). This is because a "kenotic" model allows greater emphasis to placed on the notion that Jesus Christ himself was empowered by the Holy Spirit (Luke 4:18–19; Acts 10:38).

Risen Christ to the eleven disciples is this: "Go, therefore, and make disciples of all nations" (Matt 28:19). The Risen Christ immediately goes on to describe what this command entails, and he itemizes just two things. The first thing is what concerns us here: "*baptizing* them in the name of the Father and of the Son and of the Holy Spirit . . . ."[4] The participle (βαπτίζοντες; *baptizontes*) is in the present tense, which means that it takes place at the same time as the main verb ("make disciples"). In short, a fundamental and integral part of the Risen Christ's final command to his disciples in Matthew's Gospel is for us to baptize (in water) new disciples.

In the second proof text, Acts 2:38, the apostle Peter is addressing thousands of people on the Day of Pentecost. Having heard the message—that God has made the person they crucified, Jesus of Nazareth, both Lord and Christ—the listeners are "pierced to the heart," and ask the apostles what they should do (v. 37). Peter's reply is this: "Repent, and be baptized, every one of you, in the name of Jesus Christ for the forgiveness of your sins. And you will receive the gift of the Holy Spirit." In other words, he requires them to do just two things—(1) repent, and (2) be baptized (in water).[5] Three thousand of them do as Peter tells them: and notice how the description of them begins (v. 41)—"So those who welcomed his message were baptized . . . ."

The third proof text, Acts 10:47–48, again involves Peter. Peter has been proclaiming the message of "peace by Jesus Christ" (v. 36) to a number of gentiles in the house of Cornelius. He reaches the point that everyone who believes in Jesus of Nazareth receives forgiveness of sins through his name, when, suddenly, the Holy Spirit "falls upon" all the listeners (vv. 43–44). The implication is clear—God has accepted these gentiles! It is the astonished Peter's immediate response that is of interest to us here (v. 47): "Can anyone keep these people from being baptized with water? They have received the Holy Spirit just as we have." The inference is unavoidable: the very first thing that should happen to these new believers—indeed, the only thing Peter mentions here—is that they should be "baptized with water." That is exactly what happens (v. 48): "So he ordered them to be baptized in the name of Jesus Christ."

These texts, then, describe the essential position adopted by Pentecostals: baptism in water is a required act of obedience for everyone who has made a conscious decision to follow Christ.

---

4. The second thing, of course, is this: ". . . teaching them to obey everything I have commanded you" (Matt 29:20).

5. Peter mentions two further things here—(3) forgiveness of sins, and (4) receiving the gift of the Holy Spirit. These two things, however, are the result of the two actions—repenting, and being baptized (in water).

How Should We Be Baptized in Water?

a. Full Immersion

What, then, does the rite of baptism in water look like? In other words, how should we be baptized? Again, the Pentecostal view on this is the one adopted from the wider Baptist tradition. In short, it is a brief "full immersion" in water. This can be in the sea, in a river, in a swimming pool, in a lake, in a specially constructed tank (a "baptistery")—it really does not matter. The essential point is that it is "full immersion."

This practice of baptism by "full immersion" might look a little strange. It is visually quite distinct from the form of baptism practiced in Orthodox, Roman Catholic, and other "established" denominations—that of "sprinkling."[6] So what is the reasoning behind "full immersion"?

One reason is simply the meaning of the Greek verb, "I baptize" (βαπτίζω; *baptizō*). It is widely accepted that the semantic domain for this verb and its conjugates is "dipping" or "plunging." It is not, "sprinkling." This sense of the word is supported by ancient practice. The rite of baptism took on new significance in the early church, for sure, but it would be wrong to think that Christians were the first to practice it. On the contrary, it was a very common religious practice in the first century Near Eastern world. While it has no Old Testament precedent, by the first century CE, it was widely practiced in both Jewish and non-Jewish circles. In both circles, moreover, it was invariably practiced by "dipping," or "plunging," or even "pouring over"; but never by "sprinkling."[7]

A second reason is New Testament practice. Without exception, every New Testament description of baptism in water involves "dipping" or "plunging." Three passages, in particular, bear this out. The people are baptized by John the Baptist "in the river Jordan" (Mark 1:5). When Jesus himself is baptized by John the Baptist, it is "as he was coming up out of the water" that the Holy Spirit descends into him (Mark 1:10). The baptism of the Ethiopian eunuch is especially telling: ". . . the eunuch said, 'Look, here is water! What is to prevent me from being baptized?' . . . both of them, Philip and the eunuch, went down into the water, and Philip baptized him. When

---

6. Its increasingly common practice in Christian churches, however, has perhaps made it a less unfamiliar event within contemporary society than in times gone by.

7. In Jewish contexts this manifests itself in the abundant presence of ancient "mivkehs"—ritual baths that would have steps leading into them. (These can be seen, for instance, at Qumran.) One particularly gruesome non-Jewish form of baptism was the Taurobolium—here a bull was stood on a grate over the initiate, cut open, and it entire internal contents allowed to pour down onto the initiate. (This description, however, only goes as far back as a Christian, anti-pagan poem in the late fourth century.)

they came up out of the water, the Spirit of the Lord snatched Philip away . . ." (Acts 8:36–39).

A third reason is, perhaps surprisingly, linked to an association made with baptism in non-Jewish contexts. This association appeared especially in the many Mystery Religions that were practiced throughout the Roman Empire (e.g., Mithraism). This association was essentially with death and resurrection. So much becomes clear with the help of a question. What does baptism by "fully immersion" look like? It looks like a burial! Someone is put under the water, just like someone is buried under the ground. That person, however, is also brought out of the water! So baptism by "full immersion" also looks like a resurrection. This association was not lost on the Mystery Religions.

That is to say, in the Mystery Religions especially, bathing in water had mythical connotations. When the initiate was bathed in the pagan temple (or the public baths), they became "identified" with that temple's god or goddess. Death and resurrection were often associated with the temple deities. (Examples include Osiris, Tammuz, Adonis, Attis, and Dionysus.) And so through ritual bathing, the initiate was also identified with—and participated in—the death and resurrection of their deity. (The second-century Apuleius describes a lengthy initiation into the mysteries of Isis, which was preceded by bathing in the public baths; and he describes a similar initiation into the cult of Osiris.)

This language may sound familiar to you, and that may be because similar language appears in Paul's letters in the New Testament. Indeed, this might have been a deliberate ploy on the part of Paul, to connect with the non-Jewish part of his audience (1 Cor 9:19–23). Paul's words in Romans 6:3–4 are especially poignant: "Do you not know that all of us who have been baptized into Christ Jesus were baptized into his death? Therefore we have been buried with him by baptism into death, so that, just as Christ was raised from the dead by the glory of the Father, so we too might walk in newness of life" (Compare Col 2:12; Gal 3:27).

In short, the third reason for why the earliest Christian believers practiced baptism "by full immersion"—and why we do too—is because of the resonance it offers with our new life "in Christ." Baptism in water by full immersion offers a visually powerful expression of a spiritual reality—that when we become Christians our old life is buried with Christ, and we rise into a new life "in Christ." This distinctly Pauline concept is best described by Paul himself! "I have been crucified with Christ; and I no longer live, but Christ lives in me" (Gal 2:19b–20a). Baptism by "full immersion" demonstrates this death and resurrection wonderfully.

b. The Wording

In terms of how we should be baptized in water, two further matters also warrant some attention: the wording and the setting. In terms of the wording we should use when we baptize someone, Pentecostals are typically open-minded. Some words, however, are overwhelmingly seen as required. These are the words Jesus gives to the eleven at the end of Matthew's Gospel: ". . . baptizing them *in the name of the Father and the Son and the Holy Spirit*" (28:19). Indeed, these words are generally referred to as a "baptismal formula."

We could leave this here. There is, however, a minor controversy in this area that is worth noting. This baptismal formula does not actually appear anywhere elsewhere in the New Testament. On the contrary, in the Book of Acts, whenever any new believer is baptized in water they are said to be baptized simply "into the Lord Jesus" (e.g., Acts 8:16; 10:47; 19:5; compare 1 Cor 1:13). For this reason, certain Pentecostal groups insist that this is the language we should use when we baptize someone. It remains, however, that the majority Pentecostal view by far is that we should use the baptismal formula of Matthew 28:19.

The reason for the majority view is clear. First, the minority view is championed by groups that are in fact not Trinitarian, but are instead "Modalist."[8] That is to say, the minority view is principally motivated by groups that are, in the true sense of the word, heretical. Second, it is certainly the case that new believers are described as being baptized "into the Lord Jesus" throughout the Book of Acts. This language, however, is never *prescriptive*; rather, it is essentially *descriptive*. That is to say, we are never *commanded* to use these words. Rather, they *describe* what baptism visually expresses—that as believers we are indeed identified specifically with the crucified and risen Lord Jesus Christ. In the words of Colossians 2:12: "When you were buried together with him [Christ] in baptism, you were also raised with him through faith in the power of God, who raised him from the dead."

Third, by contrast, it is only the words in Matthew 28:19 that are *prescribed*. They are specifically *commanded* by the Risen Christ—and you can't get more "prescribed" than that! (Indeed, they have been described as "red letter" words in the New Testament.) And no matter if they are given once, or a hundred times—a command is a command! It has to be said, moreover,

---

8. These groups are usually known as "Oneness Pentecostals" or "Jesus Only." They believe that only "One Person" is God, and that this Person appears in different "modes" (as Father or Son or Holy Spirit).

that the wording in Matthew 28:19 does sound intentional and "formulaic," right down to the ordering of "the Father and the Son and the Holy Spirit."

It has been suggested that, in fact, we could use both sets of words when we baptize believers—the *prescribed* proto-Trinitarian language of Matthew 28:19, and the descriptive language of Acts. In other words, when we baptize someone we baptize then in the name of the Father and of the Son and of the Holy Spirit into the Lord Jesus Christ. We need always to keep it in mind that we are saved "by faith," not "by words." So, it is as an expression of faith that baptism has spiritual significance, not as a ritual in and of itself. Nevertheless, inasmuch as we want to "get it right," and we want disciples to understand their faith, this seems like a good suggestion to me.

c. The Setting

In terms of the setting, it will help us momentarily to return to the pre-Christian practice of baptism. Within the Jewish context, the primary reason for baptism was to indicate that the person was now following a (new) rabbi. That is to say, it was a mark of discipleship. This is evidenced by the disciples of John the Baptist. It is common knowledge that John baptized many people (Mark 1:5, etc.); but it is perhaps less well known that in all this he was making disciples (e.g., Matt 9:14; Mark 6:29; Luke 7:18–19; John 1:35, 40). Perhaps the greatest indicator of this appears, funnily enough, in Acts. In Acts 19:1–4, Paul meets twelve "disciples" that have experienced only "John's baptism". And this happens far, far away from Judea, in modern-day Turkey (Ephesus).

New members of the Qumran community were also baptized in water (1QS 3:4–9; 5:13–14; 6:14–23), as were Jewish proselytes generally. This is why the Ethiopian eunuch is so keen to be baptized (a rite with which he is clearly familiar)—as a "God-fearer" (see Acts 8:27–28), he would have been hitherto denied access to full proselytism because of his "damaged" condition. This (Jewish) practice of baptizing new disciples is also, interestingly enough, adhered to by Jesus. Indeed, there is a record that both he and his disciples were out-stripping John the Baptist in this respect (John 4:1–2).

What, then, is the relevance of this in terms of how we should practice baptism? The answer lies in the fact that, as much as Christian baptism was a mark of *identification* with Christ (especially in the Pauline texts), following predominantly non-Jewish baptism, it was also a mark of discipleship. This discipleship theme is present especially in the Synoptic Gospels and Acts and follows predominantly Jewish baptism. It is reflected in the Matthean Great Commission ("make disciples . . . baptizing them." Matt 28:19). It is also reflected in the earliest Christian practice generally of baptizing new converts, something that goes right back to that first post-Resurrection Day of Pentecost (Acts 2:41). Again, what is the relevance of this in terms of how we should practice baptism?

Quite simply, it surely means that the most appropriate setting for Christian baptism as a mark of discipleship is *the local church!* It is in the local church that genuine discipleship takes place—within the context of the believing community, the body of Christ, and accountability and submission to church leadership. It is worth noting that the local church is not a building per se. Rather, it is people—believers—submitted to a recognized Christian leadership. So, this is not an insistence on the use of a "sacred building" or a particular physical location, as such. Rather, it is an insistence that, as a mark of discipleship, baptism should occur under the auspices of, and in submission to, a local church leadership and family.

Pentecostals are not the only group to see things this way. Virtually all church denominations are of this same persuasion. Most "non-conformist" Christian denominations, Pentecostals included, do not accept the notion of an "elite" priesthood. This means that there are no "priestly" bars on who can administer the "sacrament" of baptism. Any member of the body of Christ can do so. We have already seen, however, that baptism, as a mark of discipleship, should be administered by the local church, under whose leadership the individual is being discipled. So in fact, there *are* some bars as to who can administer baptism. It is limited to those approved and appointed for the role by the local church. Remember, the purpose of this is to ensure that baptism occurs within the setting of authentic, biblically based, discipleship.

Why Should We Be Baptized in Water?

All this brings us on to the second of our three questions—"Why should we be baptized?" Much of what we have already covered will be relevant here. We know that in the wider religious context, people were baptized primarily for two reasons: one was the predominantly Jewish reason, as a mark of discipleship; the other was the predominantly non-Jewish reason, as a mark of (mystical) identification. Both these reasons were adopted by the earliest Christians—we see baptism as a mark of discipleship, especially in the Synoptic Gospels and Acts, and we see baptism as a mark of identification (with Christ) especially in Paul's letters.

And so it remains that we should be baptized for these two reasons. First, baptism in water is a mark—and indeed a declaration—of discipleship.

We have decided to follow Jesus Christ. He is our rabbi! Second, baptism in water is a mark of identification. We are now identified with Jesus Christ. We were buried with him, and we have been raised in newness of life with him. We are "in Christ!"

Let me say a little more about identification with Christ—because it is so wonderful! It is not simply that we have decided to follow Christ; it is also that he now "owns" us—we belong to him (1 Cor 6:19–20). We are now, mystically, united with and identified with him. The old "us" has gone, and the new "us" is "in Christ" (2 Cor 5:17). We were "buried" with Christ, and we are "raised" with him (Rom 6:5–11). And it is this total identification with Christ that is expressed when we are baptized (by full immersion) in water. The thought is summed up in Galatians 3:27: "For as many of you as were baptized into Christ have 'put on' Christ." Indeed, we have already seen this descriptive language throughout the Book of Acts—believers are baptized "into Christ."

These, however, are not the only two reasons for why we should be baptized. There are three further simple reasons. The first of these is that Jesus was baptized! Time and again in the Gospels disciples are commanded to follow Jesus. We too are commanded to follow him (e.g., John 12:26; 1 Pet 2:21). The inference is clear: since Jesus was baptized in water, so should we be! Indeed, if the sinless Christ did this "to fulfill all righteousness" (Matt 3:15), how much more should we!

The second of these is that Jesus commanded it! This perhaps is the simplest and strongest reason for baptism in water. Remember those "red letter" words: "Therefore go and make disciples of all nations, baptizing them in the name of the Father and the Son and the Holy Spirit . . ." (Matt 28:19–20). To refuse to be baptized is to disobey Jesus. To delay one's decision to be baptized is to continue in disobedience!

The third of these is that the earliest Christians practiced it. The inference in the Book of Acts is that, right from the beginning of the church, this was a universal practice. There would appear to have been no such thing as a "non-baptized" believer. Paul makes a similar inference to the Corinthians, that all believers should be united because we are all baptized in the name of Christ (1 Cor 1:13: "Has Christ been divided? Was Paul crucified for you? Or were you baptized in the name of Paul?") Later in the same letter, he makes much the same point: "For in the one Spirit we were all baptized into one body—Jews or Greeks, slaves or free—and we were all made to drink of one Spirit" (1 Cor 12:13).[9]

---

9. One Pentecostal interpretation makes the case that this verse is in fact a reference to "baptism in the Spirit." While this interpretation is grammatically possible, the usual interpretation—that it is a reference to baptism in water—is to be preferred.

Let me also offer one, final, reason for why we should be baptized—and for why the New Testament is so insistent on it. Faith always finds expression (Gal 5:6): it finds expression through words (Rom 10:9–10), actions (Mark 5:27–29), and deeds (Jas 2:18). And baptism in water is a way for us to express—to declare publicly—that we are followers of Christ and that we belong to him. Indeed, as an expression of faith, baptism has genuine spiritual significance. Furthermore, inasmuch as baptism in water (by full immersion) is a visual and physical expression of what salvation is, it also has a teaching function. It visually and dramatically reinforces to the individual what being a follower of Christ is, and what being identified with Christ is: the old life is gone; a new life has begun! It reinforces these things, moreover, to everyone present as well. In short, baptism has both a declarative and a didactic purpose!

What Happens If a Christian Is Not Baptized in Water?

Before we move on from this second question, it is useful to address a related question. "So what happens if a Christian is not baptized in water?" Pentecostal churches are, by some definitions, non-sacramental. That is to say, we do not believe that physical things or actions have any spiritual value in and of themselves.[10] (It is only as expressions of faith that they have spiritual value.) So, it is easy for us to say that, even without baptism in water, someone who genuinely puts their faith in Christ is indeed "in Christ" (Rom 10:9; Gal 3:2, etc.). The example invariably cited in this respect is "the dying thief on the cross." Having expressed a level of recognition of who Jesus actually is, and having asked Jesus to remember him when he comes into his kingdom, Jesus himself replies, "Truly I tell you, today you will be with me in Paradise" (Luke 23:43).[11]

---

10. Many Pentecostals would understand sacrament as a "means of grace," and thus have an aversion to the term. However, it is true that some Pentecostals even refer to the Ordinances as Sacraments. Furthermore, our dear Catholic friends have seven Sacraments, which they do understand that "by them men are disposed to receive the chief effect" (*Catechism of the Catholic Church* #1667). I am fully aware that a sincere Catholic understands that Sacraments need to be accompanied by faith for full effect, however, visible practice discloses belief. In addition, given the Latin roots for the word *sacrament*, we would prefer to retain the distinction between Ordinance and Sacrament.

11. This example is perhaps not as "water tight'" as it might first appear, since this a pre-resurrection event. That is to say, specifically *Christian* baptism had not yet been initiated. Nonetheless, it may be seen as establishing the principle—that God will receive anyone who, in faith, turns to him.

So, much is clear. Nonetheless, two balancing points are also worth making. First, most Pentecostals would accept the above argument for someone that simply has not "had enough time" to be baptized in water. However, what about someone that simply refuses to be baptized in water? This is a slightly different scenario: and some might question how much "saving faith" that person actually has. That is to say, has that person actually embraced the notion that to be a Christian is to be a follower of Christ and to be identified with him?[12]

Second, Acts 2:38 is a relevant verse in this regard. Here Peter tells the convicted crowd what they need to do: "Repent, and be baptized everyone of you in the name of Jesus Christ so that your sins may be forgiven; and you will receive the gift of the Holy Spirit." This verse is not simply descriptive; it is prescriptive. Indeed, it has been described as a normative verse for the "normal Christian birth." That is to say; there are four essential components to that birth—(1) repentance, (2) baptism in water, (3) forgiveness of sins, (4) receiving the Holy Spirit. If one accepts this as the normative Christian experience, then the issue no longer revolves around "life after death"; rather, it revolves around "life before death." Quite simply, if I am not baptized in water I may be able to rest secure in the knowledge that I am in Christ; but it remains that I am losing out' on something that should be part of my Christian experience.

When Should We Be Baptized in Water?

All this brings us, in turn, on to our third question—"When should we be baptized in water?" Given all the above, the answer seems fairly obvious: "Upon conversion." As we have already seen, the Book of Acts makes it clear that this was New Testament practice—whether for people who were complicit in the actual crucifixion of Jesus (2:38, 41); or an Ethiopian eunuch (8:38); or a persecutor of the church (9:18); or first-time gentile converts (10:48); or disciples in Ephesus who have never heard about Jesus before (19:5). Indeed, baptism in water is the *only* visible rite of passage for believers in the New Testament. All the modern markers we have to indicate conversion—hands raised, "coming to the front," the "sinner's prayer," etc., may be perfectly fine. Yet none of them appears in the New Testament. In the New Testament, rather, the exclusive and the universal marker that someone is in Christ is baptism in water! The only condition for baptism

---

12. There are always pastoral caveats to bear in mind. One obvious example relates to people that have received "infant baptism"—they may have a genuine struggle in questioning their spiritual heritage, etc.

in water, moreover, is that there has been a genuine act of repentance and faith in Christ.

This last point is worth emphasizing—consistently in the New Testament, it is assumed that baptism happens *after* repentance and faith. Just a sample of texts helps to draw this out. On the Day of Pentecost, Peter tells the crowd, "Repent and be baptized" (Acts 2:38). So repentance comes before baptism. In the "Longer Ending" in Mark's Gospel, Jesus says, "Whoever believes and is baptized will be saved" (Mark 16:16).[13] So belief comes before baptism. At the end of Matthew's Gospel, Jesus commands the disciples to "make disciples of all nations, baptizing them . . ." (Matt 28:19). So being a disciple is a pre-requisite for baptism. When the Ethiopian eunuch asks Philip if he may be baptized, Philip answers, "If you believe with all your heart, you may" (Acts 8:36–37). So "believing with all your heart" is a pre-condition (the only pre-condition) for baptism. Finally, in Acts 18:8 many of the Corinthians listening to Paul "believed and were baptized." The point is clear.

In some ways, we could finish this third question here! There are, however, two related issues that need some attention: baptismal regeneration and infant baptism.

a. Baptismal Regeneration

So *integral* is baptism in water to the salvation experience of being "in Christ" in the New Testament, that it has led to the notion of "baptismal regeneration." That is to say, it is in and by the act of baptism in water itself that the individual is regenerated—"born again." Two verses, in particular, are used to support this position. In Acts 22:16, Paul is recounting Ananias's words when they first met, and notes the words with which Ananias finishes: "And now why do you delay? Get up, be baptized, and have your sins washed away, calling on his name." In 1 Peter 3:21 the writer has been describing Noah's ark, in which eight people were saved, and continues, "And baptism, which this prefigured, now saves you—not as a removal of dirt from the body, but as an appeal to God for a good conscience, through the resurrection of Jesus Christ."

Let me note something about these two verses before we come back to "baptismal regeneration."

---

13. Textual criticism makes it apparent that this is likely not part of Mark's Gospel as originally written. Nonetheless, it is certainly a very early Christian text, which intentionally reflects the reality in Acts.

It is apparent that they both make reference to baptism in water as a form of "washing." This reflects a secondary association that existed in Jewish baptisms especially. Indeed, "baptism" at Qumran especially was more a daily ritual, so much so that some scholars refer to it instead as "ablutions."

In the New Testament, this "washing'" connotation is associated more with general holiness and the effect of the Word of God (e.g., Eph 5:26). Nonetheless, the above two verses indicate that its associations with baptism in water are not altogether gone.

Returning to the subject of baptismal regeneration: Pentecostal churches reject such a notion. As we have noted, there is a strong association between baptism and regeneration in the New Testament—because the latter never occurs without the former. The above two verses are understood against this backdrop. That is to say, they refer to the New Testament reality that baptism in water is the only (the exclusive and universal) physical rite of passage' for all new Christians. So, someone is baptized at the same time as their sins are "washed away"; and their baptism in water *is* the physical expression of this. Nevertheless, association is not the same as cause. And Pentecostals reject the notion that baptism is the cause of regeneration.

Baptism, then, is not the cause of regeneration. Rather, *faith* is the cause of regeneration! This is in fact not just a Pentecostal stance. It is the stance of Protestant, evangelical churches generally, and may be described as essentially "non-sacramental." The exclusive primacy it gives to faith as the cause of regeneration goes back as far as the Lutheran and Reformed axiom of *sola fide*. One New Testament passage in particular that may be used to support this view—that baptism in water is not the cause of regeneration—is in Acts 8. Here we read about someone (Simon the sorcerer) who is baptized (v. 13); and yet it is at least arguable that he is not regenerated (vv. 20–24). Indeed, Peter makes it clear to Simon that, at present, "you have no part or share in this" (v. 21)–"this" being God's gift of salvation.

We also need to give attention to another passage in the New Testament that is traditionally associated with baptism in water, and is used to support the notion of "baptismal regeneration"—John 3:5. Here Jesus says to Nicodemus, "I tell you the truth, no-one can enter the kingdom of God without being born of water and Spirit." Johannine scholars have been divided for over a century as to whether this has a sacramental or non-sacramental meaning. In other words, it is contested that this verse refers to baptism at all. I am persuaded that within its immediate literary context, the meaning of the phrase "born of water" (ἐξ ὕδατος; *ex hudatos*) is, in fact, a reference not to baptism but to "natural birth." Both this phrase and the phrase "born of blood" (ἐξ αἱμάτων; *ex haimatōn*) were euphemisms for natural birth. Indeed, the writer himself uses the latter in such a sense in John 1:13.[14]

When read this way, Jesus' reply to Nicodemus makes plain sense—yes, it is not enough to have a natural birth, you need a spiritual birth too if you are to enter God's kingdom. This surely is what Jesus goes on to reiterate in the very next verse (v. 6: "Whatever is born of flesh is flesh, and whatever is born of the Spirit is spirit"). And it also explains why, when Jesus repeats himself later, he omits the reference to water (v. 8: "So it is with everyone who is born of the Spirit"). That is to say, being born of the Spirit is the critical point he is making—Nicodemus, you must be born "from above," you must be "born again."

b. Infant Baptism

We have given the Pentecostal (and wider Protestant/evangelical) answer to the question, "When should we be baptized in water?" Our answer is: upon conversion. This, however, raises an interesting dilemma about something widely practiced in Roman Catholic, Orthodox, Anglican, Methodist, and other Christian churches: infant baptism.[15] Given the Pentecostal acceptance of *sola fide*—the need for personal faith for regeneration to occur—this can make the notion of infant baptism problematic. Infants (i.e., babies) are not capable of personal faith, and so baptism in water for them is not appropriate. Quite simply, as a marker of discipleship and identification with Christ, baptism in water does not apply pre-conversion.[16]

In support of this, it may be noted that there is no New Testament evidence of infant baptism. There are, however, five New Testament instances of household baptism; and it might be argued that these household baptisms include the baptizing of babies. So, let us look more closely at these five instances. They appear in: Acts 10:24–48; 16:14–15, 32–34; 18:8; and 1 Cor 1:16.

In Acts 10:24–48, Cornelius and his household are baptized (v. 48). Notice the description of the household: Cornelius calls his relatives and

---

14. A similar use of this language appears in the Johannine letters, See 1 John 5:6–9; compare 1 John 4:2; 2 John 7. Whatever the precise meaning here, there is certainly no sense of it being a reference to baptism in water.

15. This is also referred to as, "paedobaptism."

16. None of this is to say that babies cannot receive "divine blessing." Jesus places his hands on children and blesses them (Mark 10:16); and Paul notes that the children of a believing parent are "clean" (1 Cor 7:14). Indeed, Jesus says concerning children, "of such is the kingdom of God" (Mark 10:14); and this surely is reason enough to believe that babies, whether baptized (i.e., sprinkled) or not, go straight to heaven if they die.

close friends together (v. 24); they gather to listen to everything Peter has to say (v. 33), and the Holy Spirit falls upon them, and they speak in tongues and praise God (v. 46). I suggest that this description precludes the presence of babies in this group. In Acts 16:14-15, Lydia and her household are baptized. But there is no suggestion that she has children, or is even married, and so to argue for the presence of babies here really is an argument from silence. In Acts 16:32-34, the Philippian jailor and his household are baptized. But we are told that he and his whole household believe (v. 34), so this description too seems to preclude the presence of babies. In Acts 18:8 the household of Crispus is baptized; but once again the point is made that Crispus and his whole household believe. Finally, in 1 Corinthians 1:16 Paul recalls that he baptized the household of Stephanas. At the end of the letter, however, he notes that this same household devoted themselves to the service of the Lord's people (16:15)—and this is hardly a description that applies to babies.

Let me be clear. None of this is to suggest that there are not babies in any of these households! The point is that any babies are manifestly not included among those who are baptized.

This can create a dilemma for Pentecostals, which in reality is as much pastoral as it is theological. Namely, given that infant baptism is not appropriate, how are Pentecostals to consider followers of Christ who have been baptized as babies? As already intimated, pastoral concerns can rightly weigh as heavily as theological concerns. But the theological reality is invariably clear. Pre-conversion baptism is, in the final analysis, not baptism at all. And so precisely the same injunction applies to new converts that have undergone infant baptism as those that have not. That is to say, for all the spiritual benefit that being born into a believing family may undoubtedly bring (see 1 Cor 7:14), when someone who has undergone "infant baptism" becomes a Christian, it remains that they need to be baptized in water for the first time. This is not in any way to make them "second-class" Christians—there is no such thing! It is simply following New Testament faith and practice.

Conclusion

Let me offer a summary of the Pentecostal position on baptism in water. This is, in fact, the position of many evangelical churches more generally, albeit not all of them. Above all, baptism in water is a required act of obedience for everyone who has made a conscious decision to follow Christ. It should be practiced by full immersion, it should include the baptismal formula of Matthew 28:19, and should be carried out under the auspices of the local church. Above all, it is the physical enactment of the reality that, as Christians, we are disciples of Jesus Christ, and that we are fully identified with him. It is a normative part of the Christian experience. While it is necessarily associated with regeneration, it is not the cause of regeneration. It should occur at the time someone truly repents and believes in Jesus Christ—ideally not long after, and certainly not before.

In all this analysis, let us make sure that we retain the joy, the reality, and even the mystery of what baptism in water is. We must be careful not to reduce it to mere symbolism. Any act of faith is more than symbolism! As a biblical act of obedience and faith, it has genuine spiritual value. Jesus Christ never just "went through the motions"; he himself says that baptism in water was necessary for him! And it is not simply a "going through the motions" for us either. It is necessary for us too! It is a wonderful, graciously God-given, empowering action. It provides us with an opportunity physically to express and visually to declare the very core of our life and purpose: we have decided to follow Jesus Christ in everything we do and say; our old life is over, and we have begun a brand new life in Christ. Indeed, it provides us with the only biblically mandated opportunity to do this; and in so doing we share in a practice that goes back to the very first generation of Christian believers. Hallelujah!

Bibliography

Albretch, D. E. *Rites in the Spirit: A Ritual Approach to Pentecostal/Charismatic Spirituality*. Sheffield, UK: Sheffield Academic Press, 1999.

Alexander, K. E. "Matters of Conscience, Matters of Unity, Matters of Orthodoxy: Trinity and Water Baptism in Early Pentecostal Theology and Practice." *Journal of Pentecostal Theology* 17.1 (2008) 48–69.

Anderson, A. *An Introduction to Pentecostalism*. Cambridge: Cambridge University Press, 2004.

Astley, J., and B. Pickering. "Who Cares about Baptism?" *Theology* 4 (1986) 264–67.

Beasley-Murray, G. R. *Baptism in the New Testament*. Exeter, UK: Paternoster, 1962.

Bicknell, R. "The Ordinances: The Marginalised Aspects of Pentecostalism." In *Pentecostal Perspectives*, edited by Keith Warrington, 204–22. Carlisle, UK: Paternoster Press, 1998.

Burkett, D. *An Introduction to the New Testament and the Origins of Christianity*. Cambridge: Cambridge University Press, 2002.

Grudem, W. *Bible Doctrine: Essential Teachings of the Christian Faith*. Leicester, UK: IVP, 1999.

Hogsten, C. D. "The Monadic Formula of Water Baptism: A Quest for Primitivism via a Christocentric and Restorationist Impulse." *Journal of Pentecostal Theology* 17.1 (2008) 70–95.

Hollenweger, W. "Liturgies. Pentecostal." In *A Dictionary of Liturgy and Worship*, edited by P. F. Bradshaw, 241. London: SCM, 2013.

Jacobsen, D. *Thinking in the Spirit: Theologies of the Early Pentecostal Movement*. Bloomington, IN: Indiana University Press, 2003.

Kay, W. K. *Pentecostalism. A Very Short Introduction*. Oxford: Oxford University Press, 2011.

Landry, T. E. "Water Baptism as It Relates to Repentance and The Infilling of the Holy Spirit." In *Symposium on Oneness Pentecostalism 1988 and 1990*, 321–49. Hazelwood, MO: Word Aflame, 1990.

Macchia, F. D. "The Nature and Purpose of the Church: A Pentecostal Response." Paper presented at the 34th Annual Meeting of the Society for Pentecostal Studies, 2005.

Owen, P. C. "A Study of the Ecumenical Nature of Charismatic Renewal: With Particular Reference to Roman Catholic and Anglican Charismatic Renewal in England." PhD diss., University of Birmingham, 2007.

Pawson, D. *Explaining Water Baptism*. Tonbridge, UK: Sovereign World, 1992.

———. *The Normal Christian Birth*. London: Hodder & Stoughton, 1989.

Prince, D. *Foundations for Righteous Living*. Harpenden, UK: Derek Prince, 1998.

Robeck, C. M., and A. Yong, eds. *The Cambridge Companion to Pentecostalism*. Cambridge: Cambridge University Press, 2014.

Tomberlin, D. *Pentecostal Sacraments: Encountering God at the Altar*. Cleveland, TN: Pentecostal Theological Seminary, 2010.

VanderZee, L. J. *Christ, Baptism, and the Lord's Supper*. Leicester, UK: IVP, 2004.

Warrington, K. *Pentecostal Theology*. London: T. & T. Clark, 2008.

7

The Baptism in the Holy Spirit

FRANK D. MACCHIA

Introduction: Jesus Imparts the Spirit

> When the day of Pentecost had come, they were all together in one place. And suddenly a sound came from heaven like the rush of a mighty wind, and it filled all the house where they were sitting. And there appeared to them tongues as of fire, distributed and resting on each one of them. And they were all filled with the Holy Spirit and began to speak in other tongues, as the Spirit gave them utterance. (Acts 2:1–4)

ACTS 2 DESCRIBES FOR us the Day of Pentecost. Jesus had been crucified and raised from the dead only a short time prior to this event. He had also been exalted to the throne of God to reign forever. The first thing Jesus does upon his enthronement as God's reigning Messiah is to pour forth the Holy Spirit upon his followers (Acts 2:33). The kingdom of God was the main topic of Jesus' discourse just before his ascension (1:3), so it is indeed significant that the Spirit is poured out directly upon Jesus' enthronement and the inauguration of his reign. The implication of all of this is that Holy Spirit will bear witness of the reigning Christ and fulfill the kingdom of Christ in the world.

The earliest followers of Jesus had described the work of their Messiah in the context of God's earlier promise to pour out the Spirit on all flesh in the latter days before all things come to fulfillment (e.g., Joel 2:28–32). The holy Son of God was conceived in Mary's womb by the presence and power of the Spirit (Luke 1:35), and he was installed as Messiah at his baptism through the Spirit's mighty anointing (Luke 3:21–22). Though he was the eternal Son of God, he was also a man whose very life was anointed and led by God's Spirit. His journey in the Spirit took him from the baptismal waters to the desert to be tested by the devil (Luke 4) and then to the cross where he faced his greatest trial in bearing our sin and death. Though he was the Son of God and man of the Spirit, he took our place by descending into our alienation from God on the cross. But the story does not end there. The Son rises victoriously over sin and death, being declared the Son of God according to the Spirit of holiness at his resurrection (e.g., Rom 1:4). He offered himself up for us by the Spirit (e.g., Heb 9:14) in order that we who are alienated from God may be able to be brought into the life of God's Spirit and find divine favor. The Spirit brings the reign of God to people's hearts and forms liberating communities dedicated to the mission of God and Christ in the world (Matt 12:28; Rom 14:17). Jesus, the reigning Messiah, bore the Spirit in order to impart the Spirit. He is the "life-giving" Messiah (1 Cor 15:45), the *Spirit Baptizer*.

Why Spirit *Baptizer*? The term comes from the ministry of John the Baptist. John the Baptist baptized in water as a sign of the hope that can be grasped through repentance. John noted, however, that one greater than he would come to "baptize" in the Spirit, meaning that Jesus would fulfill the hope inspired by John's water rite by ushering people into the reality of the Spirit. John inspired hope by placing people into water; Christ fulfilled hope by placing people ("baptizing" them) into the reality of the Spirit. This is not to say that the Spirit and the water rite cannot coincide; it just means that the one (the rite) lacks substance without the reality of the Spirit that is to come. This is also not to say that the Spirit requires the water rite to be present, only that there is a theological link between them. The entry into the life of the kingdom of God implied by the water rite comes to fulfillment in the reality of the Spirit. Jesus, the one baptized by John in water, will baptize his followers into the reality of the Spirit.

Spirit Baptism and Christian Initiation

How does one receive the Holy Spirit from Jesus? How does one enter into the reality of the Spirit, the reality of Christ's liberating reign? The answer in the New Testament is clear: The Spirit is received by faith in Christ and not by works of the law (Gal 3:1–5). No one could ever be worthy to receive God's Holy Spirit. The Spirit is the gift by which God's love is poured forth within us by faith (Rom 5:5). In fact, one first receives the Spirit at the moment one is initiated into the Christian faith, or the moment one receives Christ as Savior and Lord by faith (Rom 8:9). Water baptism then confirms and witnesses of this new life of the Spirit, for we crucify the flesh and rise to newness of life in the act of baptism (Rom 6:1–5). Yet, though the Spirit indwells us from the moment we belong to Christ and confirms our participation in Christ through water baptism, there are still rich experiences of Spirit filling and empowerment that await God's people. We can thus speak of the Spirit as continuously coming upon us so as to open us to deeper and more expansive experiences of the Spirit's presence within and through us. We may also speak of this experience as the "release" of the Spirit in life. Among those who believe, the Spirit will flow like a mighty river out from their innermost beings (John 7:37–39). They are "filled" to overflowing time and again to minister to one another in the love of Christ (Eph 5:18) or to bear witness to the world of Christ (Acts 2). This experience is desperately needed today.

How do we describe Spirit baptism in relation to our initial reception of the Spirit by faith in Christ? Evangelicals commonly view the two as the same. They refer to Spirit baptism as the moment one receives the Spirit through faith in Christ. In this view, Spirit baptism is one's "baptism" or incorporation spiritually into Christ and his body by faith (bringing about the "born again" experience).[1] Catholic and other sacramental theologians also believe that Spirit baptism incorporates one into Christ and his body, but they attach the event to water baptism (and perhaps confirmation) rather than merely the act of faith. Most classical Pentecostals, however, have historically held that the baptism in the Holy Spirit is an experience of empowerment or "filling" for the witness that is distinct from incorporation into Christ by faith and water baptism. They argue that the believers who were baptized in the Spirit in Acts were already born again believers (Acts 2; 4; 8; 9; 10; 16). In certain cases, believers are baptized in the Spirit as an experience of power distinct from water baptism (Acts 2; 4; 8; 10). Some charismatics have sought a middle ground between sacramental and classical Pentecostal positions by defining Spirit baptism as incorporation into Christ through baptism but also as something to be "released" in life later in the context of an empowering experience.[2] Some "third wave" evangelicals are seeking a similar middle ground between evangelical and Pentecostal positions (the Spirit received by faith at the born-again experience is experienced with power at a subsequent moment). A more expansive mediating position on Spirit baptism is possible that views it as "multidimensional," namely, as God's multifaceted self-impartation through Christ and in the Spirit. Spirit baptism is viewed as rooted in the born-again experience,

---

1. Incidentally, some Pentecostals have taken the evangelical view of Spirit baptism, such as Oneness Pentecostals and some German and Chilean Trinitarian Pentecostals.

2. For a thorough treatment of various views of Spirit baptism among charismatics, both sacramental and nonsacramental, see Lederle, *Treasures Old and New*.

confirmed in water baptism, and experienced in power at the moment of one's charismatic gifting and call to witness.[3]

Regardless of how one comes out on this larger issue, the classical Pentecostal view of Spirit baptism as a post-initiation experience of power for witness is not to be neglected. This accent has received new scholarly support from the work of Roger Stronstad and Robert Menzies.[4] Both of these New Testament scholars have written works that attempt to show how unique Luke's theology of the Spirit is. In their view, Luke's pneumatology accents the missionary or charismatic rather than the salvific (saving) work of the Spirit. Rather than incorporate one into Christ, Luke's description of Spirit baptism empowers the church for witness.[5] The problem in their view is that evangelicals have taken Paul's view of Spirit baptism (which accents incorporation into Christ by faith and water baptism, 1 Cor 12:13) as the standard by which to interpret Luke's understanding of Spirit baptism. The end result is that Luke's unique theology of Spirit baptism is never heard. These authors do not believe that Luke and Paul contradict each other, only that the two complement one another in their definitions of Spirit baptism. One should not forget when speaking of this complementarity, however, that Paul's voice on this issue is important too. The baptism in the Spirit that empowers us must also be related in some way to our initial reception of the Spirit by faith in Christ.

It is thus important in *distinguishing* between the indwelling and empowerment of the Spirit not to lose the continuity between them. The Holy Spirit is not a liquid that can be received in parts (one-quarter, one-half; two-thirds!). The Spirit is a divine *person* who enters a believer's life at the moment of his or her faith in Christ and remains to do a deeper and more expansive work. In order to protect the *continuity* of the Spirit's presence and work in the lives of believers, some recent Pentecostal theologians have maintained that the baptism in the Spirit is indeed rooted in the born-again experience (one's initial reception of the Spirit by faith) but is fulfilled in deeper and more expansive experiences of the Spirit.[6] Some are thus justified in describing the experience of Spirit baptism as a "release" of the Spirit in life in greater power and fullness. Such a trend would be consistent with the reference of Donald Gee, the British Pentecostal pioneer, to

---

3. Macchia, *Baptized in the Spirit*, 19–60.

4. See Stronstad, *The Charismatic Theology of St. Luke*; Menzies, *Empowered for Witness*.

5. I do not think that Luke's pneumatology is confined to the charismatic and missional work of the Spirit, though I agree that this is his overwhelming emphasis and focus.

6. See Macchia, *Baptized in the Spirit*; Yong, *The Spirit Poured Out on All Flesh*.

the baptism in the Spirit as a "bubbling forth" of the life of the Spirit that one entered into at the moment of conversion to Christ.[7] The Spirit comes upon believers afresh to open them to deeper and more outward-flowing experiences of the Spirit who already resides within. According to the Book of Acts, this baptism in the Spirit would be an overwhelming experience in the Holy Spirit (hence, a "baptism" or an "immersion" in the life of the Spirit), as a result of which believers would glorify God and exclaim God's deeds with great power (2:11; 10:46). Most striking, however, is that this Spirit baptism would also cause the people of God to share God's gift of new life with all peoples.

Spirit Baptism and Empowerment for Witness

The Spirit not only brings the church into fellowship with God and one another—the Spirit also empowers the church for global mission. The kingdom of Christ can come to earth only once this mission is fulfilled. The church is "filled" with the Spirit to overflowing for this purpose. The Spirit's filling is too powerful to be contained within the walls of the church's fellowship. It spills forth like a mighty river, thrusting the church outward in its witness before the world. This empowerment for witness is to be vast in its outreach, for it was always God's plan to bless *all nations* with redemption and new life. The promise to Abraham was so that "all the families of the earth will be blessed" (see Gen 12:3). Israel was chosen as a missionary people to be a light to the nations. This challenge was dramatically given in the Book of Jonah when God compelled the prophet to be a witness to the despised and feared Ninevites. Even the most hated gentile nations were to receive the light of the gospel. Israel struggled, somewhat unsuccessfully, over the centuries to cross such vast boundaries and to fulfill God's missionary purpose. Israel ultimately failed and, as God had planned, the Messiah came from Israel to fulfill the nation's mission. The Messiah won the victory needed to launch this mission and then handed this mission to his body, the church. The church has also struggled in the Christian era to be faithful to this mission. How will the church fulfill what Israel failed to fulfill?

In Joel 2, Israel was promised that there would be a great outpouring of the Holy Spirit upon the earth in the latter days (or the messianic era). This would result in the turning of the people of God into a community of prophets so that whoever calls upon the name of the Lord would be saved (v. 28.). This prophetic witness, empowered by the Spirit in the latter days, would cross barriers of age, gender, and social status. It would also

---

7. Gee, *Now That You've Been Baptized in the Holy Spirit*, 27.

nullify unjust privileges. Those who would be blessed to share God's new life in the power of the Spirit would include servants, women, and the aged, along with those of greater social privilege (vv. 28, 29). The Spirit would also overflow national and cultural boundaries as the miracle of tongues implies. A Galilean sect of Jews speaks in the tongues of the nations, pointing to the global thrust of the Spirit's work. The Spirit is to be poured out upon *"all* flesh."

Luke is careful to make clear that these tongues are not incidental to the Pentecost event or to the baptism in the Spirit that occurred at Pentecost. He devoted ten verses to a description of this language miracle in Acts 2. These tongues are, without question, decisively symbolic of the nature of the Spirit baptismal experience for Luke—an experience that transcends human capacities and causes people to cross boundaries for the glory of God in unexpected ways. There are classical Pentecostals historically who have insisted that one will speak in tongues if empowered by the Spirit, at least eventually. This view has been most popular among white American Pentecostal denominations (and their satellite churches). Prominent American Pentecostal leader Jack Hayford, however, maintained that Spirit baptism opens up the *capacity* to pray in tongues, for the Spirit through empowerment penetrates deep into the soul of the believer, opening up the capacity to groan in ways too deep for words (Rom 8:26). Tongues are thus the characteristic sign of Spirit baptism, but God will not force those who have this capacity to speak in tongues (it is a privilege that one is free to exercise when the moment is right). Thus, Hayford is not surprised to hear folk speak in tongues at moments of empowerment, but he does not want to make a "law" out of the link between Spirit baptism and tongues.[8] In the context of this debate, it is important to note that Spirit baptism is manifested primarily through deeper and more expansive love, as well as through a more diverse flourishing of spiritual gifts or avenues for edifying others (Eph 4; 1 Cor 12–14). At times, the church of Jesus Christ has been too lifeless in its praise, too shallow in its awareness of the divine presence, and too culturally monolithic to fully appreciate the depth and breadth of Spirit baptism as symbolized by the miracle of speaking in tongues on the Day of Pentecost. The church has yet to fully understand the significance of Spirit baptism for its life and mission. It has yet to understand what speaking in tongues symbolizes about the experience of Spirit baptism. The Pentecostal movement, which draws its name from the event of Pentecost, also needs to look more deeply into what this marvelous baptism in the Spirit should mean for the church today.

---

8. See Hayford, *The Beauty of Spirit Language.*

The Contemporary Challenge of Spirit Baptism: A Preliminary Consideration

Just think of this: How many bench warmers do we have in our churches who rarely think about a personal relationship with the Holy Spirit and who have never felt engulfed in the Spirit's presence? How many have not allowed the Spirit to dislodge them from their comfort zones and move them forth in gifted ministry to reach others with the new life of the resurrection? How many who believe in Christ have rarely felt the Spirit-inspired passion to share the goodness of God with others or the sensation of being carried by the winds of the Spirit across boundaries to do things for God not entirely explicable in natural terms? Obviously, the experience of Spirit baptism, of being mightily filled with the Spirit to overflowing as described in the Book of Acts, presents an urgent challenge to churches today.

Unfortunately, the church has misunderstood the enduring challenge of the experience of Spirit baptism by assuming that it was merely a one-time event. Though Spirit baptism is arguably a one-time event in the life of a believer, it is arguably a complex event that is rooted in faith, confirmed in baptism, and decisively (though not ultimately) fulfilled at charismatic calling and empowerment. The experiential life opened up by Spirit baptism must be furthered and renewed. The story of the entire Book of Acts reveals that the experience of Spirit filling or empowerment opened up by Spirit baptism is repeatable (chs. 4, 8, 9, 10, 19), on both a corporate (ch. 10) and an individual (ch. 9) level, and is meant to affect the people of God continuously. Will we open ourselves more meaningfully to the Spirit? Will we pray, seek, and wait on God to fill us anew? The challenge inherent in the experience of Spirit baptism is ageless and always relevant because we all tend to resist a deep or intensive experience with God, due to the powerful changes that this necessitates in our lives. We tend to resist change. Yet, we need to change in order to grow in our effectiveness for Christ.

There is something within all of us that wants to avoid such an overwhelming boundary-crossing experience of the Spirit. It seems to be human nature to want to stay safe and secure among those we know and love. Family and friends can provide a support structure for life and provide us with a familiar net of relationships to which we tend naturally to grow deeply attached. Such attachments are good and may be seen as gifts from God. Naturally, such a familiar surrounding for life extends often to include a particular subculture. Such a tendency is not necessarily problematic. God wants us to be a blessing to those who move in circles familiar to us.

The problem arises when we *confine* ourselves to such contexts and never cross boundaries to be touched by the voices and needs of others different from ourselves. Such a confinement becomes all the more problematic when it causes us to callously enjoy social privilege at the expense of those less advantaged. More problematic still is our disobedience to the Great Commission to evangelize (Matt 28:18–20) and the church's neglect of its social responsibility. We are challenged by the Scriptures to share the goodness of God with all peoples, first to those closest to us, but also to those "afar off" (Acts 1:8; 2:39). Besides evangelism, the gospel mission of the church must consider the poor and oppressed as a priority. This cause united Paul with his Jewish brothers and sisters in the early missionary efforts of the church (Gal 2:9, 10). Do we feel the burden to share God's offer of new life across social boundaries, especially those cut deep by stories of injustice and suffering? Do we know the power of God necessary to do this?

The power of God must be at the base of our crossing such boundaries to be agents of life and recipients of the same. Crossing boundaries is never easy. Christians know all too well how easy it is to ignore the challenge without the power of the Holy Spirit waking us up and dislodging us from our comfort zones. Though not all Christians are gifted to lead in such boundary-crossing, all Christians are to have a missionary heart and engage in the missionary task of the church whenever God opens the door of ministry.

It may seem impossible to minister across cultural barriers. We have a hard enough time ministering to those who live in cultural contexts familiar to us. We cannot simply jump out of our cultural skins to fully understand people different from ourselves. Linguistic, cultural, and social barriers can appear as vast ravines between people—especially if they are ingrained by stories of injustice and suffering. Also, differences of gender, age, and education can create boundaries that need to be crossed if we are to minister in the power of the Spirit. How can there be reconciliation across such separations? How can there be ministry and mutual blessing across such divisions? Pentecost gives us the answer. The experience of Pentecost is timeless. It is just as relevant and urgent today as it ever was. We need a fresh experience of Pentecost today. We need to be baptized in the Holy Spirit according to Acts 2:4. Once we've had the experience, we need a renewal of it again and again. The church lives out of such power. We can never claim to possess it once and for all. It must continuously be renewed.

The Pentecostal focus on Spirit baptism also has profound theological significance. Catholic theology has tended historically to emphasize the role of the church hierarchy in the sacramental life of the church when discussing the work of the Spirit in and through the church. The sacraments of baptism and Lord's Supper are indeed to be viewed as deep experiences of the Spirit that confirm one's born-again experience (baptism) and reaffirm its significance for life (Lord's Supper). But Spirit baptism also implies a wider circle of gifted involvement among the people of God in the ministry and mission of the church, one that goes far beyond the reception of the sacraments at the hands of the ordained clergy. Hans Küng popularized the notion of the "charismatic structure of the church" in his classic book *The Church*, where he made it the overall context in which the church's gifts of oversight are to be discussed.[9] He noted that juridical thinking is mistrustful of movements of the free Spirit of God for fear of a non-regimented enthusiasm. The tendency has been to "sacramentalize or make uniform the charism, and hence the workings of the Spirit."[10] The result is a clericalism in which the notion of charism (gifting) is overwhelmingly discussed in the context of ordained ministry. Neglected are the richness, variety, and exuberance of spiritual gifts as pictured in such texts as 1 Corinthians chapters 12 to 14 and exercised throughout the lives of "ordinary" Christians. Küng wished to reverse the historical trend toward clericalism. Rather than subsume charism under church office, Küng thus wished to do the opposite, namely, subsume office beneath charism.[11] Since everyone exercises charisms, as all in the church are called and commissioned to serve as bearers of the Spirit, the charisms are not peripheral but are rather essential and central elements of the church. Küng concludes that the charismatic structure of the church "includes but goes far beyond the hierarchical structure of the church."[12]

Küng does not deny the unique role played by clergy who exercise the charism of oversight, but he places both gifts of oversight and other giftings within an overarching concept of the church as a fellowship of faith in which all members (including ordained clergy) as bearers of the Spirit are gifted to bless one another. For Küng, "the church must be seen first as a fellowship of faith and only in this light can ecclesiastical office be properly understood."[13] Küng was to some degree responding to the breakthroughs of Vatican II, which had sought to break open the narrow focus on the gifting of the clergy to involve a greater emphasis on the Spirit's larger work among the spiritually-gifted laity. The Pentecostal theology of Spirit baptism pushes precisely in the direction suggested by Küng, for

9. See, Küng, *The Church*; Volf, *After our Likeness*, 231; Kärkkäinen, *Pentecostalism and the Claim for Apostolicity*.
10. Küng, *The Church*, 184.
11. Ibid., 187.
12. Ibid., 188.
13. Ibid., 363; Volf, *After our Likeness*, 231.

Spirit baptism involves "all flesh" and proliferates the calling and gifting of the Spirit among all; no one is excluded; all become ministers for God. As Clark Pinnock stated so well,

> As well as receiving the sacraments from the Spirit, we need to cultivate openness to the gifts of the Spirit. The Spirit is present beyond liturgy in a wider circle. There is a flowing that manifests itself as power to bear witness, heal the sick, prophesy, praise God enthusiastically, perform miracles, and more. There is a liberty to celebrate, an ability to dream and see visions, a release of Easter life. There are impulses of power in the move of the Spirit to transform and commission disciples to become instruments of the mission.[14]

In Protestant movements, the emphasis on the proclamation of Scripture tends to confine the work of the Spirit to the individual discernment of the text. The Spirit-baptized church implies a more robust and diverse role for the Spirit in the practice of biblical preaching. Because the church is the company of the Spirit-baptized, the gospel is proclaimed within a community that is expanding and deepening in its charismatic life. The gospel of the Scriptures bursts forth with signs of life in the charismatic structure of the church. Signs and wonders accompany preaching. There is a sense in which all in different ways "speak the truth in love" to one another (Eph 4:15). Expanding spiritual gifts then help to keep the apostolic word of the Scriptures alive and relevant within the ongoing gracious and gifted interactions of the people of God as they grow up into the full stature of Christ. Furthermore, spiritual gifts are always accountable to the living witness of the apostolic word of the Scriptures as Paul clearly notes in his struggle with the pneumatically gifted members of the Corinthian congregation (1 Cor 14:37). Within the charismatic structure of the church, the Spirit functions through the Scriptures as a living book of both freedom and order to guide our gracious interactions with one another. In fact, the Scriptures themselves are a universally relevant and binding gift of the Spirit to the church in order to guide the particular and diverse charismatic structure of the church in its ongoing life and mission.

Moreover, the Protestant way of salvation tends to accent the forensic understanding of justification by faith as foundational. An emphasis upon this can grant the impression that the gift of the Spirit is some kind of "added bonus" granted by God to those who believe. Spirit baptism, however, implies that the Spirit is at the foundation and goal (*telos*) of salvation. We are saved by Christ to become the dwelling place of the Spirit,

---

14. Pinnock, *Flame of Love*, 129.

thus being fully conformed to the man of the Spirit, Jesus Christ. We are justified not only through the atonement of Christ but also in the gracious embrace of the Spirit of life; we are sanctified or consecrated for a divine purpose (the purposes of the kingdom of Christ in the world) and empowered to carry out this purpose by the Spirit of God. We are "baptized" or engulfed by the Spirit for this entire complex initiation into the worship and service of Jesus as Lord and King. The end goal is a risen body that is "spiritual" (1 Cor 15:44) or perfectly permeated and led by the Spirit.[15] The empowerment of the Spirit that Pentecostals rightly call the experience of Spirit baptism is based on the born-again experience and reaches towards a new body and a new world, the kingdom of Christ on earth. The Spirit is to be poured out on all flesh. This, in sum, is the theological horizon of the baptism in the Holy Spirit.

Bibliography

Gee, Donald. *Now That You've Been Baptized in the Holy Spirit*. Springfield, MO: Gospel, 1972.

Hayford, Jack. *The Beauty of Spirit Language*. Nashville, TN: Thomas Nelson, 1996.

Kärkkänen, Veli-Matti. "Pentecostalism and the Claim for Apostolicity: An Essay in Ecumenical Ecclesiology." *Ecumenical Review of Theology* 25 (2001) 323–26.

Küng, Hans. *The Church*. New York: Sheed & Ward, 1967.

Lederle, Henry P. *Treasures Old and New: Interpretations of Spirit Baptism in the Renewal Movement*. Peabody, MA: Hendrickson, 1979.

Macchia, Frank D. *Baptized in the Spirit: A Global Pentecostal Theology*. Grand Rapids: Zondervan, 2006.

———. *Justified in the Spirit: Creation, Redemption, and the Triune God*. Grand Rapids: Eerdmans, 2010.

Menzies, Robert. *Empowered for Witness: The Spirit in Luke-Acts*. JPTS 6. Sheffield, UK: Sheffield Academic, 1991.

Pinnock, Clark. *Flame of Love: A Theology of the Holy Spirit*. Downers Grove, IL: IVP, 1996.

Stronstad, Roger. *The Charismatic Theology of St. Luke*. Peabody, MA: Hendrickson, 1988.

Yong, Amos. *The Spirit Poured Out on All Flesh: Pentecostalism and the Possibility of Global Theology*. Grand Rapids: Baker Academic, 2006.

Volf, Miroslav. *After our Likeness: The Church as the Image of the Trinity*. Grand Rapids: Eerdmans, 1997.

---

15. See Macchia, *Justified in the Spirit*.

8

The Gifts of the Spirit

KEITH WARRINGTON

Introduction

THE SPIRIT IS IDENTIFIED in the OT as enabling, among others, Elijah and Elisha to function charismatically.[1] This theme is significantly developed in the NT where a wide variety of people are given the opportunity to partner with the Spirit and manifest his gifts in and through their lives. This relationship of the Spirit with miraculous activity is clearly and particularly identified by Paul (1 Cor 12, 14). Pentecostals strongly assert a belief in the existence of charismata (more popularly referred to as "spiritual gifts"), given not on merit but as a result of the grace of God. Not only are the gifts of the Spirit bestowed by the Spirit to believers but the Spirit manifests himself through those gifts. They are not derived remotely from a distance as a result of divine initiation from heaven so much as resulting from his being present in believers.

The term *pneumatikos* emphasizes the fact that the gifts are related to the Spirit (*pneuma*) (Rom 15:27; 1 Cor 2:13; 9:11; 12:1; 14:1; Eph 1:3; 5:19; Col 3:16), the former term literally meaning, "spiritual man/one" and hence "spiritual gift"; it is preferable to identify them as gifts of the Spirit in order to emphasize the place of the Spirit in the process of them being manifested. The manifestation of spiritual gifts does not necessarily indicate a superior spirituality on the part of the one who manifests them. Rather, they are designated as being "spiritual" because the Spirit is the source, not because those so gifted have passed a certain threshold of spirituality; of course, the

---

1. This presentation was originally published in Keith Warrington, *Pentecostal Theology: A Theology of Encounter* (London: T. & T. Clark, 2008), used by permission of Bloomsbury Publishing Plc.

believer who walks with the Spirit is more available to the Spirit as s/he is attuned to his guidance.

The other main term used by Paul to describe these phenomena (*charismata*, Rom 1:11; 11:29; 12:6; 1 Cor 12:4, 9, 28–31; 1 Pet 4:10) is generally translated as a "(free) gift" or "gift of grace." It is possible that Paul uses the different terms interchangeably (Ephesians 4:11 uses neither in referring to the ministries mentioned therein). Ellis believes that while Paul uses *charismata* for all gifts, he refers *pneumatikoi* to "gifts of inspired utterance or discernment."[2] Menzies supports this perspective, suggesting that although the terms are apparently used interchangeably (in 1 Cor 12:1, 4, 31; 14:1), the *pneumatikoi* may be best understood as a subgroup of the *charismata*. Thus, Paul would be understood to be using the former term in responding to the questions concerning the "speech" gifts by the Corinthians (1 Cor 12:1) and in introducing the gift of prophecy (1 Cor 14:1, 37), both references relating to a narrow range of speech orientated gifts. In response to Menzies, it may be proposed that Paul uses the term *pneumatikos* when referring to the questions of the Corinthians because this was their preferred term, possibly because of the emphasis on the Spirit (*pneuma*) (1 Cor 12:1), while Paul prefers to educate them by replacing it with the term *charismata* with its relationship to grace, in his response (1 Cor 12:4). A difficulty with this position is that if Paul is less comfortable with *pneumatikos*, it is unclear as to why he should use it in 1 Corinthians 14:1 to introduce the discussion of tongues, interpretation, and prophecy. Other words are also used for spiritual gifts including *dōrea* (Eph 3:7; 4:7), *domata* (Eph 4:8), *energēmata* (1 Cor 12:6, 10), and *diakonioi* (Rom 12:7; 1 Cor 5:5).

Cessationism

Pentecostals reject any notion that spiritual gifts and other supernatural phenomena recorded in the NT were restricted to the early church era.[3] Their early decrease in the church era is largely believed to be due to the unwillingness of believers to accept their validity and to facilitate their operation. At the same time, occurrences of the manifestation of spiritual gifts throughout the centuries have been well documented, though their appearances are irregular. Pentecostals dispute the claim that 1 Corinthians 13:8–10 undermines the ongoing nature of spiritual gifts. Against those who believe that some of the gifts are temporary (healing, tongues, prophecy) while others are permanent (teaching, administration), Pentecostals

---

2. Ellis, "Prophecy in the New Testament Church—And Today," 48.
3. See Ruthven, *On the Cessation of the Charismata*.

react by stating that Paul makes no such distinction. Against the suggestion that 1 Corinthians 13:8–10 indicates that prophecy, tongues, and knowledge are no longer in existence, being replaced by love, the following responses may be offered:

The contrast between these three gifts and love is in the context of the superiority of love over all other manifestations of the Spirit. It is not that the former are insubstantial, but that love is supreme, the impermanence of the former being evidence of that fact.

Impermanence does not indicate that the gifts associated with it are at fault; it relates to the fact that they will not be necessary in the age of completion which is to come.

The timing of the demise of these gifts (13:10) is believed to be the return of Jesus, not the closing of the canon of Scripture. This deduction is based on the fact that Paul nowhere refers to the NT canon, but he does refer to the return of Jesus in ways that demonstrate that such gifts are no longer necessary (1 Cor 1:7; 13:12). Furthermore, to suggest that the word "perfect" (13:10) refers to the closure of the NT canon is improbable since that notion would not have been understandable to the readers of the letter since, at the time, there was no indication that there would be a NT.

Principles

Some principles concerning these gifts may be gleaned from 1 Corinthians 12:4–11.

- Paul asserts that spiritual gifts should be operated harmoniously in diversity, not uniformity, but as a result of a dynamic relationship with the Spirit, resulting in beneficial relationships with each other (1 Cor 12:4–31). The fact that these gifts are given by the Spirit should increase the sense of responsibility felt by those who administer them and, in particular, encourage them to do so appropriately, as indicated by the nature of the Giver of the gifts. Paul associates the gifts with the words "service" (12:5) and "working" (12:6). They are described as being given for the benefit of the corporate group (12:7; cf. Eph 4:12). Thus, they are not to be administered selfishly but selflessly, not for personal gain but for the benefit of others. When the manifestation of a gift ceases to exalt the person of Jesus (1 Cor 12:3) or to edify or develop other believers (Rom 1:11; 1 Cor 12:7), it ceases to be divinely inspired. When there is an absence of a manifestation of love, there is an absence of a manifestation of God through the gift (1 Cor 13:1–3).

- Each member of the Godhead is involved in the charismata being given to the church (12:4–6).[4] Paul is not necessarily assuming that the bestowal of the gifts is the responsibility of the Spirit only, as opposed to Jesus or the Father. He does not separate them so functionally. Nevertheless, given the presence of the Spirit in the life of the corporate church and the individual believer, it is logical that he should focus on the Spirit as representatively functioning in the distribution of the gifts.

- Every Christian receives a manifestation of the Spirit to facilitate their service in and on behalf of the local church (12:6, 11; Rom 12:4–6; Eph 4:7, 15–16; 2 Tim 1:7; 1 Pet 4:10). By definition, all Christians are people of the Spirit and in that respect they are eligible to function as channels through whom he can minister to others. But with the privilege comes the responsibility of maintaining a close relationship with the Spirit. Although the potential is that all believers may manifest any of the gifts, Paul is clear that not all should be expected to manifest any in particular (1 Cor 12:29–30). The concentration of Paul in 1 Corinthians 12 is not on the gifts referred to or even on their diversity. Rather, it is on the diversity of their distribution. The fact that the Spirit controls the manifestation of the gifts is a major factor in the context of an attempt to identify how one might function as a channel of the gifts (1 Cor 12:7–11). Pentecostals have always believed that one of the roles of the Spirit in empowering believers is to enable all to function in the Christian community. However, in practice, this has rarely resulted in many, or even a majority, of the believers in a local church manifesting the gifts in the way indicated by Paul. This is often because of the lack of a framework for identifying how individuals may be used by the Spirit and limited provision for opportunities to function thus.

Thus, although it is recognized that the Spirit inspires gifts in all believers, there is value in believers, in the context of the Christian community,

---

4. Although it is possible that Paul may have referred to each member of the Godhead in order to identify their differing functions with regard to the provision of the gifts referred to (1 Cor 12:4–6), it is as likely that he is seeking to emphasize that although these gifts are varied (thus described as "gifts," "service," and "working" [vs. 4–6]), they are all divinely motivated. To attempt to divide them between the members of the Godhead seems unnecessary and counterproductive to Paul's theme in the chapter, namely a diversity of gifts but a unity of purpose. Thus, to conclude, for example, that the Spirit provides the gifts while the Son administers them and the Father provides the power to manifest them is too nuanced a perspective and compartmentalizes the function of the Godhead unnecessarily.

helping to identify gifts that have already been granted to others. There are dangers with this in that a rather mechanistic procedure may be devised to help associate gifts with individuals. However, with sensitivity, this can enable believers to recognize that they are manifesting gifts of the Spirit in their lives more than they may have realized, as well as help others to discover gifts that the Spirit has already given that can be developed and exercised. Some Pentecostal churches are developing ways whereby believers are being encouraged to identify their passions, gifts, and strengths and then to discover how they might use them for the benefit of others. In this respect, they are seeking to apply to the contemporary church the Pauline recognition that diverse gifts are presented to believers for the benefit of the local church and the wider community. Pentecostals have generally distrusted the notion that one may transmit one's gifts to another or bestow a gift on another, Romans 1:11 being interpreted as not relating to the spiritual gifts as discussed above. Neither has it been accepted that 2 Timothy 1:6 should be interpreted as indicating that one may grant to another a gift via the laying on of hands.[5] But this perception does not undermine the value of recognizing or affirming gifts that have been bestowed on others and encouraging their use. It is in this regard that Paul encourages Timothy to develop his gift (2 Tim 1:6), and Barnabas and Paul were entrusted to fulfill the mission delegated to them by God (Acts 13:3), both occasions incorporating the laying on of hands. Similarly, the purpose behind the presentation of the gifts in Romans 12:6–8 is to encourage the readers to use those gifts that God has given to them and to do it in ways that are appropriate.

In order to ensure that such a process does not lead to self-centeredness and arrogance, it is important to identify needs that are to be met by the manifestation of certain gifts and the latter sought in order to minister to those issues. For some, this may be a permanent capacity to function in a particular way, though it is possible for all to function in any gift, depending on the sovereign plan of the Spirit who delegates the gifts when and to whom he wishes. Although the notion of a gift is that it belongs to the recipient and not the one who has given it, Pentecostals prefer to accept that the charismata are on loan from the Spirit; they are manifestations of the Spirit through believers that are expected to be used in ways that are appropriate to his character and will. Even when an individual frequently manifests a particular gift, it is still preferable to understand this as a manifestation of the Spirit through that person and not that s/he is using the gift of her/his own volition. It is difficult to be entirely clear in the formulation of a precise practical framework for the use of the charismata; some (miracles, healings)

---

5. Tipei, "The Function of the Laying on of Hands in the New Testament," 113–14.

are manifested more infrequently than others (administration, teaching) that are more permanent. Flexible, rather than rigid, contexts of use need to be embraced.

- The manifestation of the gifts in a public context must be subject to careful assessment. Sanctified common sense, the shared wisdom of the Christian community, a comparison with the teachings located in the Bible and receptivity to the Holy Spirit will help to confirm or reject the manifestation.

- The gifts are intrinsically equal to each other. The appropriate manifestation of any gift is determined by its value as compared to other gifts on any given occasion. Thus, Paul identifies prophecy as having greater value than tongues without interpretation because the former benefits those present while uninterpreted tongues do not (1 Cor 14:1–6). It is not that prophecy is intrinsically superior to the gift of tongues since both are manifestations of the Spirit but that the former is more valuable to the community since it is understandable and therefore beneficial. Similarly, on occasions, some gifts are more valuable to the Christian community than others; in that restricted sense, they may be identified as having greater value. Paul is not, therefore, seeking to demonstrate a hierarchy of gifts. Nevertheless, some Pentecostals, unfortunately, assume a hierarchy of sorts in which the more sensational and publicly demonstrated gifts are accorded more honor than others that are less spectacular. Paul, on the other hand, identifies the important underlying principle of ensuring that the gifts are administered for the greater good of the community.

- Gifts may be manifested in association with others. Thus, in healing, it is appropriate to expect the gifts of faith and discernment to be also operative; similarly, the exercise of the gift of administration would anticipate the presence of the gift of wisdom.

- The gifts are varied (12:4–6), Paul providing five major lists of gifts (Rom 12:6–8; Eph 4:11; 1 Cor 12:8–10, 28, 29 cf. 13:1–3; 14:6, 26), none of which are intended to be comprehensive but representative (1 Cor 7:7 which refers to the gifts of celibacy/singleness or being married). One of the main purposes of these lists is to demonstrate the diversity of gifts available to believers. Hollenweger questions the distinction between "natural" and "supernatural" gifts, preferring to identify a spiritual gift on the basis of its value to the Christian community, deducing that "a charism is a natural gift that is given for the common good."[6] Others have refused to identify natural talents as spiritual gifts.

---

6. Hollenweger, "Gifts of the Spirit: Natural and Supernatural," 667–68.

However, many deduce that a spiritual gift may be a natural talent that has been invested with supernatural energy by God, Lim concluding, "God touches all our abilities and potential with supernatural power."[7]

It is better, with many Pentecostals, to acknowledge the possibility that the Spirit can empower believers to function in ways that are beyond their normal powers and/or to enable them to utilize the gifts that they have already been granted as part of their personalities as created by God. After salvation, these gifts and sensitivities may be enhanced and supernaturally energized so as to achieve a higher potential of benefit for others. Thus, the abilities of individuals prior to their conversion may be channeled by the Spirit for the benefit of others as well as the possibility of irregular or frequent manifestation of gifts that may not have been present in their lives hitherto.

Some Pentecostals have sought to separate the gifts mentioned in 1 Corinthians 12:8–10 from other gifts while others have preferred a more inclusive understanding of the gifts. The danger with the former assessment is that some of the gifts are viewed as being of greater intrinsic value than others. As well as attempting to differentiate between the lists of gifts, others have sub-divided the gifts within the lists though this is not a particularly helpful or easy exercise, especially because it is not supported by Paul and such attempts at categorisation are tentative at best. An examination of the variety (See also 1 Pet 4:9–10) within the five main lists of gifts illustrates the difficulty in determining a pattern:

1 Cor 12:8-10	1 Cor 12:28	1 Cor 12:29-30	Eph 4:11	Rom 12:6-8
Wisdom	Apostles	Apostles	Apostles	Prophecy
Knowledge	Prophets	Prophets	Prophets	Service
Faith	Teachers	Teachers	Evangelist	Teaching
Healing	Miracles	Miracles	Pastor / Teacher	Exhortation
Miracles	Healings	Healings		Giving
Prophecy	Helps	Tongues		Mercy
Discernment	Administration	Interpretation		
Tongues	Tongues			
Interpretation				

---

7. Lim, "The Incarnational Nature of the Gifts," 15.

Although most Pentecostals tend to treat the individual gifts as they are referred to by Paul as distinct gifts with discrete definitions, it is not always clear that this is the most appropriate way of understanding them. Indeed, if Paul is not seeking to be comprehensive in his presentation of the gifts but simply remarking on the plurality and diversity of gifts, they may overlap with one another more than may have been assumed. Thus, to distinguish prophecy, wisdom, revelation, and knowledge as if each was a separate manifestation of the Spirit may be an unnecessary exercise since Paul may rather be intending to emphasize the fact that the Spirit is the source of all divinely imparted communication however it may be designated. Notwithstanding the fact that Paul explicitly identifies nearly thirty different gifts of the Spirit, most are self-explanatory. However, those identified in 1 Corinthians may benefit from more explication because of their prominence to most Pentecostals.

A Collection of Charismata

Word of Wisdom

Most Pentecostals view this gift as relating to the inspiration of Spirit-inspired revelation for a particular occasion rather than a natural propensity towards wisdom. However, a number of suggestions have been offered for the content of such wisdom, including the spiritual development of the one to whom it is given, the interpretation of the Bible, in preaching and teaching and in determining the future. This gift is often associated with the gift of knowledge; where the latter relates to familiarity with facts, the gift of wisdom is assumed to relate to the application of those facts in a particular way. The fact that the word "wisdom" is used elsewhere with reference to the wisdom available from Christ (1 Cor 1:23–24, 30; Col 2:3) may indicate that this refers to knowledge concerning the person and mission of Jesus. However, there appears to be little reason to be restrictive in this regard, and it is probably safest, in the absence of Pauline guidance, to keep the definition of the anticipated wisdom wider rather than narrower.

Word of Knowledge

Closely related to the word of wisdom, it is generally assumed that the word of knowledge is a supernatural awareness of facts that would be otherwise unknown to the recipient (Acts 5:1–2; 9:10–12). Because the word *gnōsis* (knowledge) is used elsewhere in contexts that relate to the knowledge of

God (2 Cor 2:14; 4:6; Eph 1:17), it is possible that this gift reflects those occasions when some aspect of God is being revealed. However, there is evidence of supernaturally inspired knowledge being recorded in other settings (John 1:48; 4:17–18; Acts 5:1–6; 27:10), and this suggests that a broader base of knowledge may also be appropriate.

Discernment of Spirits

Although discernment can occur naturally as a result of experience and maturity, Pentecostals believe that Paul is here referring to a charismatic gift of God. It is generally believed by Pentecostals that this gift describes the supernatural ability to identify the presence of an evil spirit (Acts 8:9–23; 16:16–17),[8] or the Holy Spirit,[9] or to identify the source of power motivating an act or word.[10]

Faith

Pentecostals distinguish the gift of faith from the fruit of faithfulness and saving faith. The faith referred to may be identified as the facility to trust God in a particular situation (Acts 3:2–19; 13:6–12)[11] and the gift of faith refers to a God-given assurance to undertake a particular action or offer a specific prayer (often in the absence of a biblical mandate or promise). The gift of faith is identified as a readiness to believe that which God has promised or stated will occur. It is particularly present in contexts when a biblical promise or guideline is unavailable. In those settings, the Spirit may choose to support a believer to follow a particular course of action by providing a "burst" of supernatural assurance or faith that their proposed action is the correct one. Thus, even though there may be no biblical mandate, the Spirit grants confirmation prior to the action being undertaken. It is this that protects the believer from functioning precipitously, precociously, or presumptuously (Rom 10:17; Eph 2:8). The confidence provided by the Spirit to support one's actions or words is to be understood as a gift of faith. It is not to be identified with the belief that God *can* do that which is needed but that he *will* do so. That which Paul refers to is a particular acknowledgment

---

8. Corsie, "The Ministry Gifts," 106–7; King, "Searching for Genuine Gold," 174–76.
9. Yong, *Beyond the Impasse*, 152–54.
10. Hernando, "Discerning of Spirits," 6–9; Martin, "Discernment of Spirits, Gift of," 582–84.
11. Martin, "Faith, Gift of," 629–30.

Gifts of Healing

The term *charismata* (gifts) prefaces *iamatōn* (healings) in a combination that occurs only in the Pauline literature. The fact that both terms are in the plural has resulted in a range of explanations. It is possible that Paul believed that each healing was to be identified as a gift of healing; thus, the person who is healed receives a gift of healing.[12] It may be that he is demonstrating the comprehensive power of the Spirit to provide restoration for all kinds of illnesses. It is possible that some believers are enabled by the Spirit to facilitate the healing of particular illnesses. Although some have claimed this to be a true reflection of their own healing ministries, it begs the question as to what one should do if the particular restorative capacity is not available to those wishing to minister to someone in need of specific restoration. It is also not reflected in the healing narratives in Acts or in James 5:14–18. Although it need not be assumed that such ability resides permanently in a believer, Paul assumes the presence of healers in the church (1 Cor 12:28). Such a definition may be applied to those who function in this gift more than other people. Pentecostals are prepared to identify individuals with a more prominent God-given gift of healing (1 Cor 12:28), though the ministry of healing would be more generally understood as being available to all and effected through (m)any believer(s) (1 Cor 12:7, 14). Gifts of healing are most appropriately manifested in conjunction with the gift of faith (1 Cor 12:9), and words of wisdom and knowledge or prophecy (1 Cor 12:8–10).

Miracles

This is viewed as a reference to the ability to perform miracles other than healings. Thus, although without NT justification, many Pentecostals particularly associate this with the ability to conduct exorcisms, though other miraculous interventions may also be included.[13]

---

12. Ervin, *Healing. Sign of the Kingdom*, 29; Warrington, "Major Aspects of Healing with British Pentecostalism," 40.

13. See Martin, "Miracles, Gift of," 876.

Prophecy

The association of the Spirit with prophecy has long been recognized and is still being explored both with regard to the OT,[14] the NT, and the early church.[15] In general, Pentecostals have distinguished prophecy before the Day of Pentecost from that which is referred to afterward. Thus, the death penalty for a false prophet (Deut 13:1–5, 18, 20) is not applied to NT prophets who speak in error and the prophecies recorded in the NT are mainly intended for believers. The ecstatic prophecies and somewhat bizarre behavior sometimes associated with some OT prophets (Isa 20:3–5; Jer 4:5; Ezek 1:24) is much less prominent in the NT church (Acts 21:10–11), where sensitivity, care, and good order are essential elements of the manifestations (1 Cor 14:32, 40).

Pentecostals increasingly view themselves as people through whom prophecies can be offered,[16] though they rarely anticipate that this will be of a foretelling nature, though that does sometimes occur, as it did in the NT (Acts 11:28; 21:10–11). Fundamentally, Pentecostals acknowledge that prophecy is a gift given by the Spirit according to his will (1 Cor 12:11).

In general, most Pentecostals identify prophecies as those occasions when an individual, inspired by God, speaks spontaneously and extemporarily with an emphasis on edification and or exhortation, thus reflecting the NT norm (1 Cor 14:3–5). Prophecy of a personal nature has generally been offered with care or even cautioned against, though many look to prophecy as a means of determining the direction or confirmation in decision making and for encouragement. Increasingly, the expectation and practice are for prophecies to be offered by a variety of believers in a congregation rather than a set few, although some individuals and Pentecostal denominations prefer to identify prophets through whom it is expected the Spirit will speak to the community. Pentecostals accept that prophecies and other verbal utterances of a charismatic nature are often associated with or preceded by mental pictures, images, words, or physical sensations, the person who receives them then describing or explaining them to the congregation. The form of the prophecy is moving away from the use of the language that assumes that the words are directly spoken by God (in

---

14. David (2 Sam 23.2); Saul (1 Sam 10.9–12); Amasai (1 Chr 12.18); Azariah (2 Chr 15.1); Jahaziel (2 Chr 20:14); Zechariah (Zech 7:12); Micah (Micah 3:8); Ezekiel (Ezek 11:5); for all (Num 11:29; Joel 2:28–29); Daniel (Dan 4:8, 9).

15. See, Robeck, *Prophecy in Carthage*.

16. L. Lugo records that 37 percent of Pentecostals in the countries researched testified that they had given a prophecy (ranging from 27 percent in the USA to 55 percent in South Africa). Lugo, "Spirit and Power," 16.

the first person singular) to a presentation that recognizes the importance of their being examined as to the quality and relevance of their content, as anticipated in 1 Cor 14:29-32.

The fallibility of prophecy is generally assumed to be due to its impermanent nature (1 Cor 13:8). It is generally left to individual believers to decide for themselves the authenticity of the information delivered, the prophecy rather than the prophet being the subject of scrutiny, though the lifestyle or the way in which the prophecy was offered may count towards its legitimacy. It is unclear from 1 Corinthians 14:29 whether the prophecy should be scrutinized by other prophets or by the wider congregation, though, in practice, the latter is assumed by most Pentecostals. The means whereby the prophecy is to be examined are manifold. A basic premise is that it should not contradict that which is contained in the Bible. Since most prophecies offer little more than representations of truth that are already contained in the Bible, such an exercise is rarely problematic. Where the prophecy is foretelling or unrelated to the Bible, other tests are needed. These relate to the confidence that people have in the one prophesying, common sense, the perception of the community of believers and personal discernment that may be manifested by the Spirit. In accordance with the guidelines of Paul (1 Cor 14:29), most Pentecostals prefer to allow no more than two or three prophecies in a given meeting, though, increasingly, it is assumed that Paul's guidance may have had relevance for the Corinthian context in particular and that contemporary application needs careful contextualization.

Pentecostals prefer not to identify preaching with prophecy, suggesting that the latter is offered independently of the Bible and thus to be contrasted with preaching and also reckoned to be inferior to the Bible. They refer to preaching as transmitting the words of God and the Bible as the Word of God. However, many are prepared to accept that, on occasions, a person may preach prophetically, even without their knowledge that they are so operating. Indeed, many Pentecostals would aspire to preach in a way that the Spirit is inspiring their words and infusing the message with a supernatural dimension reflective of the Spirit and not merely defined by the speaker, however good a communicator s/he may be.

Tongues and Interpretation

Glossolalia has been associated with (and understood to be a defining aspect of) Pentecostalism since the earliest days of its existence.[17] The popular

17. Mills, "Glossolalia: A Survey of the Literature," 13-31.

term used is "speaking in tongues" rather than the more technical term of glossolalia (from *glōssa* [tongue] *lalein* [to speak], 1 Cor 14:2, 6). The descriptions of "new tongues" (Mark 16:7) and "tongues of angels" (1 Cor 13:1) are also believed to refer to glossolalia. Pentecostals have spent minimal time exploring the actual science or theology of tongues. MacDonald robustly concludes "Biblical glossolalia has no antecedents, no precedents, no parallels—in the Old Testament, or paganism, or pathology."[18] Pentecostals dismiss suggestions that it is socio-psychologically induced, the result of a subconscious awareness of the languages being aroused by the experience of being filled with the Spirit or due to learned behavior, ecstasy, or hysteria or to be identified as gibberish or babbling. Indeed, Ervin concludes that "there is nothing inherently emotional in glossolalia."[19] They also reject the claims of some that it is satanically inspired, though they are aware of its presence in pagan religions. Instead, they prefer to believe that although it has certain inexplicable elements, the gift of tongues is best understood if it is viewed functionally. In other words, its *role* is more important than its internal mechanism. Indeed, although the topic has been the subject of significant interest to some non-Pentecostals, until recently it has received little other than pastoral and historical comment by Pentecostals. This may be due, in part, to the pragmatic recognition that this is a gift to be used rather than discussed. Even its linguistic properties are viewed as having little significance and therefore little time has been spent on attempting to analyze or explore it phenomenologically. Pentecostals are less interested in determining whether it can function as a language, it has linguistic forms or can be accurately translated. It is less important to define glossolalia and more important to experience and realize that which it does for the speaker and hearer.

The gift of tongues is best understood as an extemporaneous or spontaneous manifestation in a form that is a quasi-language. The speaker is in control of her/his speech and the forming of the sounds; the Spirit does not manipulate or coerce the speaker into a particular speech pattern. It is possible that the sounds themselves already existed in the mind and experience of the speaker, being reconstituted in the form of the tongues s/he employs though it also possible that they are previously unimagined phonetic forms. Most Pentecostals have concluded that speaking in tongues is a phenomenon that has divine and human elements in that the Spirit inspires the manifestation, but the person articulates the sounds.

It is difficult to be certain as to the percentage of Pentecostals who regularly speak in tongues, Poloma writing, "In some Classical Pentecostal circles, glossolalia is in danger of becoming a doctrine devoid of experience

---

18. MacDonald, "Biblical Glossolalia," 7.
19. Ervin, *Healing. Sign of the Kingdom*, 126.

with an estimated 50% or more of followers reporting that they do not speak in tongues."[20]

The Rules of Tongues and Interpretation

Most Pentecostals assume that the Pauline advice that a manifestation of tongues should occur no more than three times in a given setting (1 Cor 14:27) is to be taken literally, though some assume that the issue of orderliness rather than frequency of use is most important. Increasingly, it has been questioned whether his advice should be viewed as timeless or specifically for the Corinthian church that had abused the gift of tongues. Although the one speaking in tongues may pray for the ability to interpret those tongues, others may also appropriately do so. The form of the interpretation has also received some inquiry. The general assumption is that an interpretation may be shorter or longer in length than the original glossolalia.

Speaking and singing in tongues corporately without any interpretation is a phenomenon that often occurs in Pentecostal gatherings, generally as an expression of worship or prayer and many Pentecostals testify to its emotional and spiritual benefits.[21] Although 1 Corinthians 14:13–20 indicates that such a practice is inappropriate (at least, in Corinth), it nevertheless still occurs, the reference to "spiritual songs" in Colossians 3:16 (1 Cor 14:15) being used to support the phenomenon. It could be suggested that Paul's advice concerning its circumscribed use was specifically intended for the first-century Corinthian church because they had so severely abused it.

Underlying Significance and Purposes

Although it is often, with the gift of interpretation, placed at the end of the Pauline lists of charismata (1 Cor 12:10, 30), Pentecostals value speaking in tongues and recognize that it is intrinsically equal to other charismata. Pentecostals generally understand speaking in tongues as having a number of purposes:

- Many believe that it signifies that one has experienced the baptism in the Spirit,[22] though others are less convinced.[23] The evidence for it

---

20. Poloma, "Glossolalia, Liminality and Empowered Kingdom Building," 151.

21. Ma, "Doing Theology in the Philippines," 220; Cartledge, "The Practice of Tongues-Speech as a Case Study," 210; Johansson, "Singing in the Spirit," 20–23.

22. Dempster describes it as "an indigenous part of Spirit baptism" and not "only a sign." See Dempster, "The Structure of a Christian Ethic Informed by Pentecostal Experience," 111; See also, Petts, *The Holy Spirit*, 70–78.

23. Kärkkäinen, *Spiritus ubi vult spirat*, 379; Poloma identified, among US AoG

being a sign of the baptism in the Spirit tends to be drawn from Acts while the references concerning tongues in the Pauline literature are generally viewed as information provided to guide the believer in its use in personal and public worship. In other words, the gift of tongues is viewed by many as having two distinct purposes, the one as a sign of the baptism in the Spirit, the other offering ongoing personal benefit for prayer and praise.

- The use of tongues in a private context is often described as a prayer-language.[24] Thus, it provides an opportunity for a personal union of the human with the divine.[25] Paul, in particular, provides evidence for this (1 Cor 14:2, 4, 28), referring to praying in tongues (1 Cor 14:15). Fundamentally, the manifestation of the gift of tongues thus functions as a symbol of the presence of God, his closeness and his mystery, his immanence and his transcendence, in the Christian community.

- Paul declares that the use of tongues has the capacity to edify the speaker (1 Cor 14:4), though he does not clarify the specific nature of that edification. In speaking in tongues, the speakers anticipate that the Spirit will be empowering them and, in that respect, there is the potential for their being edified. In this regard, speaking in tongues provides believers with the opportunity to express prayer or praise to God without the restrictions posed by human language.

- Glossolalia is also valuable as a sign that the tongues speaker is now part of a charismatic community and therefore is expected to function in charismatic ministry. In particular, whenever glossolalia was experienced, in its historical setting in Acts, it removed barriers of class and race, affirmed non-Jews as valid members of the new Christian community and allowed for the integration of all into the newly constituted community of God (Acts 10:46; 11:15). In this regard, it may be viewed as a reversal of Babel, where language became the reason for the disintegration of the society,[26] and a remaking of

---

believers, that 77 percent expressed a belief that they had been baptized in the Spirit while only 66 percent reported they spoke in tongues. In the same survey, 51 percent agreed or strongly agreed that tongues are the initial evidence of the baptism in the Spirit while 20 percent disagreed or strongly disagreed, 18 percent being uncertain. However, only 32 percent agreed or strongly agreed that a person who has never spoken in tongues cannot already be baptized in the Spirit. See Poloma "Pentecostal Prayer as a Complementary Healing Practice within the Assemblies of God," 275–78.

24. Hayford, *The Beauty of Spiritual Language*, 95–98.

25. Chan, "The Language Game of Glossolalia," 86; Hutch, "The Personal Ritual of Glossolalia," 381–95; Yong, "The Truth of Tongues Speech," 107–15.

26. Edwards, "Babel or Pentecost?" 4–9.

history by the Spirit in the initiation of the church.[27] The Spirit's gift of tongues, available to all believers, is a means of reminding individuals of their equal place within the church, breaking through all racial and economic divisions.[28]

- Although some anticipate their value to unbelievers (1 Cor 14:20–22), most Pentecostals are wary of this perspective. Paul identifies tongues as having the potential of confirming unbelievers in their unbelief (1 Cor 14:20–22), a negative, not a redemptive, sign. Thus, Paul quotes from Isaiah 28:11 where the Jews did not listen to God's prophets when they spoke of judgment, so he sent the same message actualized through the invading armies of foreign nations who spoke different languages. The Jews did not understand the languages of the foreign invaders, but the content was of judgment, the same as that previously spoken by their prophets. Speaking in tongues that could not be understood did not lead to repentance but ushered in judgment. Likewise, although some assume that the crowds referred to in Acts 2 became believers having heard the believers speaking in tongues, their salvation is recorded only after Peter preaches his sermon (Acts 2:41).

- In early Pentecostalism, the gift of tongues was assumed incorrectly to provide the means whereby missionary activity could take place without the need for the learning of languages, the gift of tongues being assumed to be a divinely inspired ability to communicate in a given language. However, this belief did not last long as the expectation was not fulfilled in the lives of the vast majority. Nevertheless, many testimonies of human languages being spoken in the form of tongues are available that support the notion that the gift of tongues can function as *xenolalia* (speaking [human] languages).

- The gift of tongues has also been identified as a liberating or empowering act. Similarly, Dempster indicates that since glossolalia is one particular expression of the divine-human encounter, as a result of which the flawed believer engages with the morally sacred divine, it provides "a spiritual encounter with the God who is, and a moral encounter with the God who values."[29] As a result of this, a change is expected in the morality of the believer.

---

27. Dempster, "The Church's Moral Witness," 1–7.

28. Ibid.; Ayers, "Can The Behavior of Tongues Utterance still function as Ecclesial Boundary?" 274–79.

29. Dempster, "The Structure of a Christian Ethic Informed by Pentecostal Experience," 115.

Content of Tongues and Interpretation

The NT, other than Acts 2:6, indicates that an earthly language is not being assumed by the writers when they refer to glossolalia. Acts 2:6, which details an occasion when people heard their languages being spoken by others who did not naturally know them, is generally understood to describe *xenolalia* whereby the verbal expression is understandable to the hearer without the need for an interpretation.

For many years, the common perception of many Pentecostals has been that tongues and interpretation are equivalent to prophecy in that both result in information being presented to the hearers.[30] Thus, the concept of "a message in tongues" has been common among Pentecostals, the message being from God to people. This perspective has increasingly been called into question.[31] Part of this shift has been due to the fact that (possibly excluding Acts 2:6) on the occasions when tongues are referred to in the NT, the contents are prayer or praise (Acts 2:11; 10:46; 1 Cor 14:2, 14–16) and are directed *to God*, not believers (1 Cor 14:2, 14–16, 28). MacDonald concludes, "Glossolalia is always directed to God, and only to Him."[32] There is no biblical support for the suggestion that the gift of tongues was intended to be a means whereby God communicated with believers, neither is there any indication that when a tongue is interpreted, it becomes equivalent to prophecy.[33] Those who argue that interpretations of tongues should be viewed as expressions of prayer or praise to God have also suggested that the interpretations that often occur in Pentecostal gatherings more likely result from well-intentioned but mistaken believers who assume they have received them from God, or may be prophetic utterances mistakenly linked with tongues. It is possible that received Pentecostal traditions that have assumed that interpretations of tongues are intended to be prophetic messages have resulted in the promulgation of this practice. Alternatively, it may be argued that the NT does not provide all the information needed to comprehensively identify the purpose of the gift of tongues; thus, the practice of many to associate interpretation with a message to believers may be appropriate even though NT evidence does not support it.

---

30. Spittler, "Interpretation of Tongues, Gift of," 801–2.

31. Caldwell, "A Pastor's Reaction to William MacDonald's 'Biblical Glossolalia,'" 22–25.

32. MacDonald, "Biblical Glossolalia," 1; Levang, "The Content of an Utterance in Tongues," 14–20.

33. Fee, "Towards a Pauline Theology of Glossolalia," 33.

Conclusion

The Spirit is a limitless resource for believers with regard to their spirituality while he also provides resources for all believers and expects them to be used, and used sensitively for every task he sets, diversely distributing gifts to function for the benefit of all in the development of the church. The more that believers are controlled by him, the more they will benefit from his influential presence, his fruit being personally and corporately experienced.

Bibliography

Ayers, A. "Can The Behavior of Tongues Utterance Still Function as Ecclesial Boundary? The Significance of Art and Sacrament." *Pneuma* 22.2 (2000) 271–301.

Caldwell, B. "A Pastor's Reaction to William MacDonald's 'Biblical Glossolalia.'" *Paraclete* 29.1 (1995) 22–25.

Cartledge, Mark J. "The Practice of Tongues-Speech as a Case Study: A Practical-Theological Perspective." In *Speaking in Tongues*, edited by M. J. Cartledge, 206–34. Milton Keynes, UK: Paternoster, 2006.

Chan, S. K. H. "The Language Game of Glossolalia, or Making Sense of the 'Initial Evidence.'" In *Pentecostalism in Context: Essays in Honor of William W. Menzies*, edited by Wonsuk Ma and Robert P. Menzies, 80–95. Sheffield, UK. Sheffield Academic, 1997.

Corsie, E. R. "The Ministry Gifts." In *Pentecostal Doctrine*, edited by Brewster, 95–111. New York: Greenhurst, 1976.

Dempster, M. W. "The Church's Moral Witness: A Study of Glossolalia in Luke's Theology of Acts." *Paraclete* 23.1 (1989) 1–7.

———. "The Structure of a Christian Ethic Informed by Pentecostal Experience: Surroundings in the Moral Significance of Glossolalia." In *The Spirit and Spirituality: Essays in Honor of Russell P. Spittler*, edited by Wonsuk Ma and Robert P. Menzies, 108–40. London: T. & T. Clark, 2004.

Edwards, T. B. "Babel or Pentecost?" *Paraclete* 25.1 (1991) 4–9.

Ellis, E. Earl. "Prophecy in the New Testament Church—And Today." In *Prophetic Vocation in the New Testament and Today*, edited by P. Panagopoulos, 46–57. Leiden: Brill, 1977.

Ervin, H. M. *Healing. Sign of the Kingdom*. Peabody, MA: Hendrickson, 2002.

Fee, Gordon D. "Towards a Pauline Theology of Glossolalia." In *Pentecostalism in Context: Essays in Honor of William W. Menzies*, edited by Wonsuk Ma and Robert P. Menzies, 24–37. Sheffield, UK. Sheffield Academic Press, 1997.

Hayford, J. *The Beauty of Spiritual Language: My Journey Toward the Heart of God*. Dallas, TX: Word, 1992.

Hernando, J. D. "Discerning of Spirits." *Paraclete* 26.2 (1992) 6–9.

Hollenweger, W. J. "Gifts of the Spirit: Natural and Supernatural." In *New International Dictionary of the Pentecostal and Charismatic Movements*, edited by Stanley M. Burgess and Eduard M. van der Maas, 667–68. Grand Rapids: Zondervan, 2002.

Hutch, R. "The Personal Ritual of Glossolalia." In *Speaking in Tongues: A Guide to Research on Glossolalia*, edited by Watson E. Mills, 381–95. Grand Rapids: Eerdmans, 1986.

Johansson, C. M. "Singing in the Spirit." *Paraclete* 24.2 (1990) 20–23.

Kärkkäinen, Veli-Matti. *Spiritus ubi vult spirat: Pneumatology in Roman Catholic-Pentecostal Dialogue (1972–1989)*. Schriften der Luther-Agricola-Gesellschaft 42. Helsinki: Luther-Agricola Society, 1998.

King, P. L. "Searching for Genuine Gold: Discerning Spirit, Flesh, and Demonic in Pentecostal Experiences." Society of Pentecostal Studies conference paper, Cleveland, TN, March 8–10, 2007.

Levang, R. K. "The Content of an Utterance in Tongues." *Paraclete* 23.1 (1989) 14–20.

Lim, D. "The Incarnational Nature of the Gifts." *Paraclete* 26.3 (1992) 14–19.

Lugo, L. "Spirit and Power. A 10-Country Survey of Pentecostals." In *Pew Forum on Religion and Public Life*. Washington, DC: Pew, 2006.

Ma, Wonsuk. "Doing Theology in the Philippines: A Case of Pentecostal Christianity." *Asian Journal of Pentecostal Studies* 8.2 (2005) 215–33.

MacDonald, W. G. "Biblical Glossolalia. Thesis 3." *Paraclete* 27.2 (1993) 7–14.

———. "Biblical Glossolalia. Thesis 7." *Paraclete* 28.2 (1994) 1–12.

Martin, F. "Discernment of Spirits, Gift of." In *New International Dictionary of the Pentecostal and Charismatic Movements*, edited by Stanley M. Burgess and Eduard M. van der Maas, 582–84. Grand Rapids: Zondervan, 2002.

———. "Faith, Gift of." In *New International Dictionary of the Pentecostal and Charismatic Movements*, edited by Stanley M. Burgess and Eduard M. van der Maas, 629–30. Grand Rapids: Zondervan, 2002.

———. "Miracles, Gift of." In *New International Dictionary of the Pentecostal and Charismatic Movements*, edited by Stanley M. Burgess and Eduard M. van der Maas, 875–76. Grand Rapids: Zondervan, 2002.

Mills, W. E. "Glossolalia: A Survey of the Literature." In *Speaking in Tongues: A Guide to Research on Glossolalia*, edited by W. E. Mills, 13–31. Grand Rapids: Eerdmans, 1986.

Petts, D. *The Holy Spirit: An Introduction*. Mattersey, UK: Mattersey Hall, 1998.

Poloma, Margaret M. "Glossolalia, Liminality and Empowered Kingdom Building—A Sociological Perspective." In *Speaking in Tongues*, edited by Mark Cartledge, 147–73. Milton Keynes, UK: Paternoster, 2006.

———. "Pentecostal Prayer as a Complementary Healing Practice within the Assemblies of God." Society of Pentecostal Studies Conference paper. Cleveland, TN, March 8–10, 2007.

Robeck, Cecil M., Jr. *Prophecy in Carthage: Perpetua, Tertullian, and Cyprian*. Cleveland, OH: Pilgrim, 1992.

Ruthven, J. *On the Cessation of the Charismata*. Sheffield, UK: Sheffield Academic Press, 1993.

Spittler, R. P. "Interpretation of Tongues, Gift of." In *New International Dictionary of the Pentecostal and Charismatic Movements*, edited by Stanley M. Burgess and Eduard M. van der Maas, 801–2. Grand Rapids: Zondervan, 2002.

Tipei, J. "The Function of the Laying on of Hands in the New Testament." *Journal of the European Pentecostal Theological Association* 20 (2000) 93–115.

Warrington, K. "Major Aspects of Healing with British Pentecostalism." *Journal of the European Pentecostal Theological Association* 19 (1999) 34–55.

———. *Pentecostal Theology, A Theology of Encounter*. London: T. & T. Clark, 2008.

Yong, A. *Beyond the Impasse: Toward a Pneumatological Theology of Religion*. Grand Rapids: Baker Academic, 2003.

———. "The Truth of Tongues Speech: A Rejoinder to Frank Macchia." *Journal of Pentecostal Theology* 13 (1998) 107–15.

9

The Church

CECIL M. ROBECK, JR.

Introduction

IT MAY COME AS a surprise, but until quite recently, Pentecostals wrote very little about ecclesiology, the doctrine of the church.[1] That is not to say that Pentecostals did not think about this doctrine—they did. But the first generation of Pentecostals had experienced the Holy Spirit in a powerful way that seemed to be different from that seen in congregations outside the Pentecostal movement. As a result, they were far less interested in writing theology than they were in sharing their experience and winning others to Christ. The return of the Lord seemed to be so imminent that early Pentecostals believed that they had to carry forth the message of the gospel as broadly as they could in as little time as possible. As a result, the earliest generation of Pentecostals went throughout the world, bearing witness to Jesus Christ and to their experience of the Holy Spirit.

During its second generation, the Pentecostal Movement established Bible schools that were intended to pass along this message. Bible school teachers were rightly first *Bible expositors* and, to a lesser extent, they became *biblical theologians*. Typically, these teachers were not trained in the ancient biblical languages or in the classical theological disciplines, though they were often insightful and gifted teachers. Myer Pearlman in the United States and Donald Gee in England are examples of such teachers. Often, they were also charged with teaching the practice of ministry through many "how to" courses on preaching, soul winning, establishing Sunday Schools, and the like. It was during this second generation that Pentecostal *historians* began to appear as they searched their foundational documents to explain

---

1. See Kärkkäinen, *An Introduction to Ecclesiology*; Shane, *Pentecostal Churches in Transition*; Thomas, *Toward a Pentecostal Ecclesiology*; Chan, "Pentecostal Ecclesiology."

to present and future generations the development of their Pentecostal fellowships, denominations, doctrines, and ministry practices.

Only toward the end of the third generation did *systematic theologians* begin to develop, people who were classically trained, who would explore the full range of theological doctrine, including the doctrine of the church, often in conversation with those outside Pentecostalism. They would engage or interact with historical, biblical, and theological developments through the centuries.[2] This progression of disciplines within Pentecostalism parallels quite closely the developments that took place among the first generations of Christians in the early church.[3] It is a sign of the growing maturity of Pentecostalism as a movement.

The Church in the Book of Acts

The doctrine of the church is best explained beginning with the specific details, metaphors, and descriptions it receives in Scripture, and the place to begin is at the beginning. The birth of the church is most commonly recognized as taking place on the Day of Pentecost (Acts 2:1–41). It began among those who had followed the direction of Jesus to wait in Jerusalem, where they would receive the promise of the Father (Acts 1:4–5, 8). They waited, prayerfully anticipating the promise, and on the Day of Pentecost they received their answer. "This is what was spoken through the prophets," proclaimed Peter (Acts 2:16). "This is that"!

That first Christian Pentecost was sufficient to attract an initial hearing for the gospel, and Peter rose to the occasion, proclaiming that what those who were witnesses to the event now saw, was God's answer to his long-awaited promise. God was doing something new among his people; something for which Moses could only yearn (Num 11:29). Yet God had promised through the prophets (Ezek 37:12–14; Joel 2:28–29) and ultimately through Jesus (Acts 1:8) that it would take place. When it finally took place on the Day of Pentecost, Peter urged the people to repentance

---

2. Clark and Henry, *What Is Distinctive about Pentecostal Theology*, 68.

3. The earliest contributors to the faith were the first-century apostles, who with Luke (1:1–4; Acts 1:1–5), served as historians who bore witness to what they had seen and heard during their earthly walk with Jesus (1 John 1:1–3). By the earliest years of the second century, they were followed by various bishops who passed along the *apostolic tradition* to subsequent generations. Pastoral care became a primary concern of these apostolic fathers and fixed liturgical forms were increasingly set in place (cf. Didache 7:1–4; 9:1—10:7). The apologists of the late second century became the first philosophical and systematic theologians. Justin Martyr, *Apology I-II*; Irenaeus, *Against Heresies*.

and baptism, and that day, some 3,000 people joined the 120, and together they became the church (Acts 2:22–41).

What Did It Mean for Them To Be the Church?

What were the implications of this event for them, and ultimately for us? How were they to make sense of it? It is in the midst of such questions that they discovered several things about themselves, and thus, about the nature of the church. First, they recognized that they had received the Holy Spirit in a new and vital way. Just before he left his disciples, Jesus promised in his "Paraclete sayings" that he would send the Paraclete, who would strengthen them, encourage them, teach them, and remind them of all that Jesus had said. The Paraclete—that is, the Holy Spirit—would guide them into all truth, glorify Christ, and also declare new things to them (John 14:16–17, 26; 15:26–27; 16:13–15). The church was the people of God who were now indwelt by the Spirit of God (Rom 8:9), a fact that would lead them to further discoveries regarding the power that the Holy Spirit brought to their lives and the ways that they were to engage with the Holy Spirit and with one another. As they began, all they had in common was a singular commitment to the God and Father of our Lord Jesus Christ, to the Lordship of Jesus in their lives, and a newly shared spiritual experience rooted in the person of the Holy Spirit, which they saw manifested in one another.

It is fascinating to realize that Jesus had left them with no specific design that they were to follow. There was no constitution to which they had to adhere, no doctrinal statements that would provide them with boundaries, and no texts from which they might take their identity other than what they found in their local synagogues—the books of Moses, the Prophets, and the Wisdom books. It would be at least fifteen years before the earliest book of the New Testament would even be written. There were no Christian theological books, no leadership seminars, and no Bible schools or seminary programs that would help to define the church. These new believers were forced to rely upon what they had.

The Apostolic Teaching

They quickly realized that they had direct access to the apostles, those men who had been called and had spent three years with Jesus, watching him, listening to him, and doing what he had asked of them, men who would prove to be invaluable resources. As they sat with the apostles, they quickly recognized the importance that the *apostolic teaching* held for them. But what was this apostolic teaching? It consisted of the testimony of those who had walked and talked and sat at the feet of Jesus for three years. As the apostles reflected on their lives with Jesus, the memories of what Jesus had said to them or done before them, as well as accounts of their experiences with him were passed along to all of those who sat at their feet. These oral narratives or testimonies would form the collective memory of all who were present, initially made possible because these new Christians sat at the feet of the apostles. Jude would later call it, the faith "once for all entrusted to the saints" (Jude 3) that they received.

Thus, the church began with an oral narrative, based upon the testimony of the apostles. "We declare to you what we have seen and heard," John would later write, "so that you may have fellowship with us; and truly our fellowship is with the Father and with his Son Jesus Christ" (1 John 1:3). The apostolic teaching bore witness to what the apostles had seen and heard, and they passed along this tradition, which made fellowship possible, not only with the apostles, but also with the Lord. The first fellowship experienced by these new Christians came through the proclamation of the apostles, through their sharing of the apostles' teaching together. Later, the memories and teachings of the apostles and a few of their closest associates like Mark and Luke would be written down, collected, and after considerable discussion, published to form the New Testament, but in the beginning, it was the oral testimony of their lives with Jesus that brought these early believers together. This *apostolic teaching* given through apostles and prophets provided a rich foundation for the church (Eph 2:20–21), aligned with the chief cornerstone, Christ Jesus.

Koinonia

As the earliest Christians gathered at the feet of the apostles, they also recognized that they were forming new relationships, not only with the Lord and with the apostles but with one another. These relationships were described by the Greek term *koinōnía*, which is typically translated as "fellowship." It is not easy to find an equivalent that does justice to the concept of *koinōnía*. These people were strangers at one level, but they quickly found themselves being transformed as they sat together at the feet of the apostles. They began to recognize their need for one another. Jesus had not told them exactly what to do or how to live in so many words, but as they gathered together, they understood what needed to be done. They had a desire *to be with* one another. They wanted to learn together. They found it important to pray together. They wanted to break bread together. They found that their new relationship led to mutual nurture and to mutual sharing. They were a new creation (2 Cor 5:17) and they began to recognize themselves as being a new people (Eph 2:15) who were to live under a new commandment (John 13:34; 1 John 3:23–24) under Christ and in the power of the Holy Spirit.

This new relationship led them to do things that they might never have anticipated doing before, not for themselves, but for one another. The Great Commandment to "love the Lord your God with all their heart, and with all your soul, and with all your strength, and with all your mind; and your neighbor as yourself" (Luke 10:27) took on new meaning. By recognizing their life together, their *koinōnía*, as constitutive of who they were as the church,[4] they quickly realized that this new relationship inevitably led to new actions. They found that the ways that they had related previously, marked by more worldly standards such as selfishness, or animosity, or competition, or envy, were being transformed. In place of these earlier standards, they found a new ability to share, to give to one another, to consider all things as belonging to the God who now lived among them through the Holy Spirit. They sold their possessions and goods and distributed the proceeds from them to everyone who had a need (Acts 2:45). Their actions were now based on the needs of others rather than on their own needs and desires, clearly following the teaching of Jesus to serve, rather than to be served (Mark 10:4–45; Luke 22:24–27).

When the church began in Jerusalem, there was much more fellowship, much more togetherness than what would later be found in the Corinthian congregation.[5] There was genuine *koinōnía*, which made it possible for the needs of all, even those of the Hellenist widows (Acts 6:1–6) to be met. They reached out to their sisters and brothers, helping to meet their physical needs. Luke testifies that "There was not a needy person among them" (Acts 4:34–35). This level of *koinōnía* led further to the spread of the gospel and to an increase in the number of converts to the Christian community.

---

4. Over half a century ago, the Swiss pastor/theologian Emil Brunner noted that "The Body of Christ is nothing other than a fellowship of persons. It is 'the fellowship of Jesus Christ' [1 Cor 1:9] or 'fellowship of the Holy Ghost' [2 Cor 13:13; Phil 2:1], where fellowship or *koinonia* signifies a common participation, a togetherness, a community life. The faithful are bound to each other through their common sharing in Christ and in the Holy Ghost, but that which they have in common is precisely no 'thing', no 'it', but a 'he', Christ and His Holy Spirit." Brunner, *The Misunderstanding of the Church*, 10–11.

5. Paul wrote two letters to the Corinthians, urging unity among them. This congregation seems to have ignored Paul's counsel. Sometime between AD 92 and 101, Bishop Clement of Rome wrote another *Epistle to the Corinthians* to address what he described as "that shameful and detestable sedition, utterly abhorrent to the elect of God which a few rash and self-confident persons have kindled to such a pitch of frenzy that your venerable and illustrious name worthy to be universally loved, has suffered grievous harm." *Epistle to the Corinthians* 1.2.

As good as this new community was it was not perfect. There were those such as Ananias and Sapphira, who attempted to deceive the rest, but the exposure of their sin and their very public deaths (Acts 5:1–11) led to this new fellowship breaking new ground (Acts 5:12–16).

Sharing Bread

These early "Pentecostal" Christians also realized that their fellowship was tangible. It was evidenced in their breaking bread together. They enjoyed their fellowship with one another to such an extent, that they ate together with glad and generous hearts (Acts 2:46), sharing the meal with one another. That action was symbolic not only of what their Lord had done for them, but it also helped them realize that *they were one body*. It made them eager to be *with* one another, to nurture, to uplift, to aid, and to affirm one another. They came to realize that there is no room in the church for the isolated Christian. The table is a place for serving, for eating, and for enjoying the fellowship of one another together. We are typically very selective about who it is that we invite to eat with us, and these earliest Christians were no different. The table is a special place that we open up to our family and friends. Their "life together," if I can borrow a phrase from the Lutheran theologian Dietrich Bonhoeffer,[6] was clearest when they broke bread together, when they shared with one another the most basic item that provides sustenance and life.

The table would become a powerful symbol of their unity. When the apostle Paul was later confronted by the Corinthian congregation's violation of that table fellowship he was appalled at their actions and he refused to commend them. "When you come together," he wrote, "it is not really to eat the Lord's Supper. For when the time comes to eat, each of you goes ahead with your own supper, and one goes hungry, and another becomes drunk" (1 Cor 11:20–21). He would go on to note that "Whoever, therefore, eats the bread or drinks the cup of the Lord in an unworthy manner will be answerable for the body and blood of the Lord. Examine yourselves," he urged the Corinthians, "and only then eat of the bread and drink of the cup" (1 Cor 11:27–28).

---

6. See Bonhoeffer, *Life Together*.

The Prayers

These earliest Christians quickly realized that in addition to sitting at the feet of the apostles, enjoying the fellowship of one another, and participating in a common table, they needed to *pray* together. They were eager to pray with and for one another, with no secrets between them. Acts 2:42 specifically notes that these new Christians devoted themselves not simply to prayer as a discipline, but to "*the prayers.*" This term referred to "set" prayers, that is, regularly prescribed liturgical prayers offered at certain times or on certain days.[7] Today, Pentecostals place a high premium on spontaneity in their prayers, and the apostles prayed spontaneously on many occasions.[8] But these early believers also recognized that there was a place for prayer in their lives together that went beyond either individuality or spontaneity. It also included prayers of studied reflection, written, formal prayers, prayers that were said together. At times it included praying from the Psalms or other prescribed prayers that these believers inherited from their life and the liturgy found in the synagogue and temple.[9]

On the one hand, their prayers together bore witness to their *continuity* with Israel. Jesus had made it his custom to attend the synagogue each Sabbath during his ministry (Luke 4:16). The apostles, following his example, continued to attend the prayers and instruction in the synagogue and temple on a regular basis (Acts 2:46; 3:1; 13:14–16; 22:17). Among the earliest Christians, there is clear evidence that they viewed their life as standing in continuity with Jewish community life that had contributed to their self-understanding as followers of Israel's God (Deut 6:4) and his Messiah, Jesus.

On the other hand, these prayers soon enough pointed to their *discontinuity* with Israel. While the Christians understood themselves in some ways as continuing within the larger boundaries of the Jewish religious community, Jewish leaders soon viewed them differently. Luke reported that they were recognized soon enough as "Christians" (Acts 11:26), or as belonging to the "sect of the Nazarenes" (Acts 24:5). Between AD 70 and 100, the Jewish community adopted a new line in its series of prayers known as the "Eighteen Benedictions" that signaled discontinuity between Jews and Christians. One of these benedictions now contained a curse against Christians. It read, "And for apostates let there be no hope; and may the

---

7. Horton, *The Book of Acts*, 48.

8. Ralph P. Martin, calls such prayers "*ad hoc*," that is, they were offered with specific contexts and needs in mind. Martin, *Worship in the Early Church*, 30.

9. Haenchen, *The Acts of the Apostles*, 191.

insolent kingdom be quickly uprooted, in our days. And may the Nazarenes and the heretics perish quickly; and may they be erased from the Book of Life; and may they not be inscribed with the righteous. Blessed art thou, Lord, who humblest the insolent."[10] This curse was intended to ferret out those in the midst of the synagogue that held sympathies for followers of Jesus, the "Nazarenes" (Acts 24:5). While personal conversations between Christians and the Jewish community would remain open, fellowship between them was no longer possible.[11]

From the beginning, however, the prayer life together bore witness to their unity as the new people of God. Their thanksgiving and praise to God were connected with their fellowship with God, now made possible in a new way through Jesus Christ and in the power of the Holy Spirit. Their prayer together declared that they were those who gathered together in the name of Jesus Christ. Their identification with his name indicated their submission to Jesus, the crucified and risen Christ, and their acknowledgment of his authority in their midst. As a result, their earliest confession became "Jesus is Lord," made possible only by the Holy Spirit (1 Cor 12:1). In their confession of faith, in their submission to the Lordship of Jesus, in their breaking of bread, in their prayers together, and in their discipleship as they gathered to hear the apostolic teaching, they had become the church, a community or fellowship of "pentecostal" believers, and their understanding of the nature of the church would henceforth define their actions.

Our understanding of the church is always dependent upon our presuppositions and the definitions with which we work. As we look at the nature of the church, we find that what it means to be the church and what it means to do what the church does are very closely related to one another. How we define the church holds implications for what the church does. A definition of the church arising from Acts 2 demonstrates that the church is the community of believers, who have submitted their lives to the Lordship of Jesus Christ. Through baptism (Acts 2:38, 41; 8:12, 36–38; 10:47–48; 16:15, 33; 18:8; 19:5; 22:16), they have identified themselves in relation to his death and resurrection (Rom 6:3). They have discovered one another in a new way; a Spirit-inspired way, as sisters and brothers who now recognize and identify themselves as being in a new relationship with God and with one another that is described as "fellowship" or "*koinonia.*"

---

10. Schürer, *The History of the Jewish People in the Age of Jesus Christ*, 457.

11. Many of the early Christian apologists continued to speak with Jews who were open to dialogue. See, for example, Justin Martyr, *Dialogue with Trypho*, or Origen, *Against Celsus*. In many cases, the apologists attempted to explain that what was promised to Israel had been fulfilled in the church. The key came in accepting Jesus as the Jewish Messiah.

Some Pauline Contributions to Ecclesiology

Called to Be One

Just as a diamond has many facets, each of which contributes to the greater beauty of the whole, so do the many metaphors used by the apostle Paul add greater complexity as well as beauty to our understanding of the church. Paul is the first New Testament writer, for instance, to use the word *ekklēsía* to describe the early Christian community. *Ekklēsía* translates the Hebrew *qāhāl* in the Greek version of the Old Testament, the Septuagint. As a noun, it refers to an "assembly" or a "gathering." In its Greek verbal form, *kaléō*, it describes those who are gathered into such an assembly, whether for secular or for religious purposes, those who are "summoned" or "called forth" (Lev 8:4). This designation reveals that the church is never a self-selecting community that gathers itself for its own purposes. It is composed of those who have been "called" or "summoned" by God (Eph 1:18; 2 Tim 1:9). God takes the active role, the initiative through his calling, which suggests according to Paul, that the followers of Jesus have been chosen, they are the "elect" (Eph 1:4, 11–15), those who have responded to God's call. They have been summoned through the proclamation or heralding of the gospel of salvation through Jesus Christ (Acts 8:35; 16:17; 1 Cor 1:21–25; 2 Tim 4:2); they are those who have been gathered into an assembly or community over which the Lord Jesus is the Head (Rom 1:6; Eph 1:22–23). In turn, they also become heralds of the good news by proclaiming it to others (Rom 10:13–15; Matt 28:19–20). Paul urged Timothy, for instance, to pass along Paul's teaching to others who would continue to pass along what can only be described as the apostolic tradition (2 Tim 2:1–2).

There are many other metaphors that the apostle Paul used to describe this new community, including the fellowship of his Son (1 Cor 1:9), the building of God (1 Cor 3:9, 16), the bride of Christ (Eph 5:22–33), and on several occasions the "body of Christ" with Christ Jesus as the head of the body (Rom 12:4–5; 1 Cor 12:12–27; Eph 5:22–33). While each metaphor reveals some unique insight into the church, what all of these metaphors have in common is the fact that *there is only one church*. When God looks at the church, he sees only *one* people. It is a people that he has called out of the world to be his own people, redeeming them through the sacrificial death of Jesus (Titus 2:14), and placing the Holy Spirit within them.

Given human nature, it is not surprising that the potential for division should pose such a large problem for the church. From the Day of Pentecost onward, the church was a diverse body, including first Jews, and then ever-widening groups of gentiles (Acts 2:9–11; 8:26–39; 10:1–48). With such a potential for division, and with so many divisive issues raising their heads in the church, it is little wonder that Paul should beg the Ephesians "to lead a life worthy of the calling to which you have been called, with all humility and gentleness, with patience, bearing with one another in love, making every effort to maintain the unity of the Spirit in the bond of peace" (Eph 4:1–3).[12] Unity is easily broken if it is neither valued nor constantly cultivated. Indeed, the issue of unity within the church lies at the heart of the Epistle to the Ephesians. Through the church, God makes visible his work of reconciliation accomplished by the blood of Christ. Those who were far off have been brought near. Through Christ, Jews and gentiles have been reconciled (Eph 2:11–13).

Paul lifts up the unity issue to the Philippian community as well. And once again he exhorts them to "live your life in a manner worthy of the gospel of Christ, so that . . . I will know that you are standing firm in one spirit, striving side by side with one mind for the faith of the gospel and are in no way intimidated by your opponents" (Phil 1:27–28). He goes on to urge them to "be of the same mind, having the same love, being in full accord and of one mind. Do nothing from selfish ambition or conceit, but in humility regard others as better than yourselves. Let each of you look not to your own interests, but to the interests of others. Let the same mind be in you that was in Christ Jesus" (Phil 2:2–5). The ability for the Christian community to be of the same mind, thereby sustaining their unity, is a sign of their maturity (Phil 3:15).

The diversity that emerged so quickly in the earliest Christian community was not merely confined to race or ethnicity. Paul's letter to the churches serving the province of Galatia made clear that while the church included diversity in race, social class, and gender, such categories were not relevant within the church (Gal 3:28). While these categories no longer played a role in the church, the church was still to value some forms of diversity.

In 1 Corinthians 12:4–11, the apostle informed the Corinthians that the Holy Spirit sovereignly distributes a variety of charisms or gifts, and then activates them so that the faithful may use them for "the common good." This passage makes clear that from the beginning, there has been diversity within the church, a diversity that stems from the sovereign action of the Holy Spirit. That diversity is present within every congregation and within the whole church. And yet, even as the apostle recognizes and notes the role of the Holy Spirit in engendering that diversity by distributing various charisms or gifts to whomever the Spirit wills, he also notes that there is unity. There is only

---

12. A similar list of character traits that those who are part of the church are expected to exhibit may be found in Colossians 3:12–15. Paul also calls attention the fruit of the Spirit in Galatians 5:22–26.

one body, and it comes under the headship of Jesus Christ. Yet each of those who are members of Christ represent a diversity in the gifts they have been given and the gifts that they, therefore, contribute to that one body. Thus, while Paul clearly prizes unity in the church, he also recognizes its diversity within which the Holy Spirit chooses to work.

Pentecostals should be able to understand better than most what it means to be *one* while at the same time being *many*. They should understand that unity within the church does not require uniformity precisely because of the emphasis that Paul places upon the metaphor of the body. "For just as the body is one and has many members, and all the members of the body, though many, are one body," Paul reminded the Corinthians, "so it is with Christ" (1 Cor 12:12). Repeatedly, the apostle speaks of the body, when describing the church (1 Cor 12:12-27; Rom 12:4-8; Eph 4:11-16) and especially in those places where he speaks of the gifts or charisms of the Holy Spirit. A charism is a specific manifestation of grace (*charis*) that has been sovereignly given by the Holy Spirit to individual Christians (1 Cor 12:11). The people of God are given various gifts, and there must be an orderly expression of these gifts within the congregation for they are to be useful to the *one body* of Christ in which they are used (1 Cor 14:26-33). It may be in its charismatic dimension, where unity expressed in diversity may most easily be seen within the church.

Called to Be Holy

No designation is more frequently used by Paul to describe those who make up the church than "those sanctified in Christ Jesus" or those who are called "saints" (1 Cor 1:2; 2 Cor 1:2; Eph 1:1; Phil 1:1; Col 1:2, etc.). Rooted in the Hebrew *kādôsh* and its Greek equivalent *hágios*, meaning "holy" (Isa 6:3; Eph 1:4), this term designates those who have been called by God, made holy, set apart, and sanctified to do the work of the Lord in the world. The apostle notes that since the followers of Jesus have been called to be "saints" they should live in imitation of him as he imitates Christ (1 Cor 11:1; 1 Thess 1:6). Even in our bodies, we are holy when we give ourselves to God (Rom 12:1-2).

With respect to holiness, Paul often employs indicative statements of fact, followed by the imperative, instructing his readers how they should live in light of that fact. Since the church is made up of holy people, a sanctified people, a people who together are the temple of the Holy Spirit (1 Cor 3:16), their lives are to reflect or provide evidence of that fact (Cf. Col 3:1-17, especially 12-17). Ephesians 4:1-3 reverses the order, but with the same intention. They have received a "calling" (*klēseōs*) with which they have been "called" (*eklēthēte*). As a result, they are to live their lives in a manner that is worthy of that calling. This discovery of who they are or who they have become, those who have been called out of the world and into Christ, holds clear implications for how they are now to live and what they are now to do together.

In a sense, the apostle holds up before the people of God, what might best be described as an idealized portrait of the church even as he writes to less than ideal people. Part of our problem in understanding the nature of the church as holy is that we tend to individualize holiness as something that we as human beings do. While it is true that in Acts, the church is very early confronted by challenges like the duplicity of Ananias and Sapphira (5:1–11), bickering between Hebraist and Hellenist Christians over the care of the widows (6:1), suspicion when Saul claims that he is now a follower of Jesus, and he wants to join the disciples in Jerusalem (9:26), and strong differences of opinion over whether gentiles must become Jews in order to be part of the Christian community (15:1–2). While in his epistles Paul addresses various congregations as "saints," he also chides them for their many divisions (1 Cor 1:10–13; Gal 1:6–19; Phil 1:15–18; 4:2–3; Col 2:20, 1 Thess 2:1–3; 3:11–15, etc.). The congregation in Corinth seems to have been particularly plagued by the failure of some to live in light of their calling as "saints" (1 Cor 5:1–2; 6:1–8, 15–18; 7:1–5, 8:4–13; 11:17–22; 14:37–40; 15:12–19). Yet while all of these challenges and failures exist in the Christian community, Paul still insists upon addressing them as "saints." He never stops there; he goes on to hold up the ideal towards which they are to strive. But in the end, it is Christ who has made his church *a holy church*, and it is this church that will ultimately appear at Christ's return without spot or wrinkle (Eph 5:25–27).

Called to Be Catholic

It must be acknowledged that the term "catholic" sometimes raises questions in the minds of Pentecostals. When the fathers of the church decided that one of the historic marks of the church was its catholicity, they did not have in mind what many Christians have in mind when they see the word "catholic." It is not a reference to the Catholic Church, headed by the bishop of Rome, the pope. Nor does it refer to Greek Catholics. The term "catholic" has a much more basic meaning than any denominational designation. At one level, the notion of catholicity refers to the universality of the church. It appeared for the first time in the letter of Bishop Ignatius to the congregation at Smyrna, about fifteen years after the apostle John completed the Book of Revelation. "Wherever the bishop shall appear, there let the multitude also be; even as, wherever Jesus Christ is, there is (*hē catholicē ekklēsía*) the catholic church" (*To the Smyrnaeans* 8). Its meaning within the context clearly refers to the universal character of the church.[13]

While the church may have begun in Jerusalem with Pentecost, it quickly spread to the ends of the earth (Acts 1:8). Paul's observation is that in spite of any geographical distance between congregations, because every Christian within those congregations has been baptized into one body (1 Cor 12:13), that is, into Christ, then every congregation is present in the whole church. There is no separation between them. There is nowhere that the church is present in this world, where your congregation is not in some way present.

At another level, catholicity conveys the idea that the church universal —made up of all who have placed their faith in the promise of God (Heb 11:1–2, 39–40) that has been manifested in Christ Jesus (Heb 12:1–2) regardless of time or place, that is, all who have been made spiritually one with the people of God in all ages and in every place—is in some way present in each local church. It is only with this concept of catholicity that Paul's remark, "If one member suffers, all suffer together with it; if one member is honored, all rejoice together with it" (1 Cor 12:26), makes sense. This fact is quite easy to see at the local level. At the universal level, one needs to think only of Christians who are suffering for one reason or another throughout the world to recognize that *their* suffering is *our* suffering as well. For this reason, the Christians in the congregation at Antioch took up an offering for the church at Jerusalem because of an impending famine (Acts 11:27–30). For this reason, Paul encourages the Galatians to bear the burdens of one another (Gal 6:2), thereby fulfilling the "law of Christ." That is why the apostle charges the Ephesians to "pray in the Spirit" and to "persevere in supplication for all the saints" (Eph 6:18). The whole church is present in each local assembly, and the suffering, as well as the honor that comes to any one congregation of Christians, is to be embraced by all, while the suffering and the honor given to the whole is to be felt by each congregation.

Called to Be Apostolic

Among the earliest names that Pentecostals took for themselves was that of the Apostolic Faith Movement. This choice of names was intended to convey the idea that Pentecostals are those who are truly apostolic, that is,

---

13. Lightfoot, *The Apostolic Fathers*, 310–12, fn2.

they contended that they believed what the apostles believed, and they did what the apostles did.

Apostolicity is a term that is used by some historical denominations, such as Catholic and Orthodox churches, to describe the process known as apostolic succession, which they understand has guaranteed the faithfulness of the church to the teachings of the earliest apostles. In the early centuries of the church's existence, Christians were concerned to follow the lines of succession through the bishops, to guard against heresy. There is no question but that as the apostles died, their successors in the church were bishops. The bishops provided stability for the congregations they served. As Paul noted, the bishop would serve as "God's steward" who "must have a firm grasp of the word that is trustworthy in accordance with the teaching [of the apostles], so that he may be able both to preach with sound doctrine and to refute those who contradict it" (Titus 1:7–9). In this way, the bishop was to "take care of the church" (1 Tim 3:5).

That the role of the bishop in guaranteeing the apostolic character of the church was assumed may be seen in the writings of Ignatius, bishop of Antioch. Ignatius wrote to the church at Smyrna about AD 105, "See that ye all follow the bishop, even as Jesus Christ does the Father, and the presbytery as ye would the apostles; . . . Let no man do anything connected with the church without the bishop" (*To the Smyrnaeans* 8–9). He conveyed similar instructions to the congregations in Magnesia and in Philadelphia (*To the Magnesians* 7; *To the Philadelphians* 7). Similarly, Irenaeus, bishop of Lyons, wrote about AD 180 that the "knowledge of the truth," that is, faithfulness to the "teachings of the apostles" had been guaranteed through the succession of bishops from the time of the earliest apostles (*Against Heresies* 4.33.8). Thus, the rules of faith (*regulae fidei*) and creedal formulations, such as the Nicene-Constantinopolitan Creed (AD 381) were intended to provide summaries of the apostolic teaching that the faithful could understand and confess together.[14]

What is clear, however, is that in subsequent years, all bishops did not live up to their calling, and the result was that at the time of the Reformation, nearly all Protestants broke with the Catholic Church over what they understood to be the episcopal office (the bishop), which they felt had become unfaithful to the apostolic teaching. The result was that the Protestant community appealed to Scripture alone, *sola scriptura*, as their all-sufficient source of authority, rather than to Scripture and the teachings of the apostles as interpreted by the bishops. Pentecostals have joined this tradition, rejecting apostolic succession in favor of Scripture as their written authority.

---

14. Robeck, "Canon, Regulae Fidei," 65–91 especially 73, 86–90.

But they have gone further than their Protestant sisters and brothers and allowed for the Lord's continuing guidance within the church through other means, namely through the various word gifts that were given to the church during apostolic times, prophecy properly discerned, tongues with interpretation, words of wisdom, and words of knowledge.[15]

Some Johannine Contributions to Ecclesiology

Just as Paul provided various metaphors for the church, so too, does the apostle John. Many of his metaphors come from the teachings of Jesus found in John's Gospel. Jesus noted that those who continue in his word are his disciples, the true descendants of Abraham (John 8:31), a theme developed later by the writer to the Hebrews (Heb 11:1—12:2). Jesus likened himself to "the good shepherd" who "lays down his life for the sheep" (John 10:11). Concern for his sheep led Jesus, shortly before his ascension, to place the ongoing care of his sheep into the hands of the apostle Peter (John 21:15–17). Jesus also equated himself to a gate through which those who entered would be saved (John 10:9). He claimed, "I am the way, the truth, and the life, no one comes to the Father except through me" (John 14:6). And Jesus used agricultural imagery, describing the Father as the vine grower, himself as the true vine, and those who abide in him as his disciples. Abiding in him is critical if the branches are to bear good fruit (John 15:1–11). While these metaphors were given to Jesus' disciples prior to Pentecost, they may be understood as applying not only to the twelve but to all who follow him. Thus, these are valid metaphors for the church today.

In his first epistle, John reminds those who read his letter that their lives must reflect the fact that they have fellowship with God, through Jesus Christ. At one level, since he is in the light, those who follow him must also walk in the light (1 John 1:6–7). The church, therefore, must be a body that lives in transparency, neither walking in darkness, nor living with unconfessed sin, nor lacking in love for one another. Indeed, John spoke repeatedly of love as a hallmark of those who follow Jesus. He quoted Jesus as commanding his followers to "love one another" (John 13:34–36). Those who love him, Jesus said, keep his commandments (John 14:15; 1 John 2:3). It is not surprising, then, that John should repeat this same expectation. The church is made up of those who love their sisters and brothers (1 John 2:9–11). Indeed, it is the love of the Father that has made us his children (1 John 3:1–2a). The church is the people in whom God's love is perfected

---

15. See Gee, *The Ministry-Gifts of Christ*; Gee, *Spiritual Gifts in the Work of the Ministry Today*; Gee, *Concerning Spiritual Gifts*.

(1 John 4:12). That is why, John exhorts us as little children, "Let us love, not in word or speech, but in truth and action (1 John 3:18). Unity requires visible demonstration of what we claim to believe namely, that the church exists as one. Here it may be understood as the one family of God.

John is the only writer to record Jesus' prayer for the church (John 17:1–26). Of particular note is Jesus' concern that all who follow him, including those who follow him through the words of his earliest disciples, should be one (John 17:20–21). Thus, according to John, the unity of the church was important to Jesus. This prayer of Jesus does not make sense if the type of unity possessed by the church is only spiritual unity. It is that, but it must also be something that is visible, for the result for which Jesus prayed was "so that the world may believe" that the Father had sent Jesus (John 17:21) out of love (John 17:23).

Some Petrine Contributions to Ecclesiology

The apostle Peter used other metaphors such as "living stones" (1 Pet 2:4), a "chosen people, a royal priesthood, a holy nation, the people of God" (1 Pet 2:9–10). The church is those who have been ransomed through "the precious blood of Christ," enabling them to place their faith and trust in God (1 Pet 1:18–21). The church is called to be holy (1 Pet 1:15–16) and to free itself from those things that are not consistent with holiness (1 Pet 2:1–3). It is to have "unity of spirit, sympathy, love for one another, a tender heart, and a humble mind" (1 Pet 3:8). Like Paul and John, Peter exhorts the church to "maintain constant love for one another, for love covers a multitude of sins" (1 Pet 4:8). The purpose of the church is to "proclaim the mighty acts of him who called you out of darkness into his marvelous light" (1 Pet 2:9). In a passage that is quite Pauline, each member of the church has received a gift (*charisma*) over which he or she is a steward. Thus, whoever speaks must faithfully proclaim the words of God and whoever serves must acknowledge that they do so with the strength that God supplies" (1 Pet 4:11).

Conclusion

The church continues to find its strength, its power, its purpose, its proclamation, its fellowship, its table, its prayer today in "Pentecost." Jesus Christ continues to speak to us directly, through the written Word and by the Holy Spirit, especially through the exercise of various charisms. If we understand the nature of the church as it has been described in this chapter, we need to ask ourselves several questions. What will be important to our congregation as we gather together for worship? What should take priority in our community life together? What will the theological curriculum look like for a person training for full-time ministry among us? What does this mean for the way we relate to the world around us?

Bibliography

Bonhoeffer, Dietrich. *Life Together: The Classic Exploration of Christian in Community.* New York: HarperOne, 2009.

Brunner, Emil. *The Misunderstanding of the Church.* London: Lutterworth, 1952.

Chan, Simon. *Pentecostal Ecclesiology: An Essay on the Development of Doctrine.* JPTS 38. Blandford Forum, UK: Deo, 2011.

Clark Matthew S., and Henry I. Lederle, et al. *What Is Distinctive about Pentecostal Theology?* Pretoria: University of South Africa, 1989.

Gee, Donald. *Concerning Spiritual Gifts.* Springfield, MO: Gospel Publishing House, 1972.

———. *The Ministry-Gifts of Christ.* Springfield, MO: Gospel Publishing House, 1930.

———. *Spiritual Gifts in the Work of the Ministry Today.* Springfield, MO: Gospel Publishing House, 1963.

Haenchen, Ernst. *The Acts of the Apostles: A Commentary.* Philadelphia: Westminster, 1971.

Horton, Stanley M. *The Book of Acts.* Springfield, MO: Gospel Publishing House, 1981.

Kärkkäinen, Veli-Matti. *An Introduction to Ecclesiology: Ecumenical, Historical and Global Perspectives.* Downers Grove, IL: IVP Academic, 2002.

Lightfoot, Joseph Barber. *The Apostolic Fathers, Part II,* 2. New York: Olms, 1973.

Martin, Ralph P. *Worship in the Early Church.* Grand Rapids: Eerdmans, 1975.

Robeck, Cecil M. Jr. "Canon, *Regulae Fidei*, and Continuing Revelation in the Early Church." In *Church, Word, and Spirit: Historical and Theological Essays in Honor of Geoffrey W. Bromiley*, edited by James E. Bradley and Richard A. Muller, 65–91. Grand Rapids: Eerdmans, 1987.

Schürer, Emil, Geza Vermes, Fergus Millar, and Matthew Black, eds. *The History of the Jewish People in the Age of Jesus Christ (175 B.C.–A.D. 135), Vol. II.* Edinburgh: T. & T. Clark, 1979.

Shane, Clifton. *Pentecostal Churches in Transition: Analyzing the Developing Ecclesiology of the Assemblies of God in Australia.* Global Pentecostal and Charismatic Studies 3. Leiden: Brill, 2009.

Thomas, John Christopher, ed. *Toward a Pentecostal Ecclesiology: The Church and the Fivefold Gospel.* Cleveland, TN: CPT, 2010.

10

A Pentecostal Proposal for Discipleship

Christopher J. Scobie

Introduction

Discipleship is identified by Jesus as the mission of the church (Matt 28:19) and for Pentecostals it is deeply connected with one's individual experience with the person of the Holy Spirit. Yet the role and responsibility of discipleship making cannot be abdicated or transferred to another. In this chapter, we will define discipleship and identify contemporary challenges. Moreover, we will briefly consider the history of discipleship within the Pentecostal movement and offer praxis for building disciples in our contemporary communities. This chapter will demonstrate that praxis for developing disciples stands on the four legs of (1) faith, (2) the Spirit, (3) Scripture, and (4) community. In order to disciple followers of Christ as he instructs, leaders will need to foster the context within their communities were faith is challenged, practiced, and engaged. The Holy Spirit must be given room to speak, lead, and empower followers. Communities that make disciples must hold the Scripture as the standard and allow it to shape and fashion each vessel. Finally, disciples are only disciples within the context of community; it is the contribution of gifts and talents, exercised in humility, that builds *kingdom people*. If any of these legs are missing the stool will be out of balance and impoverished discipleship is envisaged.

What Discipleship?

Discipleship is understood by Segovia in a more general sense as the whole of Christian existence, the self-understanding of Christians as believers.[1] The use of discipleship among Jesus' contemporaries is understood in the context of a relationship between teacher and disciple.[2] Traditionally, Pentecostals have seen discipleship as part of the process of sanctification.[3] Sanctification is in one aspect instantaneous and yet in another aspect it is "practical and progressive" as the Holy Spirit is progressively at work in the life of the believer.[4] Sanctification sets the believer apart and at the same time is evident in the transformed life.[5] Moreover, in sanctification there is a "leaving and a cleaving," as followers leave what is not beneficial (old sinful life) and cleave to righteousness (Christ).

Successful discipleship in churches must not be defined by numbers in attendance or levels of enjoyment, certainly these factors can indicate problems, but the goal is actually individual identity "in" and "with" Christ. Neither does discipleship refer to denominational unity, but it is a march towards *koinōnia*, a fellowship with Christ and his followers. Discipleship is about adherence to Christ and having Christ formed in all aspects of the follower's life as the believer lives out daily life within a context. When Jesus washed the feet of his disciples he told them that as their Lord and Teacher he washed their feet and has given them an example, they should go and do likewise (John 13:14–15). Most commentators accept that the cultural understanding of the day defines the meaning here. It was the slave's task to wash the feet of visitors, thus in Jesus' example he is teaching them of the need for disciples and leaders to humble themselves to do the least of the tasks or the undesirable tasks, to serve others and share hospitality. In this way, recipients are invited into this *koinōnia*. Paul continues this thought when he says, "be imitates of me, just as I also am of Christ" (1 Cor 11:1).[6]

---

1. The German term *nachfolge* (disciple) is used to describe discipleship as a "following-after," "emulation," "imitation," and "to convey a teacher-pupil relationship." Segovia, *Discipleship in the New Testament*, 2.

2. Ibid.

3. Cartledge, *Encountering the Spirit*, 86.

4. Menzies and Horton, *Bible Doctrines*, 147.

5. Warrington, *Pentecostal Theology*, 206.

6. Also see 1 Thess 1:6,7; 2:14; Eph 4:32–5:2, Jesus' injunction to his disciples was to be followers or imitators of his example.

Contemporary Challenges Pentecostals Face in Discipleship

Early in the Gospel narratives of the life of Jesus, He gives the general invitation to, "come and see." As the narrative takes Jesus closer to the cross the demands increase, "love your neighbor as yourself" and "love your enemy." Until, finally, Jesus declares, if you want to follow, "take up your cross daily and follow" (Matt 8:18; Mark 8:34; Luke 9:23). Knowledge of Christian doctrine and beliefs such as faith, forgiveness, grace, sanctification, justification, and redemption, etc., does not necessarily make followers. A Christian faith where Christ is not formed as the center of one's life is Christianity without discipleship, this type of faith is a Christ-less faith. Challenges to discipleship, as they have been through the ages, all seek to place Christ on the sidelines and remove him from the center of the disciple's life.

1. Since the time the Bible was penned, false discipleship-making has been an issue in the church. In Acts 20:30 Luke recounts Paul's warning of men rising up and drawing disciples away to themselves. Paul rebukes his beloved church in Corinth for creating divisions around following certain individuals (1 Cor 1:11–13). There are many examples of this down through history from the formation of cults and sects to aberrant teachings even within the Pentecostal movement itself.[7] Christ's call is to follow him, and discipleship is about moving people to be closer followers of Christ, not puppets of some present-day "anointed" leader. Jesus seems to warn against this when said, "But do not be called Rabbi; for One is your Teacher, and you are all brothers" (Matt 23:8).

2. Throughout history discipleship has seen the danger in following programs, where knowledge and even Bible knowledge is inappropriately exalted. Knowing the Bible is not synonymous with knowing Christ. Programs and knowledge in and of themselves do not disciple people. When young people come to faith there is a window of opportunity to feed and nourish them on real spiritual food. They are hungry and desire teaching. This window of opportunity perhaps lasts about two years before the culture of the local church or some other ideas disciple them. It is not that young believers stop growing, but there is a hunger of youth, which must be feed. Moreover, cultures have different challenges and the appropriateness and precision of

---

7. The "discipleship movement" or the "shepherding movement" was considered to emphasize unhealthy allegiance to the leader. See Yeakley, *The Discipling Dilemma*; Moore, "Shepherding Movement," 1060–62.

certain material changes over time. Thus, it is not uncommon to find programs that might have been effective to one group or generation outdated and ineffective with another.

3. Since the birth of the church in Acts 2, she has been antagonized by individuals who claim special and private spiritual understanding. Gnosticism leads to a rejection of the physical world and teaches that people must receive special knowledge, leading to spiritual enlightenment. This form of spiritual elitism was problematic to John and identified in his Epistles in the late part of the first century.[8] Diotrephes did not have Christ formed as his center, and his deeds and words were wicked. Today there is no shortage of people with gnostic leanings, who raise themselves to be leaders and influencers. Pentecostals, because of the self-identification as a Spirit-led people, can be susceptible. Disciples learn to discern Christ in community and "imitate what is good" (3 John 11).

4. Pentecostalism developed significantly last century in the context of increasing theological liberalism.[9] If we discuss liberalism and fundamentalism as at both ends of a continuum, Pentecostals have been accused of both extremes. We can all think of circumstances were a more discerning voice should have prevailed. Liberalism at its best could be identified as humble, open minded, and teachable. Fundamentalism at is best would be marked by maintaining courage in the face of adversity and steadfastly holding firm to its convictions. In a prevailing culture of relativism in which religious truth has been rejected by mainstream culture, Pentecostalism's claim for truth is also often rejected as arrogance. Similarly, the Pentecostal experience cannot be reduced to subjective experience.[10] Modern disciples demand affirmation of both what is true and a God who can be experienced.

---

8. Diotrephes who opposed John was considered to have gnostic sympathies. Marshall, *The Epistles of John*, 12.

9. Theological liberalism was birthed in the nineteenth century. Immanuel Kant is credited as its philosophical father. Theological liberalism subjugates doctrine to ethics and allows experience to interpret Scripture. Modern liberal scholars have embraced *form criticism* and other forms of *higher biblical criticism*, which at its extreme has attempted to remove miracles from Scripture.

10. Pentecostals believe that it is vital that every Christian experience God, since believers are sealed in the Holy Spirit (Eph 1:13). All believers should experience or grow to experience: joy, peace, freedom from guilt, God's approval, love, revelation of God and his purpose, fruits of the Spirit (Gal 5:22), etc. However, all experiences are subject to God's word, subjective experience is not determinative of truth.

5. The high cultural value of education has migrated its way into the church communities, often at the expense of discipleship. Early Pentecostalism was chided for its lack of scholarly development, and marked by anti-intellectualism. However, with a wealth of talented and well-respected Pentecostal scholars around the world, which is growing, this claim no longer holds water. The problem is particularly highlighted in Europe where culture places a high value on education. Education can be seen to replace discipleship, which shapes character and praxis. Education facilities concentrate on rote learning, academics, and bestow diplomas and degrees upon people whose character remains in its infancy. As Warrington points out, Jesus' model was ". . . 3-year, intensive, on-the-job training with a high reliance on example, character development, and practice, whilst being rooted in community."[11] Church communities abdicate their responsibility to discipleship when they send a person away for a degree or diploma and expect they will return discipled.[12]

6. Advances in technology and communication has brought our world so much closer together. According to Bower, this "Global Village" effect contributes a further culture challenge to discipleship, which is identified as a lack of realized identity.[13] Often discipling occurs across cultural barriers, across wide socioeconomic differences, and often multiple ethic groups. After the collapse of communism in 1989 parts of Russia, Eastern, and South Eastern Europe were opened up to a multitude of missionary endeavors in new ways. Mission and evangelism has always been at the very core of Pentecostalism as the Spirit empowers and enables people for witness. However, when discipling across ethnicities and conducting formal theological training, disciplers must be aware of *missionary imperialism*.[14]

---

11. Warrington, "Would Jesus Have Sent His Disciples to Bible College?" 43.

12. "A partnership between the local church and a residential College for intensive, dedicated sessions may be a suitable framework" suggests Warrington (ibid., 43).

13. Bowers, "A Wesleyan-Pentecostal Approach to Christian Formation," 58. Bowers argues that the crisis in Pentecostal discipleship is a crisis of identity, and there are five symptoms of this lack of identity: (1) Pentecostals lack theological definition. (2) In the wider Pentecostalism, there are conflicting versions of spirituality and (3) socioeconomic difference across the world. (4) Bowers raises the concern about the identity by the media (although not all Pentecostals would be overly concerned about this) and finally he identifies (5) differing understandings of hermeneutics. Bowers, "A Wesleyan-Pentecostal Approach to Christian Formation," 55–86.

14. Missionary imperialism is the idea that missionary activities and or education is directed towards the creation of churches, Christians, or ministries which look and act like those back home. Furthermore, as Vondey argues, education is biased towards

7. Finally, as this is a contribution from the Pentecostal side of the Christian family we must allow for self-examination to critically reflect upon additional areas of potential weakness. In an interview in Laidlaw College NZ, one of Pentecostal's leading scholars, Amos Yong, shares some concerns. He explains that such a rapid growth in the Pentecostal church over the past century understandably raises some questions, which need to be reflected upon when considering growing disciples:

   i. Unity—where has all the growth come from? In those situations where believers have come from another faith tradition, what is the perception of unity among Christian communities?

   ii. Discernment—are all the works attributed to the Spirit really works of the Spirit or of human excitement?

   iii. Healing/Wealth—Pentecostals see Jesus as Savior, Sanctifier, Baptizer in the Holy Spirit, Healer, and Soon-to-come King (the fivefold gospel). In some parts, healing has moved towards wealth. How do Pentecostals speak about wealth?

   iv. Poverty—the emphasis on healing creates a challenge for disciples to speak about the poor in society and the church's approach to the poor.[15]

Early Pentecostals spoke of the baptism of the Holy Spirit as a *baptism of love* or the *baptism of power*, thus, Yong speaks of a baptism of the Holy Spirit that not only emboldens and empowers for witness but is also transformational. Any discussion on discipleship needs to grapple with its present challenges.[16]

The overemphasis on healing and prosperity has been referred to as an "over-realized eschatology." This propagates the claim that the kingdom of God is manifest in an ethical and spiritual reality here now[17] and people just have to receive their healing or finances. In 1 Corinthians 15:29–42 Paul provides a rebuff to the Corinthian's over realized eschatology, a rebuff which is shaped by Paul's Christology. Discipleship in the Pentecostal con-

---

content and meaning, which is not holistic. Vondey "Pentecostal Identity and Christian Discipleship," 3.

15. Yong, "Interview by Rod Thompson."

16. Ibid., also see Kendall who writes a critique. Kendall, "Holy Fire, A Balanced, Biblical Look," 56–78.

17. Bultmann, *History and Eschatology*, 37; Dobschutz, *The Eschatology of the Gospels*, 150; Dodd, *The Parables of the Kingdom*, 35. Although we regard Bultmann's view as primarily existential.

text needs to raise hope, faith, and the work of the Spirit, in believer's life. However, this must be in the context where community discerns, the Spirit guides, and the Scriptures speak in unity.

Pentecostal's Journeying in Discipleship?

Early Pentecostalism grew out of the holiness movement in the latter part of the nineteenth century. When we speak of the modern Pentecostal movement commentators tend to speak of Topeka Kansas 1901, The Welsh Revival 1904, and Azusa Street Revival 1906.[18] Revival grew as the Spirit fell across both social and religious divides. Early leaders within the Pentecostal movement came from differing backgrounds, thus the work of the Spirit was emphasized over form and structure. In this way, the work of the Spirit was perceived as preeminent in discipleship. Furthermore, the early hermeneutical process was formed by personal and direct experience with the indwelling of the Spirit, which was interpreted through the Acts narratives. Thus, personal testimonies in conjunction with biblical texts became important in the narratives of disciples.

As the Pentecostal movement grew, the emphasis on form permitted parts of the Pentecostal family to stray towards a fundamentalist dispensational reading of Scripture, which notably shaped its understanding of discipleship. The emerging postmodern developments within Pentecostal hermeneutics have reemphasized the role of the Spirit and the role of community in reading Scripture together. Hermeneutical developments have significantly affected the development of discipleship, moving away from a focus on form, which was often accused of being legalistic. Such individual readings were most graphically noted in Europe where *classical* Pentecostals rebuked the congregation for certain haircuts, dress styles, movie watching, breaking the Sabbath, sport playing, socializing, etc. Pentecostal theology has now come of age. From the growth and development of Pentecostal scholars, a Pentecostal hermeneutic has emerged that provides a shape to reading the Scripture and thus its application in discipleship.[19]

Developing scholarly contributions have rescued Pentecostal discipleship from self-impalement on the sword of fundamentalism or from falling off a cliff and into the abyss of liberalism. Truth for Pentecostals bears reality to the context with which it speaks to. In the same way, Pentecostals are careful to avoid the ridged modernism of earlier evangelicalism, which can lead

---

18. Synan, *The Century of the Holy Spirit*, 1–68.

19. See Archer, *A Pentecostal Hermeneutic*; Noel, *Pentecostal and Postmodern Hermeneutics*; Stronstad, *The Charismatic Theology of St. Luke.*

to pharisaical legalism. Moreover, the gospel of Christ must not be related to particular political ideologies, for it is dangerous for its integrity and identity. Religion must not be used by the powerful to manipulate the vulnerable and pacify those ostracized. Throughout history, religion has been unjustly used for blatant exploitation. While Marxism is rejected as an ideology, principles such as taking care for the underprivileged can be embraced.[20] The Word of God must speak with fresh authority to its contemporary disciples, which is discerned within its community. When the Word is allowed to speak with a fresh voice, the identity of "Christ's body" can be formed among Christ's disciples with fresh and sustained witness.

Identity is the distinguishing characteristics that shapes individuals and are shared in community. It is this lack of identity, which Vondey laments, has contributed to the "disappearing disciples."[21] In a direct response to Liberation Theology Vondey argues that discipleship is a quest to understand and appropriate one's Christian identity within the cultural and environmental context and then communicate this identity.[22] The Christian faith is communicable, however discipleship "begins with self-cognitive development before it can move to socio-cognitive action."[23] The search for Pentecostal identity, which shapes the disciple, must seek an identity: (1) Spirit-centered in formation, (2) theologically informed, (3) transformational for self and community, and (4) unifying, to enhance the corporate character of Christianity in an ecumenical sense.[24]

The development and growth of Pentecostal scholarship have correctly raised the emphasis on Scripture. However, one legacy of the modern area was the accentuated quest for single correct interpretations. Jesus is the revealed Word and discipleship cannot be reduced to a search for correct understanding but a search for a deepening relationship with God, which is illuminate and mediated by the Spirit. Thus, disciples are disciples of the Word and also of the Spirit. A relationship is not a managed clinical process,

---

20. Kuzmič, "Pentecostals Respond to Marxism," 155.

21. Vondey, "Pentecostal Identity and Christian Discipleship," 1.

22. Vondey recognizes that education is biased towards content and meaning. Moreover, there is preference given to one education setting over another, which often disregards the cultural situation. In this way often discipleship is seldom holistic. Freire introduced the term *conscientization*, whereby individuals become aware of their social-cultural reality. However, socio-cultural awareness without identification of the Christian identity first is an attempt of the speaker (discipler) to produce consequences with their teachings (*perlocutionary*). This ignores the necessity of establishing identity and thus a Christian goal apart from intended effect (*locutionary*). Vondey, "Pentecostal Identity and Christian Discipleship."

23. Vondey, "Pentecostal Identity and Christian Discipleship," 3.

24. Ibid., 4–5.

but growing and dynamic. "Disciples of the Spirit display the fruits of the Spirit, which reflect the quality life of Jesus...."[25] Jesus' discipleship was to demonstrate a relationship of obedience to the Father, complete submission to the work of the Holy Spirit, by modeling the fruit of the Holy Spirit in his life. Jesus imparted character into the lives of his disciples by "example and modeling."[26] After washing the feet of his disciples, he declared, "If I then, the Lord and Teacher, washed your feet, you also ought to wash one another's feet" (John 13:14). Modeling the work of the Spirit in his life, Jesus modeled service and humility, showing not only the role of disciples but a role of disciple-making.

For Pentecostals empowerment by the Spirit is intended to manifest itself in a tangible expression of witness. Empowerment by the Spirit for witness to the gospel is not limited to congregational settings, but intended to be an overflow of the life in the Spirit in local communities and workplaces. Often there is a dichotomy between faith and application; Self recognizes this as a failure of discipleship. Discipleship is nothing less than the transformation of believers through spiritual formation, personal wholeness, relational integrity, and vocational clarity.[27] This transformation occurs as the new identity in Christ is lived out in the daily rigors of life.[28] The local church is the primary incubator of transformation,[29] but if it is limited to the church, discipleship is not complete.

Within Pentecostal scholarship, a paradigm of discipleship has emerged that shapes identity, is holistic, transformational, and participational. The paradigm includes the work of the Spirit, shaped and founded upon Scripture, in a relationship of dependence upon the Father, all grounded in a dynamic community.

The Authority for Discipleship

A Catholic is discipled through the sacraments; an evangelical is discipled through Bible studies and community involvement; a Lutheran is discipled through the catechesis.[30] Some professing Christians do not seem to be discipled at all. Pentecostals are discipled through the praxis of *faith*,

---

25. Kimber, *Disciples of the Holy Spirit*, 24.
26. Ibid., 22–25.
27. Self, *Flourishing Churches and Communities*, 71–78.
28. Ibid.
29. Ibid., 81.
30. Mattes, *Disciples in Lutheran Perspective*, 142–63.

Spirit, Scripture, and *community,* resulting in a transformed life, which demonstrates fruit.

Answers to the question of discipleship cannot be removed from conclusions to the question of authority within the believing community. The early Pentecostal hermeneutic was guided by an emphasis on the supernatural experiences within their communities.[31] Evangelism was a significant emphasis, which was often assisted by personal testimonies within the community, which allowed the community to participate in the hermeneutical process.[32] Experience has always been significantly attached to the interpretation of the Scriptures and the formation of theology. Fundamentalism did enter Pentecostalism, and this did lead to anti-intellectualism. However, although this mindset remains in certain quarters, numerous gifted Pentecostal scholars have arisen to challenge it.[33] Kärkkäinen identifies the historical development of Pentecostal hermeneutics in four basic movements: "(1) the oral, pre-reflexive stage of early Pentecostal Bible reading; (2) the trend towards fundamentalist-dispensational interpretation in alliance with evangelicalism; (3) the quest for a distinctive pneumatic exegesis; and (4) emerging postmodern developments."[34]

Archer has written at length on Pentecostal hermeneutics. He finds that the starting point was the emphasis on the spiritual experience within the community, which formed the genesis of its approach to hermeneutics. As Pentecostalism developed, it embraced modernistic approaches from an evangelical perspective. In Archer's opinion, this is a limiting aspect for Pentecostals and moves Pentecostalism away from its original missional focus. Pentecostal hermeneutics initially developed as a response against liberalism and fundamentalism. On one side was the danger of following the evangelicals too far into modernism and on the other too much attention

---

31. Archer, "Pentecostal Hermeneutics: Retrospect and Prospect," 64.

32. Kärkkäinen, *Towards A Pneumatological Theology,* 5.

33. Ibid., 4.

34. Ibid. The use of the Bible in the early development of the Pentecostal movement remains the dominant force in Pentecostal hermeneutics. Kärkkäinen summarizes as follows: Firstly, Scripture is understood as the inspired word of God, which led to it being understood as wholly dependable. Moreover, this had the effect of leaving the biblical authors in the background with a reduced role. Secondly, given the emphasis on experience, the word of God was emphasized in their context without the full weight of the distance in time between writing and the present context. Thirdly, literal interpretations of the text were preferred and little significance was given to the historical and cultural context. Fourthly, Jesus stood at the center of worship for the Pentecostals and theologically colored much of the interpretation. Fifthly, local pastors, many of whom were uneducated, were the principal interpreters. Kärkkäinen, *Towards A Pneumatological Theology,* 5–6.

was given to experience ahead of exegetical methodologies. However, Archer finds that Pentecostalism has forged a new direction that neither fully accepts the "pluralistic relativism of postmodernism nor entirely affirms the objectivism of modernism."[35] Archer has concluded that the Pentecostal hermeneutic is a tridactic negotiation for meaning between "the readers in community, the story world of the text, and the leading of the Holy Spirit."[36] In this way, experience, the narrative, and the work of the Spirit are primary legs upon which the stool of Pentecostal hermeneutics stands.

Yong is considered to be a leading thinker among the Pentecostals. While he does not delineate in detail his hermeneutics, he speaks of a theological and philosophical approach to hermeneutics.[37] Yong understands that there is a relationship between the Spirit, the Word, and the community that forms an interplay, which establishes no hierarchy.[38] Moreover, the Spirit through charismatic gifts illuminates divine truths.[39] In this way, the scriptural interpretation is discerned incorporating the religious experience of the community, theological tradition, and the Spirit.[40] Community gives the Spirit and the Word context, in this way the identity of the community is developed and shaped by the Spirit, the Word, and their own collective experience.

In making disciples, Jesus gave sermons and instructions, he discussed, asked questions, told stories, and even delegated tasks, as he communicated a vision for what his followers should be like. However, the average pastor is ill equipped and requires a little more methodology if we are to avoid the previously discussed weaknesses. Koessler presents a methodology for discussing discipleship; although not necessarily a Pentecostal contribution, in the absence of a Pentecostal methodology, this perhaps gives as a starting position (see Fig. 1).[41] Discipleship cannot be discussed apart from faith. Moreover, we should take into account Vondey, who rightly includes transformation as a fruit of discipleship. Thus, it is essentially the cultivation of faith and authority within the life of believers that forms discipleship. Finally, we find Vondey's *unifying* function of discipleship within the expression of community. Figure 1 tries to bring these accounts together.

---

35. Archer, *A Pentecostal Hermeneutic*, 198–210.

36. Ibid., 260.

37. Yong's hermeneutics is not limited to biblical theology, as he argues it incorporates the understanding of the Christian or the community within the role of narrative and tradition. See Yong, *Spirit-Word-Community*.

38. Ibid., 17–18.

39. Ibid., 222.

40. Ibid., 229.

41 Koessler, *True Discipleship*.

Fig 1. Chart of Discipleship Methodology

Koessler's methodology for discussing discipleship	Pentecostal Hermeneutics (authority)	Vondey's foci for discipleship	A Praxis for Pentecostal Discipleship
			(1) Faith
(1) Relationship with teacher	(1) Spirit	(1) Spirit-centered	(2) Spirit
(2) Instruction	(2) Word	(2) Theologically Informed	(3) Scripture
(3) Context to be lived out	(3) Community	(3) Transformational	(4) Community
		(4) Unifying (ecumenically)	

The Four Legs of Discipleship

1. Faith

Faith is authentically a human response and thus an act of the will, it is also an act of cooperation. Scholars argue that discipleship starts pre-conversion as a person contemplates how Christian believers live and behave before they enact their own faith. It is perfectly reasonable to understand that an individual modifies their behavior as a volitional act; however, in order for authentic discipleship to occur, the Spirit must be welcomed with faith in order to be transformational. God has given each person a measure of faith—thus it is a gift. Each individual has the ability to respond to God, who is the first mover, as by his Spirit he calls people.[42] In his discussion regarding faith and the reception the Spirit, Fee has argued that faith is in itself a work of the Spirit. The believer comes to faith by the Spirit, but the believer also receives the Spirit by faith. In this way, the Spirit is seen as "both the cause and effect of faith."[43] "The object of faith, as always, is Christ; the Spirit is the means whereby such faith is sustained."[44] "Faith then, is the attitude of confident, obedient trust in God and in his faithfulness that characterizes

---

42. Pinnock, *Flame of Love*, 161; Pecota, "The Saving Work of Christ," 363.
43. Fee, *Paul the Spirit, and the People of God*, 86.
44. Ibid.

every true child of God."[45] Pecota claims that the believer cannot exercise this saving faith without divine enabling.[46] While faith is a human response to the revelation, it is made possible by God.[47] The believing aspect of the will is our's, but the gift of faith and ability to believe is God's gift. Summerall argues that there are two things in particular required as responses in order for the conversion process to take hold. Firstly, one must believe (Rom 10:9) that ". . . Jesus is God from heaven in human flesh."[48] Secondly, faith believes that after Jesus was put to death on the cross, God through his Spirit raised him from the dead.[49] In this way, faith is seen as both belief and hope. Belief establishes Christ as Lord and God—"head of the body," and hope trusts and depends upon God for deliverance.

Possibly the closest biblical definition of faith is provided by the writer of Hebrews. "Now faith is the assurance of things hoped for, the conviction of things not seen" (Heb 11:1). The Greek word *hupostasis*, which is translated as "assurance," also means substance, foundation, and support. In this way faith is a foundation, which underpins the hope that believers share. Faith is a persuasion or acceptance that God is who he said he is and will do what he says he will do. Moreover, we see that there are three elements to the faith that the individual must exercise:

i. The Intellect. The writer of Hebrews describes God as the creator and cites the visible evidence that the "worlds were prepared by the word of God" (Heb 11:3). Faith is not a blind leap in the dark. Faith is the consequence of considered and a reasoned investigation. "So faith comes by hearing, and hearing by the word of God" (Rom 10:17). In this way, the disciple grows through hearing the word of God and a diligent search of God's word.

ii. The Volition. Faith reaches out and appropriates what is known and understood. Knowledge affirms the reality, but it is the engagement of the individual's will to apply these things that is the application of faith. The writer of Hebrews explains that "by faith Abraham obeyed by going out to a place" (Heb 11:8). Faith requires acts of obedience, "by Faith he [Abraham] lived as an alien" (Heb 11:9). In this way, we see that Abraham had to exercise his will. Engaging one's will comprises

---

45. Pecota, "The Saving Work of Christ," 363.
46. Ibid., 364.
47. Ibid.
48. Summerall, *Such A Great Salvation*, 173.
49. Ibid.

of two elements: the surrender of your own will or desires and the appropriations of God's will.

iii. The Emotion. There is a certain order here which must be observed: faith beholds facts and gives rise to obedience. The result of the obedience to faith brings joy. This is the correct order, faith does not look at feelings; otherwise, faith could well tremble. We note from the Psalmist that when the children of Israel believed they sang praises (Ps 106:12), however when they grumbled in their tents, they did not obey (Ps 106:25).

Therefore, discipleship must create the context to foster and develop and protect this faith. The context creates teaching and learning opportunities to develop the reasoning capacity of the believer, increasing their understanding of God's Word. The context must create opportunities for one to exercise the volitional element. Jesus fostered the faith of his disciples by calling them to follow, he demonstrated the example to them, and then as their faith developed he delegated responsibilities, sending out the seventy-two in pairs. In this close relationship, Jesus protected them, fostered their faith, responded to their doubts, encouraged them, and eventually released his disciples to the responsibility for world evangelization.

2. Spirit-led

Pentecostals affirm the role that the Spirit has in the construction of the Scriptures. The Spirit played the vital role in the transmission of Scripture, and Pentecostals believe the Spirit has a role in the illumination of Scripture. As the Spirit moves upon individuals to lead them to salvation, it is also the Spirit who mediates salvation. It follows then logically that the Spirit's role in the life of the disciple is to lead him towards maturity. Discipleship for Pentecostals is not so much assenting to creeds or ritual as it is surrendering to Christ and allowing the Holy Spirit to form Christ in the life of the believer. Pentecostals understand that they are to bring people into spiritual relationship with Jesus Christ, a relationship that is mediated by the Holy Spirit.

> Luke's notion of conversion involves not merely the salvation of souls but also radical discipleship. . . . What is the Holy Spirit doing today? Nothing more or less than what he did in the lives of Peter, Levi, and Paul: he is calling sinners to repentance, enabling the renunciation of all ties that would enmesh us with

the systems of the world, empowering the proclamation of the kingdom, and sustaining faithfulness in the way of Jesus....[50]

The Spirit is essential in the development of the life of a disciple. The Spirit sanctifies (Rom 8:13) the life of a believer, which is what Pentecostals understand as discipleship. However, more specifically, the Spirit intercedes (Rom 8:26), assures (Rom 8:16), indwells (John 14:16–17), guides (Rom 8:14), convicts (John 16:8), witness to Christ (John 15:26; 16:13), teaches (John 14:25–26; John 16:13), enlightens (1 Cor 2:10–16), encourages (John 14:25), empowers (Luke 24:49; Acts 1:18; Eph 5:18), and equips (1 Cor 12:7–11). There is little debate on the role of the Spirit in discipleship, as the disciple surrenders to the Spirit, in ever-increasing ways so that Christ is more completely formed.

In order for this discussion to carry meaning, we must theologically reflect on what is being discussed. Perhaps the more pragmatic question is this: how do faith communities create the context where the Spirit is free and unrestricted in the life of believers? The sixteenth-century Reformation refreshed the doctrine of the priesthood of all believers. The notion that all believers have direct access to God also carries certain responsibilities. The function of the priest was threefold: firstly, the priest is to intercede on behalf of the people; secondly, the priest is to carry the people's burdens before God; thirdly, the priest is to bring blessings from God back to the people. Thus, each person carries this role to meet with God, to intercede, to carry burdens before God, and to bring blessings. Recent work by Self has highlighted the transformational role of the Spirit in the life of the disciple affecting all areas of life.[51] The challenge for pastors and community leaders is how to engage congregations and disciples into this meaningful dialog, directly with the Spirit. Traditionally, this as seen as a key purpose of coming together corporately for worship: to worship together in song, to worship together in the preaching of God's word, to worship together in ministry and the flow of gifts, and to worship together in fellowship.

It has been affirmed that the summit and pinnacle of worship in the life of the church for Pentecostals is *koinōnia*,[52] where the Spirit is the source

---

50. Yong, *Who is the Holy Spirit?* 107.

51. Self, *Flourishing Churches and Communities.*

52. *Koinōnia* is portrayed in Acts 2:42 as "they [the believers] devoted themselves to the apostles' teaching and *koinōnia* [fellowship] . . . ." Moreover in Paul's corrective correspondence to the aberrant Corinth community he speaks of the cup in the Lord's Supper as "a *koinōnia* [sharing] in the body of Christ." This *koinōnia* is rooted in Pentecostal's understanding of the triune Father, Son, and Holy Spirit (1 John 1:3). *Koinōnia* is found in the Word of God as God's Son, the Eternal Word of God, became flesh (John 1:14). *Koinōnia* is refreshed in the ordinance of baptism, as the washing

of this koinōnia (2 Cor 13.13). For good reason, the Scriptures do not give us a defined order of service. Paul prescribes that when you assemble there is a time for praise, a time for teaching, a revelation, a tongue, and an interpretation, as charismatic gifts are released in community (1 Cor 14:26). However, what we do understand from Scripture is that all of these elements whether praise, preaching, testimony, or ministry, are "all done for edification" (1 Cor 14:26). All activities are to lead believers to *koinōnia*. The Holy Spirit is both the mediator of Christ and the sanctifier. In order for effective discipleship, leaders must create space for the Spirit to lead disciples to *koinōnia* where transformation occurs.

3. Biblically Informed

The third leg on the stool of discipleship is a scripturally informed disciple. It has been argued that all the Scripture is beneficial, but a disciple does not need all the Scripture. It is more important that disciples learn the practical application and benefits of forgiveness, as opposed to some of the Leviticus laws regarding the weaving together different materials (Lev 19:19). A teenager might be better served if they learn principles of honoring their parents and leaders rather than some of the available metaphorical images in the Song of Solomon. Pentecostals have long seen discipleship as part of the process of sanctification.[53] We know that Bible study programs in and of themselves do not disciple; however, in order to be a disciple and grow one must be biblically informed. The question posed here is this: What might a biblical writer consider to be key information? What should we place on the curriculum for young disciples?

Elsewhere, I have demonstrated that Paul wrote 1 Corinthians with the overall purpose of leading the aberrant Corinth congregation towards sanctification.[54] When 1 Corinthians is examined under the light of first-century deliberative rhetoric, the text is unified and shows a logical, coherent progression towards sanctification. "The body of Christ" is used as a major image in 1 Corinthians, which is designed around the theme of sanctification or bringing the church to maturity, sanctified in Christ. Paul's goal is demonstrated

---

is a symbol of the believer being cleansed by the Holy Spirit (Ezek 36:25; Col 2:13). *Koinōnia* is to embody the life of the church (1 John 3:24; 1 Cor 10:16), the communion of the believers (John 17:21; 1 Cor 10:16–17), and reflect this unity as a witness to the world (John 13:35).

53. Cartledge, *Encountering The Spirit*, 86.

54. Scobie, "A Deliberative Rhetorical Critical Approach to the Structure and Argument of 1 Corinthians."

by the rhetorical structure of the epistle and it is expressly stated in his subsequent writing. "I promised you to one husband, to Christ, so that I might present you as a pure virgin to him" (2 Cor 11:2). In addition, a survey of patristic literature shows the adaptation of and emphasis on sanctification in catechetical works, which address the historical, cultural, and pastoral concerns of their authors. Irenaeus (AD 202), Origen (AD 185–254), and Tertullian (AD 160–220) all associated sanctification as an image of the transformation accompanying the Christian life. It is this image of sanctification in 1 Corinthians which is Paul's vision for discipleship, established particularly in 3:1; 6:13–14; 10:16–17; 11:24–26; and 12:12–27.

We argue here that *discipleship is sanctification*, as the structure of Paul's argumentation to correct the aberrant believers in Corinth and bring the community towards perfection reveals.[55] For Paul sanctification addresses eight areas.

Step One: A Disciple Is Grounded in Christ: Introduction: 1:10–2:16

Narratio is the basis and purpose for a disciple. In the first two chapters, Paul delineates what is foundational to being "in Christ." For Paul the foundations, introduction, and vision for Christian living rests on being "in Christ," gaining the "wisdom of Christ," having the "mind of Christ" being able to "discern" spiritual things. As a *spiritual man* (*pneumatikos*) is contrasted with *a natural man* (*psychikos*), Paul clearly lays the foundations of what is needed to live successfully as a disciple.

Step Two: A Disciple Knows Where He Is Aiming: Main Purpose and Vision: 1:30

Prothesis is sanctification for the disciple. For Pentecostals, sanctification represents the goal of discipleship and is the goal of Paul's letter here as he corrects and teaches his readers how to live wisely and successfully.

---

55. In the first century, writers commonly wrote either *judicial*, *deliberative*, or *epideictic* arguments to convince readers of their case. Arguments would be presented with the following components: *exordium* (introduction), *narratio* (statement of facts), *probatio* (main body or proofs), and *peroratio* (conclusion). In this way Paul's first letter to Corinth follows the structure of first-century deliberative rhetoric, what Paul considered necessary to move towards sanctification.

Main Arguments of Paul: 3:1–15:58

Five *probatio* are Paul's five key sections for developing a disciple.

Step Three: A Disciple Develops Personal Standards (or Morality): 3:1–4:21

In order to grow to maturity disciples must change their personal behavior, and imitate leaders and parents in the faith, as personal behavior is foundational and an outward expression of an inner change.

Step Four: A Disciple Develops Community Standards (or Ethics): 5:1–7:40

Paul addresses the community at large and calls them to purity, devotion to Christ, and communal relationships. Christian ethics are founded on Christ's *Sermon on the Mount*, where Jesus taught, "Do unto others as you would have them do unto you" (Matt 8:12). As disciples uphold a standard of care for the other, community is built and strengthened.

Step Five: A Disciple Develops Maturity: 8:1–11:34

Paul calls for his disciples to grow into mature believers, not to misuse personal liberties, and to bring order to their communal gatherings.

Step Six: A Disciple Grows in Their Giftings: 12:1–14:39

After addressing morals, ethics, and maturity, then they are presupposed to be ready to handle the "spiritual gifts." Paul progresses through four logical steps or areas were one must reflect Christ or allow Christ to be formed. What is particularly noteworthy is the logical development of Paul's discussion, noting that personal standards must be addressed before corporate standards, morals before ethics. It is only then that one is able to speak of community worship and spiritual gifts. Moreover, in Paul's writing he understood that he had the Spirit (7:40); therefore, his instruction was actually God's instruction, in this way it was authoritative.

Step Seven: A Disciple Needs Motivation and Orientation: 15:1-58

In responding to questions of the Corinth church, Paul explains that discipleship will be completed and salvation consummated in the resurrection body. Paul discusses the four characteristics of the heavenly and glorified body. In this way, Paul not only answers questions, but also motivates believers to finish the race, which is marked out for each person.

Step Eight: Discipleship Is Personal: 16:1-24

As Paul concludes his epistle he identifies personal issues, he deals with the church and her mission. Paul demonstrates that the life of a disciple is lived out in a physical sphere, in the context of relationship. Discipleship is lived out in relationship with the church and society.

The argument for discipleship here is certainly not that one needs to follow 1 Corinthians, but that Paul wrote to correct an aberrant community and bring maturity into the lives of readers. Thus, what is important is Paul's logical development. Many of the misuses of spiritual gifts and criticisms of the Pentecostal movement would be avoided if disciples gain Paul's commitment to develop firm Christian foundations, a sense of identity and purpose, morality, ethics, and community maturity so that spiritual gifts would be handled with wisdom and maturity. For Pentecostals, Scripture is a crucial part in the disciple's development. However, in order to grow healthy disciples, Scripture must be illuminated by the Spirit, it must be interpreted and lived out in community. Faith must be watered and encouraged with increasing steps of trust and commitment. What we have demonstrated here with the use of 1 Corinthians is a logical flow of development in the life of a disciple.

4. Community Involvement

Community[56] provides the vital context in which discipleship occurs. Chan argues that it is obedience to following Christ with a life of faith that causes

---

56. Here when we speak of community we speak of the relationships within the edifice of a church. Pentecostalism generally practices a Free Church ecclesiology, which have a Congregationalist constitution and maintain a separation between church and state. See Volf, *After Our Likeness*, 9 fn. 2. (As an aside, one should not understand Jesus words "For were two or three have gathered together in my name, I am there in their midst" (Matt 18:20) as speaking about a church. The subject is prayer and that the

the believer to then connect to the church.[57] Indeed, following Jesus is what joins one to the church.[58] Using Paul's imagery of a body from 1 Corinthians, a hand cannot say they are a believer and perform the function of a hand without being connected to the rest of the body. Community is an essential aspect for discipleship as God does not want faith to be expressed in an inferior way. Human experience is social, so there needs to be a corporate expression.

The call to discipleship is also a call to discern what the Spirit is saying. As Paul is laying the foundation for what it means to be a believer, he declares that the *spiritual man* "discerns" the will of God. While this carries a soteriological content,[59] it also has moral and ethical implications. Moreover, Free Church ecclesiology calls for a plurality of leaders to discern the will of God. As a person activates faith in what God has done in Christ, the community that they join is one that extends backwards in time to before Moses and all the way forwards through history until Christ returns. Thus, when we speak about being around the table to discern the Scriptures, to discern the will of God, we are sitting at the table with Moses, Abraham, David, Daniel, Luke, Paul, saints from the early church fathers through the Reformation leaders until the present day. Thus, we allow them to speak and in community recontextualize the Word of God so that it may speak with authority. In such a way, individual interpretations are to be avoided and disciples grow in the safety and security of community.

A recognition that community refers to all those "in Christ" allows Pentecostals to foster unity on greater levels. Insecurity and a lack of Pentecostal identity have encumbered the church and led to finger pointing and name calling. However, disciples of the Spirit foster and look for opportunities to build bridges and create unity. This allows us to gain fresh strength for the building of unity, to gain afresh from Jesus' promise. "If they will be one, I give no guarantee that they will be one, but if they will be one then I guarantee that

---

spiritual authority among them is the source of their authority in prayer).

57. Chan, *Multiply, Disciples Making Disciples*, 74.

58. The doctrine of the priesthood of every believer emanating from the sixteenth-century Reformation has been an entrenched doctrine of the Pentecostal movement. However, it has been one that has often caused more liberty than Scripture permits. Paul used "the body" twenty times in 1 Corinthians—but particularly in 10:16, 11:24, and 12:27—to refer metaphorically to Christ's body, the church. Paul's use reminds us of the unity of the church, its permanence, God's plan and purpose for his church, its sanctity and sacredness, which are not always observed when we witness the church splits and divisions that have existed among Free Church ecclesiologists.

59. Fee, *The First Epistle to The Corinthians*, 117; Fee, *Paul the Spirit, and the People of God*, 83, fn. 3.

the world will know" (my paraphrase John 17:21). Unity found in genuine community of the Spirit exponentially increases witness.

Community creates the context where young disciples are able to stretch their legs and take their baby steps of faith and ministry. A loving community affords people the opportunity to grow by experiencing and practicing what has been taught. It provides safety so that if and when mistakes are made a loving and understanding community gently lifts, encourages, supports, and occasionally corrects, so that the saints are built up and equipped for ministry (Eph 4:12). Paul's vision for community is shaped by his comments to the church in Galatia, where all worldly values are removed. In God's community there is no ethnic superiority, there is no status where rich or educated gain favor over poor, and education and gender objections are removed (Gal 3:28).

The church community is God's chosen instrument, where Christ is confessed and men and women are able to participate in the divine life. In addition, God has given power to her. The church community will play a part in God's ultimate justice. In reconciling people back to himself, God reconciles relationships between humans to reflect the reality of the triune God. At Pentecost, the church was birthed and empowered, the receiving of the Holy Spirit and a continuation of the work of Christ. Thus, the church exists not for itself, but as an instrument of God.

The Path Forward

In striving to be relevant we do not want to lose our identity in the world. Moreover, in attempts to be accepted, we cannot lose the church's mission mandate. Pentecostalism was born amid the tensions of the Holy Spirit's visible work through people, a sense of the imminent return of Christ, and the needs of a vast, unsaved, and unreached world—this has not changed. Our practices and traditions need to maintain their connection with God's metanarrative as he continues to write his story in each of our lives. The error of holding onto form as sacred entrenches believers in legalism. Equally destructive and divisive is presumption and moving beyond God in practice and application of faith. It is the call of every believer to go forth and multiply, to make disciples—disciples of Christ. As we give serious attention to this, we need to declare, announce, foster, and encourage genuine faith and hope in Christ. Leaders will need to create communities of the Spirit, where he is given the freedom to lead, renew, and transformed lives. Moreover, as leaders are also disciples, they join the community of God's people through the ages to discern the voice of God in Scripture and give clarity in contemporary contexts. The Word illuminated by the Spirit in community will create opportunities for ministry and discipleship, as unity is entered into, which witnesses to the truth and person of Christ—this is discipleship!

Bibliography

Archer, Kenneth J. "Pentecostal Hermeneutics: Retrospect and Prospect." *Journal of Pentecostal Theology* 8 (1996) 63–81.

———. *A Pentecostal Hermeneutic: Spirit, Scripture, and Community*. Cleveland, TN: CPT, 2009.

Bowers, James P. "A Wesleyan-Pentecostal Approach to Christian Formation." *Journal of Pentecostal Theology* 3.6 (1995) 55–86.

Bultmann, Rudolph. *History and Eschatology: The Presence of Eternity*. New York: Harper and Brothers, 1955.

Cartledge Mark. J. *Encountering The Spirit: The Charismatic Tradition*. London: Darton, Longman & Todd, 2006.

Chan, Francis. *Multiply, Disciples Making Disciples*. Colorado Springs, CO: Cook, 2012.

Dobschutz, Ernst von. *The Eschatology of the Gospels*. London: Hodder and Stoughton, 1910.

Dodd, C. H. *The Parables of the Kingdom*. New York: Scribner's, 1961.

Fee, Gordon D. *Paul, the Spirit, and the People of God*. Peabody, MA: Hendrickson, 1996.

———. *The First Epistle to The Corinthians*. The New International Commentary on the New Testament. Grand Rapids: Eerdmans, 1987.

Kärkkäinen, Veli-Matti. *Towards A Pneumatological Theology: Pentecostal and Ecumenical Perspectives on Ecclesiology, Soteriology, and Theology of Mission*. Edited by Amos Yong. Lanham, MD: University Press of America, 2002.

Kendall, R. T. *Holy Fire: A Balanced, Biblical Look at the Holy Spirit's Work in Our Lives*. Lake Mary, FL: Charisma House, 2014.

Kimber, George P. *Disciples of the Holy Spirit*. Bloomington, IN: Crossbooks, 2011.

Klaus, Byron D. "The Mission of the Church." In *Systematic Thology, A Pentecostal Perspective*, edited by Stanely M. Horton, 567–95. Springfield, MO: Gospel, 1994.

Koessler, John. *True Discipleship: The Art of Following Jesus*. Chicago, IL: Moody, 2003.

Kuzmič, Peter. "Pentecostals Respond to Marxism." In *Called and Empowered: Global Missions in Pentecostal Perspective*, edited by Byron Klaus et al., 143–64. Peabody, MA: Hendrickson, 1991.

Marshall, I. Howard. *The Epistles of John*. New International Commentary on the New Testament. Grand Rapids: Eerdmans, 1978.

Mattes, Mark. "Disciples in Lutheran Perspective." *Lutheran Quarterly Volume XXVI* (2012) 142–63.

Menzies, William W., and Stanley M. Horton. *Bible Doctrines: A Pentecostal Perspective*. Springfield, MI: Gospel, 1993.

Moore, S. D. "Shepherding Movement." In *The New International Dictionary of Pentecostal and Charismatic Movements, Revised and Expanded Edition*, edited by Stanley Burgess, 1060–62. Grand Rapids: Eerdmans, 2003.

Noel, Bradley Truman. *Pentecostal and Postmodern Hermeneutics*. Eugene, OR: Wipf & Stock, 2010.

Pecota, Daniel B. "The Saving Work of Christ." In *Systematic Theology: A Pentecostal Perspective*, edited by Stanely M. Horton, 325–73. Springfield, MO: Gospel, 1994.

Pinnock, Clark H. *Flame of Love: A Theology of the Holy Spirit*. Downers Grove, IL: IVP Academic, 1996.

Scobie, Chris J. "A Deliberative Rhetorical Critical Approach to the Structure and Argument of 1 Corinthians." *Bogoslovni vestnik* 71 (2011) 411–24.

Self, Charlie. *Flourishing Churches and Communities: A Pentecostal Primer on Faith, Work, and Economics for Spirit-Empowered Discipleship*. Grand Rapids: Christians Library, 2013.

Segovia, Fernando F., ed. *Discipleship in the New Testament*. Philadelphia: Fortress, 1985.

Stronstad, Roger. *The Charismatic Theology of St. Luke*. Grand Rapids: Baker Academic, 1984.

Summerall, Henry Jr. *Such A Great Salvation*. Mustang, OK: Tate, 2009.

Synan, Vinson. *The Century of the Holy Spirit: 100 Years of Pentecostal and Charismatic Renewal, 1901–2001*. Nashville, TN: Thomas Nelson, 2001.

Volf, Miroslav. *After Our Likeness: The Church as the Image of the Trinity*. Grand Rapids: Eerdmans, 1998.

Vondey, Wolfgang. "Pentecostal Identity and Christian Discipleship." 2013. http://www.pctii.org/cyberj/cyberj6/vondey.pdf.

———, ed. *Pentecostalism and Christian Unity: Ecumenical Documents and Critical Assessments*. Eugene, OR: Pickwick, 2010.

Warrington, Keith. *Pentecostal Theology: A Theology of Encounter*. London: T. & T. Clark, 2008.

———. "Would Jesus Have Sent His Disciples to Bible College?" *The Journal of the European Pentecostal Theological Association* XXIII (2003) 30–44.

Yeakley, Flavil R. Jr., ed. *The Discipling Dilemma*. Nashville, TN: Gospel Advocate, 1988.

Yong, Amos. "Interview by Rod Thompson of Laidlaw Collage 19 August 2003." http://vimeo.com/71310350.

———. *Spirit-Word-Community: Theological Hermeneutics in Trinitarian Perspective*. Reprint. Eugene, OR: Wipf & Stock, 2002.

———. *Who Is the Holy Spirit? A Walk with the Apostles*. Brewster, MA: Paraclete, 2011.

11

Fulfillment of God's Promise in the Soon-to-Return King

Van Johnson

Eschatology has always maintained an important position within a theological discussion on Pentecostalism. No one who wants to understand Pentecostalism should underestimate the formative influence of eschatology on the movement.[1] The early Pentecostals' conviction about where they stood in relation to the end of all things impacted how they thought, how they acted, and how they felt. They saw their genesis as a fulfillment of Joel's prophecy about that eschatological moment when God's Spirit would be poured out on all people. This chapter, then, would not have been out of place as an introduction to this entire volume.

Biblical eschatology concerns itself with the fulfillment of God's promises. Although we readily identify eschatology with what has not yet happened, the church has been in the eschatological age since the time of Christ, when God began to fulfill his promises to redeem Israel and to bring salvation to the nations by sending the Messiah. The word "New" in New Testament (NT) is a witness to this understanding: the NT books testify that a new day in God's timetable has begun. The promises made in the Old Testament (OT) covenants find their fulfillment in the establishment of the new covenant, which Jesus said, in referring to the cross, was in his blood (Luke 22:20).

Consequently, NT eschatology refers to what God has already done as well as what he is yet to do. The focal point, of course, is the work of God in

---

1. See Anderson, *Vision of the Disinherited*; Faupel, *This Gospel of the Kingdom*; Land, *Pentecostal Spirituality*. D. Jacobsen, who credits Charles Parham with being the "founder of pentecostal theology," noted that his "apocalyptic vision . . . set the context for Parham's theology as a whole." Jacobsen, *Thinking in the Spirit*, 20.

Christ. When Messiah came, so did the eschatological age. Before he went to the cross, Jesus spoke of the things still to come, manifestations in the heaven and the earth that would precede the end of the age (Matt 24; Mark 13; Luke 21). Before he returned to heaven, he promised to return (John 14.3), and he promised to send the Holy Spirit, who would remain with them in the meantime (John 14:26). For Luke, the coming of Messiah and the pouring out of the promised Holy Spirit signaled the arrival of the last days, but not the completion of God's work. While he introduces his gospel as a narrative about "the things that have been fulfilled among us" (Luke 1:1), he later summarizes it as "all that Jesus *began* to do and teach" (Acts 1.1). The church continues what Jesus began until, as Revelation depicts with such unforgettable scenes, the final phase of God's work in the world is finally brought to glorious completion.

The type of eschatology we are examining in the NT and in Pentecostalism, which incorporates present and future aspects of fulfillment, is part of a larger category called *apocalyptic eschatology*. In what follows we will consider the nature of apocalyptic eschatology in early Judaism and early Christianity in order to know which type of eschatology Pentecostalism adopted and to appreciate how this influenced their self-understanding. We will then look at the emergence in the 1800s of a modern form of apocalyptic eschatology known as dispensationalism, which has a long history in the global Pentecostal movement. How eschatology functioned in Pentecostalism, affecting its beliefs and practices, will then be considered, including how the tendency of Pentecostals to experience what they believe made eschatology a part of their daily lives. Finally, we will give some attention to the various eschatological elements of traditional Pentecostalism, and how the book of Revelation might be redeemed from centuries of misunderstanding so that its message might be heard again.

1. Apocalyptic Eschatology

Pentecostals identify with the first followers of Jesus; what happened to the disciples on the Day of Pentecost happened to them. Such a close identification with a critical eschatological moment in the early church helps explain why Pentecostals are so at home within the eschatological worldview of the NT. They have made it their own, albeit with the aid of some modern systems to help them understand it and teach it (more on this below). The eschatological perspective of the early church derived from a form of Jewish expectation about the end-times that was circulating in Jewish apocalypses at the time of Jesus.

In general, the apocalyptic perspective is highly pessimistic about this world—a world that appears beyond even God's redemption. How does such pessimism about the present state of things align with biblical promises about God's future work in the world? What one finds in the genre of Apocalypse is a solution that originates in a "revelation," which is what the word "apocalypse" means. Typically, a selected individual or seer (or, one who sees) is given a vision or dream, or is taken up into the heavenly realms, and what he sees (e.g., God's throne, or the place prepared for the wicked and the righteous) transforms his perception of reality on earth. The message of apocalyptic literature is this: though present circumstances inspire little hope, God is on the throne, and the day is coming when the new world will appear, either by bringing the old world to an end or by transforming it.

Apocalyptic eschatology may be distinguished from prophetic eschatology,[2] which was the primary form of eschatology in the OT, where the concern was with the ongoing work of God in history. These two perspectives need not be seen as contradictory, but as complementary: apocalyptic eschatology builds on and then transcends the earthly horizon of the prophetic vision.[3] When the OT prophets declared that God would remember his covenantal promises, their reference point was the land promised to Abraham (Gen 12, 15). The glorious future anticipated by the Israelites was this-worldly rather than otherworldly. God's judgment and reward were to be dispensed within history, whether it was God's blessing upon the faithful in Israel or his judgment on those who opposed him. Even the Day of the Lord (e.g., Isa 2:12; Mal 3:1–2), an OT term for that anticipated day when God would intervene decisively on earth, was a day *within* history, not the end of it. Future hope anticipated improved *earthly conditions*, where "the wolf will live with the lamb, the leopard will lie down with the goat" (Isa 11:6) and "the earth will be full of the knowledge of the LORD as the waters cover the sea" (Isa 11:9).[4]

The OT only hinted at the existence of an afterlife. What we are familiar with from the NT—a great final judgment, resurrection to a new world

---

2. Hanson, *The Dawn of Apocalyptic*, 11. Although apocalyptic literature shows continuity with prophetic literature, and there were elements of an apocalyptic worldview beginning to emerge in prophetic literature (e.g., Zech 1–8), they are different enough to merit separate classification. Helpful here is the identification of John Collins of the conceptual elements of apocalyptic material: "supernatural revelation, the heavenly world, angels and demons, and eschatological judgment." Collins, *The Oxford Handbook of Apocalyptic Literature*, 7.

3. Murphy, *Apocalypticism in the Bible and Its World*, 1–2.

4. The Israelites were slower than their ancient Near Eastern neighbors to ponder what might lie beyond the grave. God had promised them that his glory would be seen on the earth, and so a restored Israel was the focal point of a glorious future.

for the faithful, punishment in a fiery hell for the wicked—only came into popular thinking among the Jews in the Intertestamental period, that is to say, during the time of Second Temple Judaism. These otherworldly elements were speculated about in the Jewish apocalypses. Toward the end of the OT period, however, a number of prophetic voices were being heard that God's restoration of Israel would include an afterlife dimension, and of course, this involved talk about resurrection so that the faithful could be raised to participate in it. In Isaiah 26:19 a resurrection of the righteous back to life (on earth) is depicted.[5] In this text, resurrection is itself the reward, enabling the righteous to enjoy what had been promised—the restoration of God's glory on the earth.

It is in Daniel, in particular, that we catch a glimpse of the heavenly horizon: we see the throne room scene, where the Son of Man approaches the Ancient of Days (7:9–14); we hear about a book of life that contains the names of the righteous (12:1); and we learn about a resurrection of the wise to shine like the stars in heaven (12:3). Daniel catches a glimpse of what is above and beyond at a critical moment in the nation's history: "a time of distress such as has not happened from the beginning of nations until then" (12:1). His writing laid much of the groundwork for what would become an influential literary form in Second Temple Judaism, the Jewish apocalypse.[6] Visionary scenes, such as we see in Daniel and hundreds of years later in Revelation, are a primary characteristic of apocalyptic literature. It is the immediate access of the chosen one into the presence of God and his surroundings that distinguishes the type of supernatural revelation found in them from those in the prophetic books. It is one thing to be inspired to prophesy; it is another to be granted access to the throne room itself and then given a guided tour of the heavens.[7]

To restate a point made earlier, in apocalyptic eschatology, it is the end of history that bears the hope for the people of God. Hope is transferred away from the work of God in history and toward the final judgment and the afterlife, when reward and punishment are dispensed. Like Jewish apocalyptic writers, the earliest Christian writers envisioned that the end was near. In Jewish apocalyptic literature, there was often a messianic figure

---

5. The commentators debate as to whether Isaiah 26:19 refers to a national resurrection (like Ezek 37 and the vision of the dry bones) or to a personal resurrection (like Dan 12.2–3), but I think this is a clear reference to the resurrection of those who have been faithful to God. Israel's oppressors, on the other hand, will not rise. Isa 26:13–14.

6. Jewish apocalyptic literature was written over a four-hundred-year span, from about three centuries before Christ until a century after his death.

7. J. J. Collins notes that this is a crucial element distinguishing prophetic as opposed to apocalyptic revelation. Collins, *The Oxford Handbook of Apocalyptic Literature*, 7.

involved in the consummation of world history. In Christianity, hope centers on the Messiah, the one who had come and the one who would return. Thus, the recurring cry through the ages of those who have put their trust in Christ is: "Come Lord" (1 Cor 16:22)—a cry that continues to echo around the globe in the Pentecostal movement.

The early Christians would continue writing apocalypses after the literature fell out of favor in Judaism, either by adopting and adapting Jewish writings (e.g., there are Christian additions to 4 Ezra), or by writing their own (e.g., Apocalypse of Peter, Shepherd of Hermas, and of course, Revelation).[8] Throughout the New Testament, not just in Revelation, an apocalyptic vision of what God was doing in the world and what he was about to do pervade its chapters,[9] providing the early Christians with hope as persecution threatened to destroy them.

The signs for the first Christian community that they were situated in the last phase of human history were all around them. As Jesus had said, the world was being shaken, and the faith of many in the process (Matt 24). As Jesus had said, the Comforter had come (John 15:26). The significance of the Spirit as an eschatological indicator may be described in several ways, and each of them is pertinent for a Pentecostal way of understanding the Spirit.

The presence of the Holy Spirit was an indication both that the kingdom of God had come and was about to come. Paul captures both aspects in Romans 8:23: "we ourselves, who have the firstfruits of the Spirit, groan inwardly as we wait eagerly for our adoption to sonship." The presence of the eschatological Spirit among us indicates the beginning of the end, for he is the firstfruit (or the first taste of the harvest), but his presence also causes us to groan, because having tasted of the firstfruit of the kingdom, we know the full harvest is coming soon. Our longing to see Jesus is increased, because the taste of heaven has ruined our earthly appetite. The presence of the Spirit indicates, then, that God's kingdom has come and is coming in all its fullness. Moreover, as Pentecostals know well, the power of the Spirit was also given for the expansion of the kingdom. What is described in Acts 2:4 when the Spirit came upon the 120 was a fulfillment of Jesus' promise that "you will receive power when the Holy Spirit comes on you; and you will be

---

8. It was the disaster of the Jewish rebellion against the Romans that began in 66 CE, which led to their total defeat and even the destruction of the temple itself in 70 CE (as Jesus had predicted), and then the further devastation that ensued from the short-lived subsequent rebellion under Bar Kochba in 132–35, that caused Apocalyptic Literature to fall out of favor with Jewish leadership in the second century CE. What good is there in books that engender hope but precipitate disaster?

9. See Collins, *The Oxford Handbook of Apocalyptic Literature*.

my witnesses in Jerusalem, and in all Judea and Samaria, and to the ends of the earth" (Acts 1:8). Furthermore, the gifts of the Spirit were another sign that God's restoring power was at work in the world, and they functioned to strengthen the early Christian community. They experienced the effects of exhortation and encouragement and guidance as the Spirit spoke to them in prophecy, in tongues and interpretation, and with words of wisdom and knowledge. In short, the early Christians knew the Spirit as the one who strengthens the church and brings others into it.

This potent combination of an apocalyptic view of the future and an experience of the future in the present energized the early Pentecostals. They adopted the same outlook as the early Christians—the kingdom is breaking in now with power as a precursor to the soon return of Christ.

2. Pentecostal Visions of the Eschatological Age

Pentecostalism is a restorationist movement, that is, it sees itself as restoring the faith of the apostles by recapturing the ethos of the Book of Acts. In North America, this self-perception originated with the Holiness Movement of the late 1800s, a movement that intended to return to Christianity the type of holy living prescribed in the Bible and emphasized by John Wesley and early Methodism. Since many of the first Pentecostals came out of the Holiness Movement, it is important to track its influence on the eschatological perspective of Pentecostalism.

A. B. Simpson, founder of one of the denominational offshoots of the Holiness Movement, The Christian Missionary Alliance, popularized the idea about an impending Latter Rain of God's blessing upon the church. The Former Rain was what the church in Acts experienced; the Latter Rain, what the Holiness people were experiencing. As evidence for this, Simpson pointed to the return of the gift of healing—a spiritual gift, along with the others, that was thought to have waned after the first few centuries of church history. The return of healing was the indication that the church was entering the Latter Rain, when all the other spiritual gifts would be restored as well. It should be noted that their experience of the Spirit in healing was connected to a belief in Jesus' soon return.[10]

---

10. "We may . . . conclude that we are to expect a great outpouring of the HS in connection with the second coming of Christ and one as much greater than the Pentecostal effusion [Acts 2] as the rains of autumn were greater than the showers of spring. . . . We are in the time . . . when we may expect this latter rain." Blumhofer, *The Assemblies of God*, 151.

It is not surprising, therefore, that the emergence of tongues as a widespread phenomenon in the Pentecostal Movement in the early 1900s led those within it to interpret the proliferation of tongues among them as the evidence that they had fallen heir to the Latter Rain blessing. What Simpson had foreseen—the day when tongues and other gifts would be poured out on the church—had become their reality. Pentecostal identity is linked to their experience of what Joel had prophesied. As Peter understood Joel's promise about the return of Spirit-inspired or prophetic speech as the explanation for what happened to the 120 disciples at Pentecost, Pentecostals conclude that the reappearance of tongues explains why God raised them up as a latter-day movement. As Spirit baptism empowered the first Christians to witness effectively, so Spirit baptism with the evidence of tongues indicated to them that they too were to be empowered witnesses.

Early North American Pentecostals expressed their apocalyptic worldview in a number of ways in the early years. One of the first was an adoption of Simpson's Former and Latter Rain terminology (which was said to be based on the rainfall patterns in Israel, where the early rain accompanied planting and the latter rain preceded the harvest). No one developed this more thoroughly than Wesley Myland in his 1910 publication *The Latter Rain Covenant and Pentecostal Power with Testimony of Healings and Baptism*.[11] The terminology fell out of favor among Pentecostals when it was seized by a schismatic movement in the 1940s (the Latter Rain Movement), which emerged in central Canada and soon spread to the US and elsewhere.

Along with many other evangelicals, Pentecostals would also adopt a much more complex eschatological system called dispensationalism—a schematization of world history laid out in distinct periods of time or dispensations, and built upon a collation of Scripture texts from various regions of the Old and New Testament.[12] It featured an end-times scenario that included the rapture of the church, a seven-year tribulation, the return of Christ and the judgment, then a 1,000-year millennial reign of Christ and Christian martyrs on the earth (Rev 20). The system, which originated with J. N. Darby in the UK in the mid-1800s, reached a widespread audience in North America in the early 1900s because of its inclusion in the Scofield

---

11. Chicago: Evangel Publishing House, 1910. While former/latter rain terminology became a common expression, there were other metaphors used to illustrate the lateness of the hour. In *Apostolic Faith* (Sept. 1906) we find an eschatological framework modeled on the first week of creation. As God worked for six days then rested, so after 6,000 years since the creation of the world, our millennial rest is at hand ("The Millennium," 3). See Myland, *The Latter Rain Covenant and Pentecostal Power with Testimony of Pentecostalism*.

12. Commonly depicted as seven periods. Wilson "Eschatology, Pentecostal Perspectives," 601.

Bible.[13] Some of the first Pentecostals had become convinced of the relevance of this widely popular schematization before becoming Pentecostal, and they brought its tenets and periodization charts into the new movement. Overall, the role that dispensationalism played in early Pentecostalism (and among many Pentecostals since) was a supportive one, serving to confirm what they believed from reading Acts 2:17 ("and in the last days I will pour out my Spirit") and what they were experiencing in their meetings. It had staying power within the emerging movement because it championed the imminent return of Jesus, which Pentecostals were convinced about. In particular, it was the most well-known part of the system, the rapture of the church, that proved irresistible for many Pentecostals—irresistible because the rapture could occur at any time.

Rapture doctrine refers to a catching away of believers into heaven before the great tribulation—that seven-year period preceding the return of Christ when the Anti-Christ would emerge and the wrath of God would be poured out on all humankind. The biblical text used to support this is from Paul's pastoral counsel to the Thessalonians about the fate of Christians who died before the Lord returned. To assure them that the delay in the Lord's return did not jeopardize the eternal destiny of the departed, Paul wrote that the dead in Christ would actually rise first (1 Thess 4:16), and then "we who are still alive and are left will be caught up together with them in the clouds to meet the Lord in the air" (1 Thess 4:17). The being "caught up" to meet the Lord is understood to be the rapture event. It is presumed that the saints accompany Christ back to heaven and then the tribulation begins.[14] That it must occur before the tribulation is taken from 1 Thessalonians 5:9, where Paul assures the believers that they will not suffer God's wrath.

The popularity of dispensationalism among Pentecostals is a bit ironic because the system itself rules out the existence of a modern-day Pentecostal movement. Dispensationalism limits the period of miracles to the time of Jesus and the early church, which prohibits any return of speaking in tongues and spiritual gifts later in church history. Obviously, the early Pentecostals ignored such a limitation because they were experiencing the restoring presence of the Lord with signs and wonders. Nevertheless, the dispensational belief that miracles had ceased served to affirm a critical

---

13. See Scofield, *Scofield Reference Bible*.

14. Since the idea of a rapture of the saints before the tribulation originated from a revelation given in a charismatic prayer meeting in the early 1800s, it is fair to say that the Thessalonians might have interpreted Paul's meaning differently: the saints meet the Lord in the clouds before he comes to the earth. This would accord with an ancient practice where the people of a city would go out to meet the king and escort him back into the city.

aspect of Pentecostal self-identity as a restoration movement. If what they had been told was true, that the gifts of the Spirit had ceased ("cessationism") shortly after the time of Jesus, but it was also true that the Pentecostals were experiencing the gifts, then the logical conclusion was this: God was doing it again, restoring what had been lost and completing what he had begun at Pentecost in Acts 2.

3. Pentecostal Movement and Its Eschatological Ethos

"Pentecostals do not simply affirm a list of biblical beliefs; they have encountered them experientially," wrote Keith Warrington.[15] As with other Pentecostal beliefs, eschatological ones have an experiential component. How could Pentecostals experience the truth of what had not yet occurred? As in the early church, the belief in the soon return of Jesus was so fundamental to them that all of their beliefs and practices were influenced by this central hope. What motivated the early Pentecostals was a longing to see Jesus, and this affected everything else about them.

They lived out the implications of the future in the present, and in so doing, reinforced their belief in Christ's future return, or the *parousia*. They acted in accordance with their belief about the future by encouraging the faithful to persevere, exhorting the wandering to come home, and evangelizing the sinner to repent. Time, for them, was short. If Pentecostal belief and practice were to be diagrammed by the use of a wheel, with the spokes depicting the various beliefs and practices of the movement, the axle would be the soon return of Jesus. Although belief in the soon return of Jesus is not the characteristic that Pentecostals are most known for—that honor belongs to speaking in tongues—this conviction was the integrating belief of their spirituality. It was an idea so deeply embedded in their collective consciousness that it affected all other dimensions of their spirituality.

This section is concerned with how eschatology functioned in Pentecostalism. To begin with, the early Pentecostal experience with tongues and the gifts of Spirit intensified their belief in the imminent return of Christ. As the early Christians experienced their eschatology, so did these first Pentecostals. As early Christians understood the baptism of the Spirit, the outpouring of the Spirit as first described in Acts 2, as eschatological, so did the Pentecostals. If Peter could say on the Day of Pentecost that what they were experiencing was the sign of the last days (Acts 2:17), then early Pentecostals were convinced that it must be the last of the last days because

---

15. Warrington, *Pentecostal Theology*, 22.

God was pouring out his Spirit again. The formation of their identity as a people raised up by God to participate in an end-times revival draws heavily on Peter's declaration in Acts 2.[16]

They experienced their eschatology in their worship. A common thread in the early testimonies was the degree to which the shared experience of the presence of God in worship resulted in their sense of being drawn closer to Jesus. The Christocentric direction of their affections comes out in their testimonies and songs of praise. When they expressed love for God or sang praise, it was typically not addressed directly to the Spirit of God. That is not to say they did not recognize the presence of the Spirit and cherish the gift of his presence. A favorite chorus at Azusa Street (which echoed around the globe in Pentecostal gatherings) was "The Comforter Has Come." They welcomed the Spirit, they relied on the Spirit, they sensed his moving, but they understood that the Spirit was directing them to Jesus. As the early Pentecostals experienced the presence of Jesus, it reinforced their belief that his return was near. As they felt him near, they thought his return was near. In other words, the belief in Jesus' soon return (his imminent return) and their experience of him in worship (his immanent presence) were mutually reinforcing. Let us examine a few specific aspects of the Pentecostal ethos and note how eschatology shaped each of them.

Spirit Baptism

As said above, the restoration of Spirit baptism among them influenced their self-perception as an end-times movement. More than this, they saw Spirit baptism with tongues not only as a sign of the end but also the means by which the end would come. The empowerment for witness, which was what tongues speech evidenced, would enable them to be part of a last great harvest of souls before Jesus returned. They thought Acts 1:8 was about to be fulfilled in them: empowerment to go to the ends of the earth. For this reason, speaking in tongues was not reduced to something personal and recreational. Pentecostals, when true to their tradition, remember that the precious gift they have been given is not for personal edification, even though

---

16. For example, this eschatological conviction infused the beginnings of Pentecostalism in Canada. The first Pentecostal newsletter (May 1907), which announced the beginning of the revival in Toronto, was named *The Promise*. Underneath the title was the text from Acts 2:39, which is the conclusion of Peter's exhortation to the crowd on the day of Pentecost. Having just mentioned the gift of the Holy Spirit (Acts 2:38), Peter proclaims "the promise is for you and your children and for all who are far off" (Acts 2:39). In naming their newsletter *The Promise*, they reveal their eschatological self-understanding as the fulfillment of Joel's prophecy.

they rejoice in how praying in the Spirit has reenergized their Christian lives. The return of Jesus gives urgency to this experience, with the result that Spirit baptism becomes outward-focused rather than inward-focused. This is one of the distinguishing marks of the Pentecostal movement.

Here we may distinguish a traditional Pentecostal understanding of Spirit baptism from a charismatic one. Generally speaking, where a charismatic is likely to see the work of the Spirit, including speaking in tongues, as enabling church renewal, a Pentecostal is more likely to see the natural outcome as revival. The former sees a strengthening of the church; the latter, a growth of the church as revival leads to conversion. One is prone to draw on Pauline references to the work of the Spirit in strengthening the body of Christ, and the other, the Lukan perspective on the Spirit and mission to the world.

Gifts of the Spirit

How they perceived and exercised the gifts of the Spirit was influenced by their focus on the return of Jesus. A clear distinction was made early on between the tongues accompanying Spirit baptism (evidential tongues) and the gift of tongues (in tandem with the gift of interpretation) that Paul describes in his lists of spiritual gifts (1 Cor 12:10, 30). While Pentecostals saw tongues accompanying Spirit baptism as available to all and as the indication of individual empowerment for witness, they put in a different category the gift of tongues, which required interpretation to be of benefit in a church service. Since none of the gifts are given to all (1 Cor 12:30, "do all speak in tongues?"), not everyone was expected to use the gift of tongues as a means of conveying a message in church. As a gift of the Spirit, it was for the benefit of the body (1 Cor 7:12, "the common good"). Tongues and interpretation along with other speaking gifts brought exhortation and encouragement to the early Pentecostals. Healings and other miracles served to reinforce the belief that the transforming power of God was in their midst. Pentecostals know from experience how the power of spiritual gifts renews a community of believers.

While Pentecostals share this understanding of the edifying role of gifts with others in the charismatic movement, it was the Pentecostal anticipation of the *parousia* that gave them an evangelistic perspective on the spiritual gifts. If Jesus is coming soon, every opportunity must be seized for witness, even in regards to the gifts of the Spirit. As was the case in the time of Jesus, where signs and wonders drew a crowd, so it has happened, time and time again, with Pentecostals. Whether by their testimonies to friends and strangers, or because of the newspaper reports that soon circulated (about their "strange practices"), the presence of outsiders has been normative in Pentecostal meetings. This has kept the gifts of the Spirit from being reduced to a benefit for Christians alone. Appropriately, an altar call for salvation is a standard fixture of a Pentecostal service.

One of the reasons the Lord blessed the early Pentecostals, surely, was their sense that what the Lord did for them in their meetings was to be testified about to others. The practice of spiritual gifts afforded opportunities for witness. It may be the case that a decline in the incidents of healing in some parts of the globe is related to a loss of vision for God's purposes in administering his grace. Perhaps we grieve the Holy Spirit when eschatological urgency no longer orients our perception of the gifts of God, and we misinterpret God's grace to us as a simply personal blessing rather than as a sign to be seen by others that the kingdom is here. May we not lose sight of the power of the testimony of one who has been touched by the power of God.

One of the more dramatic examples of a gift of the Spirit serving evangelistically is the gift of tongues as *xenolalia*, or a foreign language (as opposed to *glossolalia*, which is speech in an unidentifiable language). Reports have circulated throughout the Pentecostal world about incidents in church of *xenolalia* (sometimes called "missionary tongues"). The reports go something like this: a visitor attending a Pentecostal meeting hears an individual declaring a word from God in his or her own native language, only to find out later that the speaker had no idea what he was saying or what language she was speaking. The story usually ends like this: the individual becomes a believer. Our experience has shown us that this function of tongues is not a regular occurrence, but when it does occur it reminds us how every work of God testifies to his redeeming presence in the world.

Witness

Having considered the evangelistic orientation of the practice of Spirit baptism and the gifts of the Spirit among Pentecostals, we now discuss this evangelistic orientation itself. Their belief in the soon return of Jesus ignited a movement to win the lost. Whether evangelism at home or missions abroad, the Pentecostal tradition is to respond to the lateness of the hour by proclaiming the good news with the empowering of the Spirit. It has been said that Acts 1:8 ("you will receive power when the Holy Spirit comes on you; and you will be my witnesses in Jerusalem, and in all Judea and Samaria, and to the ends of the earth"), rather than Matthew 28:19-20, is the Great Commission of Pentecostalism.

Charles Parham, a Holiness preacher turned Pentecostal, played a central role at the beginning of Pentecostalism in popularizing the view that tongues were the biblical evidence of Spirit baptism (establishing in American circles an association made earlier by Edward Irving in London).[17] He thought that all who spoke in tongues when they were baptized in the Spirit were speaking an earthly language that was unknown to them, but would be understood by the right audience. Parham saw *xenolalia* as normative rather than occasional, enabling the cause of missions to be expedited. Missionaries would span the globe without being slowed down by language training. It wasn't long before the majority of Pentecostals realized that tongues indicated that power for witness had been given, rather than Parham's idea that tongues were the means of witness. Tongues speech in Acts 2 by the 120 drew an audience and sparked curiosity, but it was the sermon of Peter, a newly Spirit-baptized individual, which he preached in the language common to them all (Aramaic) that resulted in 3,000 conversions. Although Parham was mistaken about the role and frequency of *xenolalia*, his connection of tongues to evangelism has proven invaluable for the Pentecostal movement.

Holiness

The Pentecostal movement emerged in many parts of the globe from some variant of the Holiness movement. That explains why a Holiness code of behavior is still common among Pentecostal people. What eschatological urgency among Pentecostals did was to maintain holiness as a primary way of expressing piety, and in some cases, it heightened the intensity of the holiness they practiced. As they often exhorted one another: "The Lord is coming for a spotless Bride." It is a misperception of Pentecostal holiness to view it as a rejection of all pleasure. Rather, they lived carefully so as to preserve the greater joy they had found in Jesus. The reality of the coming kingdom eclipsed the attraction of fleeting pleasure.

Otherworldly Values

The orientation of early Pentecostalism was toward the coming world rather than the present one. As it did in the NT church, the imminent return of Jesus dominated their horizon, redirecting their affections toward a coming kingdom. That does not mean that Pentecostals were so heavenly minded

---

17. McGee, "Initial Evidence," 784–85.

that they were unaware of what was going on around them. Grant Wacker contends that Pentecostalism survived and thrived because it was a movement that was both primitive and pragmatic, that is, a movement that strove for a return to things of the Spirit (the primitive), but also exhibited a realism that allowed her to adjust her otherworldly perspective to the realities of life (the pragmatic).[18] One of those realities was the delay in the return of Messiah. As the movement has passed its centennial, we now see an adjustment in the focus of some Pentecostal communities around the world. Pentecostals are now more likely to engage in the type of social engagement that requires long-term participation than in the early years when the imminent return of Jesus dominated their horizon.

Inclusivity

The inclusivity of Pentecostalism, the fact that both men and women are valued for their contributions, betrays an eschatological self-understanding. The prophetic text cited in Acts 2, where Joel's vision of the Spirit coming on all people without regard for gender, age, or status, set the social standard for the movement in its pre-denominational phase.[19] This text was taken seriously at 312 Azusa Street, Los Angeles, where a racially integrated leadership team was formed in the first few months, and at 651 Queen Street East, Toronto, where a woman, Ellen Hebden, led the beginnings of Canadian Pentecostalism. The urgency of the hour demanded full participation; the urgency of the hour would not permit half of the team to watch from the sidelines as spectators.

4. Future Events and Eschatological Systems

Premillennialism, Postmillennialism, and the Rapture

We consider now the Pentecostal understanding of future events like the parousia or the return of Jesus, the judgment, the resurrection to reward or punishment, and the millennium, and the systems they have adopted that

---

18. Wacker, *Heaven Below*, 10–14.

19. Women tend to fare better in terms of status and opportunity when Pentecostalism bears more of a resemblance to a movement than it does to a denomination. When the issue is mobilizing all resources for the sake of a cause, women gain opportunity. With denominations come hierarchies, and in hierarchies, where the issue is one of authority over others, women tend to lose out to men. Unless, of course, a woman starts her own denomination, as Aimee Semple McPherson did by establishing the Foursquare Gospel Association in 1923.

order those events into an end-times calendar. It will come as no surprise to anyone familiar with various Christian traditions that there is no one standard scheme for imagining the end of the world and what lies beyond it. The variety of expressions among believing communities reflects the difficulty in systematizing a subject that is not presented systematically in the biblical text. One may also factor in the differing social contexts of various theological traditions as a reason for the disparate views that are held. As is the case with theology in general, an eschatological understanding is shaped not only by the biblical text but also by the social situation of the interpreter. What is shared, however, is the apocalyptic worldview, according to which hope for the world is ultimately realized when history has come to its end and justice is served on the righteous and the wicked.

The return of Jesus has been and remains the great hope of the church for all believers, especially for Pentecostals. While the certainty of his return is a shared Christian conviction, the timing of his return in relation to other end-time events, particularly the millennium, is debated. A simple way to categorize some of the various scenarios of the sequence of eschatological events is to answer two questions. First, does the Lord come before the millennium (premillennial return) or after (postmillennial return)? That is, before things on earth improve or afterwards? Although there is a metaphorical interpretation of the millennium (amillennialism), which sees millennial language as a symbolic description of the blessedness of the period between Jesus' death and his return instead of an actual period of 1,000 years at the end of history, the tendency of Pentecostals to read the text literally means that they tend to envision it as a future event.[20] The book of Revelation contains the NT description of a millennium, a 1,000-year period (which is what "millennium" means) when Christ will rule on the earth with the righteous who had been martyred (Rev 20:1—21:5).

The second question: if Christ comes before the millennium (the traditional Pentecostal view), does he also come for the church even earlier than that? That is, is there a rapture of believers into heaven immediately preceding the seven years of tribulation on earth (another traditional Pentecostal view)?

In general, a premillennial view is more pessimistic about the immediate future and postmillennialism is more optimistic. For example, postmillennialism flourished in the United States in the 1700s, riding the wave of optimism created by the Great Awakening that the nation was rapidly becoming Christian. Some believed that this significant revival, which

---

20. Warrington cites Menzies and Horton, *Bible Doctrines*: "the pre-millennial view is the only one that takes the Bible as literally as it is intended to be." Warrington, *Pentecostal Theology*, 236.

is associated with Jonathan Edwards, would lead into a golden age of the church of 1,000 years, and that the Lord would return in triumph at the end of it. While postmillennialism tends to be a minority view in the Pentecostal world, its message is being carried along in the charismatic movement. Part of the reason for this is the success that the Pentecostal and charismatic movements have had in reshaping and reenergizing global Christianity. With the estimates of the numbers of Pentecostal/charismatics ranging as high as 500 million,[21] some have become convinced about the church's ability to win the world and prepare it for Christ's triumphal return.

The premillennial view, by way of contrast, is pessimistic about the immediate future. It perceives as evidence of the soon return of Jesus the signs of decay within society, the physical upheavals on the earth (e.g., famine, earthquakes), the suffering of believers, and even the departure of some from the faith (Matt 24; 1 Pet 4:12–19). Yet, underlying this worldview is great hope: deteriorating conditions on earth signal the *parousia*. And, for Pentecostals, the Lord's return is preceded by a final great revival in which they participate. What Jesus commissioned his first followers to do—be witnesses to the ends of the earth (Acts 1:8)—Pentecostals adopt as their commission.

If we decide he is returning before the millennium, is he coming in advance for believers in the rapture of the church? Whether one anticipates two returns of Jesus—one before the tribulation to take the church out of the world and another at the end of the tribulation[22]—or just one before the millennium, whether one perceives that the worst is yet to come on the earth and the church will share no part in it or that the tribulation is the present reality of the persecuted church, what must not be neglected is the doctrine of the resurrection. It is sometimes marginalized because of the debate about the when and how of Jesus' return. When Jesus returns, there is resurrection: the dead in Christ are raised to be reunited in the clouds with the saints who are still alive (1 Thess 4:13–17). In 1 Corinthians 15:42–54, Paul describes resurrection as a transformation of the earthly body into a heavenly one, that is, into a state of existence that is still bodily, but now fit for eternity. Resurrection is not the same as being revived or brought back to life in the same earthly form, which is what happened to Lazarus (John 11). Resurrection involves transformation: "we will not all sleep, but we will all be changed" (1 Cor 15:51). Nor should this biblical idea be confused with the Greek conception of the immortality of the soul, where the body is

---

21. Barrett and Johnson, "Global Statistics," 284–320.

22. The rapture return of Jesus is to be distinguished from his return to earth at the end of the tribulation, a return that triggers the judgment and leads into the period of the millennium.

discarded as the soul lives on. Resurrection is the fitting conclusion to the biblical story that began with the Genesis account of humanity's creation. In Judeo-Christian thought, one can only enjoy the blessedness of eternal life as an *embodied* being. Because Jesus was resurrected, we will be as well (Rom 6:5). Created with earthly bodies, we will be recreated with spiritual ones (1 Cor 15:44).

One of the defining characteristics of Jewish apocalyptic literature is the central role played by a great, final judgment. This belief is also central to Christianity. How could it not be? Since the character of God in both testaments is revealed to us as righteous, how could he not make all things right at the end? The judgment is consistent with his righteousness. That day will divide the ages between this world and the one to come; it will divide the righteous from the wicked, assigning to all who have lived their separate eternal destinies. In addition, the judgment day will reveal to the world the true identity of God's people, and conversely, it will show who are the enemies of God. Note, for example, Paul's conviction that creation itself is longing for the day when the people of God are revealed on the earth (Rom 8:19). Various judgments are described in the NT,[23] but it is the white-throne judgment that is portrayed in Revelation as the final one (Rev 20:11–15). That a just God would punish the wicked and reward the righteous is also a fixture in a Pentecostal worldview. With a history as a marginalized or persecuted people, Pentecostals know what it is to long for the justice of God.

While the judgment determines the final destiny of all, the resurrection equips each individual with the necessary constitution to experience heaven or hell, which Pentecostals tend to believe are both eternal states. The essence of both places hinges on the variable of the presence of God. Hell is where God's presence is not (and as such, it is a horrific place). Heaven is where God's presence is. In the new heaven and the new earth, there will be no distance between God and his people. In terms reminiscent of the fellowship God had with Adam and Eve before the fall, John wrote of the day when God would dwell in the midst of his people and wipe every tear from their eyes (Rev 20:1–4). NT authors express the beauty of God's presence and the horror of its absence with terms and symbols drawn from OT and intertestamental literature. For instance, fire in the afterlife (e.g., the Lazarus parable, Luke 16:19–31) recalls the use of fire in the OT as an instrument of judgment (e.g., Gen 19:24 [Sodom and Gomorrah]; Isa 66:24).

---

23. See Stanley and Wilkin, *Four Views on the Role of Works at the Final Judgment*.

5. Genre Apocalypse and the Book of Revelation

We have discussed the primary ideas of an apocalyptic worldview. Here we consider the type of literature that popularized those ideas in order to reconsider how we might read Revelation. One of the exciting developments in biblical studies over the last half-century has been in the area of genre analysis, which begins with the recognition that the biblical books may be categorized by the various ancient genres (or literary categories) they adopted to communicate their message. So, the book of Revelation is being re-examined as part of the genre of apocalypse.[24] This last category is foreign to the modern reader, which is one of the reasons that the history of the interpretation of Revelation is so diversified. To put it simply: we don't know what we are reading. At the heart of the problem is the tendency to read literally what was meant to be symbolic. This has been an issue for Pentecostal readers for whom a literal reading of a biblical text is usually the preferred one.

Apocalyptic literature is marked by the use of symbolism to depict visions of the realm that is above in the heavens and the realm that exists beyond time. Symbolism functions to impress a vivid image or scene upon the hearer, with the intended effect being more about impression than description. Apocalyptic literature stirs the imagination; it invites a new view of the cosmos to transform the worldview of its hearers. The apocalyptic writer did not aim for precision in detail or even consistency in the imagery that was used (why use symbols if clarity had been the intention?). Rather, the goal was to stir the heart and motivate action; these writers were encouraging the faithful and exhorting the wayward with the hope that God was about to fulfill his promises. Based on this type of genre analysis, any interpreter of Revelation who searches for a logical, linear presentation of the end-times will be overwhelmed with despair—or exhilarated at the myriad interpretive possibilities!

The book of Revelation has a long history of significance in Pentecostalism, and so its importance for the movement should motivate us to preserve its message and to experience its power. Its glorious visions of Jesus, of God on his throne, of the judgment to come, have stirred generations. A futurist view of Revelation is still quite common among Pentecostals, where the majority of events described in it are perceived as yet to occur. Pentecostals are as interested as anyone else in biblical prophecy and what the book of Revelation has to say about the conditions of the end, even though their interest goes beyond the speculative. Because Pentecostals expect to

---

24. See Collins, *The Apocalyptic Imagination*.

experience the glory of God now and because they expect to see visions now, they are very much at home in the world depicted in Revelation.[25] Their experiential approach to spirituality has allowed them to feel as if they are in those scenes depicting worship around the throne.

The danger is that speculation about the historical referents for the symbols, such as the identity of the Anti-Christ (who is not named in Revelation) and the number of the beast, may cause us to miss the central emphases of the book. Encouragement and exhortation are the intended effects (and these are also the central emphases of Jewish apocalypses). Encouragement is extended to the faithful that their sufferings and endurance are not in vain: God is on his throne, and he will reward the righteous. Exhortation is given to those who are outside the believing community that the way of the world will end in disaster: God is on his throne, and he will judge the wicked.

6. Conclusion

If the defining characteristic of NT eschatology is its already/not yet perspective (i.e., God's kingdom is here now, but not yet in its fullness), then the primary characteristic of Pentecostal eschatology is that the return of Jesus—the focal point of the "not yet"—is coming soon. The return of Jesus dominates Pentecostal eschatological expectation. This belief has been so central to the dynamic of Pentecostalism that any de-emphasis of it will alter the nature of Pentecostalism significantly. Maybe this has already occurred. The popularity of dispensationalism appears to be waning in some sectors of Pentecostalism and with it the belief in a pre-tribulation rapture of the church. Dispensationalism is, however, just one scheme within a premillennial understanding of the return of Jesus. The conviction that Jesus will return before the world enjoys a golden millennium both predates the emergence of dispensationalism and may be preached without it.

What is worrisome is that a loss of interest in the system that includes the imminent return of Jesus will spell a loss of interest in the return of Jesus himself.[26] If Pentecostals stop using the dispensational timetables, will they stop preaching about his return? If the expectation of the soon

---

25. See Archer, '*I Was in the Spirit on the Lord's Day*'; Thomas, *The Apocalypse*; Waddell, "The Spirit in the Book of Revelation."

26. "The Pentecostal movement arose in an atmosphere of fervent anticipation of the second coming of Christ; this imminent expectation is revealed in the titles of Pentecostal journals: *The Bridal Call, The Last Trump, I Come Quickly, The Evening Light and Church of God Evangel, Maranatha, The Midnight Cry, The End-Time Messenger*. As each denomination grows older, these titles for their journals tend to be abandoned." Hollenweger, *The Pentecostals*, 415.

return of Jesus has been the integrating component of Pentecostalism, what will the movement look like if it settles in for the long haul on earth? Maybe it will be something beneficial for the kingdom, but not Pentecostalism as we have known it. There are indications that the improvement in socio-economic conditions of Pentecostals in some parts of the globe is accompanied by a waning of interest in the soon return of Jesus.[27] The temptation facing Pentecostals who are moving up in the world is that the longing for the next world will decrease. And while there is much good that can come out of social action that improves the lot of the poor and the marginalized, if Pentecostals lose their next-world orientation in the process, the costs outweigh the benefits.

This movement built on the imminent return of Jesus is in its second century. Adjustments in thinking and behavior are inevitable. As the early church had to adapt to the delay in the return of Christ, so must we. Yet, like the NT community, Pentecostals are typically optimistic about the world to come and pessimistic about this one. Of greater significance for the future of Pentecostalism than the abandonment of a pre-tribulation rapture would be the loss of a premillennial disposition. May the hope engendered by the return of Jesus compel us until he returns.

Bibliography

Anderson, R. *Vision of the Disinherited: The Making of American Pentecostalism*. New York: Oxford University Press, 1979.

Archer, M. *"I Was in the Spirit on the Lord's Day": A Pentecostal Engagement with Worship in the Apocalypse*. Cleveland, TN: CPT, 2015.

Barrett, D., and T. Johnson. "Global Statistics." In *The New International Dictionary of Pentecostal and Charismatic Movements*, edited by Stanley Burgess and E. Van der Maas, 283–302. Grand Rapids: Zondervan, 2002.

Blumhofer, E. *The Assemblies of God: A Chapter in the Story of American Pentecostalism*. Vol. 1. Springfield, MO: Gospel, 1989.

Burgess, S., and E. Van der Maas, eds. *The New International Dictionary of Pentecostal and Charismatic Movements*. Grand Rapids: Zondervan, 2002.

Collins, J. J. *The Apocalyptic Imagination*. 2nd ed. Downers Grove, IL: IVP, 1998.

———, ed. *The Oxford Handbook of Apocalyptic Literature*. New York: Oxford, 2014.

Faupel, D. *This Gospel of the Kingdom: The Significance of Eschatology in the Development of Pentecostal Thought*. Sheffield, UK: Sheffield Academic Press, 1996.

Hanson, P. *The Dawn of Apocalyptic*. Philadelphia: Fortress, 1975.

Hebden, E., ed. *The Promise*. Toronto, May, 1907.

Hollenweger, W. *The Pentecostals*. Peabody, MA: Hendrickson, 1972.

Horton, S., and W. Menzies. *Bible Doctrines: A Pentecostal Perspective*. Springfield, MO: Gospel, 1994.

27. Warrington, *Pentecostal Theology*, 313.

Jacobsen, D. *Thinking in the Spirit: Theologies of the Early Pentecostal Movement.* Indianapolis: Indiana University Press, 2003.

Land, S. *Pentecostal Spirituality. A Passion for the Kingdom.* Sheffield, UK: Sheffield Academic Press, 1993.

McGee, G. "Initial Evidence." In *The New International Dictionary of Pentecostal and Charismatic Movements,* edited by S. Burgess and E. Van der Maas, 784–90. Grand Rapids: Zondervan, 2002.

Murphy, F. *Apocalypticism in the Bible and Its World.* Grand Rapids: Baker, 2012.

Myland, D. W. *The Latter Rain Covenant and Pentecostal Power with Testimony of Pentecostalism.* Vol 1. Springfield, MO: Gospel, 1989.

Scofield, C. I. *Scofield Reference Bible.* Oxford: Oxford University Press, 1909.

Seymour, W., ed. *The Apostolic Faith.* Los Angeles: Azusa Street Mission, 1906.

Stanley, A., and Wilkin, R. *Four Views on the Role of Works at the Final Judgment.* Indianapolis: Indiana University Press, 2003.

Thomas, J. C. *The Apocalypse.* Cleveland, TN: CPT, 2012.

Wacker, G. *Heaven Below: Early Pentecostals and American Culture.* Cambridge: Harvard University Press, 2001.

Waddell, R. "The Spirit in the Book of Revelation." JPT 30. Blandford Forum, UK: Deo, 2006.

Warrington, K. *Pentecostal Theology: A Theology of Encounter.* London: T. & T. Clark, 2008.

Wilson, D. "Eschatology, Pentecostal Perspectives." In *The New International Dictionary of Pentecostal and Charismatic Movements,* edited by S. Burgess and E. Van der Maas, 601–5. Grand Rapids: Zondervan, 2002.

12

Pentecostalism and Ecumenism
Past, Present, and Future

AMOS YONG

Introduction

IN THIS PAPER, I would like to raise and attempt to answer four questions.[1] First, is there a biblical ecumenism, and if so, what does that mean (§1)? Second, what are some of the classical Pentecostal objections to ecumenism, and how might these be answered (§2)? Third, does Pentecostalism have an ecumenical history, and if so, how has this related to the ecumenical movement in the mainline churches (§§3–4)? Finally, what is the future of Pentecostal ecumenism and what might be ways we could contribute to such a venture (§5)? Let us plunge right into this difficult topic.

1. The Biblical Basis of Ecumenism

The English word "ecumenism" is a transliteration of the Greek word *oikoumenē* which various forms are found fifteen times in the New Testament (Matt 24:14; Luke 2:1; 4:5; 21:26; Acts 11:28; 17:6, 31; 19:27; 24:5; Rom 10:18; Heb 1:6; 2:5; Rev 3:10; 12:9; 16:14). Derived from *oikos* (house) and *menō* (dwelling) it is invariably translated "world" or "whole world," and signifies the world's inhabitants. Clearly, *oikoumenē* most often functions as a figure of speech describing a pervasive reality. It is not used in the modern sense of the term as related to the unity of the church except

---

1. This chapter was first published as a five-part article. "Pentecostalism and Ecumenism: Past, Present, and Future," *The Pneuma Review*: Part I, 4:1 (2001) 6–15; Part II, 4:2 (2001) 36–48; Part III, 4:3 (2001) 16–27; Part IV, 4:4 (2001) 50–57; Part V, 5:1 (2002) 29–38.

in a very indirect way when referring to the widespread influence of Christian actions such as preaching the gospel (e.g., Matt 24:14; Acts 17:6; 24:5; Rom 10:18). Instances of the term in the New Testament do not, therefore, advance our understanding of contemporary ecumenism. Its current use derives more so from the etymology of the term—the whole world or the entire household or inhabitants of the world—rather than from the specific ways in which it is used in the New Testament.

Contemporary ecumenism, however, is intimately connected with ecclesiology, or the doctrine of the church. Here, of course, there is an abundant wealth of biblical material that emphasizes the unity of the body of Christ. In fact, the metaphor of household (*oikeios*) is applied to the church as well (Gal 6:10). In Paul's letter to the Ephesians, the household of God (2:19) is composed of both Jews and gentiles (2:11–22), is governed by the gospel (*oikonomia*; 3:2), and is united together "in the promise in Christ Jesus" (3:6). Later, in this same letter, he writes, "Make every effort to keep the unity of the Spirit through the bond of peace. There is one body and one Spirit—just as you were called to one hope when you were called—one Lord, one faith, one baptism; one God and Father of all, who is over all and through all and in all" (4:3–6). Clearly, for Paul, the oneness of God extends to the effects of the work of God, the church, its faith, its baptism, etc.

This Paul confirms in no uncertain terms in his first letter to the Corinthians where factions had developed among those baptized by Paul, by Apollos, by Peter, and so on (1 Cor 1:10–16; 3:4, 21–23). In response, Paul again emphasizes, among other things, the unity of the body of Christ (12:12–31). The intention of God is that "there should be no division in the body, but that its part should have equal concern for each other. If one part suffers, every part suffers with it; if one part is honored, every part rejoices with it. Now you are the body of Christ, and each one of you is a part of it" (12:25–27). Some might respond that Paul is here speaking to the various individual persons who make up the one body of Christ at Corinth. They may, therefore, say that these words provide no justification for thinking about the unity of various churches as understood by the contemporary ecumenical movement. This ignores, however, both the plain understanding of Paul's usage of the metaphor "body of Christ" to describe the church here and elsewhere in his writings, and the fact that in his salutation, he addresses not only the Corinthians but also "all those everywhere who call on the name of our Lord Jesus Christ"—their Lord and ours (1:2). It is, therefore, arguable that the "various parts of the one body" metaphor is meaningful at a number of levels, including various individual persons in one local congregation, various congregations in a city or geographic region, various groups of churches in the world, and so on.

To stop with Paul, however, would be to leave the discussion at a fairly abstract level. A much more concrete picture emerges when considering the Gospel accounts. Specifically, ecumenists have frequently pointed to Jesus' "high priestly prayer" for the disciples and all believers in John 17. God's heart for the church and the world is unmistakable as the following lengthy excerpt shows:

> My prayer is not for them alone [the immediate disciples, in vv. 19 and before]. I pray also for those who will believe in me through their message, that all of them may be one, Father, just as you are in me and I am in you. May they also be in us so that the world may believe that you have sent me. I have given them the glory that you gave me, that they may be one as we are one: I in them and you in me. May they be brought to complete unity to let the world know that you sent me and have loved them even as you have loved me.
>
> Father, I want those you have given me to be with me where I am, and to see my glory, the glory you have given me because you loved me before the creation of the world. Righteous Father, though the world does not know you, I know you, and they [the disciples] know that you have sent me. I have made you known to them, and will continue to make you known in order that the love you have for me may be in them and that I myself may be in them. (John 17:20-26)

Three points should be made about this passage. First, note that Jesus' prayer extends far beyond the circle of the twelve disciples, and embraces all of those who believe in him. The unity that is prayed for, in other words, is universally inclusive of believers in Jesus Christ, then, now, and so long as our Lord shall tarry.

Second, the unity that is expected derives from the unity between the Father and the Son. This is an important point because the Father-Son unity in the Johannine Gospel appears to be all-encompassing: ontologically in terms of shared presence (1:1-2; 10:38; 14:10-11; 16:32) and the divine name (8:58, cf. Exod 3:14); imagistically in terms of the Son revealing (1:18; 14:7-9) and representing (13:20) the Father; actually in terms of the Son doing (only) what the Father does (5:19; 8:29; 14:31); gloriously in terms of equal honor being due to Father and Son (5:23) and bestowed by each on the other (8:49-50, 54; 13:31-32); judicially, as rendered by the Son on behalf of the Father (5:22, 26-27, 30; 8:16); mutuality in terms of witness and testimony (8:18) and will and intention (6:38; 12:28); evangelistically in terms of Jesus' proclaiming and teaching (only) the Father's message

(7:16–17; 8:28; 12:49; 14:24; 15:15); salvifically in terms of Jesus being the way to the Father (14:6); communally in terms of fellowship (11:41–42) and love (14:21); and so on. This is a deep unity that cannot be simply explained in only one or another way. As prayed for by Jesus, then, the unity of believers should be understood not simplistically at any one level, but holistically, embracing every aspect or dimension of reality. As such, this unity transcends all artificial lines of demarcation that human beings so often erect to distinguish themselves from others.

Finally, it would be remiss not to mention the centrality of love to the Father-Son unity and the unity that Jesus prayed for those who believe in his name. Love is that which characterizes the Trinitarian relationship between Father and Son, between the Son and the world, and between the Father and the world. Earlier in the Gospel, Jesus had said, "By this all men will know that you are my disciples, if you love one another" (13:35). How do we show forth the salvation that we've experienced? By loving each other. Failure to demonstrate such love to the world betrays our witness to non-believers. On the other hand, the loving unity that should bind believers together in Jesus is precisely that testimony by which others realize the love of God for the world.

John does also mention another motif of the unity between Father and Son that is connected to the sending of the Spirit. Jesus promised the arrival of the Counselor, the Spirit of truth, from the Father, and foretold that "On that day you will realize that I am in my Father, and you are in me, and I am in you" (14:20). Later in the same upper-room speech, Jesus indicates that the common message of Father and Son will be made known to the disciples by the Spirit of truth (16:12–15). Yet nowhere else in the autoptic gospel is this connection between the Spirit and the ecumenical prayer of Jesus explicated.

Such explication is, however, found in volume 2 of Luke's writings. Luke, as is well known, is supremely concerned in the book of Acts with the person and work of the Holy Spirit. This pneumatological motif finds expression on the Day of Pentecost when the Spirit is, literally, poured out "on *all* people" (Acts 2:17). One should not take this "all" lightly since Luke goes to great lengths to describe the universality of peoples represented in Jerusalem who heard those in the upper room speaking to them each in their own native tongue. This gathering of Judeans, Parthians, Medes, Elamites, Cappadocians, Asians, Phrygians, Pamphylians, Egyptians, Libyans, Cyreneans, Romans, Cretans, Arabians, residents of Mesopotamia, and others (2:9–11) has long been understood to represent the re-gathering of God's people from their initial dispersal at the Tower of Babel. More importantly, however, it was individuals from each of these people groups who were baptized into the one body of Christ on that day (2:41), and who, in turn, took the gospel from Jerusalem to Judea, to Samaria, "and to the ends of the earth" (1:8).

The cumulative fruit of the Spirit's outpouring on the Day of Pentecost finds its fulfillment in the eschatological consummation of God's saving work. We are told in the revelation to the seer on the isle of Patmos that those gathered before the throne of God and the Lamb are "from every tribe and language and people and nation" (Rev 5:9; cf. 7:9). This is in part because the gospel is being sent "to every nation, tribe, language and people" (14:6). On that final day, the great multitude representing such a staggering diversity of persons will lift up one great voice to the Lord God Almighty as they celebrate the great wedding feast joining together once for all the Lamb and his bride (19:6–9). The one body of those who are saved, as this picture and that depicted at Pentecost show, knows no boundaries, whether such is conceived politically, socially, linguistically, racially or ethnically, or otherwise.

To recapitulate, then, a biblically conceived ecumenism begins with the one work of God represented during the New Testament era as and through the church of Jesus Christ. The unity of this body is—or should be—a reflection of the unity between the Father and the Son. Put another way, this unity is demonstrated in the love that members of this body have for each other, in the same way, that the Father loves the Son and vice versa. It is, therefore, appropriate to consider this love as "the unity of the Spirit through the bond of peace" (Eph 4:3), begun at Pentecost and to be completed on that great and final Day of the Lord.

2. Classical Pentecostal Objections to Ecumenism

Given this biblically defined ecumenism, then, why is it that most Pentecostals remain staunchly anti-ecumenical? While many reasons have been given, three stand out as representing a fair consensus. First, Pentecostals believe that the unity of the church should be understood spiritually rather than visibly. Second, many Pentecostals believe that the ecumenical movement represents churches that have betrayed the essence of the gospel, especially doctrinally. Finally, correlative with the previous objection, Pentecostals are generally concerned that non-Pentecostal churches are devoid of the life that is found only in the Spirit of God as "pentecostally" experienced and defined, thus fulfilling the biblical prophecy of widespread apostasy in the last days. Let me respond to each in order.

Objection 1: Spiritual Rather Than Visible Unity

Pentecostals have always valued the spiritual unity that they have found in the experience of the *charismata*, especially speaking in tongues. Manifestations of tongues and other spiritual gifts are, for them, an incontrovertible sign of the Spirit's presence and activity in their lives and congregations. The institutional, organizational, and architectural forms of non-Pentecostal churches do not impress Pentecostals. These are considered to be merely outward signs of pomp and circumstance that all human constructions can display, but which do not guarantee inward and spiritual vitality. Rather, these outward paraphernalia are symptomatic of the hierarchicalism, patriarchalism, and traditionalism endemic to the history of the church, all of which has been conveniently covered up or obscured by stain glass windows, Gothic architecture, and iconography that is distracting at best and bewitching at worst. The point is that the unity of the church is found, not in outward forms of organization and agreement, but in the spiritual togetherness that genuine Christians experience through the Spirit in the name of Jesus.

A brief response proceeds along three lines. First, Pentecostals should recognize that this argument actually has its roots in the Reformation and post-Reformation era and is driven by an ideology of individualism. The basic assumption is that God works first and foremost through individuals and not institutions or organizations. Just as *sola Christus* neglected the Holy Spirit, *sola fide* neglected sanctifying works, and *sola Scriptura* neglected the role of tradition in reading and interpreting the Word of God, so did the unspoken emphasis on the individual neglect the centrality and importance of the community of faith. Since the Reformation, the church has been struggling to counteract the influential but exaggerated importance of Luther's "Here I stand!" A myriad of individuals after the German reformer have come to similar conclusions regarding their parent Protestant churches and movements resulting in the emergence of innumerable denominations.

Pentecostals are especially prone to such developments given the restoration of the doctrine of the priesthood of all believers during the Reformation. Empowered by a dynamic and liberating experience of the Holy Spirit, Pentecostals have understood their lives and ministries as commissioned by the Spirit. This includes an emphasis on spiritual freedom that makes for an even greater tendency toward individualism, independence, and self-aggrandizement. The fragmentation of Pentecostalism into hundreds of thousands of house churches, independent churches, parachurch groups, apostolic, prophetic, evangelistic, and teaching ministries operating in isolation, not to mention denominations as well as sects and (even!) cults, is evidence of this infection with the individualist strain.

This accent on individualism, however, does not tell the entire story about why Pentecostals claim to understand the unity of the church in spiritual rather than visible terms. Now, I cannot speak for the 500 million plus Pentecostals estimated today that represent the breadth of global Pentecostalism; rather, my Pentecostal affiliation is more specifically North American, and of the classical type that traces its roots back to denominations emerging out of the Azusa Street revival. Yet I sometimes wonder if Pentecostals reject as valid outward forms of structural unity because they are motivated by fear—fear that they would be compromising their former decisions to come-out-from-among-those visible denominations; fear that pursuing such relationships would jeopardize their identity as Pentecostals; fear that visible unity would camouflage the lack of spiritual fervor; fear that outward signs would eliminate reliance on the inner witness of the Spirit. These are, along with other issues yet to be discussed, legitimate areas of concern. But to recoil from engagement simply because there are issues of concern is inappropriate, and this especially for Pentecostals who claim to be led by the Spirit.

Finally, however, I find it odd that Pentecostals object to the notion that there have to be visible signs of unity for the church given their own insistence on the import of outward signs. Most classical North American Pentecostals continue to hold to some version of tongues-speaking as evidence of receiving the baptism in the Holy Spirit. Glossolalic tongues in these cases are outward signs and manifestations—"initial physical evidence," as some denominations put it—of the Spirit's infilling. Why would the true unity of the church not be accompanied by such outward signs and evidence as well? Christians are coming to increasing agreement that the gospel truthfully proclaimed and faithfully lived out is not merely spiritual. Rather, it is most truly spiritual when practically embodied, whether in concrete acts, tangible encounters, palpable manifestations, physical healings, and, I would suggest, visible signs. Perhaps it might be objected that visible signs do not translate to structural or organizational unity, or that the evidence of Spirit baptism is biblically derived in contrast to the goals of the ecumenical movement. I have addressed the biblical issues above, and will focus on the ecumenical movement itself below. Part of my motivation for writing this piece is to present evidence for a biblical and "pentecostally" informed ecumenism to the readers of this journal. I ask you to render judgment at the conclusion.

Objection 2: The Erosion of the Gospel, Especially Doctrinally

A second reason Pentecostals have given for their anti-ecumenical stance is their belief that the ecumenical movement is built on an insecure doctrinal foundation. Specifically, the doctrinal basis of the ecumenical movement is watered-down at best and supportive of heresy at worst. At best, Pentecostals feel that the Basis of the World Council of Churches (WCC), for example, is either too hollow or admits of too much latitude in what it does not say:

> The World Council of Churches is a fellowship of churches which confess the Lord Jesus Christ as God and Savior according to the Scriptures and therefore seek to fulfill together their common calling to the glory of the one God, Father, Son, and Holy Spirit.[2]

Thus, many Pentecostals feel that this platform is minimalist in allowing agreement across a wide spectrum of churches. At worst, some denominations that adhere to doctrines clearly rejected by the historical church—such as universalism or annihilationism, or the advocacy of homosexuality as a viable lifestyle—would also be able to sign on.

Let me respond in this instance with three counter-questions. First, on a more rhetorical note, since when have Pentecostals elevated doctrinal or creedal purity above their experience of the Spirit? It seems to me that such happens among Pentecostals only as an act of self-righteous indignation against those on whom they look down. Pentecostals have always been much more interested in the demonstration of Spirit's power than in wise and persuasive words (1 Cor 2:4). I certainly do not want to minimize the importance of doctrine; as a theologian, doctrines are what concern me supremely. My point here is twofold: to highlight what appears to be the case—that Pentecostals seem to have resorted to the "doctrinal argument" as a convenient excuse for not engaging in ecumenical activity—and to suggest that such seems to be an ironic reverse application of fundamental Pentecostal intuitions and priorities.

Yet the doctrinal issue should not be ignored. To begin addressing that concern, let me pose the second counter-question. What is or should be the

---

2. The WCC Basis is functionally equivalent to denominational statements of faith. However, the WCC is also careful to insist that the Basis "is not a 'confession of faith' in the formal theological sense. But as a brief expression of the foundation of what the Council is and for what it does, it offers some important clues for understanding the WCC." Van Elderen, *Introducing the World Council of Churches*, 4.

norm by which doctrinal creeds in general, and statements, in particular, are to be measured? This is not an idle question since it is arguable that most classical Pentecostal denominations—Assemblies of God, Church of God in Christ, International Church of the Foursquare Gospel, etc.—appear to have adopted the basic framework and even wording of doctrinal statements from fundamentalism during the first quarter of the twentieth century.[3] This occurred in part because of the polemics between fundamentalists and modernist or liberals during that period of time. The emerging Pentecostal churches were confronted with few theological alternatives: either fundamentalism or liberalism. Thankfully, Pentecostal leaders during that time opted for the former rather than the latter.

This decision, however, came with a price. Whereas the liberals followed the modernist emphasis on religious experience and subjectivist feeling to the neglect of the authority of the written Word of God, fundamentalists insisted on the priority of Scripture to the neglect of sensitivity to the Spirit's illuminative inspiration. The one subsumed Scripture to contemporary experience while the other denied the validity of pneumatic experiences as false enthusiasms in favor of a wooden reading of Scripture. The result is that Pentecostal doctrinal statements have not reflected the richness of our experiences of the Spirit. Rather, they have tended to be not much more than a reproduction of fundamentalist doctrines, almost verbatim, with the addition of one or two paragraphs regarding the person and work of the Spirit, and tongues as initial evidence. Is this, however, what a genuinely Pentecostal doctrinal and theological framework should be like? Is it not the case that Pentecostals should be the first to continue the struggle for an authentic balance of the Word and Spirit?[4] Do we not need to continuously rethink about the relevance and applicability of our doctrines and theologies for each generation? Why then did we allow the primary rules and assumptions underlying doctrinal thinking and formulation to be set by fundamentalists whose worldview is articulated according to various axioms that are at odds with what we as Pentecostals believe and experience? It goes without saying that Pentecostal doctrinal construction should not bow to the pressures exerted by liberals either.

My proposal is not that we as Pentecostals should discard doctrinal reflection, but that we should go about that task according to the rules of the game that Pentecostals play, rather than abide by rules with which Pentecostals can never win. We should, in other words, set out our own terms

3. Use of the term "fundamentalism" follows Marsden, *Fundamentalism and American Culture*.

4. I have previously developed this idea at greater length. See Yong "Between Two Extremes."

for reflecting and articulating doctrine. To remain within a fundamentalist framework will force us to use their categories, restrict our theological and doctrinal methodology, and require us to continue answering their questions and concerns rather than figure out and resolve our own. That this is no figment of my imagination is demonstrated in the extensive debate over the continuance of the charismata featured in almost every issue of this journal. Even after the publication of Jon Ruthven's groundbreaking book, which effectively demolished the cessationist argument, we still have to defend the validity of the charismata.[5] I am not trying to disparage these arguments. They are important and need to be made. My point is to call attention to the fact that our doctrinal and theological agenda is driven by fundamentalist concerns. What about our obligation to engage the arguments of liberals, and to battle for the truth with those on the left instead of those on the right? Or, to return to the focus of this essay, what about our obligation to witness in the context of the wider Christian (read: ecumenical) community? What about our calling to theological and doctrinal debate with those having ecumenical concerns? More to the point, is it not time for Pentecostals to take the Pentecostal message to the farthest reaches of the Christian community? And if that question is answered affirmatively, does that not require a distinctively Pentecostal kind of ecumenism?

Having issued the challenge the way that I have, however, assumes that all ecumenists and even churches that participate in the ecumenical movement are liberals. That this is far from the truth should not need to be stated. There are Christian movements, communities, and denominations that are far from liberal theologically or doctrinally. Various Pentecostal and evangelical type churches are WCC members, as well as Eastern Orthodox churches that are stridently conservative on theological matters.[6] In fact, many of these Orthodox churches, longtime members of the WCC, have been contemplating withdrawing from the WCC precisely for these reasons. This raises the third counter-question in all its specificity: what exactly is the goal of the ecumenical movement and what role should doctrine play in this regard?

There is a widespread perception among Pentecostals that the ecumenical movement is a last days ploy by Satan to deceive the elect. In fact, the ecumenical movement in general and the WCC more specifically have been thought to be representative of the great harlot of Revelation 17–18. Pentecostals fear that the ecumenical vision of a worldwide unity is a masquerade

---

5. See Ruthven, "On the Cessation of the Charismata"; Yong, "On the Cessation of the Charismata."

6. Hollenweger, *Pentecostalism*, 384–87.

for the beast's establishing a global anti-Christian church.[7] I will return to this issue later. For now, however, it suffices to note that the WCC understands itself to be a cooperative fellowship of churches, each of which have a "'sustained independent life and organization,' including the right to decide to apply for WCC membership without the permission of any other body or person."[8] In short, the WCC operates with the understanding that local denominations and churches large enough to apply (at least 10,000 members) are fully autonomous and remain such.

Clearly, the WCC does not see itself as a church, much less the world church that Pentecostals are suspicious about. Rather, member churches retain their own autonomy, and WCC programs and initiatives are considered only as recommendations by the member churches to the churches. These are in no way binding upon individual denominations or churches except insofar as they are received as reflecting biblical truth and explicitly adopted to guide Christian practice. Given the predominance of Protestant churches in the WCC and the increasing trends toward the establishment of indigenous national churches (see also below), the trajectory of contemporary ecumenism is in the direction of an ecclesiology that emphasizes unity only amidst diversity rather than toward increasing authoritarianism, hierarchicalism, or any other kind of control (whether considered in terms of the WCC, or the Roman Catholic Church). Assuming for the moment that this is true, such an arrangement is certainly more conducive to Pentecostal participation. But what then about the role of doctrine in the quest for Christian unity?

It is here that the wide variety within Christendom needs to be appreciated. Some churches, like the Orthodox, think of theology and

---

7. The Assemblies of God, for example, "disapproves of ministers or churches participating in any of the modern ecumenical organizations on a local, national, or international level in such a manner as to promote the ecumenical movement [in part] because: . . . (c) We believe that the combination of many religious organizations into a world superchurch will culminate in the religious Babylon of Revelation 17 and 18" (Assemblies of God Constitution and Bylaws, Article 9, §11). While this position is characteristic of many fundamentalist denominations, moderate evangelical churches have distanced themselves from this kind of rhetoric. And, insofar as classical Pentecostal denominations in North America like the Assemblies of God have recently come to align themselves more so with evangelicalism than fundamentalism, this kind of reasoning regarding the ecumenical movement may need to be revisited. The International Church of the Foursquare Gospel, for example, does not have either a constitutional or position statement against ecumenical involvement. More important than mimicking one another, however, the truth is at stake. Classical Pentecostals of all types need to move beyond stereotypes they have inherited from those they have previously affiliated with and investigate the charges raised on their own terms.

8. Van Elderen, *Introducing the World Council of Churches*, 4–6.

doctrines in its literal sense as *orthodoxa*—right worship, right liturgy, right contemplation and meditation, and so on. Other, more conservative Protestant churches, think of theology and doctrines as simple biblically derived or grounded propositional restatements, without concern for right interpretation.[9] The Catholic Church, on the other hand, thinks of theology and doctrines always in terms of the conjunction between Scripture and tradition. Without making further distinctions, it should be clear that the doctrinal statement of the WCC need not be understood as a minimalist device designed to gain widespread acceptability. Rather, it should be seen as the fundamental essence of the gospel to which all Christians should adhere and from which all Christians should theologize. In this case, Christian ecumenism now becomes the arena where all of those who call Jesus Christ as their Lord celebrate their diversity and bless each other and the world with their gifts. This is a far cry from the rhetoric that castigates ecumenism as a deceitful subterfuge of the enemy focused on eroding the truth of the gospel.

Objection 3: The Apostasy of the Church in the Last Days

There is, however, one more related and frequently heard objection that Pentecostals have leveled against the ecumenical movement: the concern that ecumenical churches are spiritually dead, representing the last days apostasy predicted in Scripture (Matt 24:10–12 and 2 Thess 2:3). This is related, of course, to the apocalyptic mentality that was pervasive among early Pentecostals. First-generation Pentecostal pioneers were imbued with the missionary spirit and viewed taking the gospel to the farthest reaches of the earth as the final opportunity for the heathen to convert before the coming of the Lord (Matt 24:14). The established church was certainly in no position to be used of the Lord for this final mission, having abandoned doctrinal truth, spiritual fervor, and missionary empowerment. In fact, as the church of the last days, the established churches were, like the Laodiceans, about to be spewed out of the mouth of the Lord because of their lukewarmness (cf. Rev 3:14–22). It is for this reason that God had to raise up an obedient remnant through the pentecostal outpouring of the latter rain—so that the gospel could be taken where it had previously failed to go.

---

9. By this, I am thinking about the tendency to think of one's doctrines simply in terms of "what the Bible says," without recognizing that all biblical statements have to be interpreted—the latter resulting in the rampant denominationalism, factionalism, and sectarianism among conservative Protestants.

By way of response, I would like to make three observations. First, I think it is important to note that Pentecostals have, until very recently, uncritically appropriated the eschatological framework of a foreign theological system (again) through which they've understood the "last days." This system is called dispensationalism. What is ironic is that most turn-of-the-twentieth-century dispensationalists were also cessationists regarding the charismata precisely because of their dispensationalist framework for interpreting Scripture. Pentecostals, fundamentalists, and most Bible-believing Christians, however, were attracted to this very literal way of reading of Scripture and, therefore, swallowed dispensationalism almost without question.

The fact of the matter, however, is that Pentecostal intuitions about the "end times" derive more so from their experience of the outpouring of the Spirit in the last days than from any previously laid-out theological grid or hermeneutical framework. It is precisely because of the empowering experience of the Holy Spirit that Pentecostal have much more of an already/not-yet eschatological orientation. For Pentecostals, the present dynamism of the Spirit's reality means that the Spirit-filled believer values the embodied character of Christian life is committed to holistic forms of missionary work, and is empowered to make a difference in this world. This explains why Pentecostals believe in the physical healing power of God. It also undergirds Pentecostal convictions about the miraculous, and about the power of prayer. Certainly, Pentecostals maintain an expectancy about the coming of the Lord—the not-yet aspect of their eschatological faith. However, such is far less an otherworldly attitude that seeks to escape gloomy historical future than it is an expression of vibrant love for their Lord.

My point is not to undermine Pentecostal belief in the imminent return of Christ. Such is the proper stance the Bible indicates we should have regarding the parousia: Maranatha—"Come, O Lord!" (1 Cor 16:24). Instead, I want to raise the question again of why Pentecostals have uncritically bought into a dispensationalist system of thinking that is, at various points, wholly antithetical to their own experience.[10] I am certainly convinced that the "last days" commenced with the founding of the church on the Day of Pentecost (Acts 2:17), so I am not even suggesting that the entire dispensationalist scheme be discarded. I am only querying into the Pentecostal appropriation of the full range and details of dispensationalist eschatology. It may be the case that Jesus will return tomorrow. I don't think, however, that the dispensationalist timelines will therefore be vindicated. Too many vari-

---

10. Gerald T. Sheppard was one of the first—and by no means the last—to have raised this question. Sheppard, "Pentecostalism and the Hermeneutics of Dispensationalism," 5–33.

ants have been proposed, too many adjustments have had to be made, too many confusing speculations have been proffered, and too many mistakes have impaired the credibility of dispensationalist eschatology. If that is the case, then the uncritical correlation between the ecumenical movement and the great harlot of Revelation 17–18 is at least called into question. I say this not to baptize the ecumenical movement as an unblemished work of God. Surely this also is not the case as my exposition in the next section hopes to show. I am only asking that Pentecostals come to a fresh reading of Scripture on eschatology and other matters by beginning with Pentecostal—rather than dispensationalist, fundamentalist, or any other—premises, sensibilities, and experiences.

My next two observations will be much more succinctly stated. I am concerned that Pentecostals continue to perpetuate the idea that all mainline or established churches are spiritually dead. This is especially disconcerting in view of the charismatic renewal movement that has swept the world during the past two generations. Presbyterians, Methodists, Lutherans, Disciples of Christ, Episcopalians/Anglicans, United Church of Christ members, Baptists of all stripes, and even Roman Catholics and Orthodox Christians have all been touched and transformed by fresh encounters with the Holy Spirit. All of these denominations and churches have charismatic churches and have developed ministries designed to foster and nurture charismatic experience, piety, and mission. And while some who have experienced the Holy Spirit have left to join Pentecostal churches, many have chosen to remain committed members of these mainline churches and are fervent ecumenists. On the other hand, we have also recently begun to see many leave Pentecostal churches for mainline Protestant, Catholic, and Orthodox churches because of their depth of tradition, the richness of their liturgy, and the sense of greater connectedness that Christian life within these communities evokes. How can Pentecostals continue to believe that those involved in the ecumenical movement are apostate or lukewarm churches in the last days?

Finally, even if we grant that the established churches are, generally speaking, spiritually dead, given the revivalist fervor that the charismatic renewal movement has had in some quarters of these churches, I believe that we as Pentecostals have an obligation to engage these churches and be instruments for their further renewal and revival. We can and should take heart from the difference that even one person can make. I am thinking about the lifework of one of the first globally recognized Pentecostal ecumenists, David DuPlessis. Here was a man who was obedient to the Spirit's leading to take the Pentecostal message to the mainline churches, and he experienced rejection by his Pentecostal community in the process of doing so.¹¹ Yet it is undeniable that this one man was a catalyst for the charismatic renewal in the mainline churches. And, what else does it mean to be such catalysts other than we be Pentecostal ecumenists? How else can we hope to be used of God apart from engaging in the ecumenical task? Not to take up this challenge will render a guilty verdict on the charge that Pentecostals are guilty of continuing to perpetuate the scandal of Christian disunity before a world looking for the love of God.

3. Ecumenical Pentecostalism: A Historical Overview

I hope to have shown that Pentecostal anti-ecumenism stems in part from theological convictions imported into rather than derived from the Pentecostal experience of the Spirit. Such importations have inhibited Pentecostals from a genuine understanding of what the biblical ecumenism stands for. On the other hand, it has also certainly been the case historically that there has been a lack of spiritual fervor within the mainline churches, especially in terms of how Pentecostals gauge these expressions. Going back to the biblical material in section 1, however, this should come as no surprise. Different communities of faith bring different gifts to the one body of Christ. It goes without saying that these various communities also bring different liabilities and have diverse struggles.

My goals in this and the next section are threefold. First, I would like to demonstrate that Pentecostalism and ecumenism have not been inherently antithetical historically. This historically oriented presentation supplements the biblical and theological arguments presented in the first two sections. Secondly, I want to make a similar case on behalf of the ecumenical movement. I wish to show that historically, ecumenists have shared many of the convictions and goals of Pentecostals. Third, however, I also want to demonstrate that the devil is at work not only on "their" side but on both sides of the fence. The history of God's work among the people of God always features both triumphs and failures, and this applies to both ecumenists and Pentecostals alike.¹²

Let me begin with what I call "ecumenical Pentecostalism." I want to focus in what follows on the ecumenical character of Pentecostalism in

---

11. Du Plessis was defrocked of his Assemblies of God credentials in 1962 for his ecumenical involvement. These were restored to him much later (in 1980) after history had confirmed his Pentecostal commitment and the value of his service to the wider causes of Christ. Du Plessis, *The Spirit Bade Me Go*; Jongeneel et al., "Pentecost, Mission and Ecumenism," 143–55; Robinson, "To the Ends of the Earth."

12. So as not to bog down the reader, I will forego detailed documentation in these historical sub-sections in favor of a brief reading list at the end of this essay.

three stages. There is, first, the ecumenism of the Azusa Street revival. Second, there is the ecumenism of the charismatic renewal. Finally, there is the ecumenism now inherent within a Pentecostalism that has grown to be a global phenomenon. Let me overview each in order.

Azusa Street Ecumenism

One of the least well-known facts about the Azusa Street revival is its multiracial environment. This is especially remarkable given the segregationist mentality prevalent in North America during the first half of the twentieth century. From 1906–8, the Azusa Street mission drew persons from several races, ethnic groups, cultures, and nationalities together in worship. Blacks and whites were found worshipping and singing together, tarrying before the Lord and praying for one another, "mingling and even touching[!] in the mission."[13] One participant recollected that at Azusa Street, "the 'color line' was washed away in the blood."[14] What happened at Azusa Street, in other words, was unprecedented. The result was not only a transformation of hearts but also a tearing down of barriers to the experience of genuine Christian unity such that "there is no Greek or Jew, circumcised or uncircumcised, barbarian, Scythian, slave or free, but Christ is all, and is in all" (Col 3:11; cf. 1 Cor 12:13, and Gal 3:28 which adds "male or female").

That the ecumenical miracle at Azusa Street did not last is also a well-known historical fact. Whites and blacks formed their own denominations due to the socioeconomic and political pressures in force at that time. White Pentecostals drifted toward their Yankee (read fundamentalist and, later, evangelical) relatives, thus forging alliances that have, in more recent times, left many Pentecostals wondering what has happened to the Pentecostal fervor. Many contemporary Pentecostals complain that one can attend any Pentecostal service on a Sunday morning today, and feel as if one were in a Baptist, Covenant, Alliance, or other evangelical-type congregation. This is the case, however, only among white Pentecostal churches and denominations. Black Pentecostals have continued to emphasize the shout, the dance, the sway, the clap, and the many other electrifying features of the Azusa Street revival. This parting of ways has signified, in some respect, the socio-economic distinctions between whites and blacks in the USA. Upwardly mobile whites moved farther and farther away from lower class blacks, leaving, in places, a chasm unbridgeable (sad to say) even for a Spirit-led people. In hindsight, it is seen that Pentecostals squandered a golden opportunity to continue as a prophetic

13. Irvin, "Drawing All Together into One Bond of Love," 46.
14. Bartleman, *Azusa Street*, 54.

voice not only on racial and ethnic issues but also on socioeconomic ones as well. Racial discrimination and socioeconomic segregation would persist for another sixty plus years before being legally confronted. What might have happened if the original ecumenical character of Pentecostalism would have persisted and developed instead?

Even in light of the civil rights movements of the 1960s and '70s, however, Pentecostals have been slow to respond to the need for racial reconciliation. It was not until October 1994 when the all-white Pentecostal Fellowship of North America (PFNA) voted to dissolve and reconstitute as a racially inclusive group. The result was the emergence of the Pentecostal/Charismatic Churches of North America (PCCNA). Whites and blacks were led to seek forgiveness from and dispense forgiveness to each other, celebrate the Lord's Supper together, and, at one point, participate jointly in a spontaneous foot-washing ceremony. One should not disparage the import of this "Memphis Miracle," as it has been acclaimed.[15] Better late than never, as the old saying goes. However, one again cannot help but lament the fact that rather than being the pacesetters in this regard, Pentecostals have been sluggish in acting out the impulses inherent within its original ecumenical experience.

This original ecumenical Pentecostalism was not, however, limited to racial and ethnic distinctions in the body of Christ. As will be noted below, the modern ecumenical movement also began about the same time, and early Pentecostals were not oblivious to those developments. Further, these Pentecostals also recognized the denominationally schismatic nature of the body of Christ, especially in its Protestant forms. Their encounter with the Spirit thus led them to envision that the Pentecostal outpouring would be central to re-experiencing Christian unity. Such unity cannot emerge from structural or organizational efforts, but only through the healing presence of the Spirit of God.[16]

In short, early Pentecostals did understand the ecumenical significance of the Pentecostal experience of the Spirit. Thus, the founding of classical Pentecostal denominations like the Assemblies of God brought together individuals from a variety of backgrounds: Keswick Reformed, Wesleyan Holiness, revivalist, Baptistic, African American, and so on. Their motivation was common mission in the power of the Spirit, whether

---

15. For details, see the "Roundtable: Racial Reconciliation" articles by Frank Macchia, Ithiel Clemmons, Leonard Lovett, Manuel Gaxiola-Gaxiola, Samuel Solivan, and Cecil M. Robeck, Jr., in the spring 1996 issue of *Pneuma: The Journal of the Society for Pentecostal Studies*.

16. This vision was prominent in early Pentecostal literature such as William Seymour's Azusa Street periodical, *The Apostolic Faith*.

such be with regard to the taking of the gospel to foreign lands, social, publication or educational projects, and the cultivation of Pentecostal faith. This also explains why the Assemblies of God as well as other early Pentecostal groups saw themselves as movements rather than denominations. The latter were stigmatized as dead and lifeless organizations, whereas the former were inherently more dynamic entities conducive to the Spirit's guidance and invigoration. Inevitably, however, institutionalization processes set in, leaving groups like the Assemblies of God practically indistinguishable from established churches and mainline denominations in terms of organizational structure.

The Ecumenism of Neo-Pentecostalism

This may explain, in part, the flowering of the charismatic renewal—also called "neo-Pentecostalism"—in the mainline churches in the 1950s, '60s, and '70s, what I call the second stage of ecumenical Pentecostalism. The fact is that by this time, the Pentecostal experience of the Spirit had ceased to be a unifying force for Christians. Rather, denominational lines had hardened, and the power of the Spirit to bring people together from diverse branches of Christendom was being resisted by the various human-made boundaries that had emerged in Pentecostal churches over the course of a generation. Ironically, those who participated in the renewal movements in the mainline churches also began to see the ecumenical potential of the experience of the Spirit. These neo-Pentecostals or charismatics recognized that the vitality imparted to Christian faith by the pentecostal outpouring was a common experience that cut across creedal, denominational, liturgical, traditional, and theological/doctrinal lines.

Of course, classical Pentecostals were initially—and for quite a while, actually—rather suspicious of the authenticity of the charismatic renewal movement. These misgivings were especially intensified upon the outbreak of charismatic revival in the Roman Catholic Church in the latter half of the 1960s. Pentecostals were incredulous that followers of the Antichrist—following Luther's initial labeling of the pope—could have anything to do with the distinctive Pentecostal experience! Yet for many of these churches, ecumenical activities were sustained and furthered precisely because of the acknowledged commonality of experiencing the Spirit's presence and activity. For many Christians, the pentecostal experience of the Spirit meant a revitalized spiritual life, increased Bible reading, intensified devotional piety, the manifestation of the *charismata*, including speaking in other tongues, renewed appreciation for liturgical and sacramental worship, deeper motivation toward social action, and, most important for our purposes, stronger ties with all those who call upon the name of the Lord.

Over the past few decades, however, Pentecostal fears regarding the charismatic renewal in the established churches have been calmed. This has been enabled in part by the development of Pentecostal relationships with more evangelical-type denominations and groups. Models of Christian unity centered around common mission, such as Billy Graham crusades, World Vision famine relief endeavors, and parachurch ministries like InterVarsity, Women's Aglow, and the Full Gospel Businessmen's Fellowship International have mollified Pentecostal apprehensions and actually encouraged Pentecostal participation and koinonia with non-Pentecostals. As Pentecostals have come to know non-Pentecostals in a deeper way in these joint efforts, they have come to appreciate the diversity present in the body of Christ. And, of course, they've also begun to open themselves up to the power that a biblical ecumenism affords the church's witness.

What was lost, however, was the opportunity to influence the mainline denominations in more intentional ways. As previously noted, the onset of the charismatic renewal movement in the '50s and '60s raised many questions for the established churches. These initially turned to Pentecostals for assistance in understanding their newly-found experiences. Outside of discerning and capable individuals like David Du Plessis, however, few classical Pentecostals responded. At that time, this served only to confirm mainline stereotypes of Pentecostals as fundamentalistic and sectarian. Since then, Pentecostal relationships with the mainline churches have come a long way. What remains, however, is the long-standing reluctance among Pentecostals to be associated with structural efforts at church unity, especially those derived from organized ecumenical activities such as those of the National Council of Churches (NCC) and the WCC.

Before turning more specifically to "organized ecumenism," however, one more word must be said concerning the kind of ecumenical Pentecostalism that now permeates the movement in its global forms. The remarkable power of the Pentecostal experience to bridge not only denominational differences but also to speak to the hearts of people that come from divergent institutional, geographic, cultural, political, and religious backgrounds has recently been dawning on those perceptive to recent trends and developments. Revivals like those at Toronto, Brownsville, and Pensacola, for example, have reached staggering numbers, many of whom would never have been found together under the same roof or have broken the same bread apart from their life-transforming encounter with the Spirit of God. The masses have come from every continent to experience the power of God and have returned to their places of origin full of the Holy Spirit. This is not to affirm all that goes on at these prolonged evangelistic campaigns. It is, however, to testify to the unitive power of what I call ecumenical Pentecostalism.

Global Ecumenism and Global Pentecostalism

And this unique ecumenical Pentecostalism is by no means confined to revivalist phenomena either. In fact, Pentecostalism in its global forms has now reached such proportions that recent estimates believe the number of Pentecostals and charismatics of all stripes to exceed 500 million. The startling fact is that a very small percentage of these are of the classical type of Pentecostalism found in North America. In fact, the Pentecostal boom is taking place in such faraway places as Latin and South America, sub-Saharan Africa, and even inland China. These have not been indoctrinated into the Assemblies of God Sixteen Fundamental Truths, or any similar statement. Rather, what makes people embrace the Pentecostal message is their experience of the power of the Spirit of God. Common faith, in the global Pentecostal context, is not predicated upon the unity of doctrinal or theological beliefs, but rather on the unity of the Spirit's presence and activity.

Before being triumphalistic about the incredible growth of Pentecostal movements worldwide, however, the potential difficulties associated with such developments should be frankly acknowledged. Pentecostals are just as guilty of schisms as any other Protestant group. Such belong to the infancy of Pentecostalism as seen in the debates over the oneness or trinitarian character of God or Spirit baptism as a second or third blessing. The problematic caused by Oneness denominations remains to the present since Oneness adherents number up to one-fourth of Pentecostals worldwide. More recently, the emergence of new religious movements on the North American scene have included groups like The Way International and Christian Identity Movement which have been founded and endorsed by isolated and sectarian individuals nurtured within (among other groups) Pentecostalism.

Multiplied to a global scale, however, the phenomenon of religious syncretism is now what poses the greatest threat to worldwide Pentecostalism. Some have charged the African independent, charismatic, or Spirit-churches with being a bridge back toward native or tribal religious practices instead. The claim is that charismatic movements in Africa have so interpreted Christian beliefs and practices within the context of African indigenous religious that they have compromised distinctive faith in Christ. Such charges are far from absent in other parts of the world as well. In South American Brazil, the religious folk people go to the Catholic priest for births, marriages, and burials, to Afro-Brazilian shamans for relief from nightmares, and to Pentecostal churches when they are sick and desire healing. Most notably, in Korea, skeptics have accused Korean Pentecostal ministers of practicing a form of Korean shamanism in Christian guise. My intention here is neither to confirm or deny these allegations, but solely to bring up the importance of discernment, even of anything that might fly under the banner of "Pentecostalism." Historically, revival movements have always been accompanied by the genuine and the spurious. The contemporary global Pentecostal explosion is no different. We should rejoice in the things that God is doing upon discerning that. We should also exercise caution and discernment with regard to distinguishing the presence and activity of the Holy Spirit from that of other spirits.

The same holds true for our relationship to and participation in the ecumenical movement. The point is not to avoid the ecumenical movement since, in a very real sense, Pentecostals have always been ecumenical, even though most of us have not realized this before. Rather, ecumenical Pentecostalism should emphasize discerning participation. As a global movement, it has no other choice. There is no place left to withdraw to. Pentecostal mission, whether we like it or not, includes the ecumenical dimension.

4. Pentecostal Ecumenism: A Survey

If it is true to say that Pentecostalism has always been ecumenical, it is also true to say that in certain respects, the ecumenical movement has always been "pentecostal." In what follows, I want to tease out three elements of what I call "pentecostal ecumenism" wherein central features of Pentecostalism are highlighted. These include the missionary thrust of the modern ecumenical movement, its concern for charismatic unity, and its emphasis on what I call the "diversities of the Spirit." Let me comment on each in order.

Missionary Pentecostal Ecumenism

Few Pentecostals today realize that the ecumenical movement was initially launched as a missionary movement, and in many respects retains that focus today. As missiologists and historians have noted, while the twentieth was the century of Pentecostal missions, the nineteenth was that of the Protestant missionary enterprise. It was during the nineteenth century that what we now call the mainline churches established themselves on every continent. It was also during this same time that problems were identified, many of which were far too large for the mission agencies of these individual churches and denominations to resolve on their own. The heart of the modern ecumenical movement was thus birthed at a global mission conference which convened at Edinburgh, Scotland, in 1910, and from which the International Missionary Fellowship (IMF) was established in 1921. Meanwhile, it was realized that missionary work could not proceed apart from confronting both the social and political injustices prevalent during the inter-war years and the doctrinal differences that separated the churches. Thus emerged the Life and Work world conference (1925) and the Faith and Order world conference (1927). These combined to form the WCC in 1948.[17] In 1961, the IMF officially joined forces with the WCC, thus re-affirming the WCC's commitment to the missionary witness of the churches.

I am getting ahead of the story without having made my point which is this. The early twentieth century was a time during which churches in the West awoke to the power of ecumenical unity for carrying out the task of the Great Commission. As the various churches began to assess the daunting project of world evangelization, they realized that such could be accomplished much more efficiently if they worked together rather than separately. In short, it was the missionary endeavor that brought hitherto self-sufficient groups, movements, and denominations together. I should not need to point out that the central impetus toward Pentecostal organization was also the collaborative power of common mission. Fulfilling the missionary mandate has done more to bring the church together since the Reformation than anything else.

Moreover, this task has not been lost on the ecumenical movement today. Certainly, the world at the beginning of the twenty-first century is quite different from when the IMF was founded. Yet missions remains the *raison d'être* of the WCC, this being clearly reasserted in the WCC's *Ecumenical Affirmation on Missions and Evangelism* published in 1982. These *Affirmations*

---

17. The Faith and Order section of the WCC has been active up through to the present. Some Pentecostals who have been deeply involved in the interdenominational activities with the charismatic movement and many other large independent charismatic churches may have noticed that more often than not such "ecumenism" has emphasized experience to the neglect of doctrine! This is ironic in light of the charge leveled against ecumenical organizations such as the WCC that it has abandoned the truth of the gospel for visible unity and social programs (see my earlier discussion in §2, Obj. 2). However, the internal policies and vision of the WCC is motivated in part by the fact that its quest for unity, including the work done by Faith and Order, does not bypass serious doctrinal issues. Instead, the WCC wants to ensure that the fellowship of the churches "is not based on the illusion that differences can be overcome by ignoring them." Van Elderen, *Introducing the World Council of Churches*, 5.

emphasize the importance of conversion, the application of the gospel to every realm of life, the centrality of the churches to God's mission, mission as the way of Christ, the mandate of taking the good news to the poor, the mandate regarding global witness (to all six continents), and the challenge to witness among people of other faith and religious traditions.

Yet it goes without saying that the missionary focus of the ecumenical movement has changed over the course of a century. Clearly, the evangelistic edge has been blurred and, in some cases, been replaced among some denominations almost entirely by socioeconomic and political projects. Yet it is also the case that many of these projects, especially those that target the transformation of socioeconomic and political structures, will never be accomplished by individual churches or single denominations working alone. Instead, the resources and cumulative power of the entire church of Jesus Christ will need to be mobilized toward action if these kinds of changes are to be realized.

Now, although these kinds of organized activities are not central to Pentecostal missions, they are certainly not completely absent either. Certainly, no Pentecostal would deny that they are important features of missions and that they should remain part of the church's task. And, if Pentecostals do not take up these tasks, they can and should thank God for their missions-minded ecumenical brothers and sisters who are doing so. What I am saying is that missions is as pivotal to modern ecumenism as it is to modern Pentecostalism. And, insofar as missions is an indispensable feature of Pentecostalism, in that regard, it is appropriate to speak of a "Pentecostal ecumenism."

But, more importantly, I am convinced that both sides can provide that which is lacking in the missions efforts of the other should they come together. In fact, it is well known in ecumenical circles that there is a vitality and enthusiasm among Pentecostal missionaries that is contagious. Our ecumenical brothers and sisters have been looking to us for inspiration and would welcome joining our efforts. There lies before us another golden opportunity. Will we continue only criticizing the ecumenical movement or will we join to our much-needed criticism loving and Spirit-empowered action for the benefit of the lost in the world and for the increase of the kingdom of God? And who knows, perhaps in the process, our own missionary aspirations will also be fulfilled as we commune with other members of the body of Christ and glean from their depth and the richness of their traditions.

Charismatic-Pentecostal Ecumenism

The ecumenical movement is also "pentecostal" in a second way: with regard to its valuing the charismatic impulses to Christian unity. The onset of the charismatic renewal in the mainline churches brought about an awareness of its unitive power for Christianity in much the same way as such dawned on early-twentieth-century Pentecostals. In fact, this common experience of the Spirit has not only served to bring mainline Protestants together but also catalyzed their relationships with conservative evangelicals and Pentecostals. It is not unusual for home Bible study and prayer groups to include representatives from all the established denominations as well as independent Pentecostal and charismatically oriented individuals. Certainly, organized groups like the Women's Aglow and the Full Gospel Businessmen's mentioned earlier are powerful and concrete examples of such grassroots ecumenism. These times of Bible reading and prayer have brought out the essential unity that Christians experience in Jesus Christ by the power of the Spirit. They have also enabled the realization of the things that are trivial versus those which are important. Thus, Christians have been mobilized in these contexts to stand united on a greater front than ever before on social issues such as civil rights, abortion, and other matters. In fact, in the process, Pentecostals have even begun to realize the common convictions that they have with their Roman Catholic brothers and sisters on some of these issues.

It is also evident that the charismatic explosion in the mainline churches opened the door for Pentecostal participation in formal ecumenical activities. Beginning in 1961 when the Iglesia Pentecostal de Chile and the Misión Iglesia Pentecostal (also of Chile) joined as member churches of the WCC, there has been a slow trickle of Pentecostal churches into the ecumenical movement. Today, Pentecostal churches from Brazil, Argentina, Chile, Argentina, and various sub-Saharan churches have taken out WCC memberships. In addition to WCC involvement, various Pentecostal churches have established long-term relationships with mainline denominations, and individual Pentecostals have been active at national, regional, and other levels of ecumenical activity. Some have even served on the staffs of the WCC, the National Council of Churches (NCC), and other regional ecumenical organizations like the Latin American Council of Churches (CLAI).[18]

It is undeniable that the charismatic renewal in the mainline churches has served to raise the consciousness of its members to the centrality of the

---

18. Sandidge, "The World Council of Churches," 901–3.

Spirit's presence and activity both in the church and in the world. This was nowhere more evident than in the seventh WCC convocation held in Canberra, Australia, in February 1991. The theme of this gathering was "Come Holy Spirit, Renew the Whole Creation" (cf. Ps 104:30). Work sections were formed under the headings "Giver of Life—Sustain Your Creation!," "Spirit of Truth—Set Us Free!," "Spirit of Unity—Reconcile Your People!," and "Holy Spirit—Transform and Sanctify Us!" Reports from those who attended testified of the powerful spirit of unity present as Christians from all over the world gathered to worship, pray, sing, dance, and rejoice together in Jesus' name. Clearly, such an event would not have been possible apart from the charismatic renewal and the Pentecostal presence in the WCC. It is further arguable that events exactly like these—recall Toronto, Brownsville, Pensacola, etc.—are what transform the lives of delegates and, by extension, the congregations to which they belong.

Certainly, however, not all that has flown under the banner of charismatic renewal in the ecumenical movement can or should be endorsed by Pentecostals. Even as Pentecostals have "dropped the ball" with regard to specific issues in their own history, so have ecumenists as well. Thus, it was clear that when one of the plenary speakers at the Canberra conference invoked the spirits of war-torn and destitute Korean people and prayed for healing, that went too far for most participants and delegates.[19]

Again, however, discerning participation rather than sectarian withdrawal is in order. Pentecostal revivals have by no means been free and clear of disruptive and unholy manifestations themselves. The proper response is not to ban revivals but to sift the wheat from the dross. In the same way,

---

19. Upon returning from Canberra, Cecil M. Robeck, Jr., an ordained Assemblies of God minister and professor at Fuller Theological Seminary, penned these thoughts which may reflect the sentiments of many who witnessed that event: "The second [speaker] was a young Korean Presbyterian woman, Professor Chung Hyun Kyung, who made a stunning presentation as an introduction to the theological theme [of the conference]. She attempted to speak from the perspective of a *minjung* theology, which she believed to be especially representative of Asian women. At points, I found her to be genuinely prophetic. At other times, I was very uncomfortable. I worried that she had passed outside the bounds of orthodoxy as, for example, when she 'summoned' various spirits of *Han*, spirits of those who had been touched by anger, resentment, bitterness and grief.... To be sure, there is much to be said for the communion of saints, even among evangelicals and Pentecostals. It is also the case that our understanding of the church allows us to see ourselves in relationship with those who have gone before us in the church. Furthermore, as one who comes from a tradition which rose first among the poor, the disenfranchised, and marginalized in North American society, I could identify at points with her *minjung* concerns. But the summons of departed spirits to come to the assembly, if that is what was really intended, seemed to me to be more akin to the liturgies of Spiritism or was more rooted in ancestor worship than it was in the classical expressions of Christianity." Robeck, "A Pentecostal Reflects on Canberra," 111–12.

one can and should expect that all genuine movements of the Spirit in the ecumenical world will be accompanied by manifestations that will require discernment. This makes Pentecostal participation all the more important, given that we, of all persons, are those most sensitive to the need for discernment of spirits and to openness to that particular gift of the Holy Spirit. In any case, in all of these respects—the openness to the movements of the Spirit, the embracing of the operations of the *charismata*, and the need for discernment at every turn—"pentecostal" elements are prevailing among mainline churches to the point that in some circles, they have become a staple. To that extent, it is also appropriate to recognize the emergence of a "pentecostal ecumenism."

"Diversities of the Spirit" Ecumenism

As is always the case, however, there are two sides to every story. That which allowed the invocation of Korean *han* spirits to the WCC conference is also that which has allowed Pentecostal presence and participation in the WCC to flourish. But what is "it" that has allowed these very contrasting phenomena to "co-exist"? My hypothesis is that such can be attributed to the real presence of a genuinely Pentecostal conviction: what I call the "diversities of the Spirit." This is the commitment to seeing the full expression of the "different kinds of gifts, . . . different kinds of service, . . . different kinds of working" but all of the same Spirit, Lord, and God (cf. 1 Cor 12:4–6). Paul envisioned such diversification of giftings, of course, through the metaphor of the body of Christ having many parts, many members, many functions, and many components (1 Cor 12:12–31). And, this same diversification is intrinsic to the church itself, as its founding narrative in Acts 2 discussed earlier clearly exemplifies. The sending of the Spirit on the Day of Pentecostal resulted in the establishment of one living organism, the body of Christ, with many members. The many find their wholeness in the one, and the one's effectiveness and beauty are to be found in the diversities of its members, including not only those from around the world (Acts 2:9–11) but also all of its sons and daughters, men and women, young and old (Acts 2:17–18).

Now this emphasis on the "diversities of the Spirit" is a central value of the contemporary ecumenical movement. I need to be clear at this juncture about not approving whatever happens in the WCC—such as the controversial circumstances at Canberra—as being a genuine manifestation of the Holy Spirit. Even Paul strongly cautions the Corinthian believers that charismatic phenomena inevitably comes mixed with human and, at times, demonic influences, and requires, as has repeatedly been emphasized, discernment and judgment. No, my point is that the ecumenical movement is not about imposing a likemindedness or uniformity of belief or practices on its constituency. Rather, its goal is to lift up the name of Jesus Christ through common witness and common mission. And, its conviction is that such common witness and common mission sustains (or, should sustain) rather than destroy national, regional, local, and indigenous manifestations and expressions of the gospel. In other words, the ecclesiology of the ecumenical movement is profoundly pluralistic rather than hegemonistic, representing, ecumenists believe, the biblical emphasis on the "diversities of the Spirit."[20]

On the practical level, then, the ecumenical movement is more about affirming differences than it is about making churches the world over fit into one mold. In fact, the plurality of churches, liturgies, pieties, traditions, and expressions are affirmed. Each church is understood to play a vital role in the overall mission of the church; each contributes to the symphony that declares God's saving presence and activity in the world by the power of Spirit; each provides distinct witness to the world, and brings their own gifts to the head of the church, Jesus Christ. In fact, as the contingent of churches from the non-Western world has consistently increased in the WCC, it is becoming increasingly apparent that the traditional (read: Western) norms for discernment—whether at the level of the manifestation of the *charismata* or even at the more fundamental level of ecclesiologies as a whole—will continue to be challenged, resulting in a re-emphasis on Scriptural criteria.[21]

Of course, embracing the "diversities of the Spirit" includes with it potential problems as well. Apart from issues discussed previously, there is the important matter of an extreme tolerance that might set in such that truth is compromised. Ecumenists certainly have been charged with being pluralistic relativists, refusing to offend others who might believe or practice differently than they do. On this score, the ecumenical movement needs the Pentecostal movement, but only insofar as the latter does not mute the prophetic voice of the Spirit of God. An ecumenism without truth is simply a vacuous, outward unity. Pentecostals who are fearful on this point should be critically engaged on this front. Our obligation should be a discerning

---

20. This may explain, at least in part, why the Roman Catholic Church has never become a member of the WCC since it is rather more convinced that Christian unity includes uniformity under one head, identified of course, under the papal symbol. Since Vatican II, however, Rome has certainly been involved in ecumenical activity.

21. And, of course, it is ironic that some in the ecumenical movement are threatened by the possibility that the WCC might someday be dominated by the presence of hundreds if not thousands of independent Pentecostal churches, the majority of which would derive from the two-thirds world. Dayton, "Yet Another Layer of the Onion," 87–110.

participation and engagement, not sectarian withdrawal and unqualified condemnation. Ecumenism needs Pentecostalism in order for it to be genuinely biblical. Who among us will respond to this call?

5. Pentecostalism and Ecumenism: Future Prospects and Tasks

My conclusion is that Pentecostals need the larger church even as the larger church needs Pentecostalism. Thus, the quest for a biblically based and Spirit inspired Christian unity must include both movements. In this last section of my five-part article, I want to briefly discuss the various levels of ecumenical activity and make some practical suggestions with regard to how Pentecostals can become more ecumenically conscious and involved.

Levels of Ecumenism

There is no one correct way to either be ecumenical or to do ecumenism. In fact, although I present four levels of ecumenical activity here, it is difficult to say where one stops and the other starts. I would surmise that wherever genuine ecumenism occurs, it will include theological and doctrinal discussion (academic ecumenism), the development of interpersonal relationships between clergy across denominational lines (church leadership ecumenism) and between the laity at large (neighborhood ecumenism), and social action of some type (institutional-denominational ecumenism).[22] If we keep in mind the artificial boundaries between each level, the following is designed to provide an overview of what ecumenism-in-action looks like.

Academic ecumenism usually involves teachers, professors, and those with advanced training in biblical and theological studies. At this level, the goals of ecumenical discussion include the clearing away of stereotypes, the development of mutual understanding, and the clarification of *actual* problems confronting Christian unity (as opposed to problems that are simply the result of misunderstanding or stereotype). Pentecostal academics who have been involved in these dialogues generally are not denominationally funded since most Pentecostal churches and groups do not place such activity high on their priority list. Thus, along two fronts—financially and with regard to one's personal reputation—Pentecostals who participate at this level of ecumenism do so at some personal risk. It is therefore not unusual

---

22. Here, I follow Raymond R. Pfister's typology. See Pfister, "The Ecumenical Challenge of Pentecostal Missions."

to hear many of them attest that their ecumenical involvement proceeds from a sense of divine calling.

Nevertheless, a growing contingent of individuals from academic organizations such as the international Society for Pentecostal Studies, the European Pentecostal Theological Association, the European Pentecostal and Charismatic Research Association, the Pentecostal Theological Association of Southern Africa, the Asian Pentecostal Society, the Asia Pentecostal Theological Association, the Indian Conference of Pentecostal Theologians, the Korean Pentecostal Society, and a host of other such groups in Latin America and Oceania are now engaging in theological, doctrinal, and praxis-oriented discussions with scholars from the mainline churches.[23] Many of these are take place in formal conference settings, such as at the annual meetings of the Evangelical Theological Society, the Wesleyan Theological Society, and the American Academy of Religion. Two of the most theologically and doctrinally sophisticated conversations with churches are the Pentecostal-Roman Catholic dialogue (five sessions from 1972 to the present) and the Pentecostal-World Alliance of Reformed Churches (WARC) dialogue (1996–).[24]

However, it is misleading to think that only academics engage in theological and doctrinal conversations across ecumenical lines. One certainly does not need a graduate degree in these disciplines to do so. In fact, Pentecostal ministers and laity are frequently a part of these type of conversations. Insofar as two persons representing different Christian communities have theological and doctrinal interests, they can and do strike up such conversations. And, insofar as both come away having learned something they were not aware of before, such dialogues have to be rated as successful!

Church leadership ecumenism frequently includes theological and doctrinal discussions. Pentecostal ministers have, in recent decades, become much more involved in ministerial associations, especially in urban areas. Most pastors usually attend monthly meetings with their colleagues in Pentecostal ministry. In addition to this, many also attend minister's

23. Information about these groups is only a few clicks away: see the "Academic Societies" section of the Pentecostal-Charismatic Theological Inquiry International homepage, http://www.pctii.org.

24. The results of the Pentecostal-Roman Catholic dialogue can be perused in the pages of *Pneuma: The Journal of the Society for Pentecostal Studies*. The first three sessions (1972–76, 1977–82, and 1985–89) are found in vol. 12.2 (1990); the fourth session (1990–97) is reported in vol. 21.1 (1999); the fifth session (1998–2006) and the sixth session (2011–15) is reported on the Vatican's web page: http://www.vatican.va/roman_curia/pontifical_councils/chrstuni/sub-index/index_pentecostals.htm. For an overview of the Pentecostal-WARC dialogue. Macchia, "Reformed/Pentecostal Dialogue."

meetings organized by evangelical pastors. While the benefits of these meetings are difficult to assess in isolation, cumulatively, a miracle of perception and association has taken place. When pastors from many evangelical denominations come together, they not only have discussions on theological and doctrinal topics. More importantly, they share their testimonies, their triumphs, and struggles in ministry; they sing together, and they pray for each other and bear each other's burdens. These meetings build trust and solidarity. They clear away misunderstandings. They provide a safe and secure platform for differences to be recognized and even appreciated. They are often the inspiration and impetus for common mission.

Of course, neighborhood ecumenism also includes many of these same features. On this level, the lines between Pentecostalism and the mainline churches have all but disintegrated. Many Pentecostals now feel right at home—in fact, they are, in these situations, at home, in their back or front yards—not only talking with their evangelical, Baptist, Presbyterian, Lutheran, and even Catholic and Orthodox neighbors, but also without questioning the status of their relationship with Jesus, the latter being self-evident. Not infrequently, these conversations turn toward specifically religious matters, sometimes including theological and doctrinal themes. And, insofar as neighbors often work together in neighborhood projects, these grassroots kinds of relationships demonstrate the ecumenical fellowship in the body of Christ rather unintentionally!

This raises the question of what institutional or denominational ecumenism looks like. I have previously mentioned Billy Graham and other kinds of evangelistic crusades. Christian musicians and performers also hold concerts that attract members of very different churches. More recently, events like Promise Keepers have filled stadiums with tens of thousands of people. These kinds of activities are valuable in and of themselves. But the kind of planning that is needed to pull them off is necessarily of the ecumenical type. What usually happens is that persons from various denominations have to not only pledge their support but also be actively involved in organizing, administrating, financing, praying for—both individually and together—and following-up such events. I would argue that the relationships forged in these background activities—stuff that goes on behind the main stage, so to speak—is equally powerful in transforming lives and bringing the body of Christ together.

These kinds of overtly ministerial events, however, by no means represent the only kinds of institutional and denominational ecumenism. Other events focused on social issues are equally ecumenical. March for Jesus rallies against abortion, for example, are powerful demonstrations of the unity of the church. And, other kinds of societal changes necessarily require Christians to put aside their differences regarding inessentials in order to work together. Individual groups or churches are, by themselves, generally ineffective in bringing about large-scale transformations of socioeconomic and political structures. These can only be accomplished by prolonged engagement and strategically organized efforts motivated by Christian faith.

It is at this level that one sees academic, church leadership, and neighborhood ecumenism come together. To take just one example, the continued fight for civil rights for ethnic minorities requires, among other things, racial reconciliation. The latter cannot be legislated. It has to come about from the hearts of people in society at large and be demonstrated by concrete actions. This means that racial reconciliation cannot be the task of just a few individuals or groups. Academics have to bring to light the social, historical, and religious factors behind racial tensions. Church leaders have to explore how such tensions can be eased—perhaps by holding more interracial events, implementing a series of pulpit and choir exchanges, or even merging smaller congregations. Neighbors have to find ways to demonstrate solidarity across racial lines. And, all of this has to proceed in tandem. Neighbors cannot wait for pastors who cannot wait on academics and vice versa. My point is that racial tension as a societal problem calls for the church to awaken from its slumber and take concrete action at various levels. Such action can be nothing but ecumenical in the best sense of the word.

What Then Can and Should We Do?

I have written far more than I intended when I first accepted the invitation of the editors to address this topic. This represents both the passion I feel regarding the importance of this matter and the burden we all carry in light of the immensity of this task. I would be remiss, however, if I did not conclude with some very practical suggestions about how we as Pentecostals can and should proceed ecumenically at this time, the dawn of the second Pentecostal century.

First, Pentecostals have not been entirely truthful in their anti-intellectualism. Jesus' admonished us to love God not only with our heart, our strength, and our soul, but also with our *mind* (Matt 22:37; Mark 12:30; Luke 10:27). For those of us who are hesitant to launch out into the uncharted (for us) waters of ecumenism, the first thing we can do is to educate ourselves. In reading the Bible, look for motifs that demonstrate God's inclusive love, the universal reign of the kingdom of God, and the celebration of difference and plurality in the created order. And, of course, strive to be more knowledgeable about ecumenism in general and the ecumenical movement more specifically.

Toward that end, I have appended a reading list that includes articles and books written by both Pentecostals and non-Pentecostals.

Second, be intentional about meeting with other Christians. In fact, as pastors and church leaders of Pentecostal churches, we should lead our congregations by example, seeking out opportunities to take our Pentecostal witness to ecumenical circles, especially those involving leadership.[25] Of course, we have to earn the right to have our testimonies heard, and this is usually accomplished by listening to what others have to say. Times of mutual worship and prayer should be frequent and central to our meetings with others. And, in this process, genuine *koinonia* emerges, friendships are established, dialogue is sustained, relationships are solidified, misunderstandings and stereotypes are identified, and trust is built. The personal benefit such will have on our lives cannot be measured. From a pastoral perspective, such experience will enable us to better direct members of our congregation in building their own lay and neighborhood ecumenical networks.

Last but by no means least, the interdenominational relationships that we establish as church leaders will also allow us to plan inter-congregational activities centered around worship, prayer, and the reading and exploration of Scripture. As important will be the opportunities afforded these congregations to take on community or social projects. Relief agencies such as rescue missions, alcohol and drug rehabilitation programs, and soup kitchens are already centers of ecumenical activity. The church's presence in local communities and neighborhoods need to be more pronounced. And, rather than simply touting one congregation or denomination as "superior"—such attitudes are often communicated by Christians without intending to do so—why not convey to the world the truth that Christians love each other and those without the faith in the same way as they are loved by God and in the same way as the Father loves the Son? This comes about by concrete acts of love—the feeding of the hungry, the housing of the homeless, the clothing of the naked, the visiting of those sick and in prison, and so on (Matt 25:31–46). Churches that comprise the one body of Jesus Christ can do much more together than they can do by themselves.

---

25. In fact, even a denomination like the Assemblies of God includes a statement in its Constitution and Bylaws that leaves plenty of room for Pentecostals to engage in ecumenical activity. Concluding their denunciation of the ecumenical movement (see note 6) is a parenthetical clause: "This is not to be interpreted to mean that a limitation may be imposed upon any Assemblies of God minister regarding his or her Pentecostal witness or participation on a local level with interdenominational activities" (Assemblies of God Bylaws, Article 9, §11).

As Pentecostals, we need to ask ourselves what the Holy Spirit is doing in the world (Rev 2–3, passim). As people led by the Spirit, how can we discern what God is doing in the church and how that work affects the church's witness to the world? The world has seen enough denominational strife, abstract theological speculation, futile doctrinal disputes, and Christian polemics. What the world needs is the love of God. Pentecostals, more than others, should know what it means to have been touched by the love of God in ways that while not marginalizing theology and doctrine, certainly do not exalt its place either. And, far beyond intellectual activity, Pentecostals emphasize the empowerment of the Holy Spirit for mission. As David Bundy puts it in the closing sentences of his paper on ecumenical Pentecostalism, "there is less of a concern among Pentecostals for a unity of theological opinion . . . than for common activity for the Kingdom of God. In other words, ecumenism for mission has precedence over ecumenism for koinonia."[26] So, the question that remains is this: what is the Holy Spirit doing to break down the barriers between Christians, and how can we as Pentecostals be involved in this essential task of taking the love of God to the world?

Bibliography

Albrecht, Daniel E. "Pentecostal Spirituality: Ecumenical Potential and Challenge." *Cyberjournal for Pentecostal-Charismatic Research* 2 (1997). http://www.pctii.org/cybertab.html.

Bartleman, Frank. *Azusa Street: The Roots of Modern-day Pentecost*. Plainfield, NJ: Logos International, 1980.

Bundy, David. "The Ecumenical Quest of Pentecostalism." *Cyberjournal for Pentecostal-Charismatic Research* 5 (1999). http://pctii/cyberj/cyber5.html.

Burgess, Stanley M., Gary B. McGee, and Patrick Alexander, eds. *Dictionary of Pentecostal and Charismatic Movements*. Grand Rapids: Academic Reference Library, 1988.

Dayton, Donald W. "Yet Another Layer of the Onion, or, Opening the Ecumenical Door to Let the Rifraff in." *The Ecumenical Review* 40 (1988) 87–100.

Dempster, Murray, Byron Klaus, and Douglas Petersen, eds. *The Globalization of Pentecostalism: A Religion Made to Travel*. Oxford: Regnum, 1999.

Du Plessis, David. *The Spirit Bade Me Go*. Plainfield, NJ: Logos International, 1970.

Fackre, Gabriel. *Ecumenical Faith in Evangelical Perspective*. Grand Rapids: Eerdmans, 1993.

Hollenweger, Walter. *Pentecostalism: Origins and Developments Worldwide*. Peabody, MA: Hendrickson, 1997.

26. Bundy, "The Ecumenical Quest of Pentecostalism."

Irvin, Dale T. "Drawing All Together into One Bond of Love: The Ecumenical Vision of William J. Seymour and the Azusa Street Revival." *Journal of Pentecostal Theology* 6 (1995) 23–53.

Jongeneel, Jan A. B., et al., eds. *Pentecost, Mission and Ecumenism: Essays on Intercultural Theology*. Studies in the Intercultural History of Christianity 75. New York: Lang, 1992.

Kinnamon, Michael, ed. *Signs of the Spirit: Official Report of the Seventh Assembly of the World Council of Churches, Canberra, Australia, 7-20 February 1991*. Geneva: WCC, 1991.

———. *Truth and Community: Diversity and Its Limits in the Ecumenical Movement*. Grand Rapids: Eerdmans, 1988.

Macchia, Frank. "From Azusa to Memphis: Evaluating the Racial Reconciliation Dialogue among Pentecostals." *Pneuma: The Journal of the Society for Pentecostal Studies* 10 (1995) 3–28.

———. "Reformed/Pentecostal Dialogue." In *The Dictionary of Pentecostal and Charismatic Movements, Revised Edition*, edited by Stanley M. Burgess et al., 575–76. Grand Rapids: Zondervan, 2000.

Marsden, George. *Fundamentalism and American Culture: The Shaping of Twentieth Century Evangelicalism, 1870–1925*. New York: Oxford University Press, 1980.

Moltmann, Jürgen, and Karl-Josef Kuschel, eds. *Pentecostal Movements as an Ecumenical Challenge*. Concilium 1996/3. London: SCM, 1996.

Pfister, Raymond R. "The Ecumenical Challenge of Pentecostal Missions: A European Pentecostal Perspective for the 21st Century." Unpublished paper presented at the 29th Annual Meeting of the Society for Pentecostal Studies, Studies 16-18 March. Kirkland, WA: Annual Meeting of the Society for Pentecostal Studies, 2000.

Quebedeaux, Richard. *The New Charismatic II*. San Francisco: Harper & Row, 1983.

Robeck, Cecil M., Jr. "The Assemblies of God and Ecumenical Cooperation: 1920–1965." In *Pentecostalism in Context: Essays in Honor of William W. Menzies*, edited by Wonsuk Ma and Robert P. Menzies, 63–64. Journal of Pentecostal Theology Supplement Series 11. Sheffield, UK: Sheffield Academic Press, 1997.

———. "Growing Up Pentecostal." *Theology News and Notes* 35.1 (1988) 4–7.

———. "Pentecostals and Visible Church Unity." *One World* 192, January-February, 1984, 11–14.

———. "A Pentecostal Looks at the World Council of Churches." *The Ecumenical Review* 47 (1995) 108–20.

———. "A Pentecostal Reflects on Canberra." In *Beyond Canberra: Evangelical Responses to Contemporary Ecumenical Issues*, edited by Bruce J. Nicholls and Bong Rin Ro, 108–20. Oxford: Regnum, 1993.

Robinson, Martin. "To the Ends of the Earth: The Pilgrimage of an Ecumenical Pentecostal, David J. du Plessis (1905–1987)." Ph.D. diss., University of Birmingham, England, 1987.

Ruthven, Jan. *On the Cessation of the Charismata: The Protestant Polemic on Postbiblical Miracles*. Journal of Pentecostal Theology Supplement Series 3. Sheffield, UK: Sheffield Academic Press, 1993.

Sandidge J. L. "The World Council of Churches." In *Dictionary of Pentecostal and Charismatic Movements*, edited by Stanley Burgess, Gary B. McGee, and Patrick H. Alexander, 901–3. Grand Rapids: Regency Reference Library, 1988.

Sheppard, Gerald T. "Pentecostalism and the Hermeneutics of Dispensationalism: Anatomy of an Uneasy Relationship." *Pneuma: The Journal of the Society for Pentecostal Studies* 6 (1984) 5–33.

Van Elderen, Marlin. *Introducing the World Council of Churches*. Rev. ed. Geneva: Risk Book Series/WCC, 1992.

Yong, Amos. "Between Two Extremes: Balancing Word-Christianity and Spirit-Christianity" (A Review Article). *The Pneuma Review* 3.1 (2000) 78–83.

———. "On the Cessation of the Charismata: The Protestant Polemic on Postbiblical Miracles" (A Review Article). *The Pneuma Review* 3.2 (2000) 64–65.

13

The Theological Motivations for Pentecostal Mission

Wonsuk Ma

The Growth of Global Pentecostalism[1]

THE GROWTH OF THE modern Pentecostal movement is a remarkable story. During the century of its existence, it has grown from a "fringe" group congregating every day in a run-down warehouse in downtown Los Angeles whose members were branded as religious fanatics to spread throughout the world, and influence other church traditions. Although numbers vary,[2] there is a consensus that it now numbers around half a billion throughout the world in various forms and traditions, including "charismatics" well integrated into various existing church families.[3] This chapter charts the growth of the movement and its developing missiology, demonstrating the complex interplay of Bible, experience, and theology as it does so.

The significance of Pentecostal expansion was evident as the world church celebrated the centenary of the Edinburgh Missionary Conference. In its original 1910 conference, Pentecostals were in their infancy. The disappearance of the Azusa Street Mission in 1909, perhaps the most visible expression of Pentecostal Christianity, after a three-year controversial existence, may have been a relief to some Christian leaders who felt embarrassed by this "tongue-babbling cultish group."[4] So, the Edinburgh

---

1. This study was originally published in: Wonsuk Ma and Kenneth R. Ross, eds., *Mission Spirituality and Authentic Discipleship* (Regnum Edinburgh Centenary Series 14. Oxford: Regnum, 2013).

2. See Johnson and Ross, *Atlas of Global Christianity 1910–2010*.

3. Ibid., 103.

4. Robeck, *The Azusa Street Mission and Revival*, 134.

conference did not need to worry about them. They were already struggling with issues surrounding the Catholic Church. However, Pentecostals did not "die out." In fact, the dramatic expansion of Christianity owes much to the exponential growth of Pentecostal churches and their variants.[5] The African Independent Churches, most Chinese house church networks, and the majority of Latin American evangelicals are defined as Pentecostal in a broader sense.

By the time the world church came to celebrate the centenary of the Edinburgh conference in June 2010, the radical shift in the landscape of global Christianity was crystal clear. A hundred years ago, about 82 percent of all Christians lived in the global North, or the "West," including Oceania. But today, over 60 percent of Christians live in the global South, the three major southern continents.[6] A steady decline of Western Christianity and a corresponding growth of Christianity in the global South occurred between the two conferences. As much of the new Christianity in the South is Pentecostal or its variation, it is also noteworthy that in the West, growing segments of the church are Pentecostal-charismatic. For example, in the midst of a rapid decline of Christians in Great Britain, the annual New Wine conferences among charismatic churches are refreshing. In the 2010 Somerset conference, I witnessed about 15,000 participants of all ages savoring expositions of the Word, praises, and various seminars.

The expectation is that the growth of Christianity in the South will continue, and so will Pentecostal worship and spirituality. If the twentieth century was marked by the exponential growth of African Christianity, all eyes are now on Asia, where Christianity has reached only 8.5 percent of its vast population of 3.5 billion (more than half of the world's population). The main growth engine is going to be Chinese Christianity as it is moving toward a 10 percent goal of the national population.[7] When and if Asia achieves a 15 percent mark it will add 8.5 million to the current number, making Christians exactly one-third level of the world population.[8] The share of Pentecostals will be significant in this growth.

While evangelism and church expansion have been the focus of Pentecostal mission, it is also important to note that so-called "mercy ministry" has been an integral part of Pentecostal mission practice if not,

---

5. Jenkins, *The Next Christendom*, 63.

6. Based on the figures found in "Distribution of Christians, 1910–2010." Johnson and Ross, *Atlas of Global Christianity 1910–2010*, 59.

7. Johnson and Ross, *Atlas of Global Christianity 1910–2010*, 140–41.

8. Ibid., 53.

until recently, its official statements.[9] Countless orphanages, various levels of educational institutions, relief work, and others have been deeply ingrained in "soul-saving" activities. Often without any intentional or serious theological reflection, Pentecostals, perhaps as they are from lower social strata, have instinctive solidarity with the poor and suffering. Two recent publications may serve as useful illustrations. The first, *Not by Might, Nor by Power*[10] looks into the Latin American Child Care program of the US Assemblies of God World Mission. It records the growth of the educational program for poor families throughout Latin America and its impact on societies. From this success, the author constructs a Pentecostal mission theology of social engagement. The second, *Global Pentecostalism* by Miller and Yamamori,[11] is a summary of a four-year field study of growing congregations in the global South, who were intentionally engaging with issues that societies and communities are facing. It found that most of the congregations meeting these requirements were Pentecostal. This sociological study reveals that Pentecostal mission thinking and practice include care for the suffering. The book, however, challenges Pentecostals on two fronts: to move beyond the evangelism-church planting dimension; and to construct appropriate theology to provide Pentecostals with a valid conceptual ground for social engagement.

Inquiry at Hand

This study probes the theological motivation for such exponential growth. Considering that such expansion requires the agency of Pentecostal believers, the study looks at hermeneutical roots and missional theology of Pentecostalism. This two-stage inquiry is appropriate for the "grassroots" nature of Pentecostal theologization, a process which is often participatory and context-based: it is undertaken by people in the pews and responds to immediate human needs. The crux of this process, therefore, is not trained academic theologians, but preacher-pastors.[12] Consequently, Pentecostal theology is deeply embedded in prayers, sermons, songs and non-verbal expressions of its spirituality. This makes a theologian's first work a description, articulation, and analysis of embedded theological assumptions and arguments.

---

9. AOG, "Article III."
10. Petersen, *Not by Might, Nor by Power.*
11. Miller and Yamamori, *Global Pentecostalism.*
12. Ma and Ma, *Mission in the Spirit*, 227–41.

Hermeneutical values are a set of orientations inherent in Pentecostal spirituality and theology. These characteristics have critically contributed to the identity of Pentecostal believers and to their theological framework, although implicitly expressed. These values also guide Pentecostals in interpreting the Scriptures and their religious experiences. Although evolved throughout its history and expressed in various forms in different contexts, they still remain as constants among Pentecostal believers. They may provide clues to defining Pentecostalism.

Which Pentecostalism?

While Pentecostalism can be defined and characterized in various ways, for this reflection it seems to be convenient to limit to the first wave, denominational (or "Classical") Pentecostals. They are more identifiable than charismatics, whose mission theology and action are shaped by their denominations. They are less "messy" than the third category sometimes called indigenous Pentecostals or Neo-charismatics. Strictly speaking, it is not a category, but a catch-all holding bay for a great diversity of expressions that share Pentecostal core values, including Chinese house-church networks, African Independent Churches, and the Third Wave movement. Tentatively, therefore, we may be able to claim that the "values" are more broadly owned by various Pentecostal families, whereas the "theological threads" are more of the classical Pentecostal families. The longer history of first-wave Pentecostals makes them more doctrinally coherent and more articulate in their theology and spirituality than the others. However, even within this group, the matter is not that simple. There is great theological diversity among classical Pentecostals, particularly outside the Western hemisphere. For example, the Yoido Full Gospel Church in Korea, the largest single congregation in the world, is part of the global Assemblies of God family. However, some of its theological components and spiritual expressions are vastly different from its Western cousins. In the global scene, it is also important to remember that the first category is the smallest among world Pentecostal families.

Pentecostal Hermeneutical Values

Any theological investigation needs to seriously consider the hermeneutical strategies of a particular group. Pentecostal hermeneutical strategies influence how one reads Scripture and how one interpret one's own life in the light of Scripture. Obviously, much of Pentecostal's unique hermeneutical ethos was emerging in the nineteenth century. The following discussion is intended to be a brief presentation of key hermeneutical sources for Pentecostal mission theology.

"People of the Book": Scripture and Life

Pentecostals have been called the "people of the book" for their unquestioned acceptance of the authority, and their literalistic reading of the Bible.

The first characteristic is the non-critical reading of the Bible, or perhaps more accurately the post-critical reading by Pentecostal academics and the pre-critical reading by Pentecostals in the pew. Like their conservative evangelical cousins, early Pentecostals had a firm belief in the (almost mechanical) inspiration of Scripture. This was part of the general trend against the intellectual inquiries and the critical reading of the Bible, originating in nineteenth-century German scholarship and gradually spreading to Europe and North America. Hence, any attempt to critically study the Scriptures used to be viewed as a theologically "liberal" practice. This attitude has been further reinforced among the majority of non-Western Pentecostals who live in places where sacred Scriptures are never questioned. They are objects of reverence and obedience, and this "evangelical" attitude toward the Bible is believed to be the basis for the Christian dynamic of the global South.[13]

Pentecostals have maintained a notion that the more literally one takes the Scripture, the more faithful one becomes to the word of God, thus the will of God. Triggered from their reading of narratives in the Gospels and Acts, the historicity of events contained in the narratives is never questioned. Furthermore, the inclusion of certain narratives in the Scriptures was also taken as proof for a normative pattern. Speaking in tongues as "the initial physical evidence" of baptism in the Holy Spirit is based on the recurrence of Spirit-filled tongue-speaking in Acts. Naturally, Pentecostals fully subscribe, therefore, to the historicity and authenticity of supernatural events recorded in the Scripture. Their unique view of Scripture and the Holy Spirit allows Pentecostals to collapse the time gap between biblical times and their present, establishing a link between the early church and the Azusa Street Mission. They simply assume that miracles included in the biblical narratives are repeatable today. This comes with advantages as well as disadvantages. The Bible to the Pentecostals is not an ancient book at all.

The temporal truncation also collapses the distance between God and humans, or the sacred and the secular. The transcendental God is now

13. See Jenkins, *The New Faces of Christianity*.

immanent. They expect to "hear the voice of God" from the book. Narratives have a particular appeal as the process of reading will soon become the process of participation: the readers find themselves in the midst of the story, be it of healing or of miracles. This ability to "time travel" provides lively religious experiences. The God of the exodus, for example, is expected to appear here and now, allowing the believers to have a similar experience of God's intervention. Thus, the interplay of such a Bible-reading and experience-oriented religious life creates a spiral effect to enhance a highly engaged Christian life with God's reality. A Pentecostal's "pre-critical" reading of the Bible naturally results in a literal reading, leaving little room for spiritualizing or demythologizing any "irrational" record of the Bible.

Restorational Impulse: Apostolic Vision

As the twentieth century approached, there was a heightened interest in eschatology. One stream was the expectation of the early church restored with the manifestation of the spiritual gifts of prophecy, healing, and an outpouring of the Holy Spirit as recorded in Acts and 1 Corinthians. Camp meetings were a common annual feature for devout believers and their families to experience personal revival. One of the most popular words among the late-nineteenth-century Holiness and early-twentieth-century Pentecostal believers was "apostolic," reflecting the expectation and yearning for the restoration of church life as is recorded in the Book of Acts. The dawning of the new century reinforced their eager expectation of the "latter rain" to mark the end of the end time.

The modern Pentecostal movement has developed its unique mission-oriented theology of the Holy Spirit and Christian life. With their unique experiences such as baptism in the Holy Spirit and tongues as its accompanying sign, early Pentecostals understood themselves as being people called for a specific task. Considering that the advent of the Spirit gave birth to the church, the very foundation of its existence is missional. Accordingly, spiritual baptism has been closely linked to witnessing (Acts 1:8), and some early Pentecostal leaders advocated tongues as a practical missionary tool.[14] This unique theological understanding shaped a peculiar self-identity as people empowered for God's mission. Pentecostals were counter-cultural, both in the church and in society, and courageously endured ridicule and marginalization. Yet throughout its history, Pentecostalism has flourished where Christian presence had been in existence, instead of "virgin" Christian frontiers. In this sense, Pentecostalism is a

---

14. Goff, "Initial Tongues in the Theology of Charles Fox Parham," 57–71.

revival and renewal movement, challenging and energizing the church to recover its "apostolic" authority and call to witness for Christ to the ends of the earth. Evangelism and church planting have been at the core of Pentecostal mission, partly due to its eschatological orientation, and also as part of the early-twentieth-century evangelical Christianity.

Participatory Process: Place of Community

The role of community is the focal point of religious life and of the hermeneutical process. The work of the Holy Spirit in community-formation is experienced at least in two fronts: bringing people around common spiritual experience, and breaking barriers that divide God's people. In the Azusa Street Mission, the common experience of Spirit baptism brought together people of different races, social strata, and ecclesiastical affiliations. At the turn of the twentieth century, white and Afro-Americans worshipping together was a radical counter-cultural departure from the norm. The division of the movement along racial lines has become a stark reminder of human sinfulness and failure against the Spirit's intention and work. However, this amazing potential continued to appear throughout its history. In the Philippines in the 1980s, a sociologist discovered close relationships between Pentecostals and charismatic Catholics despite the hostility between Protestants and Catholics in the Philippines.[15]

At the center of Pentecostal community formation is worship. It provides a space and time for religious experiences, theological formation and the shared process of theology-making. Worship is incredibly participatory in nature, often blurring the demarcation between the pulpit and the pews. One excellent example is the "testimony" time, where anyone can be the "main speaker." By publicly sharing one's religious experience "to praise the Lord" or "to plea to the Lord," any member of the community contributes to the corporate deposit of theology and also for the community to exercise the "gift" of discernment, evaluation, and shared ownership of the presented experience and its interpretation. This "democratic" nature of Pentecostal spirituality significantly enhances the community formation process. The exercise of spiritual gifts also takes place in a community setting, often a prophecy or a message in tongues ideally accompanied by an interpretation.

Even seemingly individualistic matters are experienced in the community context among Pentecostals. I recall that my own yearning for the baptism in the Spirit, as individualistic as it may seem, became the subject

15. Kitano, "Socio-Religious Distance between Charismatics and Other Religious Group Members," 231–42.

of a community prayer. I walked through this process together with many fellow Pentecostal believers. When I finally "got it," we together celebrated in praise and worship. In Korea, it is common that a family's prayer becomes the prayer of the entire cell group and sometimes the cell leader will bring the family members to a prayer mountain for prayer and fasting for several days, while the entire cell member families are in prayer. The community-forming potential of the Holy Spirit is experienced in various dimensions.

Experience: Lived-Out Spirituality

Another important aspect of restorational thinking is the recovery of religious experience. Flowing from the Pentecostal view of Scripture, Bible stories are read to experience an encounter with God and to show the miracles that contemporary readers can experience.[16] Pentecostals never "demythologize" the miracle stories of the Bible. The Pentecostal appropriation of the biblical narratives occurs in two ways: they transport the ancient stories to contemporary life (existentialization), they also "slip" themselves into the ancient story of action (identification). The logic is simple: if the God of the Bible acted then, he can do the same today. For this reason, Pentecostals love to affirm that God is "the same yesterday, today, and forever" (Heb 13:8).

This mindset promotes an expectation of having a tangible encounter with God through worship, prayer, sermons, Bible reading, and the like. The nature of such encounters varies, but Pentecostals expect to "hear from the Lord." Hearing from God is a common feature of Christianity. The distinctiveness of the Pentecostal experience of hearing is rather concrete and tangible, even if one can argue that tangibility is a subjective notion. Pentecostals are quite open to various channels of such revelation, including dreams, visions, audible or "inner" voices, mental impressions, or a passage "being lifted from the page." Such "voices" are not limited to matters of spirituality but apply almost to any issue in life. The other area of encounter is the "touch of the Lord." This expression often refers to various experiences of God's reality, be it divine healing, an overwhelming sense of God's presence, relief from physical, emotional, or circumstantial difficulties, a deep conviction of God's truth, and the like.

Unlike the Reformers' notion of the Holy Spirit as a shy member of the Trinity, Pentecostals, based on their reading in Luke-Acts, have re-profiled the Holy Spirit as the active player in the birth of the church, initiator of

---

16. See Warrington, *Pentecostal Theology*.

mission, and overseer of the spread of the gospel through empowerment.[17] Many experiences, whether supernatural or circumstantial, are all carefully initiated by the Holy Spirit. This has led Pentecostals into two important theological conclusions: (1) The Holy Spirit interacts with God's people through a wide range of religious experiences, including prophecy (11:22–23; 19:6; 21:9), dreams and visions (9:10; 10:3), hearing voices (10:19; 16:9; 18:9), healings (3:1–8; 4:30), and the like; and (2) such experiences embolden believers in their faith and lead them to opportunities to witness to the Risen Lord. However, the role of experience in biblical interpretation is a controversial issue. Ideally, the Word should guide, inform, and set a parameter to religious experience, while experience affirms the Word. Pentecostals are called to guard themselves against the danger of placing experience over the word. Nonetheless, with their literalistic reading of the Bible, religious experiences—like baptism in the Spirit, as we shall see below—have a definite role in strengthening their sense of call and commitment to sacred vocation.

People of the Spirit(s)

Pentecostals assume a worldview distinct from many contemporary Western Christians, but closer to a non-Western understanding of life and the world. For example, Pentecostals are conscious of spiritual beings, benevolent as well as malevolent, angels, spirits, and demons, at work in human lives. For this reason, Pentecostals are the people of the S/spirit(s). With their "liberal" reading of the Bible, their emphasis on the experiential dimension of religious life, Pentecostals gravitate to the unseen and yet active world of the supernatural.

Two particular areas may be noteworthy. The first is, as noted briefly above, the development of a dynamic theology of the Holy Spirit. Pneumatology that is born out of one's radical experience of the Holy Spirit—be it baptism in the Spirit, healing, exorcism, "hearing" him, or "seeing" his work—will be explosive. The Holy Spirit has become a miracle-working member of the Trinity. He empowers the church to be victorious in the middle of a hostile world providing signs and wonders as part of Christian witness. This orientation gives a shape of empowerment theology that is unique to Pentecostalism. The second area is the similarity between Pentecostal worldview and that of many non-Western cultures where diverse spirits are perceived to operate on a daily basis, generating a clash of (supernatural)

---

17. See Stronstad, *The Charismatic Theology of St Luke*; Menzies, *Empowered for Witness*.

spirits. Only the most powerful spirit (or God) earns a right to be worshiped, and the contest of such spiritual forces has become the basis for mass conversions.[18] The explosion of Pentecostal-type Christianity in Africa, Asia, and Latin America is partly attributed to these worldview similarities[19] and to common interests in life, such as healings, blessings, curses.[20] Pentecostalism can supply functional substitutes to the felt and perceived religious needs because the worldviews have corresponding categories. This helps the missionary recognize the needs of the recipient.

Theological Resources for Pentecostal Mission

The mission implications of four theological beliefs unique to Pentecostalism will be discussed with reference to their historical development. The modern Pentecostal movement as an organized theological and spiritual tradition traces its origin to a conservative form of Protestantism found in the nineteenth-century Holiness movement of North America.[21] Charles Parham and William J. Seymour, the two most renowned Pentecostal "fathers," were Holiness preachers. To illustrate the beliefs and practices of early Pentecostals, reports will be used that were published in *The Apostolic Faith* (*TAF*) of the Azusa Street Mission of Los Angeles (1906–9), the most representative Pentecostal periodical of the formative years of Pentecostal theological construction. We will see that a number of key factors, already mentioned, are involved in Pentecostal theological construction: Scripture, the Holy Spirit interacting with Scripture, the community of believers,[22] the Pentecostal experience, and the wider social context. Context has been recognized as significant as Pentecostals in the global South become more prominent in the movement.

Baptism in the Spirit

This cardinal doctrine makes (classical) Pentecostals distinct from the rest of Christianity. Understood as an experience distinct from and subsequent to regeneration, belief in baptism in the Holy Spirit has caused a continuing

---

18. See Tippett, *People Movements in Southern Polynesia*.
19. Hollenweger, *Pentecostalism*, 18–80.
20. See Ma, *When the Spirit Meets the Spirits*.
21. I am aware of arguments on multiple "springheads" of the movement. For this reason, I used the qualifier "organized" theological and spiritual tradition.
22. Archer, *A Pentecostal Hermeneutics for the Twenty-First Century*, 156–91.

debate between Pentecostals and evangelicals. Based on the post-resurrection promise of the Lord that his followers would be baptized in the Holy Spirit, Pentecostals took it as a sign of the restoration of early church spirituality, especially the experience on the day of Pentecost (Acts 2).[23] For the present discussion, three aspects of this belief will be explored with mission as a proclamation in mind: experience, its interpretation, and consequences.

As discussed above, Pentecostalism has brought back the significant role of religious experiences. Testimonies abound to the powerful impact of experiences loosely termed "the baptism in the Holy Spirit." Various life-changing stories are shared, although most North American classical Pentecostal churches insist on speaking in tongues as "the physical and initial evidence." The sense of God's overwhelming presence is a common element of these experiences, as recorded in the first issue of *TAF*:

> Proud, well-dressed preachers come in to "investigate." Soon their high looks are replaced with wonder, then conviction comes, and very often you will find them in a short time wallowing on the dirty floor, asking God to forgive them and make them as little children. It would be impossible to state how many have been converted, sanctified and filled with the Holy Ghost. They have been and are daily going out to all points of the compass to spread this wonderful gospel.[24]

Speaking in tongues also brought tangible impact not only to the recipients of the Spirit baptism but also to those who witnessed them. It is no wonder that Pentecostalism spread like a wildfire. It is not only understood as a sign of the restoration of early church spirituality, but it also shapes the self-identity of people who are called and commissioned to bring the news of salvation to the ends of the earth. It is also interpreted as the reception of power from above for witnessing in the context of Acts 1:8. The early Pentecostal literature made it clear that, "The baptism with the Holy Spirit is not a work of grace but a gift of power . . . . The baptism with the Holy Ghost makes you a witness unto the uttermost parts of the earth. It gives you power to speak in the languages of the nations."[25] Its biblical illustrations are often taken from Peter's bold preaching in Acts 2:14–40, and Stephen's courageous sermon in Acts 7:2–53. Last, especially at a popular level, baptism in the Spirit is understood to be the "floodgate" of spiritual gifts including healing and miracles.

---

23. See Macchia, *Baptized in the Spirit*.

24. See "Pentecostal Has Come: Los Angeles Being Visited by a Revival of Bible Salvation and Pentecost."

25. See "The Enduement of Power."

The consequences of this doctrine are evident in an unbending commitment to mission. With a strong sense of calling to be witnesses "to the end of the earth," this revival movement quickly turned into a missionary movement. A catalog of heroic missionary achievements, despite little or no training or support, is attributed to this sense of call. A zeal for preaching the "full gospel" in which tongue-speaking often functions as a reinforcement is another consequence. Some early Pentecostals expected tongues to enable them to bypass laborious language-learning.[26] Third, after the pattern of Acts, signs and wonders are expected in the context of mission. This power-orientation makes Pentecostals bold witnesses with claims of healings and miracles, albeit with many controversies surrounding them. The net result is the fast spread of the Pentecostal message and the expansion of the Pentecostal movement globally. This pneumatologically-shaped missiology is well attested in a *TAF* report of an Azusa missionary in its early days:

> A Pentecostal missionary has left for foreign lands, Bro Thos P Mahler, a young man of German nationality. He has the gift of tongues besides the knowledge of several. He left here for San Bernardino. He may go by way of Alaska, Russia, Norway, Germany and to his destination in Africa. As our brother was leaving, Bro Post spoke of his call and gave a message in tongues in regard to Bro Mahler which he interpreted as follows: "I have anointed this dear one with my Spirit, and he is a chosen vessel to me to preach the gospel to many, and to suffer martyrdom in Africa."[27]

Prophethood of All Believers

This is closely related to the previous discussion on baptism in the Spirit. However, because of its significance in Pentecostal mission, a separate discussion is deemed necessary. This is almost a natural and logical outgrowth of the belief in baptism in the Holy Spirit. Peter's interpretation of the advent of the Holy Spirit on the day of Pentecost is important. In the Old Testament period, only a handful of leaders experienced the coming of the Spirit of God, such as the seventy elders (Num 11), selected judges, the first two kings of United Israel, and selected prophets. However, an eschatological expectation of the Old Testament is to break this exclusivity of the Spirit:

---

26. See "Russians Hear in Their Own Tongue."
27. Ibid.

everyone in God's community will experience the coming of the Spirit. This is the prophecy of Joel (2:28–29), which has its root in Moses' desire for the whole of Israel (Num 11:29). This democratization of the Spirit is the gist of Peter's sermon in presenting the coming of the Holy Spirit on the Day of Pentecost (Acts 2:16–21).

If anyone in God's community is baptized in the Holy Spirit, regardless of age, gender, and social status, the calling, empowerment, and commission for God's work are for every believer, thus, "prophethood of all believers." This theological paradigm should be understood within the context of Christianity in the West at the turn of the twentieth century. In spite of various expressions of "every believer's prophetic call," the dominant ministry paradigm among the established churches was clergy-oriented professionalism. Pentecostal theology was a powerful challenge to the established norm.

Of particular note is the significant contribution of women in Pentecostal mission. Later this is expressed in Korea through the mobilization of lay women leaders in David Yonggi Cho's well-known cell-group system. Young people are also mobilized for the mission in networks, such as Youth With A Mission. This liberates ministry from the exclusive hands of elite clergy. Often advocating short-term missionary service, YWAM and others have "democratized" ministry and mission for every believer. Thirdly, an extension of this radical mission-thinking is the establishment and empowerment of, and transfer to, national and local leadership at the earliest opportunity,[28] a practice that has made Pentecostalism the fastest growing religious movement in our day.

Eschatology

Early Pentecostals shared their eschatology with the late nineteenth-century-conservative premillennial orientation. The turn of the century provided a naïve expectation of the end of human history. Here is an example found in *TAF*:

> All these 6,000 years, we have been fighting against sin and Satan. Soon we shall have a rest of 1,000 years . . . . We must go on to perfection and holiness, and get the baptism with the Holy Ghost, and not stop there, but go on to perfection and maturity.[29]

---

28. See Hodges, *The Indigenous Church*.
29. "The Millenium."

The outpouring of the Holy Spirit was taken as a sure sign of the end of the end time, the last opportunity for the greatest harvest of souls before the return of the Lord. This created an incongruent theological system for Pentecostals, adopting the dispensational scheme of human history. With the fast closure of the church age, or the age of grace, the church is to be taken to heaven, before the return of the age where Jews are dealt with through tribulation. This formed the awareness of living at the "five-to-midnight" moment, giving an extremely small window of opportunity to save as many souls as possible. "One-way ticket missionaries" were strongly motivated by the eschatological urgency. It was not unusual that engaged young women broke their engagements and left for their mission field.[30] This eschatological consciousness made them other-world oriented. Coupled with the religious consciousness of call and empowerment for witness, they are the best ingredients for the significant mission movement we have seen in the last one hundred years.

In spite of the powerful and positive contribution of this form of premillennialism with the expectation of the imminent return of the Lord, such clock-setting eschatology must expire sooner or later. As the movement enters the third generation, eschatological messages from Pentecostal pulpits have gradually disappeared to be replaced by this-worldly concerns, such as church growth, the message of blessings and health.[31] Fortunately, the dynamic motive of Pentecostal mission lies in the pneumatological interpretation rather than its temporal eschatological expectation, as the global Pentecostal movement has continued its growth even after the waning of an imminent eschatology.

Primacy of "Soul" Matter

Pentecostalism has all the crucial ingredients to become an unprecedented "religion to travel," as well-evidenced in the exponential growth and spread all over the world in its wild diversity and creativity. Its evangelical heritage and the temporally oriented eschatology has focused Pentecostal missiology on evangelism and church planting. The rise of a social gospel in the middle of the twentieth century may have further encouraged the already narrowly focused attention. Mission impetus was also taken from the mission roadmap found in their favorite passage: ". . . from Jerusalem, all Judea, Samaria and (finally) to the ends of the earth" (Acts 1:8). Crossing geographical

---

30. Shemeth, "Trasher, Lillian Hunt," 1153.
31. Ma, "Pentecostal Eschatology," 227–42.

boundaries, therefore, has been part of Pentecostal mission paradigm. Many brilliant social programs have soul winning as their ultimate goal.[32]

This, however, may reveal the Pentecostal understanding of humans, sin, and salvation. Every evil, be it personal or corporate, is traced to sin, and to Genesis 3 where separation from God resulted in spiritual damnation, physical suffering, broken society, and cursed environment. The Pentecostal view of restoration, therefore, reverses the order, beginning with the spiritual regeneration, and then personal (including the physical level, such as healing), communal (social), and even environmental, if the notion is conceived in Pentecostal mission framework.[33] The upward social mobility of Pentecostals has been attributed to this paradigm.[34]

Naturally "revival" or "renewal" is an important concept in Pentecostal thinking. The Pentecostal movement itself is often classified as a revival movement. The January 1907 issue of *TAF* reveals a glimpse of the Azusa Street revival:

> The meeting went on till morning and all the next day. . . . Pentecost first fell in Los Angeles on April 9th [of 1906]. Since then the good tidings has spread in two hemispheres. . . . Wherever the work goes, souls are saved, and not only saved from hell but through and through, and prepared to meet the Lord at his coming. Hundreds have been baptized with the Holy Ghost. Many of them are now out in the field, and some in foreign lands, and God is working with them, granting signs and wonders to follow the preaching of the full Gospel.[35]

As Pentecostal missiology matures, an argument seems to gain ground that spiritual dynamism, evangelism, church growth, and social service are not mutually exclusive.[36]

Conclusion

If this short study in any way leaves an impression that Pentecostals have finally unlocked the secret of Christian mission, the reality is exactly its opposite. In the name of God's kingdom and renewal, church divisions were caused by this movement and unfortunately they have been part of

32. See, Calcutta Mercy Ministries, "History."
33. Batty and Campbell, "Teen Challenge," 14–21.
34. See Martin, *Tongues of Fire*.
35. See "Beginning of World Wide Revival."
36. Lee, *The Holy Spirit Movement in Korea*, 126–27.

its growth "strategy." Some of its serious blind spots, such as its eschatological expectation, are already presented. While they are praised for their creativity in contextualization, Pentecostals are also criticized for the ugly "prosperity gospel"[37] and their extremely "Western" outlook and ethos. All in all, there is much for further reflection and study.[38]

In the next decades, the progress of Pentecostal mission will depend on how Pentecostals preserve and strengthen their unique spiritual values and understand their changing contexts so that their theological constructs will respond to their missional call and contextual needs. The Bible will continue to play an important role, especially as the movement spreads increasingly in the global South. The expectation of the supernatural dimension of Christianity, the role of community and experience, as well as a more holistic worldview, will continue to play critical roles in Pentecostal religious life. Serious challenges and new opportunities will rise on the theological front, and any good theology will need to be locally grounded and relevant. This requires the conscious engagement of Pentecostal values and context. If frontline workers such as pastors, evangelists, and missionaries are to continue their critical role of popular theological construction, theological formation will be essential. Aided by Pentecostal theologians, frontline leaders can protect Pentecostal communities from consumerism-driven and self-serving popular religion so they can become relevant to their context. Pentecostal eschatology, as seen in the past, may not serve its earlier pivotal role, and so may be the way of the baptism in the Spirit. However, the latter's empowerment theology, incorporated in the prophethood of all believers, will remain high in Pentecostal theological agendas, if the theology is to remain "Pentecostal." The primary purpose of soul-winning is expected to continue, although the Pentecostal horizon in mission thinking and practice has become more holistic and inclusive. At the same time, more locally motivated theological agendas, such as reconciliation, should surface in places where religious and racial conflicts raise tensions.

Classical Pentecostals have the most theological and institutional resources. In non-Western lands, they look radically different from their North American or European "mothers," who are not necessarily growing. This is a serious challenge to their century-old theology and constantly institutionalizing ethos. Yet they may also empowering the rest of the Pentecostal-charismatic churches. Together they should continue their engagement in new frontiers of mission because to remain faithful to the Scriptures, to Pentecostal spiritual heritage, and yet be relevant to the immediate context

---

37. Yung, "The Missiological Challenge of David Yonggi Cho's Theology," 85–90.
38. See, Ma and Ma, *Mission in the Spirit*.

will pose a significant challenge to emerging Pentecostal mission communities throughout the world.

Bibliography

AOG. "Article III." In *Constitution of the General Council of the Assemblies of God, Revised, August 8–11, 2007, Indianapolis.* http://agchurches.org/Sitefiles/Default/RSS/AG.org%20TOP/2007_Constitution_and_Bylaws.pdf.

Archer, Kenneth J. *A Pentecostal Hermeneutics for the Twenty-First Century: Spirit, Scripture and Community.* London: T. & T. Clark, 2004.

Batty, David, and Ethan Campbell. "Teen Challenge: 50 Years of Miracles." In *Assemblies of God Heritage* 28, (2008) 14–21.

"Beginning of World Wide Revival." *TAF* 5 (January 1907) 1, col 1.

"Calcutta Mercy Ministries." *History.* http://www.buntain.org/ about.html.

Goff, James R. Jr., "Initial Tongues in the Theology of Charles Fox Parham." In *Initial Evidence: Historical and Biblical Perspectives on the Pentecostal Doctrine of Spirit Baptism,* edited by Gary B. McGee, 57–71. MA: Hendrickson, 1991.

Hodges, Melvin L. *The Indigenous Church.* Springfield, MO: Gospel, 1963.

Hollenweger, Walter J. *Pentecostalism: Origins and Developments Worldwide.* Peabody, MA: Hendrickson, 1997.

Jenkins, Philip. *The New Faces of Christianity: Believing the Bible in the Global South.* Oxford: Oxford University Press, 2006.

———. *The Next Christendom: The Coming of Global Christianity.* Oxford: Oxford University Press, 2002.

Johnson, Todd M., and Kenneth R. Ross, eds. *Atlas of Global Christianity 1910–2010.* Edinburgh: Edinburgh University Press, 2010.

Kitano, Koichi. "Socio-Religious Distance between Charismatics and Other Religious Group Members: A Case Study of the Philippines in the 1980s." *Journal of Asian Mission* 5.2 (2003) 231–42.

Lee, Young-hoon. *The Holy Spirit Movement in Korea.* Oxford: Regnum, 2009.

Ma, Julie C. *When the Spirit Meets the Spirits: Pentecostal Mission to an Animistic Tribe of the Northern Philippines.* Frankfurt: Lang, 2000.

Ma, Julie C., and Wonsuk Ma. *Mission in the Spirit: Towards a Pentecostal/ Charismatic Missiology.* Oxford: Regnum, 2010.

Ma, Wonsuk. "Pentecostal Eschatology: What Happened When the Wave Hit the West End of the Ocean." In *The Azusa Street Revival and Its Legacy,* eds. Hunter Harold and Cecil M. Robeck, Jr. Cleveland, TN: Pathway Press, 2006.

Ma, Wonsuk, and Kenneth R. Ross, eds., *Mission Spirituality and Authentic Discipleship.* Regnum Edinburgh Centenary Series 14. Oxford: Regnum, 2013.

Macchia, Frank D. *Baptized in the Spirit: A Global Pentecostal Theology.* Grand Rapids: Zondervan, 2006.

Martin, David. *Tongues of Fire: The Explosion of Protestantism in Latin America.* Oxford: Blackwell, 1990.

Menzies, Robert P. *Empowered for Witness: The Spirit in Luke-Acts.* London: T. & T. Clark, 2004.

Miller, Donald E., and Tetsunao Yamamori. *Global Pentecostalism: The New Face of Christian Social Engagement.* Berkeley: University of California Press, 2007.

"Pentecostal Has Come: Los Angeles Being Visited by a Revival of Bible Salvation and Pentecost as Recorded in the Book of Acts." *TAF* 1 (Sept 1906) 1, col. 1.

Petersen, Doug. *Not by Might, Nor by Power: A Pentecostal Theology of Social Concern in Latin America*. Oxford: Regnum, 1996.

Robeck, Cecil M. Jr., *The Azusa Street Mission and Revival: The Birth of the Global Pentecostal Movement*. Nashville, TN: Thomas Nelson, 2006.

"Russians Hear in Their Own Tongue." *TAF* 1 (Sept 1906) 4, col 3.

Shemeth, S. "Trasher, Lillian Hunt." In *New International Dictionary of Pentecostal and Charismatic Movements*, edited by Stanley Burgess, 1153. Grand Rapids: Zondervan, 2002.

Stronstad, Roger. *The Charismatic Theology of St Luke*. Peabody, MA: Hendrickson, 1984.

"The Enduement of Power." *TAF* 4 (Dec 1906) 2, col 2.

"The Millenium [*sic!*]." *TAF* 1 (Sept 1906) 3, col 3.

Tippett, Alan P. *People Movements in Southern Polynesia: A Study in Church Growth*. Chicago: Moody, 1971.

Warrington, Keith. *Pentecostal Theology: A Theology of Encounter*. London: T. & T. Clark, 2008.

Yung, Hwa. "The Missiological Challenge of David Yonggi Cho's Theology." In *David Yonggi Cho: A Close Look at His Theology and Ministry*, edited by Wonsuk Ma, 69–93. Baguio, Philippines: APTS Press, 2004.

14

Mission, Education, and Public Engagement

A Case Study in Romanian Pentecostalism

Corneliu Constantineanu

Introduction

It is acknowledged that the Pentecostal church in Romania is one of the largest and most vibrant among the Pentecostal churches in Europe.[1] After a rather difficult period of persecution and marginalization in the decades of the communist regime, the Romanian Pentecostal church has developed to become, currently, the fourth largest Christian denomination in Romania and is the only church in the context of Central and Eastern Europe to have had significant growth in various respects in the last ten years. Beyond numerical expansion, the church has also made significant progress with regard to several other areas such as foreign missions, education, economic, social, and political engagement, as well as Roma Christianity.

If in 1950 there were approximately 30,000 Pentecostal believers, by 1989 the number has risen to up to 300,000 people. These came from approximately 1,100 churches, of which 800 were authorized and 300 unauthorized (illegal).[2] An official 1992 survey showed some 220,033 registered Pentecostals,[3] and ten years later, growth rates of over 60 percent pushed

---

1. This paper is a revised and updated part of a larger project previously published. Constantineanu and Balaban, "Not by Might, Nor by Power, But by My Spirit." In *Global Renewal Christianity: Spirit-Empowered Movements Past, Present, and Future*, edited by Vinson Synan and Amos Yong. Vol. IV. Lake Mary, FL: Charisma House, 2016.

2. Bochian, *Viața unui păstor din România*, 68, 110.

3. "Penticostalii din România," *Cuvântul Adevărului*, 25.

that number up to 330,486 registered believers.[4] The growth of the Pentecostals believers continued in the next decade, and the official national census in 2011 registered 362,314 Pentecostals and some 3,000 churches. These figures place the Pentecostal denomination as the fourth largest in the country after the Orthodox, Roman Catholic, and the Reformed churches.[5] Even though in terms of absolute figures this may not look spectacular (compared with some other nations from the Southern Hemisphere), for Central and Eastern Europe it is remarkable. Already some years ago, seeing the great potential of the Romanian evangelical churches in general and of Pentecostals in particular, Peter Kuzmic, the Croatian Pentecostal scholar, called Romania "the Korea of Europe."[6]

This brief chapter intends to offer some specific features of Romanian Pentecostalism, particularly its contribution to the economic development of local communities, advances in education, and unique mission impetus in the region. I conclude with some of the specific challenges Romanian Pentecostals need to respond to.

Some Specific Features of Romanian Pentecostalism

Foreign Missions and Education

If Romania has benefited greatly from the work of foreign missionaries, in recent decades there has emerged a unique, totally Romanian mission agency, called *Agenția Penticostală de Misiune Externă* (APME or *The Pentecostal Agency for Foreign Mission*), which has sent missionaries across the world. APME currently has fifty-five long-term missionaries in twenty-one countries across three continents, most of which serve in Islamic contexts. There are an additional fifteen to twenty mission candidates, already trained, in the process of being approved by APME and who will begin their mission work soon.[7] 99 percent of the agency's budget comes from Romanian churches and believers. With less than ten years of existence, a passionate and visionary team led by Gheorghe Rițisan has developed a clear strategy for foreign missions. From the beginning, the goal of APME was to mobilize

---

4. See, "Populatia dupa etnie si religie," http://www.insse.ro/cms/files/RPL2002INS/vol4/tabele/t5.pdf.

5. See, Institutul National De Statistica, table 11. http://www.recensamantromania.ro/noutati/volumul-ii-populatia-stabila-rezidenta-structura-etnica-si-confesionala/(see table 11).

6. Kuzmič, "Why Romania has Become the Korea of Europe," 13.

7. See, Rițisan, "APME presentation."

Romanian churches for missions and "to facilitate the process of recruiting, training, sending, and supporting Romanian missionaries, especially among unreached ethnic groups."[8] It order to be effective in its mission, APME has established its own mission school—*Centrul Roman de Studii Transculturale (Romanian Center for Transcultural Studies)*—where cross-cultural mission candidates are properly trained and equipped. With its coherent and dynamic strategy, as well as the significant partnerships, APME has become an inspiring model of missions for other national churches in the region and even around the world.[9]

When it comes to education, it is not surprising to note that Pentecostals, in general, have been associated with a rather low view of the intellectual life and even with a strong anti-intellectualism. Historically, many gifted young men and women have been discouraged in their pursuit of higher education, and thus many genuine gifts for the intellectual and academic life of the church have been lost. Yet, in this context, Romanian Pentecostals have emphasized education. With freedom from the communist dictatorship since 1989, many schools opened at all levels to offer education within a Christian ethos.[10] As of 2016, the Romanian Pentecostal church had the following educational institutions, all accredited by the Romanian Government/Ministry of Education:

- two university-level Pentecostal programs, with a total of twenty faculty members and some 300 students
- thirty Pentecostal Bible schools (of two years) in each of the nine denominational districts, with 198 teachers, 2,649 students and over 16,848 alumni; these are the only programs that are not accredited, from the present list
- two post-high-school professional colleges with 734 students
- nine high schools, with 227 professors and 4,337 enrolled students
- eight gymnasium schools
- eight primary level schools
- forty kindergartens, with 119 instructors and 1,401 children

---

8. See the vision, mission and strategy, as well as other interesting facts and data at www.apme.ro.

9. For a more detailed history, strategy and development of APME. See, Ritisan and Constantineanu, "Not by Might, Nor by Power, But by My Spirit."

10. Ardelean, *et al. Monografia* învățământului *din Cultul Crestin Penticostal*, 33.

All told, the Romanian Pentecostal church has ninety-nine educational institutions with a total of 9,393 students and over 579 professors, lecturers, and instructors. In addition, there is a fast-growing community of young Pentecostal professionals at all levels and the social, economical, political, administrative, and educational sectors, an excellent illustration of the shift in understanding and appreciation of the importance of education. It is also not an overstatement to say that the Pentecostal Theological Institute in Bucharest, with its fourteen full-time faculties, all Romanians with PhDs completed and the academic rankings from full professor to lecturers, is one of the strongest Pentecostal theological schools in Europe.[11] There is, of course, much more to be done, in terms of advanced research and specific Pentecostal theology, but with its young and well-trained faculty, the school is on the right track also towards advanced research and theology.

There is yet another significant development regarding Pentecostal theological education in Romania that deserves to be mentioned here. A few years ago a special program of Pentecostal theology was established and accredited within the Faculty of Humanities and Social Sciences of the "Aurel Vlaicu" University of Arad. This is the only such Pentecostal degree, fully integrated into a secular university in Romania and where almost 100 students are studying every year and a young and qualified Pentecostal faculty is teaching. As a full-time faculty member in this institution I consider it a great privilege to be able to contribute in this way to a Christian witness in society, particularly to the public dimension of the gospel. Moreover, a plan has been submitted by the Pentecostal faculty and approved by the leadership of the university to begin a masters' program in public theology and there are very good chances that this will begin in October 2017. This will be the first time ever for Romania when a masters in public theology will be accredited and it is very significant that this is a Pentecostal initiative from within a secular university. This is yet another excellent example of the recent developments of the Romanian Pentecostal theological trajectory towards a holistic and integrative understanding of theology as a significant and important voice to the public discourse in Romania.

Public Engagement: Economic, Social, and Political Issues

Pentecostals have been rather known for their lack of concern for public engagement, and Romania is no exception to this rule. During the communist regime, when the atheist rulers realized they could not eliminate religion,

---

11. For a full picture of the Theological Institute in Bucharest see www.itpbucuresti.ro.

they attempted to limit religious manifestations exclusively to the church and private life. Believers also were unconcerned, as long as they were allowed to meet and worship God in their churches. However, over the years, Pentecostals have developed a renewed commitment to witness publicly to the lordship of Christ. Several new developments in the economic, social, and political sectors of Romanian society are underway.

Thus, in Romania, there is a robust and growing community of Pentecostal business people, some of whom have made significant contributions to the local and national economy. MG-Tec Group is a group of some fourteen companies owned by Ioan Tecar, a Pentecostal believer from Dej, that engages mostly in the production and distribution of building materials and provides retail sales of heavy trucks, hotel, and storage services. The company has a total of 1,213 employees and an annual turnover of some 145 million euros.[12] ATP Exodus is owned by Romanian Pentecostal Mircea Cirt from Baia Mare and offers a complex range of goods and services for vehicles, specializing in sales and service of Mercedes-Benz, Mazda, Opel, and MAN, with a used-car division and sale of spare parts for trucks. ATP Exodus is one of Romania's market leaders for accessories and spare parts for commercial vehicles, with a network of thirty-three national and ten international branches (in Bulgaria, Serbia, and Hungary). The company has a team of over 800 employees and an annual turnover of some 40 million euros.[13] Last but not least, Marelbo Prod-Com SRL, a family business and shoe factory owned by Aurel Bob, a Pentecostal believer from Vicovu-de-Sus, has over 200 employees, an annual turnover of some 10 millions euro, and over forty stores throughout the country.[14] Marelbo offers job opportunities for several villages in the area and together with similar companies of Pentecostal believers in the region have substantially contributed to the economic development of that area. The list could continue, even as we note that these Pentecostal business people are involved in and support financially many local churches and Christian organizations.

Pentecostal churches and organizations are also engaged in the social area. There are many examples of churches and even individual believers who felt compelled to respond to the social needs arising particularly after the abrupt change from a totalitarian regime to a free democracy. The following highlights a particular aspect of this work that came especially as a response to the plight of the abandoned orphans in Romania. The state of affairs regarding the situation of children in the former communist context

12. See www.mg-tec.ro.
13. See www.atp-exodus.com.
14. See www.marelbo.ro.

is dramatic. According to a recent UNICEF report, some 15,000 children are being abandoned annually in the former communist countries.[15]

No one can forget the disturbing images of the orphans and institutionalized children in Romania made public immediately after the collapse of communism in 1989. Twenty-five years after, there, unfortunately, remains far too many stories of child abandonment and street children, not to mention the plight of Roma (gypsy) children or the tragedy of the so-called "eurorphans," the hundreds of thousands of children left behind by their parents who migrated for work in Europe. There is still a perception that the state institutions are able to handle appropriately the plight of such children, and this contrary to the evidence that such institutionalization is against children's interest and wellbeing. It is in response to such urgency that many Pentecostal churches and individuals have begun to act on behalf of children in Romania and thus many homes and centers have been established to feed, care for, educate, and offer a future to these children. Corina Caba, a young Pentecostal woman from Oradea, is a remarkable example as she opened her own apartment for destitute children. The apartment became soon too small to host so many children in need of help, and she founded Hope House Family Center in Oradea for these abandoned children.[16] Corina is just one of many people in Romania who offer a shelter and home to children at risk.[17]

Centrul Crestin pentru Reintegrare Sociala Onisim (The Christian Center for Social Reintegration Onisim) in Bistrița is another social initiative by Pentecostal believers offered to those who have served time in prison and need to be reintegrated into society. There are only five such centers in the country, and the Onisim center has many stories of people changed and transformed. Beyond social reintegration, people who passed through the center have gone on to affect positive change in their communities. The center's significant impact led to its making the headline of a national newspaper in Romania.[18]

---

15. See Marie-Pierre, "Quinze mille enfants abandonnés chaque année dans les pays post-communistes."

16. For more details on this remarkable story see http://romania-reborn.org/news/.

17. For an excellent and in-depth study about the situation of children at risk in Romania and how the various churches and NGOs have responded, see Prevette, *Child, Church, and Compassion*.

18. The financial national newspaper *Ziarul Finaciar* and the MEDIAFAX agency devoted an entire article to highlight several of the success stories of the Onesim Centre: "Un fost deținut de la penitenciarul Bistrița a ajuns patronul unei companii de transport în Irlanda" ["A Former Prisoner from the Bistrita Penitentiary becomes the Owner of a Transport Company in Ireland"]. See, http://www.zf.ro/analiza/un-fost-detinut-de-la-penitenciarul-bistrita-a-ajuns-patronul-unei-companii-de-transport-in-irlanda-10244838.

One comment about Pentecostals and politics ought to be made. If Pentecostals were once primarily known for their intense, private spirituality and their lack of political engagement, in the last two decades the situation in Romania has changed. Thus, Pentecostal believers are running for and gaining seats in the Romanian Parliament (some ten of them over the last fifteen years). Also, at the local levels, there are many villages, towns, and even big cities in Romania where Pentecostals hold political and administrative positions, from counselors to city mayors. There was even a strong Pentecostal contribution to form a Christian-democratic political party which attempts to bring a specifically Christian alternative to the governance of the country.[19]

Roma/Gypsy Christianity in Romania

A brief note about Roma/Gypsy Christianity, another significant feature of Romanian Pentecostalism, is appropriate. Even though this phenomenon has never been thoroughly researched throughout Eastern Europe,[20] it deserves to be mentioned as Romania has the largest Roma population in Central and Eastern Europe and, arguably, the largest number of Roma Christians, with the fastest growth rate. There are many individual Roma Christians in the Romanian Pentecostal churches, individual Roma churches within the existing Pentecostal denomination, and many independent churches including, for example, the Christian Union of Roma Pentecostals in Romania (with some 200 churches). In addition, there is a large number of small, independent Roma churches in villages and towns across the country. The most renowned place in Romania is Toflea (a village known for much violence and mafia gangs), where a particular Christian movement among the Gypsy began in the early 1990s. From the testimony of radical transformation of the lives of the first Roma converts, a large number of Roma followed—there was, for example, a single baptismal service in 2002 in which over 600 gypsies were baptized—and now some 90 percent of the village are Christians and attend the local Pentecostal church, which numbers well over 1,000 members.[21]

19. For a complete description of the Christian-democratic proposal to politics in Romania, see www.ucdr.ro.

20. For an academic study about the situation of Roma Christians in the neighboring Bulgaria, see Atanasov, *Gypsy Pentecostals*.

21. For an excellent analysis of the larger phenomenon of Roma Christianity see Melody J. Wachsmuth, "Roma Christianity in Central and Eastern Europe: Challenges, Opportunities for Mission, Modes of Appropriation and Social Significance." Also see Constantineanu et al., *Mission in Central and Eastern Europe*, forthcoming.

There are, of course, other testimonies of entire gypsy villages in Romania that converted to Christianity (such as Ramnicelu, Valea Rece, Tecuci). A few years ago *The Economist* ran the story of mass conversion among the Roma people in Ramnicelu and how this phenomenon brought significant and visible changes to the community:

> Typically Romani girls drop out of school when they marry. But the director of the schools in Râmnicelu says that girls are now attending classes, and that the boys are better behaved. Locals say the conversions have helped them understand the value of education. Field-officers from the National Agency for Roma attest that conversions have reduced violence, criminality, and alcoholism in other parts of the country.[22]

Scholars of Romanian Christianity should watch developments in this area.

Evangelistic Outreach and Church Life

If one asks why the Romanian Pentecostal church is the only one to register growth in the last decade, part of the answer may be found in her evangelistic zeal and outreach efforts. Indeed, there is a special effort in all Pentecostal churches to organize at least a full week of evangelistic meetings every year and the lay believers contribute a great deal to these events. There are also many public evangelistic meetings in stadiums, sports halls, even in big tents on the streets. There are many gifted singers and music teams as well as an increasing number of excellent Pentecostal preachers and evangelists who are traveling the country for these events. The experience of transformed lives has not only motivated testimonies but also attracted others.

Similarly, many larger Pentecostal churches are organizing evangelistic outreaches and church plants in the villages around them. One outstanding example is given by the Pentecostal Elim Church in Timisoara, one of the largest Pentecostal churches in Europe, which has currently no less than thirty-three church plants in the villages around Timisoara.[23] Another example of a particularly influential youth movement that attracts many young people is Fundatia Peniel (Peniel Foundation), which is focused on the young generation. There are thousands of younger people who attend

---

22. See Ramnicelu, "Romania's Evangelical Romanies."
23. See http://www.elim.ro/filiale/.

their national, regional, and international meetings every year, and many are converted through this ministry.[24]

Pentecostal growth cannot be understood without reference to Pentecostal church life. Church services in Romanian Pentecostalism still last for three hours on Sunday morning and two hours on Sunday afternoon, and these include a full hour that is devoted to intense, fervent, intercessory prayer. Many people find that attractive as they have the chance to bring all their concerns, hopes, and aspirations to God with the entire community. Every single church service also includes a prayer for healing and deliverance, and many people are deeply touched. And there is also the element of poetry in Romanian Pentecostal church services. It would be rare that a church service excluded the recitation of poetry. These are powerful, inspiring moments for the church attendees as poets have unique gifts to evoke new possibilities and imaginatively envision the new creation in faith. These may be some of the reasons why people visit and join the church.

Conclusion: Further Challenges for the Romanian Pentecostal Church

For all the preceding, a good Pentecostal would ultimately say whatever was accomplished was done, "not by might, nor by power, but by my Spirit." This is, indeed, one of the conclusions of the most comprehensive work on the history of Pentecostalism in Romania (two volumes, with a total of over 1,300 pages), written by historian Valeriu Andreescu: "We emphasize once more that the development of Pentecostalism in Romania was due and is still due to the work of the gifts of the Holy Spirit."[25]

If we have mentioned primarily some positive aspects and opportunities for the Romanian Pentecostal church, this should not be understood as the whole story. There are, of course, many further challenges to which Pentecostals need to respond. To mention only a few of the most important ones, note that the Romanian Pentecostal church is rather isolated from the worldwide Pentecostal family, and so there is an urgent need for stronger international connections, interactions, and partnerships. Another challenge is the need for solid, biblically grounded foundations for holistic engagement in the public life. Yes, there are a few good examples of public engagement (above), but these are still far too few compared with the

---

24. See http://peniel.ro.

25. We found it significant that Professor Andreiescu subtitled his two volumes of work: "The Full Gospel and the Power of God" and "The Works of the Power of God." Andreiescu, *Istoria penticostalismului romanesc*, 667.

potential for the public contribution that the Romanian Pentecostal church has. Along the same lines, there is the challenge of developing a specifically Pentecostal way of reflection and theologizing, bringing to the fore the particular contribution that Pentecostals can make to Christian theology, spirituality, and mission. Higher degrees and more specialized research in this area are needed. Finally, there is a need to continue to search for the best alternative in the leadership structure of the denomination in order to allow more time and space for strategic planning and development. There are many leaders in the denomination who think that those who are in higher authority positions in the denomination ought to be relieved of their duties/roles as local pastors to be able to devote more time to the actual vision, mission, and ministry of the Pentecostal denomination. There was actually such a proposal presented and discussed (eventually heavily debated) at the national congress of the denomination in 2014, but it was eventually rejected. However, there are good signs that in the near future this decision might be implemented and so we will see a more coherent strategy for Pentecostal development.

Bibliography

Andreiescu, Valeriu. *Istoria penticostalismului romanesc* [*History of Romanian Pentecostalism*], vol. 1. Oradea: Casa Cărții, 2011.

Ardelean, Moise, et al., eds. *Monografia învățământului din Cultul Crestin Penticostal* [*A Monograph on Education in the Christian Pentecostal Denomination*], Cultul Crestin Penticostal din România, Departementul de Învățământ. Timisoara: Editura Dalia, 2013.

Atanasov, Miroslav A. *Gypsy Pentecostals: The Growth of the Pentecostal Movement among the Roma in Bulgaria and its Revitalization of Their Communities*. Wilmore, KY: Emeth, 2010.

Bochian, Pavel. *Viața unui păstor din România* [*The Life of a Pastor from Romania*]. București: Editura Privilegiu, 1997.

Constantineanu, Corneliu, and Ciprian Balaban. "'Not by Might, Nor by Power, But by My Spirit': Pentecostalism in Romania." In *Global Renewal Christianity: Spirit-Empowered Movements Past, Present, and Future*, edited by Vinson Synan and Amos Yong, 47–66. Vol. IV. Lake Mary, FL: Charisma House, 2016.

Institutul National De Statistica. http://www.recensamantromania.ro/noutati/volumul-ii-populatia-stabila-rezidenta-structura-etnica-si-confesionala.

Kuzmič, Peter. "Why Romania has Become the Korea of Europe." *Global Church Growth Magazine* 20 (1983) 13.

Marie-Pierre, Sofia. "Quinze mille enfants abandonnés chaque année dans les pays post-communistes" ["Fifteen Thousand Abandoned Children Each Year in Post-Communist Countries"], *Le Monde*. http://www.lemonde.fr/europe/article/2012/11/21/quinze-mille-enfants-abandonnes-chaque-annee-dans-les-pays-post-communistes_1793535_3214.html.

"Penticostalii din România" ["Pentecostals in Romania"]. *Cuvântul Adevă rului [The Word of Truth]*, series II, 14:7–8 (2003) 25.
"Populatia dupa etnie si religie." http://www.insse.ro/cms/files/RPL2002INS/vol4/tabele/t5.pdf.
Prevette, Bill. *Child, Church, and Compassion: Toward Child Theology in Romania*. Oxford: Regnum, 2012.
Ramnicelu, B. J. "Romania's Evangelical Romanies." *The Economist*, 17 January 2011. http://www.economist.com/blogs/easternapproaches/2011/01/religion_romania.
Ritisan, Gheorghe, and Corneliu Constantineanu. "APME: A Case Study in Cross-Cultural Mission Originating from Eastern Europe." In *Mission in Central and Eastern Europe: Realities, Perspectives, Trends*, edited by Corneliu Constantineanu, et al., 345–62. Oxford: Regnum, 2016.
Rițisan, Ghiță. "APME presentation." Paper given at the Consultation in Costa Rica, 13–17, April, 2015.